So lernst du mit Red Line

Dein Buch hat fünf Units. Jede Unit ist gleich aufgebaut.

Unit (Kapitel)

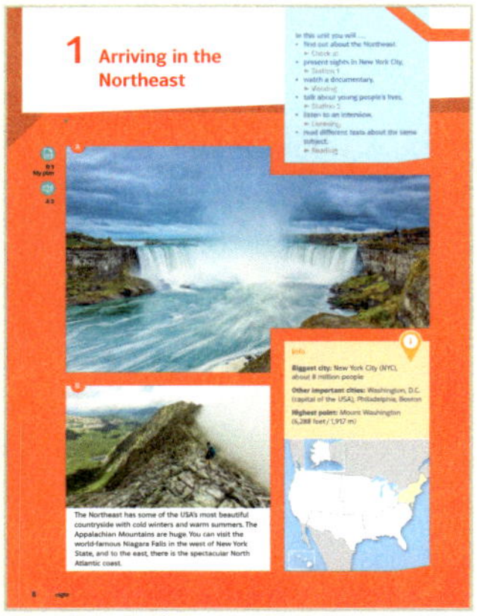

Check in

Du erfährst etwas über die Region und die Inhalte der Unit.

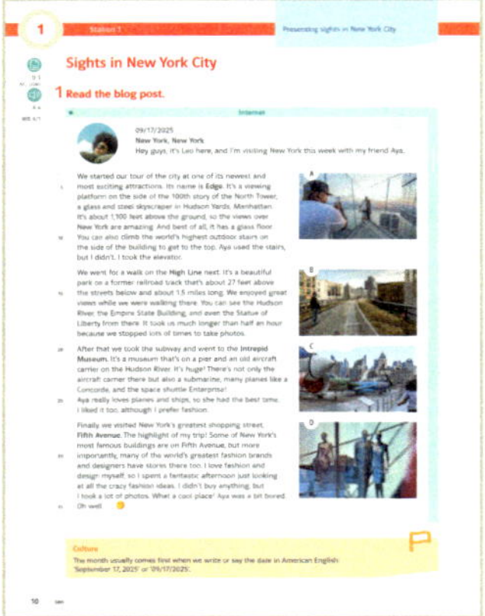

Stations

Jede Unit hat zwei Stations mit einer eigenen Your turn-Aufgabe.

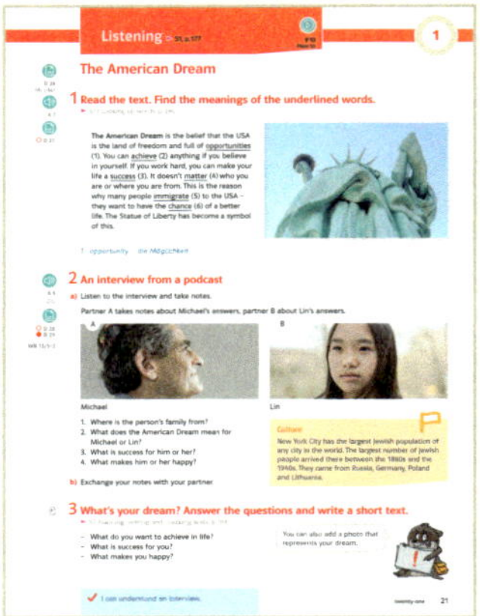

Listening

Verschiedene Arten von Hörtexten

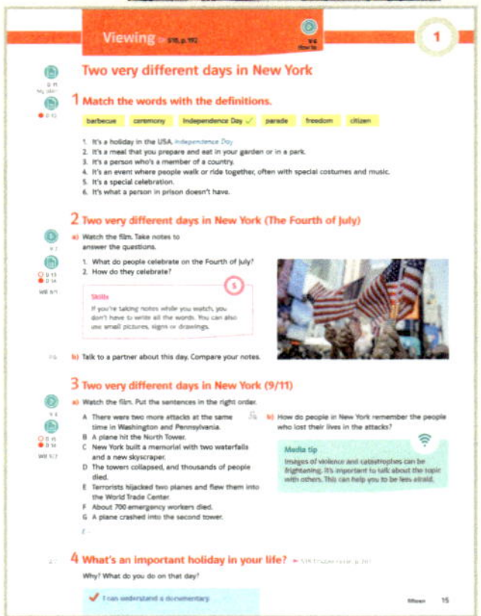

Viewing

Kurze Filme aus der englischsprachigen Welt

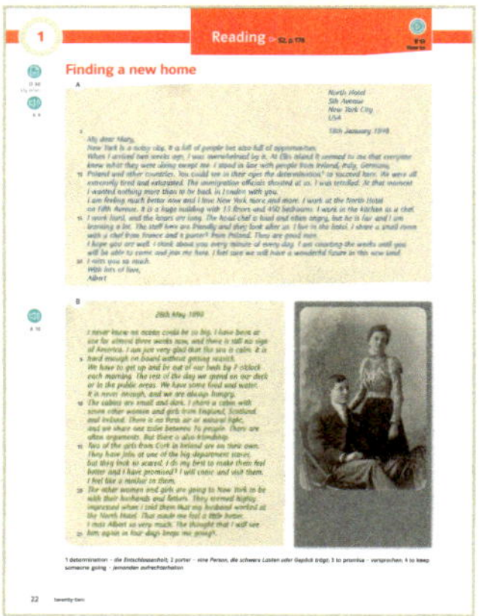

Reading

Geschichten und andere Texte

Check out

Am Ende der Unit gibt es eine Checkliste und ein kleines Projekt, die Task.

Discover

Zusätzliche Informationen über Land und Leute der USA

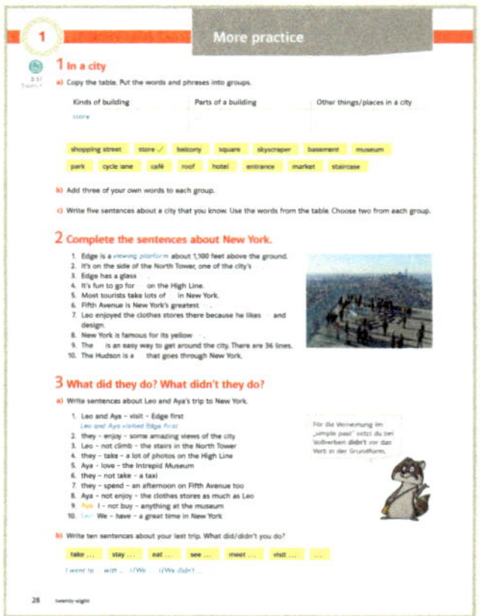

More practice

Zusatz-Aufgaben, z. B. zur Vorbereitung auf die Klassenarbeit

Anhang

Help H

In **Help** gibt es einfachere Parallelaufgaben zu gekennzeichneten Aufgaben der Unit.

Extra E

In **Extra** gibt es weitere Texte, z. B. eine Geschichte, ein Gedicht, ein Theaterstück und ein Diagramm.

Grammar G

In **Grammar** kannst du die Grammatikregeln nachschlagen. Außerdem gibt es noch mehr Übungsaufgaben.

Skills S

In **Skills and methods** bekommst du Tipps, welche Strategien oder Methoden du bei bestimmten Aufgabentypen anwenden kannst.

Vocabulary V

In **Vocabulary** sind alle neuen Wörter in der Reihenfolge aufgelistet, in der sie in den Units vorkommen. Hier findest du auch häufige Arbeitsanweisungen und nützliche Sätze für den Unterricht.

Word banks W

In **Word banks** stehen alle Wörter, die zu einem Thema gehören und die du schon gelernt hast. Du kannst sie zum Schreiben eigener Texte verwenden.

Dictionary D

In **Dictionary** kannst du Wörter nachschlagen, die in Band 1 bis 4 vorkommen. Sie sind alphabetisch geordnet: Englisch-Deutsch und Deutsch-Englisch.

Symbole und Medien

○	leichtere Parallelaufgaben
●	schwierigere Aufgaben
(Partner-Symbol)	Partnerarbeit
(Gruppen-Symbol)	Gruppenarbeit
P	Portfolio
WB 4/1	Verweis auf passende Aufgaben im Workbook
► G3	Verweis Grammar
► W11	Verweis Word banks
► V	Verweis Wortsammlungen
► S6	Verweis Skills

A 17	Audio: Hörtext
V 7	Video: Film
V 4 How to	Video: Erklärvideo
I 2	Interaktiv: Übung zur Selbstüberprüfung
I 4–6 360°	Interaktiv: 360°-Foto
I 4 Quiz	Interaktiv: Quiz
D 3 My plan	Dokument: Lernplan
D 25 Support	Dokument: Hilfe oder Vorlage
D 4 D 5 ○/●	Dokument: Einfachere oder schwierigere Übung

Die Medien (Audios, Videos, interaktive Übungen und Dokumente) zum Schulbuch sind online und offline verfügbar.

1. QR-Code scannen oder Link in einen Browser eingeben
2. Mit den persönlichen Klett-Zugangsdaten anmelden
3. Digitale Medien online nutzen oder in die **Klett Lernen App** herunterladen

Link
qr.klett.de/LC-o3A-gyN

1. Auflage 978-3-12-548924-0 (fester Einband) 1 5 4 3 2 1 | 29 28 27 26 25
1. Auflage 978-3-12-549924-9 (flexibler Einband) 1 5 4 3 2 1 | 29 28 27 26 25

Alle Drucke dieser Auflage sind unverändert und können im Unterricht nebeneinander verwendet werden.
Die letzte Zahl bezeichnet das Jahr des Druckes.

Herausgeber: Dr. Frank Haß, Kirchberg
Autorinnen und Autoren: Jeremy Bowell, Oxford sowie Annika Franzke, Baesweiler; Wolfgang Hamm, Marktredwitz
Beratung: Wilma Brings, Bedburg; Ulrich Dannenhauer, Remscheid; Peter Debray, Wuppertal; Tanja Frank, Ulm; Wolfgang Hamm, Marktredwitz; Annette Kantel, Siegburg; Christa Kathmann-Fuhrmann, Bonn; Dr. Margitta Kuty, Greifswald; Étienne Michel, Lennep; Henning Reichel, Berlin; Alexandra Schärtl, Wilhelmsfeld; Martina Sprenger, Bad Rappenau-Babstadt; Timothy Starratt, Dudenhofen; Christian Straukamp, Nordhorn; Sascha Sütterlin, Karlsruhe; Konstanze Zander, Westerengel

Entstanden in Zusammenarbeit mit dem Projektteam des Verlages.

Externe Redaktion: Birgit Piefke-Wagner, Korntal-Münchingen; Lektorat editoria: Cornelia Schaller, Fellbach
Gestaltung: Koma Amok, Stuttgart
Titelbilder: Getty Images Plus, München (Leland Bobbe); Unsplash, Montréal, QC (Caleb Perez)
Satz: graphitecture book & edition; Fotosatz Kaufmann, Stuttgart
Reproduktion: Meyle + Müller GmbH + Co. KG, Pforzheim
Druck: Firmengruppe APPL, aprinta druck, Wemding

Printed in Germany
ISBN 978-3-12-548924-0 (fester Einband)
ISBN 978-3-12-549924-9 (flexibler Einband)

9 783125 489240 9 783125 499249

Herausgeber: Dr. Frank Haß

Red Line 4

Ernst Klett Verlag
Stuttgart · Leipzig · Dortmund

Inhalt

S = Speaking R = Reading V = Viewing I = Intercultural
W = Writing L = Listening M = Mediation MC = Media competence * = fakultativ

S = Speaking R = Reading V = Viewing I = Intercultural
W = Writing L = Listening M = Mediation MC = Media competence * = fakultativ

Inhalt

S = Speaking R = Reading V = Viewing I = Intercultural
W = Writing L = Listening M = Mediation MC = Media competence * = fakultativ

Zoom in

Welcome to the USA

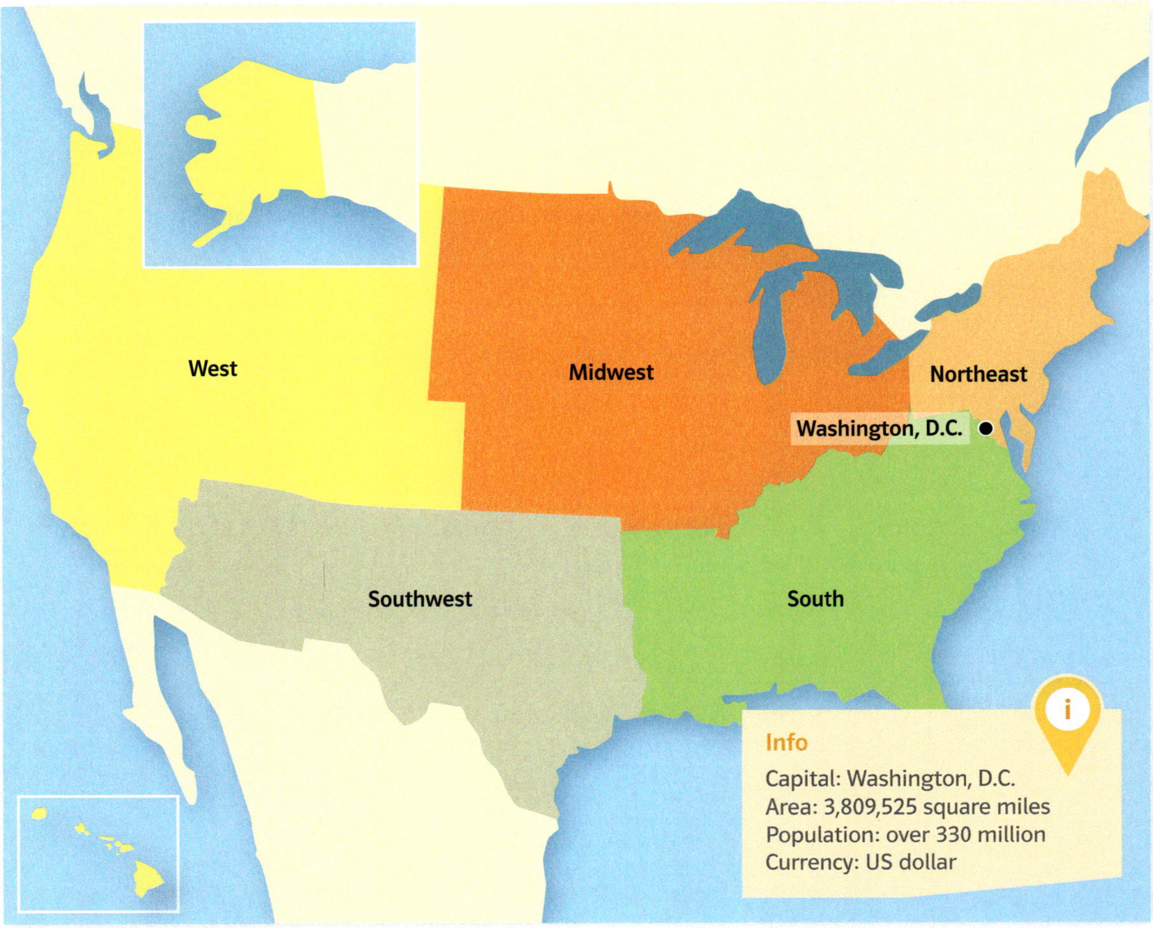

Info

Capital: Washington, D.C.
Area: 3,809,525 square miles
Population: over 330 million
Currency: US dollar

@Brad
I like cooking and new recipes.

@Luciana
My dream? A more sustainable world.

1 Look at the map. What information can you get about the USA?

2 A look at the USA

a) Think about the questions. Which answers do you already know? Make notes.

1. What is the most famous city in the USA?
2. How many states does the USA have?
3. What is special about Alaska and Hawaii?
4. What are the colours of the flag?
5. What colour are American school buses?
6. What sports are popular?
7. What food is popular?

V 1

b) Watch the film. Check your answers from a) and complete your notes.

A 1
WB 2/1

3 Listen to the five teenagers from the USA.

Take notes about their home towns and what they say about themselves.

You can find out more about the differences between British and American English on page 203.

Culture

American English (AE) and British English (BE) are a bit different. You can hear this in words like 'Thursday', where the 'r' is pronounced in American English. Some words are completely different, like 'lift' (BE) and 'elevator' (AE). Sometimes the spelling is different like in 'favourite' (BE) and 'favorite' (AE).

1 Arriving in the Northeast

In this unit you will …
- find out about the Northeast.
  ► Check in
- present sights in New York City.
  ► Station 1
- watch a documentary.
  ► Viewing
- talk about young people's lives.
  ► Station 2
- listen to an interview.
  ► Listening
- read different texts about the same subject.
  ► Reading

D 1
My plan

A 2

A

B

The Northeast has some of the USA's most beautiful countryside with cold winters and warm summers. The Appalachian Mountains are huge. You can visit the world-famous Niagara Falls in the west of New York State, and to the east, there is the spectacular North Atlantic coast.

Info

Biggest city: New York City (NYC), about 8 million people

Other important cities: Washington, D.C. (capital of the USA), Philadelphia, Boston

Highest point: Mount Washington (6,288 feet / 1,917 m)

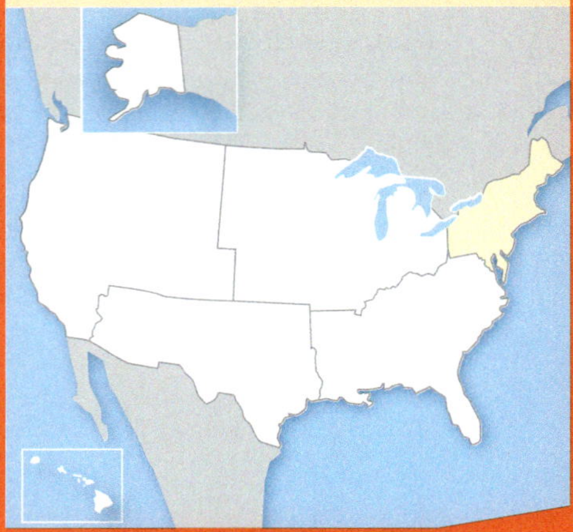

C

Native American tribes lived in the Northeast long before the European settlers came and founded colonies there. English settlers called the area 'New England'. They used names from home for cities like Boston and New York.

D

Ellis Island is in New York Harbor. Between 1892 and 1954, the island was an immigration center. Around 12 million immigrants came through the center before they were allowed into the country.

E

The Northeast coast is a great place to go whale watching. You can see different kinds of whales up and down the coast from May to October. Tourists can learn how important it is to protect the sea and all its plants and animals.

F

Around 23 % of the USA's economy is in the Northeast. It's one of the richest areas of the USA. New York City is the most important financial center. Farming and fishing are also very important to the area.

1 Facts about the Northeast

D 2 Support P

a) Read the texts. Collect information about the Northeast. Copy and complete the fact cards.

A 3

b) What information can you find out about the Northeast from the audio and the video? Add it to your fact cards.

V 2

WB 3/1–3

c) Talk about the Northeast with the help of your fact cards.

History
...

Cities
...

Nature
...

Economy
...

Other facts
...

V

Audio and video words

runner – der Läufer / die Läuferin
marathon – der Marathon
to raise money – Geld sammeln
historical – historisch
government – die Regierung

✔ I can understand information about the Northeast.

D 3
My plan
A 4
WB 4/1

Sights in New York City

1 Read the blog post.

Internet

09/17/2025
New York, New York
Hey guys, it's Leo here, and I'm visiting New York this week with my friend Aya.

A

We started our tour of the city at one of its newest and most exciting attractions. Its name is **Edge**. It's a viewing platform on the side of the 100th story of the North Tower, a glass and steel skyscraper in Hudson Yards, Manhattan. It's about 1,100 feet above the ground, so the views over New York are amazing. And best of all, it has a glass floor. You can also climb the world's highest outdoor stairs on the side of the building to get to the top. Aya used the stairs, but I didn't. I took the elevator.

B

We went for a walk on the **High Line** next. It's a beautiful park on a former railroad track that's about 27 feet above the streets below and about 1.5 miles long. We enjoyed great views while we were walking there. You can see the Hudson River, the Empire State Building, and even the Statue of Liberty from there. It took us much longer than half an hour because we stopped lots of times to take photos.

C

After that we took the subway and went to the **Intrepid Museum**. It's a museum that's on a pier and an old aircraft carrier on the Hudson River. It's huge! There's not only the aircraft carrier there but also a submarine, many planes like a Concorde, and the space shuttle Enterprise! Aya really loves planes and ships, so she had the best time. I liked it too, although I prefer fashion.

D

Finally, we visited New York's greatest shopping street, **Fifth Avenue**. The highlight of my trip! Some of New York's most famous buildings are on Fifth Avenue, but more importantly, many of the world's greatest fashion brands and designers have stores there too. I love fashion and design myself, so I spent a fantastic afternoon just looking at all the crazy fashion ideas. I didn't buy anything, but I took a lot of photos. What a cool place! Aya was a bit bored. Oh well … 🙂

Culture
The month usually comes first when we write or say the date in American English: 'September 17, 2025' or '09/17/2025'.

D 4
D 5

2 Sightseeing in New York City

a) Answer the questions in sentences.

1. Why are the views from Edge amazing?
   They're amazing because it's about 1,000 feet above the ground.
2. What did Leo like best about the platform?
3. What did Leo and Aya enjoy at the High Line?
4. Why did the walk take more than half an hour?
5. How did Leo and Aya travel to the museum?
6. Who liked the museum more, and why?
7. What time of day were they on Fifth Avenue?
8. What two things did Leo do there?

b) Which of the places would you like to visit? Why? ► S18 Milling around, p. 201

A I'd really like to visit Edge because I'd love to see New York from above.
B Me too. But I'd like to visit … too because … . What about you?
A I'd prefer to visit … because … .

WB 4/2

3 Words for parts of a building ► W1 Parts of a building, p. 232

a) Match the words with the parts of the building (A–H). ► ○ p. 122

basement | entrance | balcony | story | elevator | solar panels | ground level ✓ | staircase

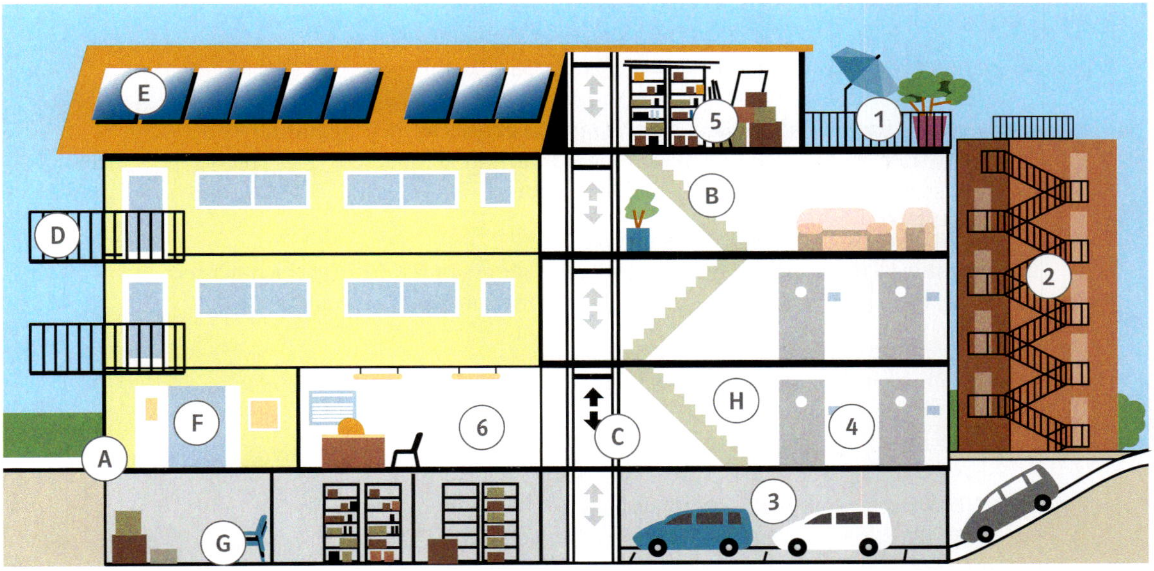

A. ground level

b) Match the words in the picture with the definitions. Check your answers with the picture.

underground parking lot | lobby | corridor | roof terrace | loft | fire escape

1. You can sit there on the top of a building.
2. You must use it in an emergency.
3. It's a place for your car that's below the ground level of a building.
4. It's the part of a building from which doors lead into rooms.
5. It's an apartment under the roof at the top of a building.
6. It's a large room that you enter in public buildings and hotels.

WB 5/3

4 New York City's tallest buildings ► S14 Using the internet, p.196

a) Find the missing information. Take notes and write sentences. ► ○ p.122

A

B

C

D

Name	Woolworth Building	Chrysler Building	Empire State Building	One World Trade Center
Opened	1913	1930	1931	...
Metres	...	319 m	...	546 m
Floors	60	...	...	94
Lifts	...	32	73	...
Tallest building in NYC	1913–1930	...	1931–1970 2001–2012	since 2012

A. 241 m, ... lifts; The Woolworth Building is 241 metres tall and has ... lifts.

● **b)** Research and write about a famous building in another city. Add a photo.

V 3
How to
WB 5/4

5 Mediation ► S9 Mediation, p.191

Du machst ein Projekt über die Geschichte der Fotografie für den Geschichtsunterricht. Gib die Informationen, die du für interessant hältst, auf Deutsch wieder.

In 1932 a New York newspaper published a photo of eleven men sitting on a steel beam eating their lunch, about 853 feet above the ground on the 69th story of the RCA Building (called the Comcast Building today). You can see Manhattan and Central Park in the background.

The photo is real. The men were all workers on the construction of the building. However, the situation is not real. The men were asked to sit on the beam and pretend to eat lunch. The photo was taken to promote the skyscraper.

The photo is one of the most famous images of New York City, and it is a piece of American history.

V 4
How to

Language revision: Simple past ► G1, p. 146

G

Test yourself: Put in the verbs in the right forms.
1. Yesterday morning we — (start) our tour at one of the city's newest attractions.
2. But I — (not walk) up the stairs.
3. Then Aya and I — (walk) on the High Line.
4. It — (be) beautiful there.
5. Later we — (go) to the Intrepid Museum.
6. What — Aya — (see) at the museum?
7. — (be) it busy on Fifth Avenue yesterday? – Yes, it —.
8. — you — (buy) anything on Fifth Avenue? – No, we —.

○ D 6
● D 7
WB 6/5–6

6 Complete the text about Madison Square Garden. ► S18 Peer correction, p. 200

On my last day in New York, my friend Aya *took* (1 take) me to the famous Madison Square Garden. It — (2 be) my first time there. We — (3 not get) tickets for a concert or a sports event there, but we — (4 do) a 60-minute tour. A guide — (5 show) us around. He — (6 tell) us about the Garden's 150-year history. I — (7 not know) that it is home to the NBA's NY Knicks and the NHL's NY Rangers. We — (8 not see) their lockers, but we — (9 go) on the court!

WB 7/7–8

7 How was New York?

a) Complete the dialogue. Act it with a partner. Then change roles. ► ○ p. 123

You Hi, *how was your trip to New York*? (1)
Aya Hi. My trip to New York was great.
You When — you — (2)?
Aya We returned yesterday.
You Who — (3)?
Aya Leo was with me.
You — you — (4)?
Aya Yes, we visited Edge.
You What — (5)?
Aya My highlight was the Intrepid Museum.
You — you — (6)?
Aya No, we didn't take a taxi.

● b) Talk to a partner about a trip to a city or other place that you visited last summer.
► S3 Speaking with other people, p. 180

You can ask questions from a) or make your own questions.

○ D 8
● D 9
WB 7/9

8 Write a blog post about a trip. ► S7 Planning, writing and checking texts, p. 184

Include:
- where you went,
- who was with you,
- what your highlight was,
- why you liked it.

Hi guys, it's … here.
Last … I went to … . We … . My highlight was … .
I … because … . …

I 1
V 5 How to
D 10 Support

9 Your turn: A blog post about a sight in New York City

Write a blog post about a New York City sight. ► S7 Planning, writing and checking texts, p. 184

Step 1

Choose a sight in New York City. It can be a building, a place or any other interesting location.

Posts about visiting sights are always very positive. You should use words like 'fantastic', 'amazing' and 'spectacular'.

Step 2

Search the internet for information.
- Where?
- What?
- Opening times?
- For free or buy tickets?
- ...

► S14 Using the internet, p. 196

- *Hudson Yards*
- *a great place to visit*
- *Vessel not open at the moment*

...

Step 3

Write a draft.
Use hashtags for the places in the blog post.

Media tip
We use a hashtag (#) on social media to identify special content. The hashtag helps people to find information about the topic, for example:
#VesselNY #NYsights

Step 4

Find one or more photos that you can add to your blog post.
► S16 How to use photos, films and texts, p. 198

Visit Vessel in Hudson Yards, New York City. It's crazy! It's still closed but great, anyway!
Have you already been here? Tell me in the comments below.
#NewYork #VesselNY #NYsights #crazystairs

Step 5

Write your blog post and add the photos.

Step 6

Read other students' blog posts.
Ask for and give feedback.
► S8 Giving and asking for feedback, p. 190

Step 7

Which of the places in New York City would you like to visit? Why? ► S18 Round robin, p. 201

Media tip
You can also use virtual reality to visit a place.

✔ I can present sights in New York City.

Two very different days in New York

D 11
My plan
D 12

1 Match the words with the definitions.

barbecue | ceremony | Independence Day ✓ | parade | freedom | citizen

1. It's a holiday in the USA. *Independence Day*
2. It's a meal that you prepare and eat in your garden or in a park.
3. It's a person who's a member of a country.
4. It's an event where people walk or ride together, often with special costumes and music.
5. It's a special celebration.
6. It's what a person in prison doesn't have.

2 Two very different days in New York (The Fourth of July)

V 7
D 13
D 14
WB 8/1

a) Watch the film. Take notes to answer the questions.

1. What do people celebrate on the Fourth of July?
2. How do they celebrate?

Skills

If you're taking notes while you watch, you don't have to write all the words. You can also use small pictures, signs or drawings.

b) Talk to a partner about this day. Compare your notes.

3 Two very different days in New York (9/11)

V 8
D 15
D 16
WB 8/2

a) Watch the film. Put the sentences in the right order.

A There were two more attacks at the same time in Washington and Pennsylvania.
B A plane hit the North Tower.
C New York built a memorial with two waterfalls and a new skyscraper.
D The towers collapsed, and thousands of people died.
E Terrorists hijacked two planes and flew them into the World Trade Center.
F About 700 emergency workers died.
G A plane crashed into the second tower.

E – …

b) How do people in New York remember the people who lost their lives in the attacks?

Media tip

Images of violence and catastrophes can be frightening. It's important to talk about the topic with others. This can help you to be less afraid.

4 What's an important holiday in your life? ► S18 Double circle, p. 201

Why? What do you do on that day?

✓ I can understand a documentary.

A day in the life of an American teenager

D 17 My plan
D 18

1 Which places are important to you and why?
► S18 Think-pair-share, p. 200

My youth club is very important to me because it's a place where I can meet my friends, try new activities, and get help if I have any problems.

A 5
WB 9/1

2 Read the website.

Internet

Making new friends online

You're just a minute away from a new friend. Our teenagers are from many different places in the USA and around the world. They like to make new friends and chat about their lives and their favorite places. Click through their posts and answer them.

Marsha, 16, Boston, Massachusetts
Hey, I'm Marsha. I'm from Boston. I live in the suburb of Charlestown, which is in the north of the city by the harbor.
There are lots of cool stores and cafés here. The harbor is one of my favorite places because I love watching the people and the boats there. It's always busy there and it makes me dream of foreign places.
I go to Elmont High School. I feel comfortable because I have lots of friends there, and the school offers some cool after-school clubs. I'm in the school band, so I go to band practice three times a week. In the evening I love to sit on my favorite sofa by the window in my room and chat online with my friends. It's so cozy. Where do you feel comfortable?

Nicolas, 17, Waitsfield, Vermont
Hey guys, I'm Nicolas. I live in Waitsfield, a small town in Vermont.
I go to Bloomfield High School. The school isn't my favorite place, but I love the sports grounds there. I play lacrosse in spring and ice hockey in fall. It's great because I've made some good friends. After practice or a game, we often go to the mall. That's my favorite place because one of my favorite restaurants is there. They sell the best seafood in town. What's your favorite place? Church is also a big part of my life. When my family moved here, the church really helped us to feel part of the community. They also organize some fun activities for young people on Sunday afternoons.

Logan, 16, Philadelphia, Pennsylvania
My name is Logan. I live in the northeastern part of Philadelphia, or 'Philly'.
My family and I live in a small apartment. I share a room with my two younger brothers, so there's not much private space. Jacob and Noah are so nosy. That's why I spend as much time outside on the basketball court as possible. That's my favorite place. I can play alone or with friends and I can forget all my problems there. My second favorite place is the Magic Gardens arts center. The art there is just so creative. I get lots of ideas for my own art projects there. I go there when I have some money left. Some people think it's crazy, but I love it. Which place makes you happy?

○ D 19
● D 20

3 About Marsha, Nicolas and Logan

a) Are the sentences true or false? Correct the false sentences.

Marsha

Nicolas

Logan

1. Marsha lives in the centre of Boston.
   That's false. She lives in Charlestown, in the north of the city.
2. Music is part of her life at school.
3. Her bed is one of her favourite places.
4. Nicolas loves the cafeteria at school.
5. The restaurant at the mall has great pasta.
6. The church is important to Nicolas.
7. Logan has his own room at home.
8. He's a basketball player.
9. You can hear concerts at the Magic Gardens.

b) Choose one of the teenagers and answer their post. ► S7 Planning, writing and checking texts, p. 184

Hi …,
I'm … . I live in … . …

WB 9/2

4 That's interesting! ► W2 Adjectives, p. 233

a) Make five groups with the adjectives. ► ○ p. 123 ► S13 Looking up words, p. 194

1. good, *great, …*
2. bad
3. sad
4. unusual
5. interesting

awful | great ✓ | strange | exciting | terrible | fantastic | miserable | fascinating | weird | unhappy

● **b)** Add these adjectives to the groups in a). You can add more adjectives too.

odd | awesome | unpleasant | impressive | heartbroken | …

WB 10/3

5 Saying it differently ► W2 Adjectives, p. 233

a) Replace the underlined adjectives with adjectives that have a similar meaning.
► ○ p. 124

1. The clubs at our school are <u>nice</u>. I'm in two clubs.
   The clubs at our school are *fantastic*. I'm in two clubs.
2. I'm <u>sad</u> that I couldn't join the basketball club too.
3. The tea that we had at school yesterday was <u>bad</u>. I won't drink it again!
4. Some people think that the Magic Gardens are very <u>unusual</u>. But I like them.
5. The people at church talked about a <u>good</u> plan this morning. I liked it a lot.
6. The film that we saw last week was <u>interesting</u>.

Using synonyms for words like 'good', 'bad' and 'nice' can make your texts more varied and interesting.

● **b)** Work with a partner. Make sentences like in a).
Your partner replaces the adjectives.

D 21
D 22
WB 10/4

6 Talk about what you think of these things.

A

B

C

D

A I think that cat is beautiful | fascinating | interesting | … .
B I don't think so. I think it looks weird | awful | strange | … .
C …

A 6
WB 11/5

7 Life in an Amish community

a) Listen to Bridget and choose the right answers. ► p. 124

1. Where does Bridget live?
   A She lives near a lake with her parents.
   B She lives in a flat with her mother.
   C She lives on a farm with her parents and brothers.
2. When did Bridget leave the Amish school?
   A She left when she was 16.
   B She left when she was 15.
   C She left when she was 18.
3. What does Bridget do most mornings?
   A She helps with the animals and in the kitchen.
   B She looks after her two younger brothers.
   C She stays in bed until 8:30 a.m.
4. Why does she enjoy her job at the store?
   A She can be on her own, and it isn't busy.
   B She meets people there and finds out what's new.
   C She can choose what the store sells.
5. When do most Amish people use a machine?
   A They use one when they work in the garden.
   B They use one when they wash the plates after a meal.
   C They use one when they wash their clothes.
6. What does Bridget say about social media?
   A Her group doesn't use it.
   B Most Amish use it.
   C She often posts videos.

b) Listen again and take notes to answer the questions.

1. What does Bridget do in the afternoon?
2. What does she do on Sundays?
3. Would she like to use social media? Say why.

Culture
The Amish are a religious group who left Europe and went to North America in the 18th century. They still speak a German dialect at home.

V 9 How to
V 10 How to

G

Language revision: Comparison of adjectives ► G2, p. 148

Test yourself: Put in the adjectives in the right forms.
1. Waitsfield is — (quiet) than Boston.
2. Boston is — (big) than Waitsfield.
3. Marsha thinks that city life is — (exciting) than country life.
4. Nicolas thinks that his new school isn't the — (bad) place.
5. He loves ice hockey because it's one of the — (fast) team sports in the world.
6. Logan thinks that it's — (good) to meet his friends outside than at home.
7. Learning traditional skills is one of the — (important) things for Bridget.
8. Modern technology has made life in the Amish community — (easy) than it was before.

8 Marsha's brother Zach: My summer as an au pair ► S18 Peer correction, p. 200

D 23
D 24
WB 11/6

a) Complete the sentences with the right forms of these adjectives (-er or -est).

hard | cool | noisy | large | old ✓ | good

I'm Zach and I work for a family in Naples, Italy. I look after two children, Matilda and Daniele, while their parents are at work. Matilda is *older* (1) than Daniele. I make their breakfast and later I help them with their English. That's the — (2) work for me. But they think I'm — (3) than their English teacher at school. Then we usually go for a walk to the park and have an ice cream. The ice cream here is the — (4)! My room is nice and it's — (5) than my room at home. The family live in a busy part of the city. It's much — (6) than where I live in Charlestown.

WB 12/7–8

b) Put in the adjectives in the right forms.

I think Naples is *more beautiful* (1 beautiful) than Boston, which is where I'm from. The people are — (2 friendly) than they are at home, but not so many people speak English. That's one of the — (3 difficult) things for me. The summer here is — (4 hot) than in Boston. The nights are also very warm. I love the food. Italy has the — (5 fantastic) pizza in the world. It's also — (6 cheap) than in Boston. So you can buy one more often. 😊

9 Boston or Waitsfield – which place do you like better?

WB 12/9

a) Use these and your own adjectives to compare the places. ► ○ p. 125

large | colourful | small | noisy | interesting | ...

A

B

A I think Boston is better. The city is larger and ... .

B I prefer Waitsfield. It's ... .

b) Find photos of other interesting cities and compare them with a partner.

I 2
V 11 How to
D 25 Support

10 Your turn: A short video about your favourite place

Make a video about your favourite place and what you do there. It shouldn't be longer than three minutes.

► S11 Making a short film, p. 193

Step 1

What's your favourite place?
What do you do there?
Why is it important to you?

- *Grandma's garden*
- *help her with the flowers, the fruit and vegetables*
- *relax after school*
- *...*

Step 2

Make a short video about your favourite place. Make your video more interesting by using different angles and zooms.

► S16 How to use photos, films and texts, p. 198

Media tip

If you want to include other people in your video, you need to ask for their permission first.

Step 3

Use the video tool on a tablet or a phone to edit your video.

Step 4

Write a short text about the place and what you do there.

► S7 Planning, writing and checking texts, p. 184

Step 5

Record your text.

Skills

After recording a text, you should listen to it and check if you can understand everything.

Step 6

Finish your video by putting everything together.

Step 7

Share your video with other people in your class. Ask for and give feedback.

► S8 Giving and asking for feedback, p. 190

✓ I can talk about young people's lives.

The American Dream

D 26
My plan
A 7
D 27

1 Read the text. Find the meanings of the underlined words.

► S13 Looking up words, p. 194

The American Dream is the belief that the USA is the land of freedom and full of opportunities (1). You can achieve (2) anything if you believe in yourself. If you work hard, you can make your life a success (3). It doesn't matter (4) who you are or where you are from. This is the reason why many people immigrate (5) to the USA – they want to have the chance (6) of a better life. The Statue of Liberty has become a symbol of this.

1. opportunity – die Möglichkeit

A 8
D 28
D 29
WB 13/1–2

2 An interview from a podcast

a) Listen to the interview and take notes.

Partner A takes notes about Michael's answers, partner B about Lin's answers.

A

Michael

B

Lin

1. Where is the person's family from?
2. What does the American Dream mean for Michael or Lin?
3. What is success for him or her?
4. What makes him or her happy?

b) Exchange your notes with your partner.

Culture

New York City has the largest Jewish population of any city in the world. The largest number of Jewish people arrived there between the 1880s and the 1940s. They came from Russia, Germany, Poland and Lithuania.

P

3 What's your dream? Answer the questions and write a short text.

► S7 Planning, writing and checking texts, p. 184

- What do you want to achieve in life?
- What is success for you?
- What makes you happy?

You can also add a photo that represents your dream.

✔ I can understand an interview.

 ▷ S2, p. 178
V 13
How to

Finding a new home

D 30
My plan
A 9

A

North Hotel
5th Avenue
New York City
USA

18th January 1898

My dear Mary,

New York is a noisy city. It is full of people but also full of opportunities.

When I arrived two weeks ago, I was overwhelmed by it. At Ellis Island it seemed to me that everyone knew what they were doing except me. I stood in line with people from Ireland, Italy, Germany, Poland and other countries. You could see in their eyes the determination[1] to succeed here. We were all extremely tired and exhausted. The immigration officials shouted at us. I was terrified. At that moment I wanted nothing more than to be back in London with you.

I am feeling much better now and I love New York more and more. I work at the North Hotel on Fifth Avenue. It is a huge building with 13 floors and 450 bedrooms. I work in the kitchen as a chef. I work hard, and the hours are long. The head chef is loud and often angry, but he is fair and I am learning a lot. The staff here are friendly and they look after us. I live in the hotel. I share a small room with a chef from France and a porter[2] from Poland. They are good men.

I hope you are well. I think about you every minute of every day. I am counting the weeks until you will be able to come and join me here. I feel sure we will have a wonderful future in this new land.

I miss you so much.

With lots of love,
Albert

A 10

B

28th May 1898

I never knew an ocean could be so big. I have been at sea for almost three weeks now, and there is still no sign of America. I am just very glad that the sea is calm. It is hard enough on board without getting seasick.

We have to get up and be out of our beds by 7 o'clock each morning. The rest of the day we spend on our deck or in the public areas. We have some food and water. It is never enough, and we are always hungry.

The cabins are small and dark. I share a cabin with seven other women and girls from England, Scotland and Ireland. There is no fresh air or natural light, and we share one toilet between 16 people. There are often arguments. But there is also friendship.

Two of the girls from Cork in Ireland are on their own. They have jobs at one of the big department stores, but they look so scared. I do my best to make them feel better and I have promised[3] I will come and visit them. I feel like a mother to them.

The other women and girls are going to New York to be with their husbands and fathers. They seemed highly impressed when I told them that my husband worked at the North Hotel. That made me feel a little better.

I miss Albert so very much. The thought that I will see him again in four days keeps me going[4].

1 determination – *die Entschlossenheit*; 2 porter – *eine Person, die schwere Lasten oder Gepäck trägt*; 3 to promise – *versprechen*; 4 to keep someone going – *jemanden aufrechterhalten*

A 11

C

WHITE STAR LINE

LIVERPOOL – QUEENSTOWN – NEW YORK CITY

Passenger ticket No. 458977 Date: 9th May 1898

Name	*Mary Backshall*	Age	*23*
From	*Liverpool*	To	*NYC*
Class	*Third Class*	Cabin	*25F*

A 12

D

Clothes: two dresses, one coat, two blouses, two skirts, one scarf, three pairs of socks, underwear
Toiletries[5]: soap, hairbrush, perfume / Documents[6]: papers, tickets
Food: dried fruit, nuts, biscuits / Other: money, blankets, books, photos, sewing box[7]

5 toiletries – *die Hygieneartikel*; 6 documents – *die Dokumente, die Papiere*; 7 sewing box – *das Nähkästchen*

1 Read the texts.

2 Types of text

► S7 Planning, writing and checking texts, p.184

D 31
D 32

a) Match the types of text with texts A–D.

list | letter | ticket | diary entry

A. ...

b) Explain your answers. What are the characteristics of each text?

Text A is a ... because ... .

3 Finding a new home

D 33
D 34

a) Read the texts again and take notes.

1. Who are the texts about?
2. What happened?
3. When, where and why did the things happen?
4. How did the people feel?

b) Tell Mary and Albert's story. Use your notes.

Albert arrived in New York in January 1898.
He was ... when he arrived at Ellis Island, but later he ... . His wife Mary left Liverpool ... .

4 Choose one of these tasks.

P

WB 15/1–4

a) Imagine you are Mary. Write an answer to Albert's letter.

► S7 Planning, writing and checking texts, p.184

Respond to his news and ask some questions about his life in New York.

My dear Albert,
I am happy to hear from you. ...
...

OR

b) Interview someone with a multicultural background about life in Germany.

► S3 Speaking with other people, p.180

Decide which questions you want to ask. Take notes during the interview or record it.

Where are you / your family from?
Why did ...?
... difficult? ...

✔ I can understand different texts about the same subject.

Checklist

D 35 My plan

WB 16

Check in: Arriving in the Northeast

✓ I can understand information about the Northeast.

WB 16

Station 1: Sights in New York City

I can name parts of a building.
► W1 Parts of a building, p. 232
I can say what happened in the past.
► G1, p. 146 (Simple past: statements, negatives, questions)

basement | staircase | solar panels | balcony | …
The building opened in 1913. | It was great. | They didn't visit the memorial. | She didn't visit Edge. | Where did you go? | Did he like the museum? | …

✓ I can present sights in New York City.

WB 17

Viewing: Two very different days in New York

✓ I can understand a documentary.

WB 17

Station 2: A day in the life of an American teenager

I can name qualities of things and people.
► W2 Adjectives, p. 233
I can compare qualities of things and people.
► G2, p. 148 (Comparison of adjectives)

strange | fascinating | awesome | great | …
The new school is better than the old one. | His life is more exciting now. | This is the hardest work. | …

✓ I can talk about young people's lives.

WB 18

Listening: The American Dream

✓ I can understand an interview.

WB 18

Reading: Finding a new home

✓ I can understand different texts about the same subject.

I 3 Quiz

?

Find the photo in the unit.
You can also do the online quiz about the Northeast.

D 36
Support

Task: A presentation

Give a presentation about a person who has been successful. It does not have to be an American.

► S4 Giving a presentation, p. 181

Step 1

Choose a person who has been successful. It can be an actor, a scientist, an artist, an athlete or somebody from your family or a friend.

Alice Augusta Ball (scientist), Sümeyye Boyacı (Paralympic swimmer), Ryyan Alshebl (from refugee to mayor), ...

Step 2

Search the internet to find out more about the person's life.
Think about the person's life and story.
What made the person successful?

► S14 Using the internet, p. 196

Alice Augusta Ball

- *born in 1892*
- *grew up in Honolulu, Hawaii*
- *first African American who graduated from College of Hawaii*
- *first female chemistry teacher there*
- *...*

Step 3

Make a draft.
Introduce the person.
Write about what makes the person special and what the person has achieved.

► S7 Planning, writing and checking texts, p. 184

Alice Augusta Ball was a scientist. She was born in 1892 and grew up in Honolulu, Hawaii. She was the first African American who graduated from the College of Hawaii. Ball was also the first female chemistry teacher there. ...

Step 4

Add some photos.

► S16 How to use photos, films and texts, p. 198

S Skills

You can make a poster or show a short film as part of your presentation. You can also use a computer to give your presentation.

Step 5

Practise the presentation.

► S18 Read and look up, p. 200

Step 6

Give the presentation.
Ask for and give feedback.

► S8 Giving and asking for feedback, p. 190

The Northeast – past and present

A 13

Native Americans had lived in the Northeast for thousands of years when the first European settlers arrived and founded colonies along the coast. By 1776, when the USA became independent from Britain, there were 13 colonies. These became the first states of the new country.

1

2

3

1 Before 1600 **the Patuxet** Native Americans lived in what later became Massachusetts. However, 20 years later European diseases had killed almost all the Patuxet. Today visitors can learn about the Patuxet at the Plimoth Patuxet Museums.

2 The ship **the Mayflower** sailed to America from Plymouth in England in 1620. There were 102 passengers on board. These men, women, and children founded New Plymouth, the first permanent[1] colony in New England. They were later called the 'Pilgrims'.

3 **Cape Cod** is a peninsula[2] which stretches out[3] into the Atlantic Ocean. The Mayflower landed here a few days before the settlers founded Plymouth. Today Cape Cod is also famous for its seafood, and tourists love its beautiful beaches.

1 permanent – *permanent, dauerhaft*; 2 peninsula – *die Halbinsel*; 3 to stretch out – *sich erstrecken*

1 What do you already know about the places and things in the photos?

2 What was new in the texts? What did you find interesting?

I knew / didn't know that … .
It's interesting that … .

I 4–6 360° Let's have a look around New York City!

4

5

6

4 The Europeans began to build settlements[4] in **the White Mountains** in New Hampshire in the mid-17th century. Today many tourists love to visit the mountains in September and October to see the beautiful fall colors.

5 **Boston** was an important city in 1773. In that year protesters[5] against British taxes[6] on tea threw chests[7] of tea into the sea in Boston. This became known as the 'Boston Tea Party'. Modern Boston is a center for artificial intelligence[8] and biotechnology.

6 Philadelphia is the largest city in Pennsylvania. On July 4, 1776, delegates[9] from the 13 colonies signed **the Declaration of Independence** there. The flag of the USA has 13 stripes[10] for the 13 original colonies and 50 stars for the 50 states of the USA today.

4 settlement – *die Siedlung*; 5 protester – *der Demonstrant / die Demonstrantin*; 6 tax – *die Steuer*; 7 chest – *die Kiste*; 8 artificial intelligence – *die künstliche Intelligenz*; 9 delegate – *der Delegierte / die Delegierte*; 10 stripe – *der Streifen*

D 37 Support

1 In a city

a) Copy the table. Put the words and phrases into groups.

Kinds of building	Parts of a building	Other things/places in a city
store	...	...
...		

shopping street | store ✓ | balcony | square | skyscraper | basement | museum | park | cycle lane | café | roof | hotel | entrance | market | staircase

b) Add three of your own words to each group.

c) Write five sentences about a city that you know. Use the words from the table. Choose two from each group.

2 Complete the sentences about New York.

1. Edge is a *viewing platform* about 1,100 feet above the ground.
2. It's on the side of the North Tower, one of the city's — .
3. Edge has a glass — .
4. It's fun to go for — on the High Line.
5. Most tourists take lots of — in New York.
6. Fifth Avenue is New York's greatest — .
7. Leo enjoyed the clothes stores there because he likes — and design.
8. New York is famous for its yellow — .
9. The — is an easy way to get around the city. There are 36 lines.
10. The Hudson is a — that goes through New York.

3 What did they do? What didn't they do?

a) Write sentences about Leo and Aya's trip to New York.

1. Leo and Aya – visit – Edge first
   Leo and Aya visited Edge first.
2. they – enjoy – some amazing views of the city
3. Leo – not climb – the stairs in the North Tower
4. they – take – a lot of photos on the High Line
5. Aya – love – the Intrepid Museum
6. they – not take – a taxi
7. they – spend – an afternoon on Fifth Avenue too
8. Aya – not enjoy – the clothes stores as much as Leo
9. Aya I – not buy – anything at the museum
10. Leo We – have – a great time in New York

Für die Verneinung im „simple past" setzt du bei Vollverben **didn't** vor das Verb in der Grundform.

b) Write ten sentences about your last trip. What did/didn't you do?

take ... | stay ... | eat ... | see ... | meet ... | visit ... | ...

I went to ... with ... . I/We ... . I/We didn't ... .

4 Put in was, wasn't, were or weren't.

Aya We *were* (1) in New York last September. The skyscrapers — (2) fantastic! The weather — (3) warm (over 25°C!) and sunny. The High Line — (4) very crowded – only a few people — (5) there that day. But the Intrepid Museum — (6) very busy, and we had to wait more than 20 minutes before we could go in. The stores on Fifth Avenue — (7) my highlight – I'm not very interested in fashion. We — (8) in New York for long, but we saw a lot!

5 Questions and answers

a) Write questions.

1. you – watch TV last night
   Did you watch TV last night?
2. you and your family – go on a trip last year
3. you – take any photos yesterday
4. your English teacher – give you any homework last week
5. your friend – chat with you yesterday
6. what – you do last Sunday
7. when – you get up yesterday
8. where – you spend Christmas Day last year

b) Write your answers. Give more information.

1. Yes, I did. I watched … . / No, I didn't. I don't usually … .

6 Put in the adjectives in the comparative (+) or superlative (++) form.

1. Nicolas is a year *older* than Logan. (old +)
2. The Magic Gardens have the — art projects in Philadelphia. (exciting ++)
3. Logan's brothers are — than him. (young +)
4. Philadelphia is a — city than Boston. (big +)
5. Nicolas thinks that ice hockey is — than school. (interesting +)
6. His favourite restaurant has the — seafood in town. (fantastic ++)
7. Being in the church made life — for Nicolas when they moved. (easy +)
8. Boston is one of the — cities in the USA. (famous ++)

old → **older**, **oldest**
big → **bigger**, **biggest**
crazy → **crazier**, **craziest**
interesting → **more / most interesting**
famous → **more / most famous**

7 Write a text for 'Making new friends online'.

Write a text about yourself for the website on page 16 of your book. Include this information:

1. Say your name and where you're from.
2. Name your favourite place and say why you like it.
3. Say how you spend your free time.
4. Give some information about your family.
5. Ask the reader about his/her favourite place.

2 Off to the Midwest

In this unit you will …
- find out about the Midwest.
  ► Check in
- talk about school life.
  ► Station 1
- listen to a radio show.
  ► Listening
- talk about holidays and festivals.
  ► Station 2
- watch a live documentary.
  ► Viewing
- read part of a short story.
  ► Reading

D 38
My plan

A 14

A

B

The Midwest is the USA's most important region for agriculture and manufacturing. It's famous for its endless fields of wheat, corn, and soy, and there's also a lot of dairy farming. The car factories in Michigan and other states of the Midwest are an important part of the economy of the USA.

Info

Biggest city: Chicago, about 2.6 million people

Sights: Mount Rushmore, the Great Lakes, Badlands National Park

Time zones: three (Eastern, Central and Mountain Standard Time)

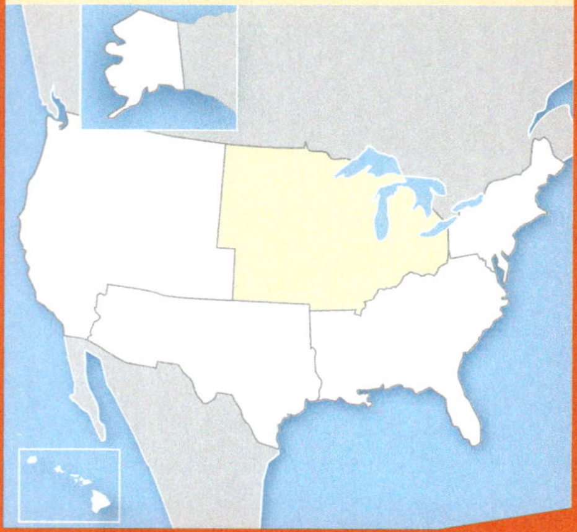

C

The Oglala Lakota Nation is a Native American tribe in South Dakota. They traditionally hunted bison in parts of the Midwest. Today visitors can learn about the culture of the tribe at a living history village.

D

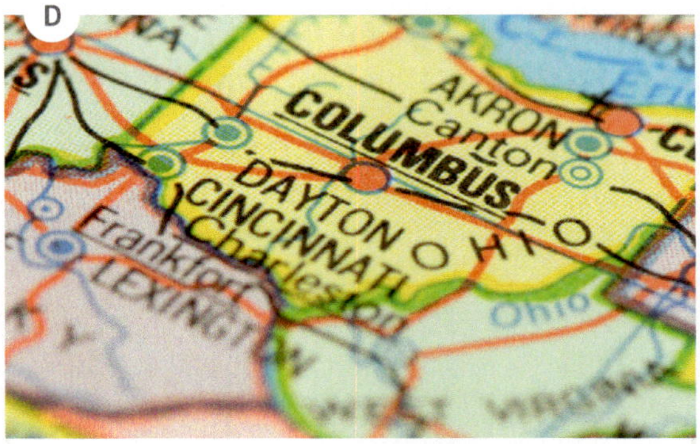

Millions of German families settled here during the 19th century. Many were farmers or craftspeople, and they brought their culture with them. That's why there are towns here with names like Augsburg and Dresden.

E

The Kansas City Chiefs are a very successful American football team. They've won the Super Bowl, the most famous sports event in the USA, four times.

F

Chicago is on the shores of Lake Michigan, one of the Great Lakes. It's one of the largest cities in the USA. Al Capone was a famous criminal in Chicago in the 1920s. There are many movies and songs about his life.

1 Facts about the Midwest

D 39 Support P

a) Read the texts. Collect information about the Midwest. Make a mind map.

A 15

V 14

b) What information can you find out about the Midwest from the audio and the video? Add it to your mind map.

WB 19/1–3

c) Talk about the Midwest with the help of your mind map.

Midwest: landscapes, sights, other facts, economy, people

V

Audio and video words

formation – die Formation
fossil – das Fossil; die Versteinerung
plain – die Ebene
president – der Präsident / die Präsidentin
crop – die Feldfrucht
tornado – der Tornado

✓ I can understand information about the Midwest.

High school life

D 40 My plan
A 16
WB 20/1–2

1 Read the text from a blog.

Internet

11/05/2024

Hey, it's Lena, welcome to my blog! I'm an exchange student at a high school in Columbus, Ohio. I started school here at the beginning of September. Let me tell you all what it's really like!

I get up at 6:30 and get ready for school. You know, there's a dress code, and students aren't allowed to wear baseball caps or crop tops, for example! I usually wear jeans and a sweater. I also check the school's online portal every morning. Then I walk to the end of the road with Paisley, my host sister. We meet our friends where the yellow school bus stops and ride to school together.

The bus arrives at school at about 7:45. We have to walk through a metal detector. That felt a bit strange at first. Then I put my bag in my locker and hang out with my friends in the hallway. At 7:55 the school gates close. If you're late three times, you have to go to detention.

We start the day with homeroom at 8:00. It's like a class meeting with our homeroom teacher. I love my homeroom group. We get information and news about school events, and we can talk if we have any problems. Students also take the Pledge of Allegiance every day. They say that they're loyal to their country.

Each student has a schedule. It has classes which everyone does, like math, English, and science, but there are also electives. These are classes which students can choose. I wanted to try out some new things, so I chose film production, creative writing, and drama. How cool is that?

The school cafeteria is where everyone eats. The food isn't as good as it is at home with my host family, but it's OK. The cafeteria is also a good place to hang out with friends. Paisley has really helped me make friends. She's awesome, and because of her I feel totally at home here.

There are clubs after school every day, so the school days are longer than they are in Germany. I go to a foreign language club on Mondays and Wednesdays and our yearbook club on Thursdays. Paisley plays volleyball and she's a member of the student council. She's organizing the prom, the dance that takes place once a year. It's a highlight for most students. I can't wait to go there in March! On Friday afternoons everyone goes to watch a big American football game at the school. It's an amazing event, and they also live stream the games on the school's social media channel.

I'm loving my time here at high school. Do you have any questions? Please post them in the comments. Maybe I can answer them for you.
Bye!

Language tip ► G5, p. 154

We meet our friends **where** the bus stops.

Culture

The most popular foreign languages at school in the USA are Spanish, French and German.

2 Lena's blog

a) Complete the sentences with information from the text. Use one or two words. ► ○ p. 126

1. Lena started school in the USA in *September*.
2. She and her host sister Paisley go to school by —.
3. Students must go through a — when they enter the school.
4. The school gates — at 7:55.
5. Students have to go to — if they are late too often.
6. Each student has different —, like film production or drama.
7. Students can go to — after school every day.
8. They can watch an — game at school or on the school's social media channel.

● **b)** Write your own headings for the paragraphs of the blog.

1. Hello from Columbus, Ohio

3 Talk about the blog. ► S18 Round robin, p. 201

○ D 41

What did you find most interesting? What was new to you?

A I was surprised that students in the USA can choose some of their subjects. …
B …

4 High schools in the USA ► W3 School life in the USA, p. 234

WB 20/3

a) Find words in the text for these definitions. ► ○ p. 127

1. some rules about what you can wear at school *dress code*
2. a website with news and messages
3. a small cupboard where students keep their bags
4. when a student has broken the rules and must stay longer
5. classes that students can choose themselves
6. an activity where students make a book about the school year
7. a group of students who meet regularly to organise things for other students

● **b)** Read the texts. Which high school club or activity would you choose?

A

Do you play an instrument? Join our orchestra! We practice on Mondays at 3:25 p.m.

B

At peer tutoring we help other students with their work. We meet on Tuesdays at 3:25 p.m.

C

If you like having arguments, try our debate club! It's every Thursday at 3:25 p.m.

D

Cheerleading is very important at our school. We practice on Fridays at 3:25 p.m.

V 3
How to
WB 21/4

5 Mediation ► S9 Mediation, p. 191

Die Schülervertretung an deiner Schule informiert sich, wie Schülervertretungen in anderen Ländern funktionieren. Ein amerikanischer Freund hat dir diesen Screenshot geschickt.
Fasse auf Deutsch für die anderen zusammen, wer die Personen und was ihre Aufgaben sind.

Introducing your new high school student council officers

Olivia Lacey

Hey guys, I'm Olivia,
your president for this year. I'm interested in drama, music, and health. One of my aims this year is to introduce regular wellbeing days with yoga, meditation, and healthy cooking classes.

Grant Pettinato

Hey everyone, I'm Grant,
your vice president. I love wrestling, football, and I'm also in the debate club. I'm going to organize the spring festival this year.

Nolan Wang

Hi, I'm Nolan.
I'm the secretary this year. I'm responsible for organizing meetings and keeping records. You can contact me with any questions you have about student council meetings.

Laura Gallo

Hello, I'm Laura,
and I'm the treasurer of the school student council. I'm in charge of managing the student council bank account. I help decide how much money each club gets.

D 42
D 43
WB 21/5

6 Complete the text from the website. ► S18 Peer correction, p. 200

trip | fill in | hallways | members ✓ | exams | meet | projects | take part in | quiet | biology

Internet

News

Science club
The science club is looking for new *members* (1) who want to work on exciting — (2) that help to solve real problems. There are opportunities to — (3) science competitions. We — (4) every Tuesday and Thursday at 3:25 p.m. in the — (5) room. Join now!

Arts and media center closed
English and Spanish — (6) will take place in the arts and media center on Friday. Please be — (7) when you walk in the — (8) on the third floor.

Calling all history students
If you want to go on the school — (9) to Indianapolis next weekend, you must — (10) the registration form before Wednesday.

D 44
D 45
WB 22/6

7 Compare Lena's school with your own school. Write about four aspects.

The school times are different at Lena's school.
Lena's school starts at … . Our school … .

school times | subjects | rules | clubs | …

V 15
How to

Language revision: Simple present ► G3, p. 150

G

Test yourself: Put in the verbs in the right forms.

1. The bus — (leave) at 7:25 a.m. every day.
2. We — (not have) English on Wednesdays.
3. What subjects — (you – have) on Mondays?
4. Paisley — (be) Lena's host sister.
5. We always — (eat) lunch in the cafeteria.
6. — (be) the meals nice?
7. Lena — (not go) to a club on Tuesdays.
8. The gym — (not be) open on Mondays.

WB 22/7–8

8 Lena's American family life

a) Write sentences. ► ○ p. 128

cook | not play | talk ✓ | hang out | write | not do

A

Lena | every Sunday

B

she and Paisley | on Saturdays

C

her host parents | sometimes | together

D

Lena and Paisley | homework | together

E

Lena | at school

F
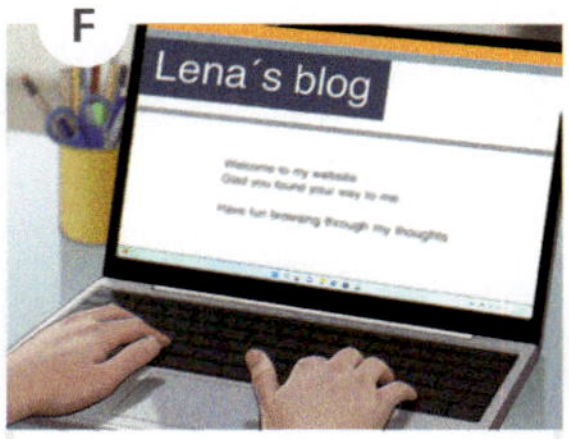

she | often | in the evenings

A. Lena talks to her parents every Sunday.

● b) Write six sentences about your family life. Use the verbs from a).

WB 23/9–11

9 How is life in Columbus?

a) Complete the dialogue. ► ○ p. 128 ► S18 Peer correction, p. 200

do | live | be | think | like ✓ | miss | spend

Todd: How *do you like* (1) life in Columbus, Lena?
Lena: It — (2) great!
Todd: Cool. Where — (3)?
Lena: In Logan Street.
Todd: What — (4) in your free time?
Lena: I often — (5) time with my host sister.
Todd: — (6) anything?
Lena: Yes, my family. I often — (7) about them.

● b) Write a dialogue with a new student at your school. Ask and answer at least five questions.

I 7

V 16 How to

D 46 Support

10 Your turn: A leaflet about your school

Make a leaflet for exchange students or new students from other countries who come to your school. Include information that you think they will need to know. ► S7 Planning, writing and checking texts, p. 184

Step 1

Get into groups of three students. Think about topics that are important to school life.
Make notes.

- *subjects*
- *sports*
- *school platform / news about school life*
- *...*

Step 2

Collect useful information that a new student would need to know. Make a table with the information and where to find it.

Things to know	Where to find out
sports (examples, when, where ...)	*visit the school's website: ...*
...	*...*

Step 3

Structure your notes and make a plan for your leaflet.

I'd like to write about ... first because ... .
It's quite important to know ... .
Maybe we should leave out ... .

Step 4

Write a short text for each piece of information.
► S18 Peer correction, p. 200

Sports

Our school has ... . You can ... .
It's open ... .

Step 5

Find photos for your leaflet. You can take your own photos too.
► S15 Taking good photos, p. 197
► S16 How to use photos, films and texts, p. 198

The school gym

Step 6

Organise all your texts and photos and make your leaflet.

Media tip
You can also use wiki software. This lets every student change the texts at any time.

Step 7

Ask for and give feedback.
► S8 Giving and asking for feedback, p. 190

✔ I can talk about school life.

D 47 My plan

Meet the farmers

D 48 D 49

1 Words and their meanings

a) Match the words with the definitions. Look in your dictionary if you aren't sure. There are three more words than you need. ► S13 Looking up words, p. 194

dairy | cherry | grass | crops | costs | to increase | acre ✓ | to produce | farmer

1. an area of land, about 4,050 m² *acre*
2. to become larger
3. about milk
4. to make products
5. the things that a farmer grows
6. a kind of fruit

b) Write your own definitions for the words that you didn't need.

A 17 D 50 D 51 WB 24/1

2 Farm stories

a) Listen to a radio show about two farmers in the Midwest. Copy and complete the notes.

Fischer's Farm
1. in *North Dakota* (state)
2. a — farm
3. about — of land
4. — people work there (number)
5. now sell — in farm store (three things)

Allen's Farm
6. in — (state)
7. grow — and other fruit (two things)
8. huge farm, — of land
9. — staff for most of the year (number)
10. want to open a — next year

b) Listen again. Take notes to answer the questions.

S Skills
When people talk, you should listen carefully to how they speak as well as what they say. Recognising how someone feels will help you understand them better.

Martin Fischer
1. Why does he think his cows produce better milk?
2. What two problems does he talk about?
3. What does he say about the new products?

Catherine Allen
4. What does she like about working on a farm?
5. Why did they lose their crops a few years ago?
6. How does she feel about the future?

WB 24/2

3 Would you like to work on a farm? Say why. Talk to your partner.

A I would / wouldn't like to work on a farm because … .
B I agree / don't agree. I think it would be … . /
I'm not sure about that.

✓ I can understand a radio show.

Happy holidays

D 52
My plan
D 53

1 Do you like family celebrations? Say why.

I like / don't like family celebrations because I like / don't like seeing my ... .

A 18
WB 25/1–2

2 Read the dialogue.

It's Thanksgiving morning, and Brad is at home with his mom, his dad, and his younger brother Lincoln, in Cincinnati, Ohio. Brad is making a video call to his sister Regan, who is in Austin, Texas.

Regan Hey Brad, what's happening at home?

Brad Hey Regan, we're all busy here! Dad is preparing the turkey. I think he wants to put it in the oven soon. Mom is baking the pumpkin pie. It's also snowing!

Regan Oh wow! What's Lincoln doing?

Brad I'm glad to say that he isn't helping in the kitchen! He's tidying the living room now. Here he is.

Lincoln Hi Regan!

Regan Hey Lincs! Good to see you! Good job with the living room!

Lincoln Very funny! Not!

Regan Brad, what else will we have for Thanksgiving dinner this evening?

Brad Grandpa has made his homemade cornbread, and Grandma has made pecan pie. You love that, don't you?

Regan Yes, I can't wait. So, who else will be there?

Brad Aunt Susan, Uncle Peter, and Cousin Moira. And Grandma Margaret, of course!

Regan Cool! I haven't seen Moira in ages. No Aunt Alice and Pedro this year?

Brad No, they're with Pedro's family.

Regan What are you doing to help?

Brad I'm making my Thanksgiving fruit punch!

Regan What's in it this year?

Brad I can't tell you that, can I? It's a secret. But it's a new recipe.

Regan That's good! Is that Mom in the background? Hey Mom!

Mom Hey Regan. Can't wait to see you later. Safe flight, honey!

Regan Thanks!

Brad What are you doing at the moment, Regan?

Regan I've just packed my suitcase, and now I'm waiting for my cinnamon cookies to finish baking. I'll leave for the airport in an hour.

Brad What time is your flight?

Regan It's at 2:25 this afternoon. The flight takes about two and a half hours, so I should be in Cincinnati at about 6 o'clock your time.

Brad Mom and I will pick you up at the airport.

Regan That's awesome. Thank you!

Brad OK, I need to make that punch now. See you later. Safe flight!

Regan Thanks. See you later!

Culture

Thanksgiving is one of the most important holidays in the USA. It's on the fourth Thursday of November. There's always a big meal, with turkey, pumpkin pie and other dishes, and people often tell each other what they are thankful for.

Language tip ► G6, p. 155

You love pecan pie, **don't you**?

D 54
D 55

3 A video call

a) Answer the questions in sentences.

1. What day is it today?
   Today is … .
2. Where is Regan?
3. Which people take part in the call?
4. What will they do together later?

Skills

Skimming a text means reading it to get a general understanding. You don't need to read or understand every word. **Scanning** a text means looking through the text to find the words or information that you need.

b) Complete the sentences with the right words or phrases.

1. Brad's father wants to — in the oven soon.
2. Lincoln is — at the moment.
3. Regan loves her grandma's — .
4. Aunt Alice and Pedro — .
5. — will travel by plane later.
6. The flight time is — .
7. — will meet Regan at the airport.
8. Brad wants to — after the call.

WB 25/3

4 Holidays and celebrations ► W4 Celebrating special days, p. 235

a) Match the words to make phrases. ► ○ p. 129

A

light *candles*

B

prepare and eat

C

give or receive

D

watch or take part in

E

wear

F

put up

presents | decorations | a parade | special clothes | candles ✓ | a special meal

b) Make phrases. Use your dictionary if you aren't sure.

donate | make | remember | watch

a resolution | a fireworks display | relatives and friends who are no longer alive | money to charity

D 56
D 57

5 Talk about the activities. When do you do them? ► S18 Double circle, p. 201

A We usually light candles at … .
I always … on my birthday.
B That's cool! I … .

If you don't understand your partner, say:
"Sorry, I don't understand." or
"Can you say that again, please?"

6 Regan's voice messages

A 19
WB 26/4

a) Listen and choose the right answers.

1. She wants to go to the airport by **train** | *bus* | **car**.
2. Her flight will leave **30** | **60** | **90** minutes later.
3. She can buy a **book** | **sweater** | **pen** for her dad.
4. The plane will leave at **3:20** | **4:20** | **8:20** p.m.
5. She doesn't have her **coat** | **ticket** | **luggage** yet.

Culture
The USA is a very big country. Going from one state to another sometimes means that you cross into a different time zone.

b) Write or record an answer to one of Regan's voice messages. ► S7 Planning, writing and checking texts, p. 184

7 British or American English?

A 20
D 58
D 59
WB 26/5

a) Copy the table. Listen and put the words in the correct lists.
Look at page 203 for help.

1. Tuesday
2. turkey
3. party
4. airport
5. water
6. afternoon
7. of course
8. tomato
9. can't
10. new

British English (BE)	American English (AE)
Tuesday	...
...	...

A 21

b) Listen to the sentences. Are they American English (AE) or British English (BE)?

1. My aunt and uncle are going by car.
2. What are we going to have for dinner?
3. I'm waiting for the bus.
4. Can't wait to see you later!

WB 26/6

8 A cartoon ► S5 Describing photos and pictures, p. 182

a) Describe the cartoon. ► ○ p. 129

A turkey and a ... .
...

"I'd like to spend November and December in a foreign country."

● b) Tell the story of what happened at the travel agency. Add your own ideas for what the woman can say. Write about 70 words.

One day a turkey went to ... .

Skills
Cartoons are often about the culture of a country. You often need to make a connection (in this example between turkeys, November and December and Thanksgiving traditions) to understand the joke.

V 17
How to

V 18
How to

Language revision: Present progressive ► G4, p. 152

G

Test yourself: Write sentences in the present progressive.

1. Aunt Susan | visit | relatives | at the moment
2. I | celebrate | my | birthday | today
3. Brad's parents | not have | dinner | in a restaurant | this evening
4. Regan and Brad | sit | in the kitchen | now
5. I | not eat | pumpkin pie | at the moment
6. you | wear | special clothes | today?
7. what | your friend | do | right now?

WB 27/7–9

9 What's happening?

a) Complete the phone call. ► ○ p. 130

Alice How *are you enjoying* (1 you – enjoy) Thanksgiving, Regan?
Regan We — (2 have) a lot of fun. I — (3 play) a game with Brad and Moira at the moment. How about you? — (4 you – visit) Pedro's family?
Alice Yes, we — (5 stay) with Pedro's parents. It's cold here, but it — (6 not rain) at the moment!
Brad Hey Regan, who — (7 you – talk) to?
Regan Aunt Alice.
Brad Oh, say hi from me. But we need you here, Regan. Moira — (8 win) the game, and we have to stop her!
Regan OK, Aunt Alice, I have to go. They — (9 wait) for me. Would you like to speak to Mom? She — (10 not play).
Alice Sure, speak soon, Regan!

● **b)** You're at a friend's birthday party. Your American exchange student couldn't come.
Write and record a voice message and say what's happening at the party. You can use these ideas:

dance | play | eat | cool | loud | …

Hi Emily, I'm … . The party is … .

WB 28/10–12

10 Photos from a Midwest carnival

a) Put in the verbs in the simple present or the present progressive. ► ○ p. 130

Moira The Saint Paul Winter Carnival last February was fun. This is a photo of the parade. Look, the people *are wearing* (1 wear) cool costumes.
Brad Wow! There's snow too.
Moira Yes, it — (2 not snow) every year, but we had a lot this time! The carnival king — (3 ride) in the parade in this photo.
Brad Cool. What about the people in this one?
Moira They — (4 take part) in the Fire & Ice Run. It's a special race.
Brad Is the food good too?
Moira Yes, they always — (5 sell) awesome burgers. Look, my friend Ben — (6 eat) one in this photo.

● **b)** Find a photo of a winter event where you live and show it to a partner. Use these phrases:

… in this photo. | I/We/They always … . | Look! … | … usually …

I 8
V 19 How to
D 60 Support

11 Your turn: A slide show

Make and present a slide show with photos from a celebration or another event.

► S4 Giving a presentation, p. 181

Step 1

Think of a celebration or other event that you enjoyed and would like to present to your class. It can be a family event or an event where you live.

Step 2

Search for photos of the event on your phone or laptop.
There should be enough photos showing different situations to make your slide show interesting.

Media tip
You can sort your photos by date. You can also add descriptions and locations or create folders to find photos more easily.

Step 3

Choose five to ten photos. Organise your photos in a presentation tool.

► S16 How to use photos, films and texts, p. 198

Skills
You should make sure that all the people look OK in the photos. It's a good idea to ask yourself if you would like others to see you like this in a slide show.

Step 4

Write a short introduction to your celebration or event. Answer the wh-questions.
Which day or event?
Who?
Where?
When?

My cousin's birthday
- *my cousin's family and 20 guests*
- *at my cousin's house*
- *after breakfast on 4th April*

Step 5

Prepare sentences to describe what is happening in the photos.
Use the present progressive.

A In this photo you can see my cousin. She is eating a piece of cake. My mum is dancing with my grandpa. …

Step 6

Present your slide show to your class. Describe the photos. Thank your audience at the end and ask if they have any questions.

A That's the end of my presentation. Thank you for watching. Do you have any questions?

Step 7

Ask for and give feedback.

► S8 Giving and asking for feedback, p. 190

✓ I can talk about holidays and festivals.

D 61
My plan

D 62
D 63

Storm chasers

1 Match the words with the sentences.

to chase | to live stream ✓ | shot | television | tornado | hailstones | to shut

1. This means to show something on the internet while it's happening. *to live stream*
2. You sometimes get these in a storm. They can be dangerous.
3. This is another word for 'to close'.
4. This means to run after someone or something.
5. This is a very violent storm.
6. This is a kind of media.
7. This is a photo or a part of a video.

V 20
WB 29/1–2

2 Storm chasers

a) Watch the film. Take notes about:

- the atmosphere of the film,
- your feelings when you watch.

exciting, ...

Media tip
People who make films often use the camera in a certain way to set the mood.
The music can also help to make parts of the film sad or exciting, for example.

A

B

b) Talk to a partner. Compare your notes.

V 20

D 64
D 65

3 Watch the film again. Complete the sentences with one or more words.

1. Reed and his team chase the storm in a *car*.
2. They find really big — on the road.
3. They want to see how — the tornado is.
4. The — make driving on the road more difficult.
5. Reed gives information to a television —.
6. Reed describes the tornado as very —.
7. They take some very good — of the tornado.

4 Talk to a partner. Would you like to be a storm chaser? Say why.

have an exciting job | be a hero | work in a team | get hurt | dangerous | ...

A I'd like to be storm chaser because … .
B Really? I wouldn't like to be a storm chaser. I … .

✓ I can understand a live documentary.

Reading ▷ S2, p. 178

V 13 How to

Fancy dancer by Monique Gray Smith

D 66 My plan

1 Talk about the pictures.

What do you think the story will be about?

A I think .... What about you?
B Maybe it .... I think the boy ....

Skills
You shouldn't give up if there is a word in the text that you don't understand.
The meaning will often become clear when you read the rest of the text.
You can also just look up the word later.

A 22

2 Read the text.

Rory lives in the Midwest. His mother is a Cree Native American from Saskatchewan in Canada. His father's ancestors came from Ireland. This is the first part of a longer story.

Mom walked a bit lighter on the earth; my little sister, Suzie, laughed louder; and I – well, I got a dad, most people would call him my stepdad, but there's nothing 'step' about him.

My father had left two years before, when I was nine.

One day, he just never came home from work. Mom tried to explain it to us, but we already knew that things weren't good between them. Kids know. Parents don't think we do, but we do.

But then he never came to see us. He never phoned. Ever. It was hard to see how much Suzie missed him. You probably think that as his son I was sad, but I wasn't. I was happy. You see, my father was not a nice man. Not to me or my sister, and he really wasn't nice to my mom. That was the hardest part. Watching how he hurt my mom.

I checked on a map once, and Saskatchewan, Canada, is pretty far from Ann Arbor, Michigan. My father never said it, but I'm pretty sure he hated that my mom was Cree. Why else would he forbid her to speak Cree in our house, or do anything that was part of our culture?

I remember my mom celebrating her culture once. I was about seven or eight. It was the middle of the night, and I was thirsty, so I went to the kitchen to get a drink. As I got close, I saw a light and heard music. The music was new to me, but the beat was powerful. Like it was calling me closer. I looked around the corner to see what was going on in the kitchen, and there was my mom, dancing.

She stood with her head high, shoulders back, and her feet quietly moved to the beat of the drum. In her hand was what looked like feathers, and, like her feet, she moved them to the sound of the drum.

I watched until the music stopped, and Mom extinguished the candle. I went back to bed. That night I learned something really important. I always knew my mom was strong, but now I understood that she was much stronger than I'd thought. In the middle of the night, she was keeping her culture, our culture, alive.

After nine years with my father, I knew almost nothing about who I really was. I'm pretty sure he was ashamed of us, or that's how it felt. He often told Suzie and me that we'd have a better life if we looked more like him and his Irish ancestors, but we didn't. Everyone could see we were Native.

I always knew Mom was proud of me, and that was all I needed. At least that's what I thought, until she brought Paul home.

A 23

Paul was often at our dinner table and around our house after that. He's Cree like us, but from Alberta. He came to teach for a year and loved it so much, he stayed. Paul and Mom both work at the University of Michigan; that's where they met. He came into the library looking for a book, and my mom, who is a librarian, helped him find it. They've been together since then.

Not long after Paul came into our lives, Mom contacted her family again. Our family. Although we couldn't go to Saskatchewan to meet them, we were talking online two or three times a week. I liked meeting everyone, and there were a lot of them! I liked knowing I was part of a big family and that I looked like them. I really loved watching how Mom laughed with her siblings. Now Mom walks every day like she did that night I saw her dancing: head high, shoulders back.

A few months after Paul came to live with us, we were driving home from a good day of fishing when he turned on some music. It was the same music that Mom listened to that night I saw her dancing in the kitchen. It went straight to my heart, and my head began to move to the beat.

"You ever been to a powwow?" Paul asked.

"A what?"

"I guess[1] that answers my question."

"What's a powwow?" I asked him.

"Only one of the greatest weekend events ever."

"And?"

"And?" He looked at me and could see I really had no idea what a powwow was. "Well, where do I begin? It's both a ceremony and a meeting, where we dance, sing, visit, and laugh. There's always a lot of laughing!" Paul smiled, "Then there's the food. I love the fry bread[2] with butter and salt. Mmm, mmm, mmm." After a moment, he added, "But really, powwow is a way of celebrating our traditions, our families, and our ancestors."

"Is it just us?" I asked. "You know, uh, Native Americans?" Our family hadn't talked about who we were for so long that I wasn't sure what to call us.

"Mostly, yes. Native people travel from all over the country to go to powwows, but non[3]-Natives are welcome too. That's part of what makes the powwow beautiful, the sharing of cultures."

He looked at me. "We have one of the biggest powwows in the United States here in Ann Arbor. It's called the Dance for Mother Earth Powwow."

"Really?"

1 to guess – *schätzen, vermuten*; 2 fry bread – *Frybread (flaches Teigbrot, das gebraten oder frittiert wird)*; 3 non – *nicht*

A 24

Paul nodded. "I saw you dancing in your seat. I think you could be a fancy dancer."

"OK, first, I don't know what a fancy dancer is. And second ..." I remembered my father's voice. *Hope you got some brains in that head of yours, 'cause[4] you sure ain't got[5] any hopes of being on any sports team.*

I put my head against the window. "I'm not good at sports. So I'd probably suck at[6] this fancy-dancing thing."

As we went along Pontiac Trail, I asked myself if I'd ever stop hearing my father's voice in my head.

We were almost home when Paul started talking again. "Your mom told me some of the stories of how your dad treated you. How he treated all of you." He looked at me for a moment and then back to the road. "I'm sorry that happened."

"Why are you sorry? You didn't do anything."

"You're right, I didn't, but I can still be sorry that it happened. No one should ever treat a child or a woman like he treated you, Suzie, and your mom. I understand why you think you wouldn't be good at fancy dancing. But I think you could be good. Dancing isn't just about being good at sports, it's about telling a story to the beat and showing the strength that is in your heart."

Paul was quiet until we arrived at our house. He turned to me. "There is a lot of strength in your heart, Rory. You can let the awful things your father said define you. Or –"

"Or what?" I asked.

4 'cause (= because) – *weil (ugs.)*; 5 you ain't got (= you haven't got) – *du hast kein/e … (ugs.)*; 6 to suck at something – *in etwas total schlecht sein (ugs.)*

3 Talk about the story. Do you like it? ► S18 Round robin, p. 201

Think about the characters, the events and the places.

4 Correct the sentences.

D 67

1. Suzie tells us the story.
   Rory tells us the story.
2. The kids' father left three years before.
3. His mother couldn't talk to her friends while their father was there.
4. Rory saw her dancing in her bedroom one night.
5. After she met Paul, she contacted her relatives in New York City.
6. Paul and Rory listen to some Native American music after a day of football.
7. Paul sees Rory dancing at school.
8. Rory's mum tells Rory about a powwow in Ann Arbor.
9. Paul says that Rory can be a volleyball player.

S

Skills

There are many stories where one of the characters tells us what happens. We call this character a 'first-person narrator'. This kind of narrator can say what he or she thinks and feels about the events and the other characters in the story. We don't find out what the other characters think, or if the narrator is right.

D 68
D 69

5 Thoughts and feelings

a) Answer the questions in sentences. Give the lines in the text where you found the information.

1. How did Rory feel when his father left them? How did his sister feel?
   He felt happy. (line 19) His sister .... (lines ...)
2. What did Rory think when he saw his mother dancing one night?
3. What were Rory's father's feelings about Cree culture?
4. How did Rory's mother feel when she contacted her family again?
5. Why doesn't Rory feel confident about dancing?
6. How does Rory feel about Paul?

b) Compare your answers. Do you agree?

6 The power of words

a) Choose the sentence with the same meaning.

"... you sure ain't got any hopes of being on any sports team." (Rory's father)

A You should work harder.
B You'll never be good at it.
C I was better when I was your age.

b) Complete Paul's sentence at the end of the story in your own words.

"You can let the awful things your father said define you. Or —"

c) Think of three English sentences that could influence someone's life in a good way.

WB 30-31/1-5

7 Choose one of the tasks.

a) Make freeze frames of the family's life with their father and with Paul.
► S18 Freeze frame, p. 200

1. Choose two scenes from the text.
2. Decide who will be which character in each scene.
3. Talk about how the characters feel about each other and how the situation has changed.
4. Use body language to show their feelings.
5. Present your freeze frames to the class.

You don't need props or costumes.

OR

b) Find out about a powwow.
► S14 Using the internet, p. 196

Take notes about:
- when and where the event takes place,
- who goes to it,
- what happens there,
- why it's important in Native American culture.

Give a short presentation about it to the class.
► S4 Giving a presentation, p. 181

✔ I can understand part of a short story.

Checklist

D 70 My plan

WB 32

Check in: Off to the Midwest

✓ I can understand information about the Midwest.

WB 32

Station 1: High school life

I can name things at a school in the USA.
► W3 School life in the USA, p. 234

student council | electives | homeroom | lockers | schedule | …

I can say what a person does or doesn't do.
► G3, p. 150 (Simple present: statements, negatives, questions)

I get up at 6:30. | We take the yellow school bus every morning. | They don't play volleyball. | Do you have any questions?

✓ I can talk about school life.

WB 33

Listening: Meet the farmers

✓ I can understand a radio show.

WB 33

Station 2: Happy holidays

I can say how people celebrate.
► W4 Celebrating special days, p. 235

put up decorations | wear special clothes | light candles | give presents | watch a parade | …

I can say what is or isn't happening at the moment.
► G4, p. 152 (Present progressive: statements, negatives, questions)

I'm waiting for my cinnamon cookies now. | Lincoln isn't helping in the kitchen at the moment. | What are you doing right now?

✓ I can talk about holidays and festivals.

WB 34

Viewing: Storm chasers

✓ I can understand a live documentary.

WB 34

Reading: Fancy dancer

✓ I can understand part of a short story.

19 Quiz

?

Find the photo in the unit.
You can also do the online quiz about the Midwest.

D 71
Support

Task: Thanksgiving in class

Prepare a Thanksgiving celebration in your class.

Step 1

Collect words for Thanksgiving dishes in a mind map. Look for more dishes online.
► S14 Using the internet, p.196

turkey sandwiches
Thanksgiving
cornbread
...

Step 2

Decide which dishes you want to prepare.
Talk about these questions:

- Are there any students with allergies?
- Are there vegetarians, vegans or students who don't eat certain kinds of food?
- Can we prepare the dish easily at home or at school?

Skills

It's important to listen carefully and think again if you need to. You can use these sentences:
I see what you mean, … .
I understand, … .
Maybe we could … .

Step 3

Get into groups of four or five. Decide which group is going to prepare which dish or dishes. Make a plan.

Ayshe, Tim, Sara, Mohamed: turkey sandwiches
Leon, Anita, ...
...

Step 4

Find a recipe for your dish or dishes on the internet.
► S14 Using the internet, p.196

Media tip

You can watch videos on social media that show you how to cook some dishes.

Step 5

Write an invitiation for the event.
Say when and where the event will take place.

Step 6

Meet to prepare your dish or dishes.

Step 7

Have a nice Thanksgiving celebration!
Talk about what you are thankful for while you are eating.
Don't forget to bring lunchboxes so that you can take home any food that is left.

The Great Lakes

A 25

1 Which famous lakes do you already know? What can you do there?

1

2

3

1 The Lakes
The five Great Lakes are Superior, Michigan, Huron, Erie, and Ontario. They are the largest group of freshwater[1] lakes in the world. Part of the border between the USA and Canada runs through the Great Lakes.

2 Water of life
The Great Lakes contain[2] 21% of the world's fresh water. Over 30 million people depend on[3] them for fresh water. The lakes also water[4] forests and farming land across the Midwest and much of Canada.

3 Wildlife
There is a lot of beautiful wildlife in the Great Lakes region. Many kinds of fish swim in the lakes, and they are also home to otters and beavers. Gray wolves, lynx[5], and moose[6] live near the shores of the lakes.

1 freshwater – *Süßwasser-*; 2 to contain – *beinhalten*; 3 to depend (on) – *abhängig sein (von)*; 4 to water – *bewässern*; 5 lynx – *der Luchs*; 6 moose – *der Elch*

2 Which facts surprised you? What would you like to learn more about?

I was surprised to find out that … .
I didn't know that … .
I'd like to learn more about … .

4

5

6

4 Storms on the lakes
In the fall, cold air from Canada meets warm, humid[7] air from the south over the Great Lakes. This can cause[8] powerful and terrible storms. Winds can reach[9] up to 100 miles per hour, and there are sometimes very large waves.

5 Crossing Lake Michigan
The SS Badger is a ferry that crosses Lake Michigan. The Badger is over 75 years old and is the last coal-powered steamship[10] in operation[11] in the USA. It takes four hours to travel the 62 miles between Michigan and Wisconsin.

6 Shipwrecks
The weather on the lakes often changes quickly, and this can make it dangerous for ships. It is possible that more than 6,000 ships have sunk there. The lakes are so large and deep that the location of many of the ships is unknown.

7 humid – *feucht*; 8 to cause – *verursachen*; 9 to reach – *erreichen*;
10 coal-powered steamship – *das kohlebetriebene Dampfschiff*;
11 in operation – *in Betrieb*

D 72 Support

1 High school life

a) Put in the school words. There are four that you don't need.

schedule | locker | electives ✓ | bus | homeroom | club | prom | Pledge of Allegiance | dress code | cafeteria | student council

1. Creative writing is one of Lena's *electives*.
2. — is a kind of meeting with the class teacher.
3. When students take the —, they say that they're loyal to their country.
4. Each student has a — for bags and other things.
5. The — is a good place to meet friends, and the food is OK.
6. The — is a big dance. It's a highlight!
7. Students have a — so that they know when they have different classes.

b) Write your own sentences with the words that you didn't need.

2 Complete the sentences with the simple present.

1. Lena *gets up* at 6:30 a.m. (get up)
2. She usually — the school's online portal. (check)
3. She — to school. (not walk)
4. She — the bus. (take)
5. She and her friends — a uniform. (not wear)
6. They — through a metal detector every day. (walk)
7. Lena — her homeroom group. (love)
8. She — volleyball at school. (not play)

3 Complete the online dialogue between Paisley and a German student.

Paisley *Do you take* the bus to school? (1)
Student No, —. (2) I usually walk.
Paisley When —? (3)
Student School starts at 7:45 a.m.
Paisley Where —? (4)
Student I usually have lunch in the cafeteria.
Paisley What — after school? (5)
Student I usually go straight home. I go to a swimming club on Wednesday evenings.
Paisley — a lot of homework? (6)
Student Yes, —. (7) Too much!
Paisley Where —? (8)
Student I usually do my homework in my bedroom.
Paisley When — to bed? (9)
Student I usually go to bed at 10:00 p.m.
Paisley Thanks for answering my questions!
Student You're welcome.

You should use a form of **do** in questions and short answers in the simple present.

4 It's Thanksgiving. What are they doing at the moment?

A

Brad's uncle | eat

B

Brad's friends | take part

C

Brad's aunt | light

D

Regan | wait

E

Lincoln | play

F

Brad and his parents | watch

A. Brad's uncle is eating pecan pie.

5 Complete the sentences (simple present or present progressive).

1. Brad *makes* a fruit punch every year. (make)
2. Aunt Alice — her husband's family at the moment. (visit)
3. Lincoln Hey, look! It —! (snow)
4. Grandma Margaret often — at Brad's house at Thanksgiving. (stay)
5. Brad's dad — at the moment. He's eaten a lot of turkey! (sleep)
6. Regan usually — home for the holiday. (go)
7. The cousins — a board game now. (play)
8. Regan and Brad always — Thanksgiving. (enjoy)

The signal words in the sentences can help you!

6 Definitions

a) Find the words for the definitions. The words are all in the story on pages 44–46.

1. a member of a person's family who lived a long time ago
   an ancestor
2. a kind of food that people often put on bread
3. to phone or write to someone
4. the part of the body above the arm
5. to use your face to show that you are happy
6. an event where Native Americans celebrate their culture

b) Write your own definitions for these words.

1. salt
2. to laugh
3. a kitchen
4. to travel
5. to dance
6. close (to something)

3 Going to the West

In this unit you will …
- find out about the West.
  ► Check in
- talk about the life cycle of a product.
  ► Station 1
- watch a report.
  ► Viewing
- present a social project.
  ► Station 2
- listen to a radio play.
  ► Listening
- read a magazine article.
  ► Reading

D 73
My plan

A 26

A

B

From the mountains, lakes and forests of Alaska, through the volcanoes of the Hawaiian islands to the deserts and canyons of Nevada, the West has some of the most spectacular landscapes in the USA. Surfing is a very popular sport in Hawaii, California, and other states in the West.

Info

Biggest city: Los Angeles, about 3.7 million people

Sights: Golden Gate Bridge, Hollywood, Pan-American Highway

Hottest place: Death Valley, California, 134°F (57°C)

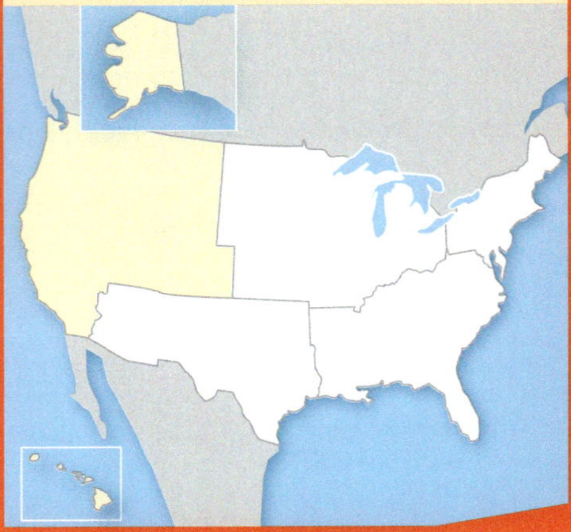

C

California has a large, multicultural population. There are many people of Hispanic or Asian background. San Francisco had the first Chinatown in the USA, and Spanish is California's second language.

D

Silicon Valley has been the world's center for technology since the 1960s. It's home to the biggest internet, social media, and online entertainment platforms, and many start-ups that hope to become leading world brands.

E

The states on the Pacific coast are the top US producers of tree nuts, dried fruit, and fresh fruit like apples, pears, grapes, and cherries. Many seasonal workers, and even some children, work on fruit farms there.

F

Higher temperatures and drier summers mean that there are many challenges in the West. For example, reservoirs are often at very low levels. There are also awful wildfires in California and other states.

1 Facts about the West

D 39 Support P

a) Read the texts. Collect information about the West. Copy and complete the mind map.

A 27

b) What information can you find out about the West from the audio and the video? Add it to your mind map.

V 21

WB 35/1–3

c) Talk about the West with the help of your mind map.

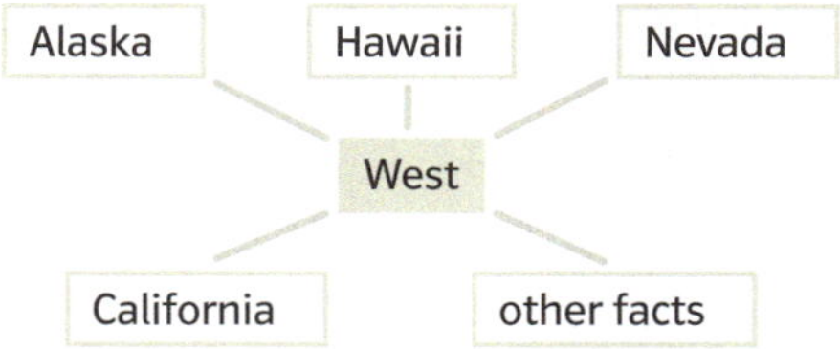

V

Audio and video words

sunrise – der Sonnenaufgang
sunset – der Sonnenuntergang
daylight – das Tageslicht
peninsula – die Halbinsel
fog – der Nebel

✓ I can understand information about the West.

D 74 My plan
D 75
A 28
WB 36/1

The life of a phone

1 How many phones have you had in your life?

2 Read Luciana's blog entry.

Internet

Luciana, Silicon Valley

Hey guys,
How many phones have you had in your life? I've already had three phones. I wanted to buy a new one two months ago, but then I thought about it again. Did you know that the average life of a phone is only about two and a half years in the USA today? Why is that a problem? It takes a lot of energy and raw materials like rare metals to produce a phone, and it can be really bad for the environment if you throw it away. It just isn't sustainable to replace your phone every two years. Look at the life cycle to find out more.

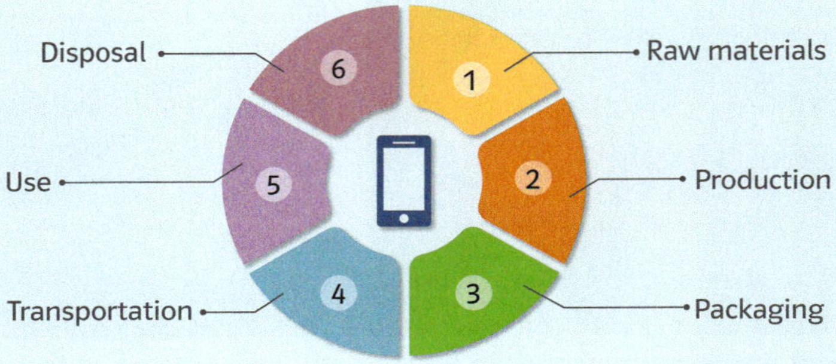

1 Raw materials are taken from under the ground. Phones are usually made of about 45 % metals, 30 % plastics, and 15 % ceramics.

2 Most phones are put together in large factories in China, usually by robots. This needs huge amounts of energy and also chemicals, which can be highly dangerous for the workers.

3 Each phone is packaged using paper, card, and plastic. Phone companies spend a lot of time designing packaging that makes it special.

4 Phones are transported tens of thousands of miles around the world from China by ship and road.

5 Most phones are used for three to four hours per day and are charged for two to three hours every day.

6 You can get back large amounts of rare metals and save energy through recycling. But fewer than 20 % of the world's phones are recycled. The rest are either kept at home or thrown away.

I think it's time for our phones to be more sustainable. Sustainable phones …

- ✓ are made from recycled materials.
- ✓ are easy to repair.
- ✓ reduce waste and pollution and save energy and money.

What do you think? You can leave a comment here.

D 76
D 77

3 Choose the right answers.

1. Two and a half years is the average time that —.
   A a phone works
   B people use their phones
   C companies need to make new phones
2. Metals for phones come from —.
   A places near the factories where they make phones
   B other larger factories
   C below the earth
3. Most phones are put together in —.
   A Europe
   B Asia
   C America
4. Recycling phones means that —.
   A phones have less packaging
   B phones are more expensive
   C we can use some of the materials again
5. More than 80% of the world's phones —.
   A aren't recycled
   B are thrown away
   C are kept at home
6. Luciana thinks that phones should be —.
   A cheaper
   B more sustainable
   C easier to use

D 78
D 79
WB 36/2

4 Write a comment on Luciana's blog. ► S7 Planning, writing and checking texts, p. 184

Say what you think about this topic. Give reasons.

good/bad for the environment | (not) expensive | easy/difficult to repair | …

I think it's (not) important to have sustainable phones because … . I think … . …

S

Skills

A comment is a statement in which you express your opinion on a topic. This means that you collect arguments and examples that support your opinion.

WB 37/3

5 What do they do? ► W5 Life cycle of a product, p. 236 ► S18 Peer correction, p. 200

a) Match the phrases with the pictures. ► ○ p. 131

program devices | process metal | produce packaging | transport products | manufacture devices ✓ | mine raw materials

A

B
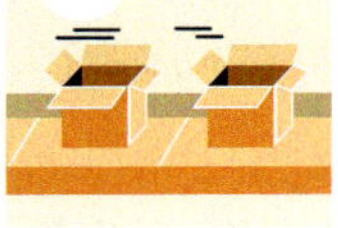
C
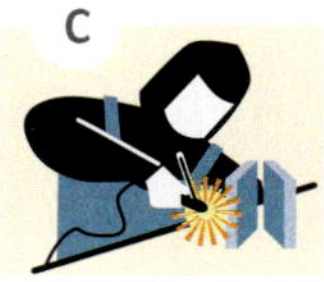
D
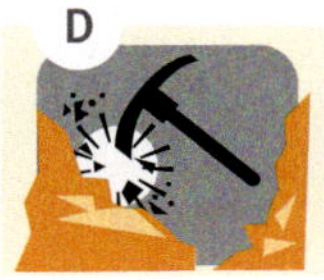
E

F

A. manufacture devices

● **b)** Replace the underlined verbs with the verbs below.

put together | throw away | transport | process | mine

1. Vans <u>distribute</u> the finished products to shops around the country.
2. Workers <u>extract</u> the rare metals from under the ground.
3. In this factory they <u>treat</u> the raw material so workers can use it to make T-shirts.
4. It takes about 24 hours to <u>assemble</u> the cars in this factory.
5. Customers should <u>dispose of</u> packaging in recycling bins.

V 22
How to

Language detectives ► G7, p. 156

G

You **package** each phone. → Each phone **is packaged**.
People **throw away** many old phones. → Many old phones **are thrown away**.
They **don't recycle** many phones. → Many phones **aren't recycled**.

Compare the sentences. When can you use the passive voice? How do you form it?

○ D 80
● D 81
WB 37/4

6 Are these sentences in the active or passive voice?

1. Many phones are stolen every year.
   passive voice
2. Luciana doesn't buy a new phone.
3. The company designs new packaging.
4. Food is processed in factories.
5. Workers transport boxes to another factory.
6. Many old things aren't recycled.
7. About 80% of phones are thrown away.
8. Some people buy a new phone every two or three years.

Are the people who are doing the action important (active)? Or is the action more important (passive)?

WB 38/5

7 How a robot is made

a) Complete the sentences. You can look up irregular verb forms on page 172. ► ○ p. 131

1. The school robot *is designed* (design).
2. The raw materials — (process) into parts in a factory.
3. The parts — (transport) to other factories.
4. The robots — (put together).
5. Then each robot — (program).
6. The robots — (check).
7. The robots — (deliver) to schools around the country.
8. I — (ask) to try the robot at my school.

● **b)** Imagine you have a school robot. Write five sentences about what is done for you by the robot.

My text is checked. ...

○ D 82
● D 83
WB 38/6–7

8 Complete an expert's presentation about sustainable phones.

John It's easy to see why sustainable phones are becoming more important. They *are designed* (1 design) to reduce waste during their life cycle. Let's look at how this — (2 do).
First, sustainable phones — (3 not make) of new metals, but of old metals that — (4 recycle).
This means that important materials — (5 not throw away).
Next, a sustainable phone — (6 not replace) after two years. It's very easy to repair and has a much longer life.
Modern technology — (7 use) to manufacture sustainable phones. The workers in the factories — (8 not treat) badly. Their work — (9 respect).
If many more sustainable phones — (10 produce), I think that big companies will start to make them too. I believe that sustainable technology is the future.

D 84
D 85
WB 39/8

9 Complete the dialogue after the presentation.

Luciana	Excuse me, can I ask a few questions?
John	Sure. What would you like to know?
Luciana	— (1 where | the raw materials | take from?)
	Where are the raw materials taken from?
John	From under the ground in about 19 different countries.
Luciana	— (2 how much | energy | use) to produce a phone?
John	The amount of energy that — (3 use) to charge 73 phones for a year.
Luciana	I see. — (4 where | the phones | put together?)
John	Many phones — (5 put together) in China.
Luciana	— (6 be | each phone | transport) by plane?
John	No, most phones — (7 transport) by ship.
Luciana	— (8 how many | phones | throw away) each year?
John	About 100 million phones — (9 throw away) in the USA each year.
Luciana	Wow, that's a lot!

Grammar ► G7, p. 156

Is this material **recycled**?
Where **are** phones **produced**?

WB 39/9

10 From apples to apple jam

a) Write sentences. You can look up irregular verb forms on page 172. ► p. 132

A

grow

B

choose

C
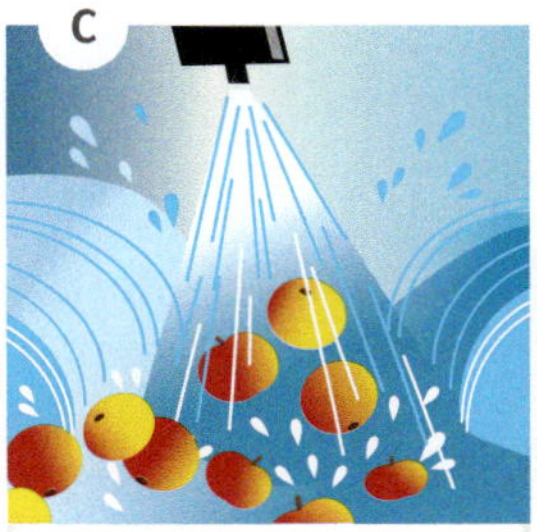
wash

D
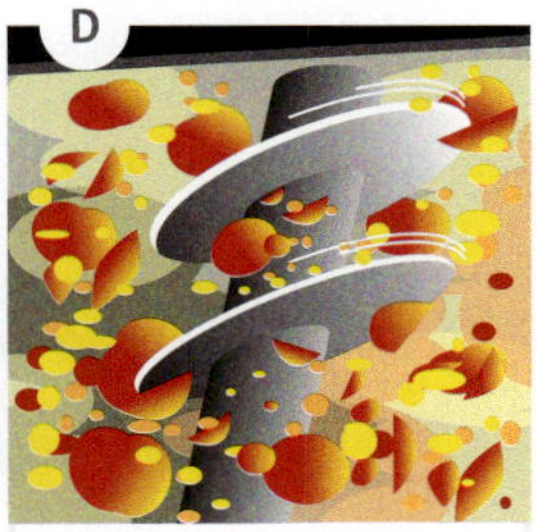
cut

E

cook

F

add

G
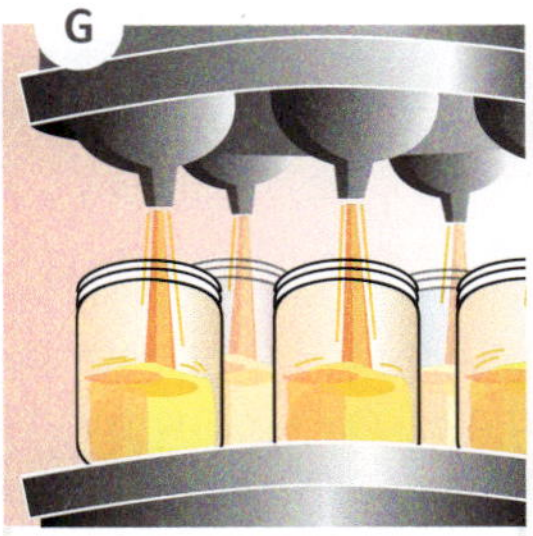
put

H

sell

A. Apples are grown on a large farm.

b) Ask five questions about the process in a). Use the passive voice.

recycle | package | transport | …

Are the jars recycled? How …

Culture

In addition to jam, the most popular spreads in the USA are peanut butter and marshmallow cream.
What are your favourite spreads?

I 10

V 19 How to

D 86 Support

11 Your turn: The life cycle of a product

Create a digital diagram to show the life cycle of a product. ► S4 Giving a presentation, p. 181

Step 1

Decide on a product.

clothes, TVs, games consoles, toys, ...

Step 2

Find out about the six stages of the life cycle of a product and take notes:
Raw materials – Production – Packaging – Transportation – Use – Disposal

► S14 Using the internet, p. 196

Raw materials: cotton, water, ...
Production: produce fibres
...

Step 3

Choose a presentation tool and create a new file. You can use any writing or presentation program on a computer, tablet or phone.

Step 4

Draw a circle or an oval. Draw lines to divide it into six segments which represent the six stages of the life cycle.

Media tip
In most writing apps look for "Insert" (Einfügen) or "Insert Shapes" (Formen einfügen).

Step 5

Use text boxes to add your notes from step 2.

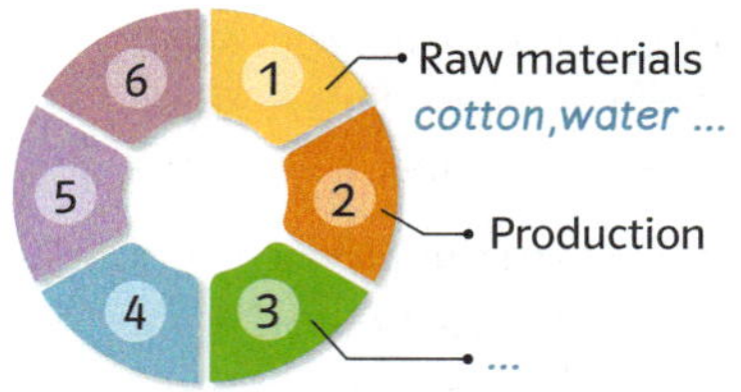

Step 6

Find symbols that represent each stage of the life cycle and add them to the text boxes.

► S16 How to use photos, films and texts, p. 198

Media tip
If you use a presentation app, you can add an animation for each of the six stages.

Step 7

Show the diagram to the others and tell them about it.

► S18 Gallery walk, p. 201

Ask for and give feedback.

► S8 Giving and asking for feedback, p. 190

A This is the life cycle of a T-shirt. Cotton is needed to make a T-shirt. The cotton is transported to .... It is then washed ...

✔ I can talk about the life cycle of a product.

Climate heroes

D 87
My plan
D 88

1 Find the places on a map of California and answer these questions.

Newcastle | Meadow Vista | Auburn

1. Where in California are they? Name a big city near them.
2. What do you already know about the climate in California?

D 89

2 Complete the sentences with these words. ► S13 Looking up words, p. 194

global | install | solution ✓ | engineer | detect | screensaver | connection

1. A *solution* is an answer to a problem.
2. Everybody knows the — between a healthy forest and good air.
3. Football is a — sport.
4. Metal detectors can — weapons.
5. You must — the program before you can use your computer.
6. I haven't used my computer for ten minutes. Now it's showing the —.
7. My uncle is a computer —. He repairs and checks computers.

V 23
D 90
D 91
WB 40/1–3

3 Watch the film and choose the right answers.

1. The kids want to work on —.
   A storms
   B wildfires

2. They choose Spain because it —.
   A has the same climate
   B has already found solutions

3. At the international competition the kids meet other teams from the USA, —.
   A Australia, Germany and Mexico
   B Australia, Germany and England

4. The kids show their project —.
   A online
   B at a live event

5. The kids' solutions are — which tell you when there's a wildfire.
   A screensavers
   B films

6. — will help the team who wins to work on their project.
   A Teachers
   B Engineers

Culture
The North American wildfire season usually runs from spring to autumn. However, because of climate change there are more and more wildfires out of season. Which regions do you know where there are frequent wildfires?

4 What happens in the film? Copy and complete the summary.

► S18 Peer correction, p. 200

Some kids from *California* take part in —. They make — which —. The kids are very — when they —. Now they can — with —.

✓ I can understand a report.

Your community needs you!

D 92
My plan
D 93

1 What can you or other people do to help your community?

► S18 Think-pair-share, p. 200

collect clothes or food, organise charity events, …

A 29
WB 41/1–2

2 Read the conversation.

Lois is a student from Portland, Oregon. She's visiting Room to Hope, an outreach center for homeless people, because she's thinking about helping there. She's talking to Bob, a member of staff at the center.

Lois May I ask you a few questions about what you do here?

Bob Sure. What would you like to know?

Lois What does the project do?

Bob Room to Hope works with homeless people in the city and tries to help and support them the best we can. Some of our staff are medically trained, some of the staff can offer counseling services for people who have mental health problems, and some of us give practical help. We also have a small café.

Lois What's your job here?

Bob I'm a first responder. That means when someone becomes homeless, I'm there to find out about their situation, explain what they can do and also help them to cope with the situation.

Lois What kind of help do you offer?

Bob Finding places for homeless people to live is one of the main things I do. I also help them by just being their friend, which is what most people need. I also ask if they need medical or mental health support.

Lois That's really interesting. Why do people become homeless?

Bob There are many different reasons. Often it's because they lose their jobs. When people are jobless, they often get into debt and then they aren't able to afford their rent. Sometimes it's because people get seriously sick or become addicted to drugs or alcohol. And sometimes it's because women get pregnant. Doing this job makes you understand how easy it is to become homeless.

Lois What's the best thing about social work?

Bob I really enjoy helping people find solutions to their problems. Helping someone find a home and a job and get back their self-respect is the best thing. It's my reason for doing this job. For example, two weeks ago we helped a single mom and her three-year-old son to find a new home in the city. Seeing their faces as they walked into their new apartment was amazing.

Lois What's the worst thing?

Bob Well, not every story is a success. Some people with serious drug and alcohol problems find it hard to stop forever. That's really difficult to see. And when I have to tell someone that we haven't been able to find them a place to live or the support they need, it's heartbreaking. But we never stop trying.

Lois Thanks for talking to me.

D 94
D 95

3 Answer the questions in sentences.

1. Why is Lois at Room to Hope?
   She's there because she's thinking about helping.
2. Who does the project try to help?
3. How do first responders help? Give two examples.
4. How can the problem start? Give two examples.
5. Why were the woman and her son happy?
6. Why is Bob sometimes very sad?

WB 41/3

4 Social work ► W6 Social work, p. 237

a) Find words or phrases in the text for these definitions. ► ○ p. 132

1. people without a place to live
   homeless people
2. another word for 'to help'
3. another word for 'workers'
4. advice about a problem
5. having no work
6. not being able to stop doing something
7. another word for 'very bad'
8. another word for 'very sad'

● **b)** Match the words to make phrases. You can use them more than once. ► S13 Looking up words, p. 194

offer | encourage | arrange | recommend | advise

a place to live | meetings | families | therapy | a sad person

WB 42/4

5 Lois' diary entries ► S7 Planning, writing and checking texts, p. 184

a) Write Lois' diary entry after her conversation with Bob. ► ○ p. 133

What did she do? Who did she meet? What was interesting? How do you think she felt? …

May 26
Today I met Bob, a very special person from Room to Hope. We talked about his work …

● **b)** Write Lois' diary entry after her first day as a volunteer.

Was the day as she expected? What did she do? How did she feel? …

June 29
My first day at Room to Hope! I was so excited and nervous. I met Bob, and he …

A 30
D 96
WB 43/5

6 Listen to Arthur's story. Are the sentences true or false?

1. Arthur worked for a car company three years ago.
   That's false.
2. He had a problem with alcohol.
3. He stayed with his dad after he lost his job.
4. Bob talked a lot at their first meeting.
5. The team helped him when he looked for a job.
6. He eventually found a job and a place to live.
7. He now plays a lot of tennis in his free time.

Culture
The legal drinking age for alcohol is 21 years in the USA. This means that you can legally own a rifle and drive a car in the USA before you can legally drink alcohol. What age limits are there in your country?

7 Mediation ► S9 Mediation, p. 191

V 3 How to
WB 43/6

a) Du arbeitest mit Nadja für ein Schulprojekt zusammen. Da sie noch nicht so gut Deutsch spricht, hilfst du ihr, ihre Fragen zu diesem Flyer zu beantworten.

Du weißt nicht, wo Du nächsten Monat schlafen sollst? Schule oder Ausbildung geschmissen? Kein Geld, keinen Plan und keiner da, der Dir hilft? Du hast das Leben auf der Straße satt? Deine Pflegefamilie kann sich nicht mehr um Dich kümmern? Du bist von zu Hause abgehauen?

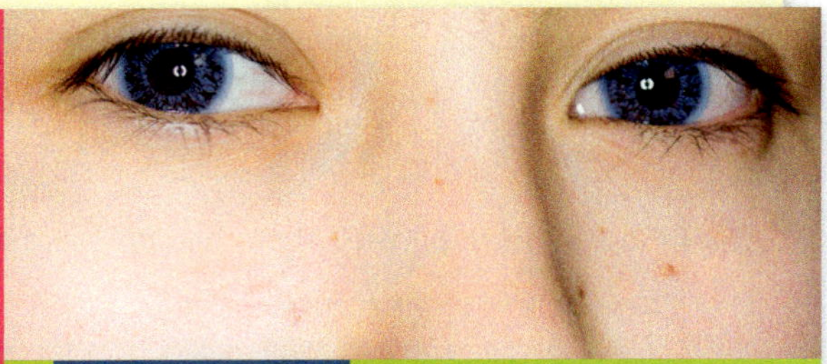

Keine Angst – es gibt Menschen, die sich mit solchen Problemen auskennen! Egal, ob online, am Telefon oder Face to Face: Wir helfen Dir – ganz vertraulich, kompetent und kostenlos.

Für wen gibt es Hilfe?
- Du bist mindestens 14 und nicht älter als 26 Jahre.
- Du hast keine Ahnung, wie Du Dein Leben eigenständig führen sollst.
- Du bist wohnungslos oder wirst es bald sein.

Worum geht's?
Darum,
- Dir zu helfen, ein selbstbestimmtes und selbstständiges Leben zu führen,
- eine für Dich passende Unterkunft zu finden, wenn Du kein Zuhause mehr hast.

Hier erhältst Du Hilfe
In Deiner Nähe gibt es professionelle Beratende, die Dir zur Seite stehen!

Wer hilft Dir?
- ✓ Streetworkerinnen/Streetworker und mobile Beratende kommen dorthin, wo Du Dich aufhältst – zum Beispiel auf der Straße, in Jugendclubs oder auch Chatforen. Sie geben dir Rat und zeigen Dir, wo Du weitere Hilfe erhältst.
- ✓ Erstanlaufstellen vor Ort beraten Dich zu Deiner Lebens- und Wohnsituation. Sie leisten kurzfristige Hilfe, z. B. bei der Wohnungsbewerbung, und begleiten Dich auf Wunsch auch zu weiteren Hilfseinrichtungen.
- ✓ Benötigst Du für einen längeren Zeitraum Hilfe, beraten und begleiten Dich erfahrene Mitarbeitende auch mehrere Monate oder Jahre.

Mehr Info auf der Rückseite.

Nadja I've found this flyer for our project. I know it's about a service for young people, but what problems can they get help with?
You (1) …
Nadja I understood that there are different people who can help these young people. Where can young people meet a social worker?
You (2) …
Nadja Do they just talk? What help do they offer?
You (3) …

b) Nadja möchte noch mehr über das Projekt wissen. Schreibe für sie eine kurze E-Mail an die Organisation auf Deutsch und stelle ihre Fragen.

Nadja This is a great project. Do you think we could ask them some questions? Would you please write to them? Do they wait until a young person comes to them or do they go to different places and talk to young people? What qualifications do you need to work there? Can you also work there as a volunteer?

V 24
How to

G

Language detectives ► G8, p.158

Losing your home must be awful.

I enjoy **helping** people in my community.

Arthur's friend is good at **speaking** to people.

Look at the marked words. How do you form them? When do you use them?

WB 44/7–9

8 Being a volunteer

a) Complete the description by a volunteer. ► ○ p.133 ► S18 Peer correction, p.200

Tessa I'm a volunteer in a local second-hand store that supports people who need help in Seattle. I started last summer and I love *working* (1 work) here. I really enjoy — (2 help) these people.
— (3 sell) clothes is fun, but — (4 talk) to the people in the store is what I like best. I think I'm quite good at — (5 make) customers feel welcome. I've made so many friends.
I'm really interested in — (6 get) a job in social work later. I'm looking forward to — (7 learn) more about the work this place does. I can say that — (8 be) a volunteer is great, both for yourself and for the community.

● **b)** Complete the sentences with a gerund. There is one verb that you don't need.

wear | talk | check | work | go | help

1. Tessa enjoys — customers to find the right clothes.
2. People who are interested in — as a volunteer can apply online.
3. — that the clothes are OK to wear is an important part of the job.
4. — second-hand clothes helps to reduce waste.
5. Fashion fans like — to second-hand shops because they sometimes have cool clothes.

○ D 97
● D 98

9 Which of these activities would you do as a volunteer?

► S18 Milling around, p.201

What are you good at doing?
What do you like doing?

play with children | look after animals | help old people | organise … | …

A What are you good at doing?
B I'm good at playing with children. What do you like doing?
A I like … .

Culture

In the USA students are encouraged to spend some time volunteering while still at high school. This isn't only good for the community – it might also help a student to get a place at their favourite college or university.

I 11
V 25 How to
D 99 Support

10 Your turn: A presentation about a social project

Give a three-minute group presentation about a social project that you want to raise money for.
► S4 Giving a presentation, p. 181

Step 1

Get into groups. Decide on a social project in Germany. It can be a project that helps animals, young people or people who are homeless.

first aid club, animal home, outreach centre for …

Step 2

Research the project:
What aims does it have?
Who does the project support?
How does the project help others?
How can you take part?
Which challenges does it have to face?

"Breakfast club"
- *help young people at school*
- *provide food*
- *help make breakfast*
- *needs volunteers, money, food*

Step 3

Think of an introduction.
The introduction should show why this project is so important that your class should raise money for it.

Everybody needs food, but some families don't have the money to prepare breakfast. That's where our project helps. …

Step 4

Write the main part and a conclusion.

S Skills
If you want to promote projects, it's important to address the feelings of the audience. You can ask questions like "How would you feel in this situation?" Photos can support your message too.

Step 5

Find and add photos.
► S16 How to use photos, films and texts, p. 198

Step 6

Decide who will give which part of the presentation. Practise your part.

S Skills
To see if your presentation works, you can film yourself practising. Then you can see what's already good and what you still need to work on.

Step 7

Give your presentation and decide on a project your class would like to support.
► S8 Giving and asking for feedback, p. 190

When you have found a project, think about what you can do to support it. Money is important, of course, but you can also help in other ways.

✔ I can present a social project.

The gold rush

D 100 My plan

1 Match the words with the photos.

ghost town | creek | luck | gold-mining tools

A

B

C

D

2 Life in Saint Elmo

A 31
D 101
D 102
WB 45/1–2

a) Listen to the radio play. Match scenes 1 to 3 with the right photos, dates and captions.

1880 | 1920 | Today | After the gold rush | Life in a ghost town | Hopes and dreams

A

B

C

Scene 1: photo C, ...

b) Listen again. Complete the sentences.

1. The tourists meet a man in front of a —.
2. Owen's family moved to Saint Elmo in —.
3. A man has come to Saint Elmo to find —.
4. Andrew and Jed think that it isn't easy to get —.
5. Harriet works as a — in the town.
6. She and her family are going to look for — in San Francisco.

3 A story based on a photo ► S7 Planning, writing and checking texts, p. 184

D 103
D 104

a) Look at the photo. Make notes before you write the story. Think:

- What was here in the past? *a house ...*
- Who is in the story?
- What happened?
- When and why did it happen?

P

b) Write your story. Use the simple past.

✔ I can understand a radio play.

 ▻ S2, p.178

V 13 How to

D 105 My plan

A 32

America's natural treasures

by Ava Jones, 04/20/2025

A The USA's 63 national parks are some of the country's most precious and important areas. They include deserts, forests, glaciers, canyons, and even volcanoes. The national parks are home to a large variety of wildlife and plants. In Yellowstone National Park in Wyoming, you can spot bison, wolves, and grizzly bears, while the Everglades in Florida are home to many bird species[1] and alligators. You also find unique ecosystems, from ancient pine[2] forests in Great Basin National Park in Nevada to the famous cacti in the deserts and mountains of Saguaro National Park in Arizona.

B One of the first national parks in the USA was Yosemite in California. John Muir, a writer and naturalist[3] who was born in Scotland in 1838, was convinced that America's wilderness had to be protected. Not everyone agreed. Large areas were used for mining and hunting, and there was a lot of deforestation[4] at that time. Muir wrote magazine articles about Yosemite Valley and about how important natural landscapes are for future generations. In 1890 the US Congress[5] passed a law to establish a national park in Yosemite Valley.

C The National Park Service (NPS) was created in 1916. The NPS manages all the USA's national parks. It employs around 20,000 people and has about 280,000 volunteers across all the states in the country. It enforces[6] rules, looks after visitor facilities, and does important scientific research on how to protect the parks in the future. So today the national parks are protected by law and cannot be used for mining, hunting, or other developments.

D Visitors to the national parks are encouraged to enjoy the natural environments carefully and responsibly. There is a saying[7] that visitors should 'take only photos and leave only footprints'. This means that visitors should take home all their garbage and not remove anything from the park, including plants and flowers. Visitors are also asked[8] not to get close to the animals or to feed them. They should also stay on paths to avoid damaging the environment. Smoking is strictly forbidden too.

National parks: fascinating facts

- The USA's largest national park – Wrangell-St. Elias National Park and Preserve in Alaska – is bigger than Switzerland.
- The world's tallest tree is in Redwood National Park in California. It is 380 feet high.
- In the early 1900s there were only 23 bison in Yellowstone National Park in Wyoming, Montana and Idaho. Now there are around 5,000.
- Coldest national park: Gates of the Arctic in Alaska with temperatures as low as −70°F.

1 species – *die Art*; 2 pine – *die Kiefer*; 3 naturalist – *der Naturforscher / die Naturforscherin*; 4 deforestation – *die Abholzung*; 5 US Congress – *der US-Kongress (das Parlament der USA)*; 6 to enforce – *durchsetzen*; 7 saying – *das Sprichwort*; 8 to ask – *bitten*

1 Read the text.

2 Find the information in the text.

D 106
D 107

1. five different landscapes
2. five animals
3. five names of national parks
4. three things that the NPS does
5. five things that visitors shouldn't do
6. three facts that you find interesting

3 Take notes on each paragraph of the text (A to D). Use keywords.

A. 63 national parks in the USA, different landscapes, ...

S

Skills

The keywords in a paragraph are the most important words. It's a good idea to use general words instead of specific words or details. You shouldn't write full sentences.

4 A group summary ► S7 Planning, writing and checking texts, p. 184

a) Get into groups of four to write a summary of the text.

Each student in your group summarises one paragraph: A, B, C or D.
Use your notes from ex. 3 and write about two sentences about your paragraph.

A. There are 63 national parks in the USA today. ...

b) Put the summaries of your paragraphs together.

You can use this introduction (1) and conclusion (2) to complete your summary.

1. Ava Jones published the text "America's natural treasures" in a magazine on 20th April 2025. The article is about the development of national parks in the USA.
2. The text shows how important national parks are and why we should protect them.

5 Choose one of these tasks.

► S7 Planning, writing and checking texts, p. 184

WB 47/1–3

a) Make a flyer for people who visit a national park in the USA.

Choose a national park in the USA and find out:
- what you can see or do there,
- what you shouldn't do there,
- when to visit,
- what's special about it.

► S14 Using the internet, p. 196

Write the text and add photos.

► S16 How to use photos, films and texts, p. 198

OR

b) Make a comic strip about a trip to a national park in the USA.

Include these words:

waste | grizzly bear | sunset

Think of an interesting story. Think about:
- when and where it happens,
- who is in the story,
- what happens.

Draw three to four pictures.
Add captions and speech bubbles.

✔ I can understand a magazine article.

Checklist

D 108 My plan

WB 48

Check in: Going to the West

✓ I can understand information about the West.

WB 48

Station 1: The life of a phone

I can name stages in the life cycle of a product.
► W5 Life cycle of a product, p. 236

mine | process | package | transport | recycle | reduce | …

I can say how things are done.
► G7, p. 156 (Passive voice: simple present)

Phones are designed. | A box is transported. | Important materials aren't thrown away. | Where are phones produced? | …

✓ I can talk about the life cycle of a product.

WB 49

Viewing: Climate heroes

✓ I can understand a report.

WB 49

Station 2: Your community needs you!

I can name aspects of social work.
► W6 Social work, p. 237

find solutions | help homeless people | cope with difficult situations | support addicted people | …

I can use verbs as nouns.
► G8, p. 158 (Gerund)

Losing your home is terrible. | I enjoy helping people. | They're good at organising clothes and food. | …

✓ I can present a social project.

WB 50

Listening: The gold rush

✓ I can understand a radio play.

WB 50

Reading: America's natural treasures

✓ I can understand a magazine article.

I 12 Quiz

?

**Find the photo in the unit.
You can also do the online quiz about the West.**

D 109 Support

Task: A slide show

Prepare a slide show to present a German national park to tourists. You're only allowed a certain number of slides and a limited time for talking.

Step 1

Read the rules for the slide show:
- 15 slides
- one visual per slide
- no text on the slides
- 20 seconds per slide
- total time of slide show: 5 minutes

This way of presenting things is fast paced. You must be well-prepared. Notes are usually not allowed.

Step 2

Get into groups. Choose a national park in Germany that you would like to present. Research information about the national park:
- where and how big it is,
- when it was established,
- what wildlife and plants you can find there,
- what visitors can do there,
- what dangers and challenges there are.

► S14 Using the internet, p. 196

Hainich
– Thuringia
– about 75 square kilometres
– established in 1997
– once the army used parts of it
– ...

Step 3

Think about how you want to distribute your information over the 15 slides. Make a plan.

Step 4

Prepare your slide show.
Add one visual to each slide. Don't add text to your slides.

► S16 How to use photos, films and texts, p. 198

Media tip
A visual does not just have to be a picture. There are other types of visuals too: charts, infographics, maps, icons and symbols.

Step 5

Decide who will present which part.

Step 6

Practise your slide show.
Start with one slide at a time. Then practise more slides until you feel comfortable.

► S18 Read and look up, p. 200

Use a stopwatch to watch the time and to see how much you can say in 20 seconds.

Step 7

Present your slide show.
Ask for and give feedback.

► S8 Giving and asking for feedback, p. 190

A look at Alaska

A 33

1 What do you already know about Alaska?

1

2

3

1 Geography
Alaska is a state of forests, rivers, lakes, mountains, glaciers, and volcanoes. But the warming climate is changing Alaska's geography. The glaciers and the sea ice are getting smaller, and wildfires are happening more frequently[1] in the forests.

2 Facts and figures
Alaska is the largest state in the USA, but only 733,000 people live there. It is about 500 miles from the rest of the USA. In the past Alaska was part of Russia. However, in 1867 Russia sold the region to the USA for $7.2 million.

3 City life
Anchorage is the biggest city in Alaska, with a population of 291,000, but Juneau is the state capital. Its population is only 32,000. Juneau's harbor is popular with tourist cruise ships[2]. The harbor has room for up to five cruise ships per day in summer.

1 frequently – *häufig*; 2 cruise ship – *das Kreuzfahrtschiff*

2 Would you like to live in Alaska? Say why.

A I would / wouldn't like to live in Alaska because … .
B I think … would / wouldn't be … .

I 13–14
360°

Let's take a road trip through California!

4

5

6

4 Nature

Alaska is a great place to see wild animals. Whale watching is popular along the coast. Visitors to Denali National Park can see golden eagles[3], caribou, and grizzly bears. Alaska is also a good place to see the Northern Lights[4].

5 Alaska Native people

There are many different Indigenous[5] groups in Alaska. Traditionally they hunted and fished and used dog sleds[6] to travel across the snow. Modern transportation has replaced the traditional ways, but dog sleds are still sometimes used.

6 Renewable[7] energy

Because of the long, cold winters, Alaskans use a lot of energy. More and more of that now comes from renewable sources[8]. Around 90% of the renewable energy comes from hydropower from the state's rivers.

3 eagle – *der Adler*; 4 the Northern Lights – *die Polarlichter*; 5 Indigenous – *einheimisch*; 6 dog sled – *der Hundeschlitten*; 7 renewable – *erneuerbar*; 8 source – *die Quelle*

D 110 Support

1 California, the Golden State

a) Complete the sentences with a word or phrase.

1. Many people of Hispanic or Asian *background* live in San Francisco.
2. — is the second language in the state, after English.
3. Silicon Valley is an important place for — and technology.
4. It has many — that hope to become famous companies.
5. California is a top — of fruit and other food.
6. — are people who only work for part of the year.
7. Summers in California have become hotter and —.
8. Because of this, there are often awful — in the forests.

b) Write a sentence about California with each word or phrase.

1. surfing
2. entertainment platform
3. Los Angeles
4. brand
5. multicultural
6. Death Valley

2 How phones are made

a) Put in the verbs in the passive voice.

1. The raw materials for phones *are taken* from under the ground. (take)
2. Most phones — by robots in factories. (put together)
3. A huge amount of energy — to produce a phone. (need)
4. Chemicals — which can be dangerous for workers. (use)
5. Most phones — with paper, plastic or card. (package)
6. They — around the world by ship or road. (transport)
7. They — by customers in shops or online. (buy)
8. A typical phone — after two or three years. (replace)
9. More than 80 % of the world's phones —. (not recycle)
10. Most phones — in Europe or the USA. (not make)

is/are + past participle
Check the list of irregular verbs on page 172 if you aren't sure.

b) Write sentences about sustainable phones.

1. design | to reduce waste
2. make | from recycled materials
3. not replace | after two years
4. not sell | in big shops
5. produce | in small factories
6. workers | treat well

3 Write sentences about a school in Nevada.

1. Spanish and French | teach at the school
   Spanish and French are taught at the school.
2. a yearbook | produce every year
3. phones | not usually use in lessons
4. the food in the cafeteria | buy from local producers
5. paper, glass, and some plastics | collect for recycling
6. football games | show on the school's social media channel

4 Complete the sentences with the right forms.

Bob helps *homeless* (1 home) people in Portland, Oregon. People often lose their homes when they get — (2 serious) sick, for example. Bob enjoys — (3 find) solutions to their problems. He also tries to be — (4 friend) when people ask him for help.
Some of the — (5 work) are medically trained, others give practical advice. The — (6 good) thing about the job is when they can help people find a new home. Unfortunately, they aren't always — (7 success). But Bob and the team at Room to Hope never stop — (8 try) to help!

5 Activities and free time

A

B

C

D

E

F

a) Write a sentence about each activity.

I like / don't like .... | I'm good / not very good at .... | ... is/isn't my favourite activity.

A. I like cooking.

b) Write about four more activities.

6 Use the words to complete the text.

about | in ✓ | for | of | to | after | its

Yosemite National Park is *in* (1) California. There was a lot — (2) mining in the area 150 years ago. Then John Muir wrote magazine articles — (3) the beautiful valley. Muir loved Yosemite and — (4) wildlife. He wanted — (5) protect the landscape. Today the National Park Service looks — (6) Yosemite. It protects the beautiful park — (7) people in the future.

4 Around the Southwest

In this unit you will …
- find out about the Southwest.
  ► Check in
- describe a role model.
  ► Station 1
- watch a film portrait.
  ► Viewing
- talk about local issues.
  ► Station 2
- listen to job talks.
  ► Listening
- read a short story.
  ► Reading

D 111
My plan
A 34

A

B

The Southwest is a region of deserts and canyons, including the stunning 277-mile-long Grand Canyon. Another sight is Monument Valley. Its beautiful rocks have been in many famous movies. The climate is mostly dry. Temperatures can be very hot during the day and extremely cold at night.

Info

Biggest city: Houston, about 2.3 million people

Sights: Monument Valley, Acoma Pueblo, Old Town Albuquerque

Important rivers: Colorado River, Rio Grande

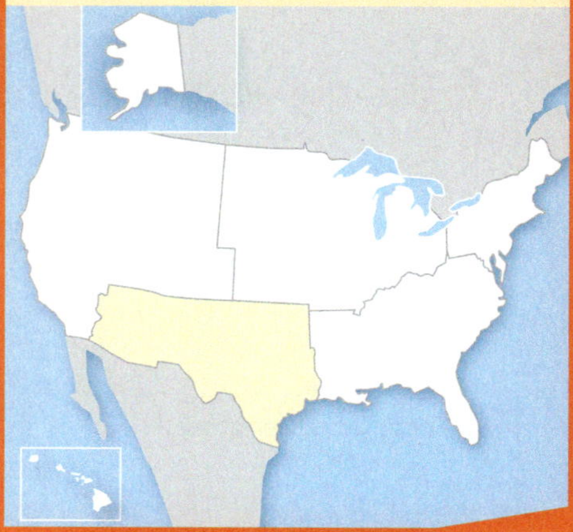

C

D

The Navajo, one of the largest Native American tribes in the USA, live on the Navajo Nation. They have a modern lifestyle, but they keep their traditions alive. There are Navajo schools, and the tribe also has its own police.

Much of the Southwest was part of Mexico until 1848. Millions more Hispanic people have migrated to the region from Latin America since then. Today the Rio Grande forms part of the border between the USA and Mexico.

E

F

The Hoover Dam crosses the Colorado River. It's 726 feet high and 1,244 feet wide. The dam provides power to Nevada, Arizona, and California. Copper mining is also an important part of the economy of the region.

Cowboys traditionally used horses when they worked with cattle. Today cowboy skills are a sport at rodeos. There are many different competitions. At one event cowboys throw a rope around a cow's neck, horns, or legs.

D 112 Support P

A 35

V 26

WB 51/1–3

1 Facts about the Southwest

a) Read the texts. Collect information about the Southwest. Make a table.

b) What information can you find out about the Southwest from the audio and the video? Add it to your table.

c) Talk about the Southwest with the help of your table.

climate	…
landscapes	…
people and culture	…
economy	…
other facts	…

V

Audio and video words

to recommend – empfehlen
Pueblo – Pueblo-; der Angehörige / die Angehörige der Pueblovölker
bean – die Bohne
plateau – die Hochebene; das Plateau
rug – der Vorleger; der Teppich

✔ I can understand information about the Southwest.

My role models

D 113 My plan
A 36
WB 52/1

1 Read Julie's blog post.

Internet

03/28/2025

Who inspires you?

by Julie

Have you ever thought about who your role models are? I want to tell you about three people who have inspired me.

My first role model is the actor Emma Stone, who was born in Arizona. I'm impressed by her because she's very talented, modest, and she has a strong character. From a young age, she was determined to become an actor. But it wasn't easy. Around the age of eleven, she took part in a local theater production, and she applied for lots of roles in Hollywood. She wasn't successful, but she still followed her dream. For example, she moved to Los Angeles with her mother and she worked part-time there. Today she's one of the most famous actors in the world and has won many awards since 2008. She's inspired me to never give up and to find a way to achieve my goals.

I'd like to talk about someone who's had a huge influence on me next. It's my high school track and field coach, Mr. Morales. When I started high school, I never thought I was a good athlete. But Mr. Morales saw that I could jump high, and he encouraged me to take part in training and competitions. I've been a member of the high school team for two years now. Mr. Morales really helped us athletes to become fitter and work as a team. He was very patient and he taught us to support each other. Last year I finished my first big race. Because of Mr. Morales, I started believing in myself and have become much more confident and ambitious.

Finally, I'd like to talk about one of my friends, Becky Carter. Becky is a little person. She's only four feet tall. This is because she was born with a genetic condition and has short arms and legs. But she doesn't let that stop her. I've known Becky since we started middle school. At first people were quite awful to her, but she was really strong. In fact, she stood up to the bullies, and now they respect her. She's always been positive, although life has sometimes been difficult for her. We've been good friends for about four years now, and she's always shown me that life is what you choose to make it.

What do you think of my role models? Let me know some of the people who inspire you.

2 Match the statements with the role models. He or she ...

D 114
D 115

1. isn't as tall as other teenagers of the same age.
   That's Becky Carter.
2. believed that Julie was talented.
3. didn't get many roles at first.
4. is a high school sports coach.
5. is a movie star.
6. is good friends with Julie.
7. helped Julie become fitter.

A

Emma Stone

B

Coach Morales

C

Becky Carter

○ D 116
● D 117

3 Answer the questions. Write short answers. ► S18 Peer correction, p.200

1. Why is Julie a fan of Emma Stone? *very talented, modest, strong character, never gives up*
2. What did Emma Stone take part in when she was about eleven?
3. Why didn't Julie join the high school track and field team when she started middle school?
4. What did Julie achieve for the first time last year?
5. What did Becky do when the bullies were awful to her?
6. What has Julie learned from being friends with Becky?

WB 52/2

4 Character traits ► W7 Describing a role model, p.237

a) Match the sentences with the right adjectives. There's one that you don't need. ► ○ p.133

ambitious | modest ✓ | fit | confident | positive | patient | determined

1. What I did wasn't special, anyone could do it.
   modest
2. I know exactly what I want and I'm going to follow my dream.
3. I always stay calm when I have to wait for something.
4. I believe that I'm good enough to do this.
5. One day I'd like to start my own company.
6. I always try and remember what's good in my life.

● **b)** Look at these words. Find a word from the same word family in the text. Check their meanings.

determination ✓ | influential | modesty | talent | ambition | patience

determination – determined

S

Skills

You can form many nouns from adjectives (and adjectives from nouns) by changing the ending. For example, the endings of nouns often look like this: -**ion**, -**ation**, -**ance**, -**ence**, -**y**.
Adjectives often end with -**ous**, -**y**, -**al**, -**ed**, -**ent** or -**ant**.

5 Talk about three important qualities that role models should have.

A I think role models should be successful and modest. And they should … .
B I agree. / I don't agree. / I'm not sure. I think … .
C …

V 3
How to

WB 53/3

6 Mediation ► S9 Mediation, p.191

Der Filmklub in deinem Jugendzentrum sucht nach Klassikern für einen Filmabend zum Thema USA. Du hast diese Filmkritik im Internet gefunden. Informiere die anderen auf Deutsch über den Film.

Internet

The Searchers

The Searchers is a 1956 western that is set during the 19th century. John Wayne plays the lonely hero Ethan Edwards. Edwards tries to find and rescue his niece, who has been kidnapped by a tribe of Native Americans. The movie, which was directed by John Ford, features lots of stunning shots of the wide, rocky landscape of the Southwest. It's very beautiful.
But it's hard to see Ethan Edwards as a hero. He's violent, cruel, and motivated by revenge. Unfortunately, the movie doesn't show real Native American life or culture. The Native Americans in the movie are either violent, stupid, or comical. From today's point of view, this portrayal of Native Americans is dangerous and unhelpful, and we need to see the movie in this context.

V 27 How to
V 28 How to

G

Language revision: Present perfect ► G9, p.160

Test yourself: Write sentences.

1. Julie | already | train | today.
2. I | not talk | to my friend | yet.
3. Julie and Becky | already | do | their homework | together.
4. Julie | not watch | the new film with Emma Stone | yet.
5. you | ever | meet | Emma Stone? – No, I —.
6. Who | inspire | you | the most?
7. Coach Morales | talk | to you | about the next competition yet? – Yes, he —.
8. Our coach | be | very busy this week.
9. My role models | have | a huge influence on me.

○ D 118
● D 119
WB 53/4

7 Complete the sentences. Use the present perfect. ► S18 Peer correction, p.200

You can look up irregular verb forms on page 172.

1. Emma Stone *has already worked* (already work) with lots of other famous actors.
2. She — (not direct) a film yet.
3. Coach Morales — (help) many young athletes.
4. He — (never teach) baseball.
5. Julie — (become) much more confident.
6. She — (never have) an accident.
7. Becky — (not try) horse riding yet.
8. Students in Julie's class — (show) Becky that they respect her.
9. Julie: I — (not make) a video for my social media account yet.

WB 54/5

8 Interview with a role model

a) Complete the interview with the right forms of the verbs. ► ○ p.134

Julie: Hi Coach. I*'ve just had* (1 just have) an idea. I'd like to write a blog about my role models. You're one of them! Can I ask you some questions?
Coach: That's awesome! Sure.
Julie: — you — (2 always be) a track and field coach?
Coach: No, I — (3). I worked in a small company after college.
Julie: — you — (4 ever lose) a really important competition with a team?
Coach: Yes, I — (5). It was a year ago. I was angry because the other team wasn't good.
Julie: That sounds awful. — you — (6 ever run) a race in another country?
Coach: Yes, I — (7). We went to Australia two years ago. It was really exciting!
Julie: Thanks for talking to me, Mr. Morales.
Coach: You're welcome.

●

b) Ask and answer two questions about each photo. Use the present perfect.

see | play | watch | visit | travel | be | try | meet | ...

A Have you ever ...?
B Yes, I have. / No, I haven't.

A

B

C

WB 54/6

9 Since or for?

a) Write sentences about Becky. Use since or for. ► ○ p. 134

A

have | six months

B

read | September

Grammar ► G9, p. 160
I've had these shoes **for** two years.
I've been a member of the basketball team **since** March.

C

know | middle school

D

play | two months

E

make | one year

A. Becky has had her dog for six months.

● b) Write sentences about yourself using the present perfect with since or for.

1. live | in my house or flat
2. be a student | at my school
3. know | my best friend
4. like | my favourite star

○ D 120
● D 121
WB 55/7–9

10 Complete the dialogue. Use the present perfect or the simple past.

► S18 Peer correction, p. 200

Becky Who's that basketball player on TV?
Julie It's Dirk Nowitzki.
Becky I*'ve never heard* (1 never hear) of him.
Julie He doesn't play any more. But he was one of the greatest players of all time.
Becky Where's he from?
Julie He was born in Germany, but he — (2 live) in Dallas since 1998.
Becky What — he — (3 achieve) as a player?
Julie He — (4 play) in lots of important games. In 2007 he — (5 win) the NBA Most Valuable Player Award.
Becky Wow! — anyone — (6 ever write) a book about him?

Julie Yes, a few people have. Thomas Pletzinger — (7 write) *The Great Nowitzki* a few years ago, for example.
Becky — you — (8 already read) it?
Julie No, I — (9), but I'm going to read it soon.

The signal words can help you!
Present perfect: already, never, not … yet, ever, since, for
Simple past: in (year), ago, last

I 15

V 11 How to

D 122 Support

P

11 Your turn: An email to a magazine

A youth magazine has a feature about teenagers' role models. Zara, one of the reporters, asks the readers to write emails about their own role models. Write an email to Zara.

► S7 Planning, writing and checking texts, p. 184

Step 1

Choose a role model to write about. It can be someone who is famous or someone who is a friend or a member of your family. The person must be important to you, however.

Media tip

Some influencers have many followers but aren't suitable role models. Some even promote hate speech, racism or conspiracy theories.

Step 2

Begin the email with a greeting, some information about yourself and the name of the role model.

Dear Zara,
My name is ..., and I go to ... School. I read your feature about role models and I would like to write about ... .

Step 3

Give more information about your role model.

- How long have you known (about) the person?
- What has your role model done and what makes the person special? Do some research if you need to. ► S14 Using the internet, p. 196
- Describe the character of your role model. Give examples.

I've known (about) ... since/for ... .
... has (already/never) ...
... always ...
... is very ...
...

Step 4

Share how your role model has influenced you. Explain in what ways this person has motivated or inspired you.

He/She has inspired me to ... .
Because of him/her, I've become much more ... .

Step 5

Write the last part of your email. Don't forget to write in a friendly way.

... has had a big influence on me. I think ... is a great role model.
Thank you and best wishes,
(Your full name)

Step 6

Check your email and ask for feedback. Write a new draft if you need to.

► S8 Giving and asking for feedback, p. 190

S Skills

You should check that your email has a good structure and put each part in a different paragraph. You could have paragraphs with:

- an introduction,
- your role model's character, with examples,
- your role model's influence on you,
- some closing words.

✔ I can describe a role model.

Multicultural USA

D 123 My plan

D 124
D 125

1 Match the words with the definitions.

Look in your dictionary if you aren't sure. ► S13 Looking up words, p. 194

have the same rights | slave | racism | plantation | continent | tribe | reservation ✓ | live in slavery

1. an area where Native Americans can live, often not where they lived in the past *reservation*
2. a group of people, for example Native Americans, with the same traditions or language
3. someone who isn't free and has to work for another person
4. be allowed to live in the same way as others
5. a way of treating people badly because of the colour of their skin
6. live without freedom or rights
7. a large area of land with crops, often in a hot country
8. Africa, Asia or Europe, for example

V 29
D 126
D 127
WB 56/1–3

2 Multicultural USA

a) Watch the film. Complete the sentences with a word or phrase.

1. More than *330 million* people live in the USA today.
2. Many Native Americans died in — and of European diseases after the settlers came.
3. The Navajo and other Native American tribes live in towns and cities or on —.
4. Millions of people had to go from — to the USA to work as slaves.
5. The slaves worked on —.
6. Black people still didn't — as other Americans after slavery ended.

b) Watch the film again. Take notes about what happened at these times.

1. before the Europeans came
2. the 1500s and the 1600s
3. from the 16th to the 19th century
4. 1865
5. the time after 1865

The times come in a different order in the film.

3 A short presentation

a) Do some research about one of the times in 2b) and add more information to your notes.
► S14 Using the internet, p. 196

b) Give a short presentation about the time that you chose. ► S4 Giving a presentation, p. 181

Culture

Black History Month takes place every February in the USA. It celebrates the history and culture of Black people and their contribution to American life in the past and the present. There are many other celebrations like this in the USA, for example Native American Heritage Month and Hispanic Heritage Month.

✓ I can understand a film portrait.

Life in a small town

D 128
My plan

1 What can you do if you want to change things where you live?

► S18 Think-pair-share, p. 200

I can ask / talk to someone who … . / I can write / post … .

2 Read what people say at a town hall meeting in Arizona.

A 37

Host Thank you for coming to our town hall meeting. Our mayor is here to listen to you and answer your questions. First we have Pablo Ramirez, a student from George Washington High School.

Pablo Hello. We've been finding out about graffiti in our art class this year. People complain about graffiti at the bus station and other places in town. Other cities have special graffiti walls where anyone can be creative. We'd like to have a wall like that in our town. Our town has good sports facilities. Can the mayor support people who like art too?

Host Thank you, Mr. Ramirez. Mayor Sanchez?

Mayor Good evening Mr. Ramirez. It's great that you have an idea to make our town better. Unfortunately, I can't say yes this evening, but we can think about this when we make our plan for next year.

Host Thank you. I'd like to ask Maria Faulkner, a store owner, to speak next.

Maria Good evening. I'm opening the Moo Moo frozen yoghurt store next to the bank on Broad Street next month. We'd like to put a large sign in the shape of a cow on the sidewalk in front of the store to celebrate. We could also organize events and activities for children. Can the mayor help us with some money for this?

Host Thank you. Mayor Sanchez?

Mayor Good evening Ms. Faulkner. That sounds fantastic! We're always happy to support new businesses and people who offer new services. However, please contact Mr. Hampson here at the town hall first so that we can talk about the plans.

Host I hope that answers your question. Our next speaker is Jason Allister, an engineer.

Jason Hello everyone. I've been talking to some friends in the last few weeks about how we can make our town greener and improve our air quality. I believe that the best way to do this is to have more trees. We should plant them in the parks, along the sidewalks, and around public buildings like the library and the hospital too. We'd like to start a program to plant 1,000 new trees. The air quality will be better if we plant trees, and they will also make it cooler in summer. What does the mayor think about this?

Host Thank you, Mr. Allister. Mayor?

Mayor I think this is an excellent idea. I'm happy to say that in our new Green Town project, we've already planned to plant around 500 new trees in the town over the next five years. But we can also talk about how Mr. Allister and other people in the town can help us.

Host That's good news!

Culture

Town hall meetings take place in town or city halls across the USA. People can meet local and national politicians at the meetings. They can ask questions and talk about problems and things that they would like to change.

D 129
WB 57/1

3 Complete the report about the town hall meeting.

Internet

Last night's town hall meeting

April 2, 2025
by Amber MacDonald

Over a hundred people came to the *town hall* (1) last night. There were a lot of questions and ideas.
High school student Pablo Ramirez would like a — (2) in our town, like the ones in other cities. Mayor Elena Sanchez wants to — (3) about the idea.
Maria Faulkner, a local — (4), asked the next question. She would like to put a large — (5) in front of her new — (6). She would like to have — (7) from the mayor to help with the project.
Jason Allister, an engineer, wants to start a program for better — (8). The mayor talked about the town's plans. They want to — (9) 500 new trees over the next — (10).

Mayor Elena Sanchez

D 39
Support
WB 57/2

4 In a town or a city ► W8 Infrastructure and services, p. 238

a) Copy and add to the mind map. Look in the text and add your own words. ► p. 135

b) Check the meanings of these words. Add them to the mind map.

athletics track | low-emission buses | optician's | sculpture park | law court | charging point | butcher's

D 130
WB 57/3

5 What should be in every town?

a) Make a list of five things. Use the words from your mind map.

b) Talk about your list with a partner. Do you agree?

everyone needs … | useful when you are …

A Every town should have … because … .
B I don't agree. Towns don't need …, but they … .

WB 58/4

6 A letter to a mayor

a) Replace the underlined parts of the letter with more suitable words and phrases. ► ○ p. 135
► S18 Peer correction, p. 200

Hi Dear *(1) Mayor Wilson,*
I am writing to you because we need better sports facilities for kids (2) and young people in our town. The sports facilities that we have are very old. Some were there when my mom and dad (3) were my age!
Sports are important to help people have healthy lives.
Every town should have awesome (4), modern facilities where young people can do their favorite sports.
I understand that new facilities are expensive, but I believe that they will help the town in the future.
Could my BFFs (5) and I have a meeting with you about this?
I hope that we can chat (6) about the problem soon.
Thanks (7) and kind regards,
Mona Abbadi

S Skills
It's important to use more formal language when you write to someone like the mayor of a town. This shows that you respect the person.

● b) Rewrite these sentences so that they are suitable for a town hall meeting with a mayor.

1. Some cool dudes started a roof garden.
2. Planting a few trees is no big deal.
3. Too many young people are broke.
4. A movie ticket is twelve bucks.

A 38
○ D 131
● D 132
WB 59/5

7 Listen to a podcast interview about the history of a town.

Are the sentences true or false?

1. Native Americans lived in the area of Show Low until the 1500s. *That's false.*
2. Corydon Cooley and Marion Clark started a farm together.
3. Five years later they played a game.
4. Cooley lost the game.
5. Cooley opened the first store in the area in 1883.
6. More than 13,000 people live in the city today.
7. You can go to Show Low by plane.

○ D 133
● D 134
WB 59/6

8 Cartoons ► S5 Describing photos and pictures, p. 182

a) Talk about the cartoons with a partner.

- Who or what is in the cartoons?
- What do the cartoons tell you about small towns and big cities?

A There is … / There are … . Some people are … / A person is … . The cartoon tells us that … .

b) Where would you like to live: in a town, in a city or in the country? Say why.

A I'd like to … because … .

A

B

"You can't miss me – I'm under the tree."

G

V 30
How to

Language detectives ► G10, p. 162

We **'ve been finding out** about graffiti in our art class **since the start of the year**.
Jason **has been talking** to his friends **for three hours**.

The actions are not complete, and the duration is also important. How do we form the new tense?

D 135
D 136
WB 60/7

9 What has been happening since the town hall meeting?

Write sentences.

get | paint ✓ | sell | organise | check | plant

A

Pablo | a large picture

B

Jason and friends | air quality

C

Maria | lots of frozen yoghurt

D

workers | trees in the town

E

weather | warmer every day

F

host | other meetings

A. Pablo has been painting a large picture.
B. Jason and his friends have ... .

WB 60/8

10 How long?

a) Ask a partner. ► p. 136 ► S18 Double circle, p. 201

take the bus to school | live where you live | use the local skate park | listen to ...
go to ... | play ... | watch ...

A How long have you been taking the bus to school?
B I've been doing that since I was ten. How long have you ...?

b) Write about what has or hasn't been happening in your village, town or city in the last few months. Use these verbs.

improve ... | install ... | build more ... | replace ...

I 16

V 31 How to

11 Your turn: Statements about local issues

Prepare and make statements in class about issues that are important in your city, town or village.

► S3 Speaking with other people, p. 180

Step 1

Work in groups. Think about what you would like to change or improve in your city, town or village. Collect ideas.

transport
sports facilities
place(s) for people who like …
…

Step 2

Agree on a topic for your group.
Think of arguments and find facts to support them.

► S14 Using the internet, p. 196

Transport
- *not enough buses at weekend*
- *buses too full at other times*
- *…*

Step 3

Choose a host to manage the meeting. (The host can be a student or the teacher.) Give the host the topic that your group wants to talk about.

Media tip
You can use an app to make and share your notes on a digital board.

Step 4

Prepare a statement about your topic with arguments and examples to support your statement. The speaker will have one minute for this.

Skills
It's important to think about how much time you have for your statement. Maybe you can start with a question ("Have you ever missed your bus and waited an hour for the next one? …").

Step 5

Decide who will be the speaker.

Step 6

The host writes the topics on the board and decides which topic goes first. Make your group's statement.
After each statement the students in the other groups ask questions (two minutes).

A Thank you for your statement.
I understand your argument, but have you thought about …?
I didn't understand when you said … .
What did you mean?

Step 7

Vote to decide which statement was best.

You can also pass on some of the ideas to the mayor or the administration where you live.

✔ I can talk about local issues.

D 137
My plan

Finding out about jobs

1 Read the questions on the flyer. Talk about your answers with a partner.

1. What kind of job are you most interested in?

- working with people
- working in an office
- making things
- working outside

2. How do you feel about these things?

- working in a team
- long working hours
- working fast
- helping people
- studying for a degree
- doing an apprenticeship
- a high salary
- using programming languages
- doing something that you enjoy

A 39

D 138
D 139
WB 61/1–2

2 Job talks

a) Listen to three people talking about their jobs. Choose the right jobs.

A

emergency medical technician (EMT)

B

police officer

C

software engineer

D

electrician

E

farmer

F

carpenter

G

bus driver

H

social worker

b) Listen again. Complete the sentences with one or two words.

1. Gina works for a — in Socorro.
2. In her job you must be good with —.
3. Ricardo helps people who have serious — in his job.
4. You have to do about — of training.
5. Jenna's company produces — for hotels.
6. People in her job can get high salaries, but she works — too.

WB 61/3

3 Find out more about one of the jobs in ex. 2. Tell a partner about it.

► S14 Using the internet, p. 196

What do people do in the job?
What are the working hours like?
What should you be good at?
Would you like to do this job? Say why.

Culture
Job titles and qualifications may be different in different countries, although the job itself may be the same or similar.

✔ I can understand job talks.

 ▷ S2, p. 178

V 13
How to

D 140
My plan

A 40

When everything changed

Beep[1] beep, beep beep, went the alarm on Robert's phone. It was a cool Monday morning in March. Robert turned his head and reached out for his phone, which was next to his bed. But as he did, something felt quite different. He slowly opened his eyes. He looked at his arm, his hand, and his fingers. They were slimmer than he remembered.

Something wasn't right. He sat up in bed, pulled the covers up, and looked beneath[2] them. He was shocked. His body wasn't his own. Robert had woken up as a girl!

Robert got up in a panic. He frantically[3] looked in his wardrobe. He couldn't believe what he saw. It was full of girls' clothes! He threw everything on the bed and looked at all the clothes for a few minutes without doing anything. He wasn't sure if he was still dreaming. But after some time he had to get dressed. He found a pair of jeans and his most comfortable sweater.

He was still living in the same house in Santa Fe, New Mexico, where he'd always lived. The house was empty when he went downstairs. He opened his front door and walked to the bus stop.

"Hey Nina! Nina!" shouted Ida and Hannah, two girls from Robert's class, when he got on the bus.

"Nina! Come and join us!" one of them added.

They were clearly looking at him, so Robert walked towards the girls. They made room for him to sit down. But he didn't know what to say to them. The whole situation was too strange.

"Is that sweater new?" asked Ida. "I haven't seen you wear it before."

"I don't know," answered Robert.

"And no make-up today," added Hannah. "Going for the natural look? Cool!"

Robert felt confused that they were so interested in his appearance. He immediately began to feel nervous. He felt as if everyone was looking at him.

"Can I ask you something?" Robert said to the girls. They looked at him. "Can you remember how long we've known each other?"

"Since elementary school[4]," said Ida. "We were in the same class, weren't we?"

"Of course we were," he answered. He understood. He was a girl called Nina, and to his friends, he'd always been a girl called Nina. It was crazy!

The school day started as always. Robert went to his science lesson. Sara, a girl he'd always liked, invited Robert to sit next to her. For a moment Robert felt happy, until he realized that she was inviting Nina to sit next to her and not Robert. Even so, Robert enjoyed how Sara was more friendly towards him than when he was a boy.

After lunch Freddie, a friend of his from tennis club, stopped him.

"Hey Nina. Can I talk to you for a second?" asked Freddie.

"Sure."

"There's a girl I really like, but I don't know how to tell her," Freddie told him.

"Really?" asked Robert.

"Yeah, I've wanted to ask her on a date for weeks, but I don't know how to. I feel really shy."

Robert was surprised to hear this. He thought Freddie was really confident and had kissed lots of girls.

Freddie had never spoken to him about his feelings before. Robert was beginning to realize that everyone treated him differently as a girl, and it wasn't too bad.

"I think it's best to be honest about how you feel," he told Freddie. "Just be yourself and be confident. I'm sure she'll say yes," he added, smiling at his friend.

Freddie smiled back. Their eyes met. Suddenly, Freddie moved his head forward and …

1 beep – *Piepsgeräusch*; 2 beneath – *unter*; 3 frantically – *außer sich, rasend*; 4 elementary school (AE) – *die Grundschule*

1 Read the short story.

2 When everything changed

○ D 141
● D 142

a) Complete the sentences.

1. When Robert wakes up, he's a *girl*.
2. At first he feels —.
3. On the bus to school he meets —.
4. He learns that his name is —.
5. Robert is happy sitting next to Sara in science because —.
6. After lunch a boy called Freddie wants to —.

b) Think of more details to fill in the gaps in the story. Answer these questions with your own ideas. Take turns.

1. Why is Robert's house empty?

A I think maybe Robert's house is empty because his parents are helping his grandma. They do this every morning. She lives in the same street.

2. What does Robert think about when he looks at his clothes?
3. What does Robert do before he leaves the house?
4. What other things do Ida and Hannah talk about on the school bus?
5. What do Freddie and Robert usually talk about in their free time?

The answers aren't in the text. Try to find ideas that add more information to the story. Your ideas shouldn't contradict the events or characters in the story.

3 Find the adjectives in the text. Give the lines.

1. surprised and upset *shocked (line 10)*
2. easy to wear
3. with no people or things
4. unusual or weird
5. not able to understand something
6. not able to relax
7. afraid of talking to people
8. saying what is true

4 Choose one of these tasks.

WB 63/1–3

► S7 Planning, writing and checking texts, p. 184

a) Add two more paragraphs to the end of the story.

Include:
what happens next,
how Robert feels,
what he says to Freddie,
what happens on a day that comes after the events in the story.

OR

b) How could the story be different if a girl woke up as a boy one day? Rewrite the first two paragraphs from a girl's perspective.

Think about:
What could be different from Robert's story?
What could be the same?
How could the girl feel?

✔ I can understand a short story.

Checklist

D 143 My plan

WB 64

Check in: Around the Southwest

✓ I can understand information about the Southwest.

WB 64

Station 1: My role models

I can name character traits.
► W7 Describing a role model, p. 237

talented | modest | ambitious | brave | honest | …

I can talk about events in the past that are still important now.
► G9, p. 160 (Present perfect: statements, negatives, questions)

Julie has known Mr. Morales for two years. | I've been a member of the team for two years.

✓ I can describe a role model.

WB 65

Viewing: Multicultural USA

✓ I can understand a film portrait.

WB 65

Station 2: Life in a small town

I can name the infrastructure and services in a town.
► W8 Infrastructure and services, p. 238

town hall | bus station | bank | sports facilities | …

I can talk about recent actions that are still continuing.
► G10, p. 162 (Present perfect progressive)

We've been finding out about graffiti in our art class this year. | I've been talking to some friends in the last few weeks.

✓ I can talk about local issues.

WB 66

Listening: Finding out about jobs

✓ I can understand job talks.

WB 66

Reading: When everything changed

✓ I can understand a short story.

I 17 Quiz

?

Find the photo in the unit.
You can also do the online quiz about the Southwest.

D 144
Support

Task: A podcast

Prepare and record a short podcast about the Southwest.

Step 1

Get into groups and decide on your topic.
Your podcast can be about the geography, culture, history, economy, wildlife, famous people, sports or natural landmarks of the Southwest.

Step 2

Research your topic.
Your podcast should include at least three interesting aspects. Find two or three facts for each aspect.

► S14 Using the internet, p.196

Natural landmarks of the Southwest:

1. The Grand Canyon
– What and where is it?
– How long is it?
– …

Step 3

Write the script of your podcast. Introduce yourselves and the podcast at the start and say goodbye at the end. Try to keep the style friendly. It's a good idea to compare things in the Southwest with things in Germany.

► S7 Planning, writing and checking texts, p.184

Welcome to our podcast about … . I'm …, and this is … .
Did you know that …? That's bigger than … / twice as big as …! That's amazing, isn't it? …
Thanks for listening to our podcast. Goodbye!

Step 4

Practise your podcast.
Decide who will speak when and who will check the recording.

Media tip
You can use an online dictionary to check how to pronounce new words.

Step 5

Record your podcast.
You can record it in short sections if you don't feel confident reading a longer text.

► S12 Making a short audio, p.193

Step 6

Share your podcast with the other groups.
Ask for and give feedback.

► S8 Giving and asking for feedback, p.190

Media tip
It may be possible to use your school's platform to share the podcasts. There are also websites where you can share large files for free.

The Southwest – deserts and more

A 41

1 Do you recognise the places and things in the photos?

What do you know about them?

1

2

3

1 Monument Valley is in the desert on the Arizona-Utah border. It is famous for its sandstone rocks that are up to 1,000 feet tall. The valley is a sacred[1] place for the Navajo Nation Native Americans who live in the area. It has also been in many movies.

2 Phoenix is the largest city in Arizona. It is located in the desert and is the hottest large city in the USA, with average high summer temperatures of around 100°F. But the city is planting trees and investing in technology to reduce temperatures.

3 Taos Pueblo is an ancient Native American village in New Mexico. Most of the buildings there are between 600 and 1,000 years old. About 150 people still live in Taos Pueblo. The buildings have influenced the architecture in Santa Fe and other cities.

1 sacred – *heilig*

2 What was new in the texts? What did you find interesting?

I knew / didn't know that … .
It's interesting that … .

4

5

6

4 The Southwest isn't all desert! There are six national forests in Arizona and five in New Mexico, for example. The **Gila National Forest** is in New Mexico. It has large areas of wilderness, which are home to wolves, cougars[2], black bears, and many bird species[3].

5 The **Gila Monster** is a lizard[4] that lives in the deserts and forests of the Southwest. The lizards are venomous[5] and can give you a painful[6] bite[7]. They can be up to 22 inches long. Fortunately, they are slow and heavy, and they rarely[8] attack people.

6 **Southwestern food** is enjoyed in many parts of the USA. Many dishes include one or more of three classic ingredients[9] – corn, squash[10], and beans. They often have lots of chili too. Burritos, enchiladas, and nachos are also very popular.

2 cougar – *der Puma, der Berglöwe*; 3 species – *die Tier- oder Pflanzenart*;
4 lizard – *die Eidechse*; 5 venomous – *giftig*; 6 painful – *schmerzhaft*;
7 bite – *der Biss*; 8 rarely – *selten*; 9 ingredient – *die Zutat*; 10 squash – *der Kürbis*

D 145 Support

1 Adjectives and nouns

a) Choose the best adjectives to complete the text. There are four that you don't need.

little | difficult | nervous | good ✓ | angry | positive | awful | ambitious | genetic | patient | strong

Julie and Becky have been *good* (1) friends since middle school. At first people called Becky names and were — (2) to her. This was because she is a — (3) person (she is only four feet tall) who was born with a — (4) condition. But Becky is a — (5) person too, and she stood up to the bullies. Now they respect her. Becky's condition means that life has sometimes been — (6) for her. She's always been — (7), however. She never forgets what's good in life!

b) Write sentences with the four adjectives that you didn't need.

2 Since or for?

a) Write sentences with the present perfect and since or for.

1. Emma Stone | win | a lot of awards | 2008
   Emma Stone has won a lot of awards since 2008.
2. Mr Morales | be | Julie's coach | two years
3. Julie | know | Becky | middle school
4. Becky | have | a pet dog | six months
5. I | not eat | chocolate | Sunday
6. our neighbours | have | a new car | six weeks
7. my friend | want | a pet cat | more than a year
8. we | not see | our cousins | November

b) Write the sentences.

1. I | be | a student at … | since … .
2. I | know | my best friend | for … .
3. I | be | a fan of … | since … .
4. My brother/sister/friend | play … | for … .

3 Copy the table. Put the signal words into two groups.

Which word don't you need?

Simple past	Present perfect
yesterday	…

just | yesterday ✓ | last year | already | at the moment | not … yet | ago | in February | since | in 2023 | on Sunday

4 Present perfect or simple past?

Put in the right forms. The signal words can help you.

Julie *started* (1 start) doing track and field in her first year at high school. Coach Morales — (2 see) that she could jump well. He — (3 help) Julie a lot since then and she — (4 become) more confident. She — (5 finish) her first big race last year and she — (6 feel) very proud that day. She — (7 already – train) twice this week, but she isn't going to train tomorrow – it's her birthday! She — (8 have) a party at home last year, but this year she's going to eat a meal at a diner with her family.

5 In a town or city

a) Find the words.

1. This is a place where sports events can take place.
   a stadium
2. People can come here to get or stay fit.
3. The mayor's office is usually in this building.
4. This is an official place for street art.
5. This is a large shop that sells food and other products.
6. This is a place where people can keep their money.
7. Buses or trains can arrive and leave from here.
8. This is a large building for people who are ill.

b) Write your own definitions.

1. a park
2. a concert hall
3. a restaurant
4. a cinema
5. a market
6. a youth club

6 What have they been doing?

Complete the sentences with the present perfect progressive.

1. Jason Allister *has been checking* the town's air quality for the last six weeks. (check)
2. Pablo's brothers — in the garden today. (work)
3. Jason's sister — in her room all afternoon. (read)
4. Amber MacDonald — about local events in the town for the last three years. (write)
5. Pablo's mother and father — Chinese since last summer. (learn)
6. His friend — a cake. (bake)
7. Jim Roberts — at the local high school for more than 30 years. (teach)
8. Elena Sanchez — and — to people in her town a lot since she became mayor. (talk, listen)

have/has been + -ing
We can use the present perfect progressive to talk about recent actions that are still continuing.

5 Settling in the South

In this unit you will …
- find out about the South.
  ► Check in
- talk about discrimination.
  ► Station 1
- watch a nature film.
  ► Viewing
- give your opinion.
  ► Station 2
- listen to a radio feature.
  ► Listening
- read an article from a history magazine.
  ► Reading

D 146
My plan

A 42

A

B

The South is a warm, fertile region with large farmlands. The huge Mississippi River flows into the sea near New Orleans in Louisiana. In Florida you can see the Everglades, a beautiful area with forests and lakes, and Cape Canaveral, the launch site for US space missions.

Info

Biggest city: Jacksonville, about 970,000 people

Sights: Country Music Hall of Fame, Kennedy Space Center

Famous national park: Everglades National Park

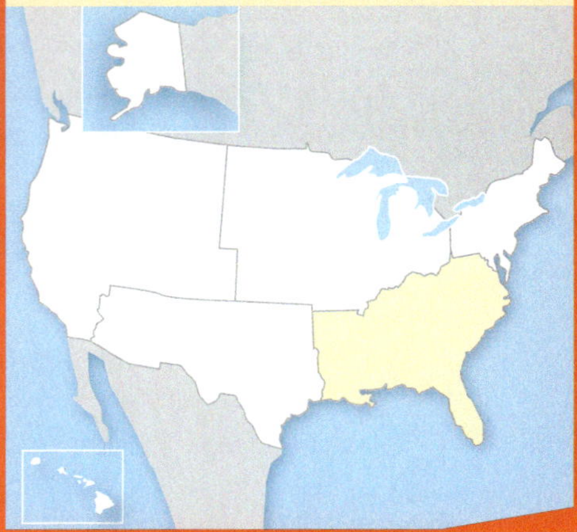

C

The climate means that people can spend a lot of time outside. The region is famous for its barbecues with smoked meat, ribs, and spicy sauces. Many Southerners are proud of this tradition. There are even barbecue competitions.

D

New Orleans is a unique city. The French founded it in 1718, and it later became part of a Spanish colony. New Orleans is famous for its Mardi Gras carnival, a big celebration with a lot of music and dancing.

E

The Civil Rights Movement started in places like Montgomery, Alabama, where Black people protested against racism and segregation in the 1950s and 1960s. Racism is still a problem in the USA and other parts of the world today.

F

The coast of the South is often hit by powerful hurricanes. The storms start over the warm water in the Atlantic Ocean. The winds damage houses and other buildings and can also cause terrible floods.

1 Facts about the South

D 2 Support P

a) Read the texts. Collect information about the South. Copy and complete the fact cards.

A 43

V 32

WB 67/1–3

b) What information can you find out about the South from the audio and the video? Add it to your fact cards.

c) Talk about the South with the help of your fact cards.

Climate	Landscapes	People
…	…	…
Traditions	**History**	**Other facts**
…	…	…

V

Audio and video words

Creole – kreolisch
ingredient – die Zutat
shrimp – die Krabbe; die Garnele
coral reef – das Korallenriff
wetland – das Sumpfgebiet

✔ I can understand information about the South.

Respecting each other

D 147
My plan
A 44
WB 68/1

1 Read the social media comments.

Internet

Macy
Charlotte, North Carolina
06:22 p.m.

They say that all men are created equal, but unfortunately, they aren't always treated as equals. When you treat someone unfairly because of what they look like or who they are … that's discrimination. This happens again and again. I'm a person with a disability. I must use a wheelchair to get around. A few years ago my city improved access to its stations by installing more elevators. Getting around has been easier for me since then. But last week the elevator at my stop didn't work, and I wasn't able to get to the platform. Most people just walked past me without looking, although I asked some for help. Some even pushed me out of their way and insulted me. I was mad. But I didn't have to wait long. Three people finally helped me, and we had a nice chat on the train. What are your experiences of difficult situations? How do you cope with them?

See all answers.

Jamar
Biloxi, Mississippi
07:15 p.m.

I'm so sorry to hear about your experience, Macy. I'm a person of color. Last month I worked as a volunteer at a summer camp. Most people were very nice, and we had lots of fun together. But there were a boy and a girl who often called me names. They didn't do it in public – just whenever we were alone. It made me feel so helpless. But I know I am strong. I couldn't prove that they said those things, so I talked to my team and my friends and family. I chose to ignore the bad words, and you know what? I felt a lot better, and the other two soon lost interest in me.

Ricarda
Savannah, Georgia
08:36 p.m.

That's so bad, Macy. I can really understand you. I hate it when people treat me differently because I have a Mexican accent. When I started school here in the USA, some of the other students thought I was stupid because I wasn't able to speak English very well. They didn't want to work with me and didn't want to make friends. But I'm very good at volleyball. You don't need many words there. After some time in the team things got better. You mustn't give up, Macy!

Jin
Knoxville, Tennessee
09:07 a.m.

When my mom first arrived in the USA 20 years ago, she had a difficult time finding a job. Her English was very good, but because she was Chinese and a woman, people didn't take her seriously. When she finally got a job in a store, she wasn't allowed to talk to customers. It was really a hard time for her. Together with other women she soon started raising awareness for women's rights. She also educates people about discrimination in our community.

Culture

The quote "all men are created equal" is part of the Declaration of Independence. It was written in 1776, when the USA became an independent country with its own laws. This statement is still talked about today because it shows how important equality, democracy and justice are. Is there something similar in your country?

○ D 148
● D 149

2 Complete the sentences with information from the text.

► S18 Peer correction, p. 200

1. Macy must use a wheelchair *to get around*.
2. She couldn't get to the platform because —.
3. A girl and a boy at the summer camp —.
4. When Jamar ignored them, they —.
5. People treat Ricarda differently because —.
6. Things got better for her when she —.
7. It was hard for Jin's mother to —.
8. Today she educates —.

WB 68/2

3 What you can do

► W9 Attitudes and behaviour, p. 239

a) Complete the flyer. ► ○ p. 136

behave | strategies | choices | discrimination ✓ | danger | tolerant | discriminated against

Be strong – Training for young people

In our training sessions we talk about all kinds of *discrimination* (1). We want to talk about why, when, where, and how people are — (2). We want to work together to learn about — (3) for coping with discrimination in your daily life.
We will show you what — (4) you have.
We will also talk about how you can — (5) in different situations without putting yourself in — (6).
Help us to live in a more — (7) world.
Visit our website for more information.

● **b)** Match the words and phrases with the definitions.

reflect | be rude | put yourself in other people's shoes | be stubborn

1. not want to change your mind
2. think carefully about something
3. imagine that you're in somebody else's place
4. not respect another person's feelings

A 45
○ D 150
● D 151
WB 68/3

4 A conversation about dealing with discrimination

a) Listen and complete the sentences.

1. Julia took part in a —.
2. The leader presented some —.
3. They made a poster to show different kinds of —.
4. Julia talks about — for difficult situations.
5. Gedeon wants to organise a workshop at —.

b) Listen again and take notes about the strategies that Julia talks about.

Number 1: stay …
Number 2: …
…

A 46
WB 68/4

5 Listen and say the words. Which parts get the stress?

1. educate – education
   educate – …
2. celebrate – celebration
3. discriminate – discrimination
4. present – presentation
5. invite – invitation
6. compete – competition
7. describe – description

V 33
How to

Language detectives ► G11, p. 164

G

They use lifts. (It's a fact.)
They **can** use lifts. (They're able to do it.)
They **may** use lifts. (It's OK for them to do it.)
They **must** use lifts. (Because they can't walk.)
They **mustn't** use lifts. (It's not safe.)
They **needn't** use lifts. (Because there are stairs.)

How would you say the marked words in German?

○ D 152
● D 153
WB 69/5–6

6 Choose the best answers.

1. We *mustn't* | **can't** discriminate against people.
2. If you have any questions, you **may** | **must** ask them at the end of the presentation.
3. In a free country people **must** | **can** say what they like.
4. You **mustn't** | **needn't** talk about it if you don't want to.
5. I **can't** | **must** go to the workshop now. I'm too busy!
6. People with disabilities **can** | **must** still think carefully about how to get around.

WB 69/7

7 You really must do it!

a) Complete the sentences. Use each modal auxiliary only once. ► ○ p. 137

must | may ✓ | can | mustn't | can't | needn't

A

People *may ride* bikes here.

B

He — the guitar very well yet.

C

You — phones in this building.

D

Students — a uniform.

E

He — very fast.

F

They — hard for their exams.

● **b)** Write sentences about yourself, your friends and your family with these verbs.

must train ✓ | may use | needn't go | can play | mustn't … | can't …

I must train before my next football match.

V 33
How to

G

Language detectives ► G11, p.164

I **can** walk to school now. → I **was able to** walk to school last week.
We **may** use this room today. → We **were allowed to** use this room two weeks ago.
Students **must** leave the building now. → Students **had to** leave the building yesterday.
They **mustn't** use their phones now. → They **weren't allowed to** use their phones yesterday.
We **needn't** study today. → We **didn't have to** study last Tuesday.

Can you find the rule?

○ D 154
● D 155
WB 70/8

8 Complete the sentences. ► S18 Peer correction, p.200

1. Macy *wasn't allowed to* (may not) use the train alone when she was younger.
2. But she and her best friend — (may) play in the park together.
3. Ricarda hurt her leg badly last summer. She — (cannot) play volleyball for three months.
4. Jamar — (must) look after his little brothers when his dad was ill last month.
5. Jin's mum — (can) find a shop to rent in the city centre three years ago.
6. Jin was happy because she — (needn't) move to a new city.
7. She — (must) help her mum in the shop before it opened.

WB 70/9–10

9 Your future

a) Complete Jin's diary entry. ► ○ p.137
Use will be able to, will be allowed to, and will have to.

G
Grammar ► G11, p.164
I'**ll be able to** make new friends.

June 24
I'll go to college in Charlotte, North Carolina soon. I'll live in my own apartment. I'*ll have to* (1 must) cook and clean for myself. I — (2 can) cook my favorite food every day and eat when I want to. I — (3 may) go out and meet my friends whenever I want. I — (4 must) get a job to pay for my car and my rent. I — (5 can) buy my own things and travel around. My parents — (6 can) come and visit me every year. I'm really excited about the future!

● b) Write a diary entry about your hopes for the future. You can write about your life, work or free time.

10 Is it discrimination or not? Say what you think. ► S18 Think-pair-share, p.200

1. A student with a disability won't be able to take part in summer camp because the building there doesn't have a lift.
2. A person wasn't allowed to work as a bus driver because she wasn't able to speak the country's language very well.
3. Someone meets a girl who looks Asian for the first time and asks where she comes from.

A I (don't) think this is discrimination. …
B I agree. / I don't agree. …

In some discussions, talking about the topic and hearing other perspectives can help you to understand the topic better.

I 18
V 34 How to
D 156 Support

11 Your turn: An anti-discrimination poster

Make a poster in groups of four to show what everybody can do to fight against discrimination.
► S7 Planning, writing and checking texts, p. 184

Step 1

In what ways are people discriminated against?
Think about problems that people have because of the colour of their skin, their gender, a disability or other things.
Collect examples.

You don't have to talk about your own experiences.
You can also talk about your friends, family or problems you've read about.

Step 2

What can you do to fight against discrimination?
Collect ideas.

- *talk to ...*
- *organise ...*

...

Step 3

What's the message of your poster?
Discuss your ideas.
Agree on a main message and make notes.

- *make people aware of discrimination*
- *stand up for equality*
- *take specific action*

...

Step 4

Search the internet for pictures that underline your message. Use your notes from steps 1 to 3 as your search terms.
The pictures can show a situation where there is discrimination or where people are protesting against discrimination. They can also show how life would be without discrimination.
► S14 Using the internet, p. 196
► S16 How to use photos, films and texts, p. 198

Step 5

Make a first draft of a text for your poster.
Arrange your pictures.
Choose short, powerful words for the message.

- *Respect other people!*
- *Stop discrimination!*

...

Step 6

Copy the text and add the pictures to your poster.

Media tip
You can use an app to design your poster.

Step 7

Present your posters. ► S18 Gallery walk, p. 201
Ask for and give feedback.
► S8 Giving and asking for feedback, p. 190

✔ I can talk about discrimination.

D 157 My plan

A trip to the Everglades

1 Find out what the underlined words mean. ► S13 Looking up words, p. 194

A 47
○ D 158
● D 159

Tips for fishing in the Everglades

- There are a lot of bugs (1), and the sun can be dangerous, so wear shirts with long sleeves (2).
- Remember the 'catch, photo, release (3)' rule. Always put the fish back into the water!
- Snook (4) are good fish to catch. They grow about a foot a year.
- Look for minnows (5) too. These small fish are an important part of the food chain (6).
- The Everglades are famous for alligators, but did you know that sharks (7) live there too?
- People who are 15 or under don't need a license (8) to go fishing in the Everglades.

1. bug – das Insekt

2 A trip to the Everglades

V 35
○ D 160
● D 161
WB 71/1–3

a) Watch the film and answer the questions.

1. Who's visiting Florida, Grace or Cedric?
2. Who takes them on the fishing trip?
3. How does Grace feel before the trip?
4. How does she feel at the end?

b) Watch the film again. Choose the right answers.

1. The cousins are **14** | *15* | **16** when they go on the trip.
2. There are over 300 **guides** | **boats** | **animals** in Everglades National Park.
3. The snook and the birds both eat **insects** | **grass** | **minnows**.
4. Snook have large **noses** | **eyes** | **legs** and they use them to find food.
5. When Ray puts the snook back into the water, they see some **birds** | **people** | **sharks**.
6. Ray says that we should **respect** | **talk about** | **learn about** wildlife in the Everglades.

3 A fact card

a) Collect facts about one of the animals in the Everglades. ► S14 Using the internet, p. 196

alligator | minnow | shark | snook

P

b) Make a fact card about the animal.

✔ I can understand a nature film.

An exciting future

D 162
My plan

1 Can you imagine living on Mars or another planet?

Do a digital survey to find out what your class thinks. Give the idea 1–10 points.

2 Read the texts.

A 48
WB 72/1

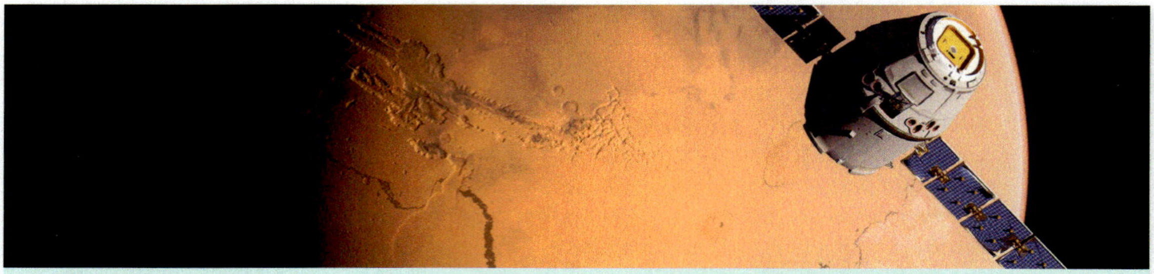

FUTURE DIRECTIONS

How will technology change our lives in the future? *The Miami News* is looking at this question during May. We've written about developments in food and farming, communication, transportation, and artificial intelligence so far. But Florida has always been important for space travel, and last week we wrote about the topic 'Our future is on Mars'. Today we're publishing some of the letters and emails which we received.

Dear Editor,

I'm writing about the topic 'Our future is on Mars'. In my opinion, having a human colony on Mars would be a good idea. There are many reasons for this.

For one thing, it's possible that war or another disaster could destroy life on Earth in the future. If we have a second home on Mars, we can survive.

Moreover, a human colony on Mars would also give us the chance to find natural resources, like rare metals. These may help us solve the problems that we have on Earth.

Finally, I wouldn't worry about leaving Earth. I think that humans could start again on Mars. There would be no countries and no wars. We could build a better, happier, and more peaceful future for everyone.

For all these reasons, I'm definitely in favor of having a colony on Mars.

Sincerely,

Delvon Andrews

Orlando, Florida

Dear Editor,

I'd like to join the discussion about our future. As a high school student who worries about the future of our planet, I don't think it's a good idea to live on Mars.

Firstly, Mars is a planet whose atmosphere is not suitable for human life. It has more extreme temperatures than Earth. It would be highly expensive to build just a small colony which could support life, with air, water, and food for the people who live there.

Secondly, Mars is a long way away. It might be possible to send four or five astronauts there in the future. But it would be too difficult to send enough people to establish a colony.

To sum up, I believe it's wrong to use resources to move to Mars instead of solving problems here. We should try to save our planet and build a better future on Earth.

Sincerely,

Cassidy Rogers

Tampa, Florida

3 Future directions ► ○ p. 138

a) Answer the questions in full sentences.

1. Who is for the idea and who is against it?
   Delvon is for the idea and … .
2. What could destroy life on Earth, in Delvon's opinion?
3. What could people find on Mars?
4. What does Cassidy say about the atmosphere on Mars?
5. Why would it be difficult to establish a colony?
6. What should we try to do, in her opinion?

● b) Do some research about Mars. Take notes about the planet's size, its highest and lowest temperatures and how far it is from Earth. ► S14 Using the internet, p. 196

○ D 163
● D 164

4 Find the phrases in the texts. ► W10 Giving opinions, p. 239

Introducing opinions: *In my opinion, …*
Structuring what you say: *For one thing, …*

○ D 165
● D 166
WB 72/2

5 Are you for or against a future on Mars? Talk to a partner.

► S18 Round robin, p. 201

A In my opinion … . I think … .
B …

You can use your answers from ex. 3 and 4 when you say what you think.

WB 73/3

6 Future developments ► W11 In the future, p. 240

a) Copy and complete the table. Put the words in the right groups. ► ○ p. 139

virtual reality (VR) | the Moon ✓ | face-to-face | drones | insects | air taxis | to connect | artificial meat | to explore | driverless cars | robot doctors and nurses | the solar system

A	B	C	D
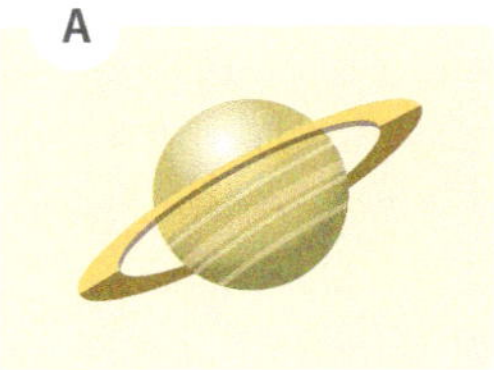	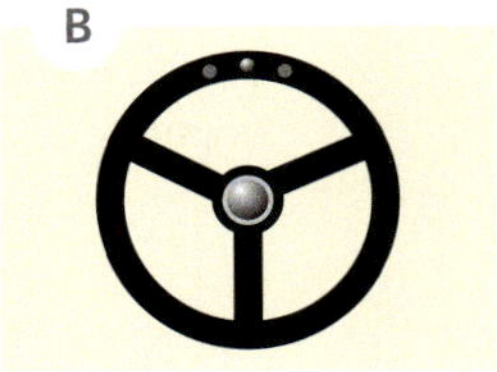		
Space	Transport	Communication	Food and health
the Moon …	…	…	…

● b) Add these and your own words to each group.

seaweed | thought transfer | zero gravity | hyperloop network

Culture

The first person in space was a Russian, Yuri Gagarin, in 1961. But the USA won the race to the Moon in 1969. Since then countries like China, India and Japan and some private companies have developed their own rockets and spacecraft.

A 49

7 A poem: A world of possibilities

a) What does the speaker in the poem think about the future?

In the near future, cars will fly.
I will have to navigate my way through the sky.
This is my prediction for you and me –
A world of possibilities, just wait and see.

We'll travel to the Moon, build a home on Mars,
But we won't get a suntan if we go that far!
This is my prediction for you and me –
A world of possibilities, just wait and see.

The future is exciting, in a very special way,
But will it be better than the life we live today?
This is my question for you and me –
A world of possibilities? Let's wait and see.

b) Practise reading the poem and perform it in class. ► S18 Read and look up, p. 200

V 3 How to
D 167
WB 73/4

8 Mediation ► S9 Mediation, p. 191

Du bist in einem Besuchercafé des Kennedy Space Centers in Florida.
Vermittle zwischen den zwei Personen, die die jeweils andere Sprache nicht so gut können.

German	You	American
Kannst du mir beim Gespräch helfen? Frag mal bitte, was sein größtes Highlight war.	↔	I really liked the bus tour. I learned lots of exciting things about space travel. What about you?
Ich habe noch keine Bustour gemacht. Aber ich habe mir die großartige Ausstellung „Race to the Moon" angeschaut.		Yes, it's very cool. There's a lot to see and explore. You're on holiday here, aren't you? Are you from Germany?
Ja, richtig. Ich komme aus Oldenburg. Die Stadt ist im Norden von Deutschland, in der Nähe von Bremen.		I haven't been to Germany, but I've heard of the Oktoberfest. My friends went last year and said it was awesome. Do you go there too?
Nein, ich war noch nie auf dem Oktoberfest. Das ist im Süden, in München, und sehr weit weg von Oldenburg. Woher kommt er?		Oh, I see. I'm from the south of Florida, from Miami. That's about 200 miles from here.
Ach, das ist ja interessant! Davon habe ich schon viel gehört. Stimmt es, dass dort viele ältere Menschen leben?		Well, yes and no. In my community there are people of all ages. I'd love to visit Germany. Where should I go?
Die Nordsee ist besonders schön. Berlin ist auch super. Frag ihn bitte noch, ob er einen Tipp für Florida hat.		The south of Florida is the best part. Everglades National Park is amazing, and Key West is stunning.
Vielen Dank für den Tipp!		You're welcome. Enjoy your time in Florida!

S

Skills

Everyone has ideas about what people from other countries are like and how they live. But you should remember that these ideas may be stereotypes, and that they may hurt the people that you're talking to.

G

V 36
How to

Language revision: Defining relative clauses ► G12, p. 166

Test yourself: Choose the right answers.
1. An astronaut is a person **who** | **which** travels in space.
2. The sun is the star **whose** | **which** is the closest to Earth.
3. Mars has an atmosphere **that** | **who** is too dangerous for human life.
4. Isaac Asimov was a writer **whose** | **who** books about space are still very popular.
5. Maybe we won't eat meat **who** | **which** comes from animals in the future.
6. People **who** | **whose** don't like driving will be able to use driverless cars.
7. Companies **which** | **whose** products are easy to deliver will be able to use drones.

○ D 168
● D 169
WB 74/5–6

9 Who, which or whose?

a) Put in the right words.

1. This is the spacecraft *which* will take tourists into space.
2. The writer — writes the best letter wins the competition.
3. She's the astronaut — space walk is online.
4. These are the drones — can fly at 50 km/h.
5. This is the chef — cooks some dishes with insects.
6. These are the scientists — book won an award.

b) In which sentences in a) can you also use that?

WB 74/7

10 Landmarks in science and technology

a) Write sentences. ► ○ p. 139

1. Johannes Kepler | a scientist | found out how planets move around the sun
   Johannes Kepler was a scientist who found out how planets move around the sun.
2. the Vostok 3KA | a spacecraft | took the first human into space
3. the DynaTAC 8000x | the phone | made the first mobile phone call
4. Neil Armstrong | the astronaut | first stood on the Moon
5. the Model T | a machine | was one of the first modern cars
6. Ada Lovelace | a scientist | wrote a kind of computer program

● **b)** Find out about these people and things. Write sentences with which, who, that or whose.
► S14 Using the internet, p. 196

the Wright Flyer | Valentina Tereshkova | ENIAC | Johannes Gutenberg | Alexander Fleming

The Wright Flyer was the plane which … .

I 19

V 11 How to

D 170 Support

11 Your turn: A comment

Write a comment about a possible future development. Give your opinion.

► S7 Planning, writing and checking texts, p. 184

Step 1

Read the statements.

A. People will spend lots of time in virtual reality.

B. People will live on the Moon.

C. Robot nurses and doctors will work at hospitals.

D. People will use air taxis.

Step 2

Choose one of the statements from step 1 and make notes.

What would change?
How would it affect people's lives?

spend lots of time in virtual reality:
- *people wouldn't experience ...*
- *people could try ...*
- *people from different places ...*
- *...*

Step 3

Do you think the development is a good idea? Think about your notes from step 2 and decide on an opinion. Write a sentence about your opinion.

I think virtual reality is a good idea. / I think virtual reality is a bad idea.

Step 4

Look at your notes from step 2. Write two to three arguments for the opinion you decided on in step 3. Give examples.

► W10 Giving opinions, p. 239

Firstly, people who spend lots of time in virtual reality wouldn't ... . For example, they ... .

Step 5

Write your comment.
You should structure your comment like this:
- Introduction
- Your opinion
- Arguments and examples
- Conclusion

We use digital media every day. In the future, we could use them even more. Maybe people will spend lots of time in virtual reality.
...
To sum up, we should / shouldn't ... .

P

Step 6

Check your draft.

Step 7

Read other students' comments about the same topic. Ask for and give feedback. ► S8 Giving and asking for feedback, p. 190

✔ I can give my opinion.

D 171 My plan

D 172 D 173

Celebrating life in New Orleans

1 Match the words with the photos. ► S13 Looking up words, p. 194

coffin | musician | cemetery ✓ | to march | hurricane | funeral

A 
B 
C 
D 
E 
F 

A. cemetery

A 50

D 174 D 175

WB 75/1–2

2 Jazz funerals

a) Listen to the radio feature. Which five things do they talk about?

history | clothes | animals | a terrible event | food | music | musicians' funerals

b) Listen again. Are the sentences true or false?

1. There are jazz funerals in New Orleans and many other cities.
   That's false.
2. Sad and slow music is played at first.
3. The music changes after the people have said goodbye for the last time.
4. People start going home in the second part of the funeral.
5. The first jazz funerals were in the 18th century.
6. When the funeral is for a popular musician, other musicians play in the parade.
7. The city remembered the people who died in Hurricane Katrina with a big football game.

3 Songs ► S14 Using the internet, p. 196

a) Go online and listen to one of the songs. How do you feel when you hear it?

- Amazing Grace
- When the Saints Go Marching In
- Down By the Riverside

b) Search the lyrics for one of the songs from a). Take notes.

- What's your favourite line from the song? Why?
- What do you think about the song?

Culture

New Orleans is famous as the home of jazz. Musicians of other styles, like gospel and the blues, have lived and worked there too. The city still has many music clubs today.

✓ I can understand a radio feature.

V 13 How to

Civil rights and the South

D 176 My plan

1 Look at the photos. What do they tell you? ► S18 Think-pair-share, p. 200

A
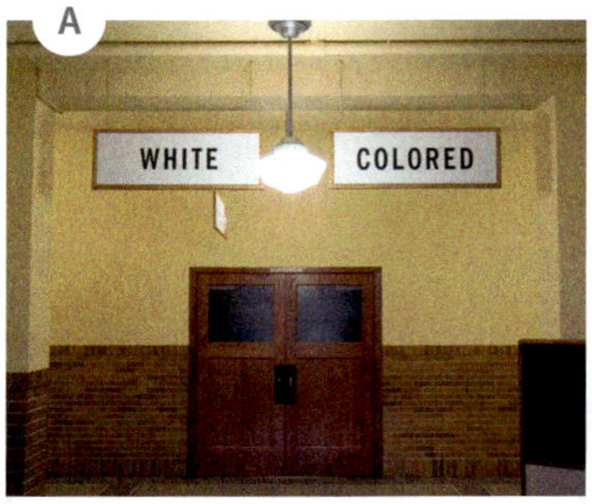

In the 1960s

B

2009–2017

C

In the 2020s

2 Read the texts.

A 51

INTRODUCTION

After slavery was abolished in 1865, Black people were free to live as American citizens. However, new laws in Southern states in the late 19th and early 20th century led to segregation. Black people weren't allowed to use the same public services as white people, including schools and libraries. On public transportation they had to sit in different seats to white people. In many cases, they also weren't allowed to vote. These racist laws, which still existed in the 1950s, led to the start of the Civil Rights Movement in 1954.

A 52

A MONTGOMERY, ALABAMA

Montgomery became famous around the world on December 1, 1955, when civil rights activist Rosa Parks got on a bus and sat down on a free seat. When the driver asked her to move so that a white person could sit down, she refused. She was arrested and had to pay $14. When people heard of this, activists began to plan their response. On December 5 they announced[1] plans to stop using public buses in Montgomery.

The National Civil Rights Museum in Memphis

A police photo of Rosa Parks

The boycott lasted a year and was hugely successful. It caused a change in the law and brought attention to the Civil Rights Movement and its new leader, Martin Luther King.

Today the Rosa Parks Museum stands on the site where she was arrested.

1 to announce – *ankündigen*

A 53

B LITTLE ROCK, ARKANSAS

Little Rock was the location of one of the most famous events of the Civil Rights Era[2]. In 1954 the US Supreme Court[3] decided that schools were not allowed to be segregated anymore. But it took three years for this to happen in Little Rock.
In September 1957 nine Black students became the first to go to the all-white Little Rock Central High School. However, many local people were against this.

Mayor of New York City with the teenagers from Central High School

A protesting crowd

Racist protestors stood outside the school and tried to stop the students from going inside. At first the governor[4] of Arkansas asked the Arkansas National Guard[5] to stop the Black students from going to school, but the US president then ordered them to protect the students and defend their right to attend school. Crowds of people shouted at the students as they bravely walked into school in scenes that are still shocking to watch today.

A 54

C BIRMINGHAM, ALABAMA

Another important place in the Civil Rights Movement was Birmingham, Alabama. In the early 1960s it was one of the most divided cities in the country. Black people faced discrimination everywhere. Although the city had a 40 % Black population, it had no Black police officers or bus drivers, for example. In 1963 James Bevel, Martin Luther King and others organized a campaign to change this. It included boycotts of stores, restaurants, and other public facilities.

Foot Soldiers statue in Kelly Ingram Park

Protests at Graymont Elementary School

James Bevel asked students, including elementary school students, to take part in peaceful protests. Images of police hitting young Black children as they walked to the mayor's office shocked the country and the world. There is now a Birmingham Civil Rights National Monument in the city. This includes some important churches and the Kelly Ingram Park.

2 era – *die Ära, das Zeitalter*; 3 US Supreme Court – *der Oberste Gerichtshof der USA*; 4 governor – *der Gouverneur / die Gouverneurin*; 5 National Guard – *die Nationalgarde (unterstützt das Militär innerhalb eines Bundesstaates)*

A 55

D MEMPHIS, TENNESSEE

Memphis was also an important place in the Civil Rights Movement. In April 1968 Martin Luther King was in the city to show his support for a strike by Black public workers. On April 3 King gave a famous speech at the Mason Temple in the city. The following evening King was shot as he stood on the balcony of room 306 of the Lorraine Motel. He died in hospital an hour later. His assassination[6] caused riots across the country.

Dr. Martin Luther King

The Lorraine Motel, Memphis

On April 9 King's funeral took place in Atlanta, Georgia. About 100,000 people watched it. At the end of the ceremony, the crowd sang the Civil Rights anthem[7], 'We Shall Overcome'.
The Lorraine Motel is part of the National Civil Rights Museum today. There is a wreath[8] on the balcony where King was shot.

6 assassination – *die Ermordung*; 7 anthem – *die Hymne*; 8 wreath – *der Kranz*

3 Answer the questions about the introduction.

D 177

1. What happened in the USA in 1865?
2. Why didn't the situation get better after that?

4 About the texts

D 178

a) Home group: Get into groups of four. Each of you chooses one of the texts (A–D).

b) Read your text again and answer the questions. Take notes.

1. What happened?
2. When did it happen?
3. What was their message?
4. What do you think? Were they successful?

c) Expert group: Find students who have read the same text. Compare your answers with theirs.

Expert group A: Montgomery, Alabama
Expert group B: Little Rock, Arkansas
Expert group C: Birmingham, Alabama
Expert group D: Memphis, Tennessee

d) Meet your home group again. Present what you have found out about your text. Take notes about the other texts.

D 179
D 180

5 Make a timeline.

Use dates and events from the texts and your notes.

1865	…	…
…		

Media tip
You can easily create timelines digitally. It can often be found under "Insert" and "Insert Process".

6 I have a dream

a) Read a famous quote from King's 'I have a dream' speech.
Has his dream come true? What has or hasn't changed?

"I have a dream that my four little children will one day live in a nation where they will not be judged by the color of their skin but by the content of their character."

b) Go online and watch and listen to 'I have a dream' by Martin Luther King.
► S14 Using the internet, p. 196

1. What's the atmosphere like?
2. What and who can you see?
3. How does it make you feel?

Media tip
The internet often offers videos with subtitles. This makes it easier to follow the content.

Culture
Martin Luther King held his famous 'I have a dream' speech during a march in Washington, D.C. on 28th August, 1963. About 250,000 people listened to him in front of the Lincoln Memorial. He called for equal rights and an end to racism.

WB 76/1
WB 77/2–4

7 Choose one of these tasks.

a) Choose one of the photos from the text. Talk about these questions.

1. What can you see in the photo?
2. How does it make you feel?
3. Find out more information about the photo on the internet.
► S14 Using the internet, p. 196

OR

b) Search the internet to find out about Black Lives Matter. Write a short text about the movement.
► S14 Using the internet, p. 196
► S7 Planning, writing and checking texts, p. 184

1. What do you know about these protests?
2. Why did they start?
3. What are their goals?

✔ I can understand an article from a history magazine.

Checklist

D 181 My plan

WB 78

Check in: Settling in the South

✓ I can understand information about the South.

WB 78

Station 1: Respecting each other

I can name attitudes and behaviour.
► W9 Attitudes and behaviour, p. 239

raise awareness | take it seriously | discriminate against | insult | ignore | …

I can talk about ability, permission and obligation.
► G11, p. 164 (Modal auxiliaries and their substitutes)

You may leave the classroom. | She needn't talk about the situation. | We mustn't insult other people. | I was allowed to walk alone. | They had to wait. | He wasn't able to find a job. | …

✓ I can talk about discrimination.

WB 79

Viewing: A trip to the Everglades

✓ I can understand a nature film.

WB 79

Station 2: An exciting future

I can structure a comment.
► W10 Giving opinions, p. 239

in my opinion | moreover | for one thing | …

I can name future developments.
► W11 In the future, p. 240

virtual reality | drones | artificial meat | …

I can give more specific information about people and things.
► G12, p. 166 (Defining relative clauses)

It would be expensive to build a colony which would support life. | There wouldn't be food for the people who lived there. | Mars is a planet whose atmosphere is not suitable for human life. | …

✓ I can give my opinion.

WB 80

Listening: Celebrating life in New Orleans

✓ I can understand a radio feature.

I 20 Quiz

WB 80

Reading: Civil rights and the South

✓ I can understand an article from a history magazine.

?

Find the photo in the unit.
You can also do the online quiz about the South.

Task: A multimedia presentation

Prepare and give a multimedia presentation to tell your class about your dream for a better future.

► S4 Giving a presentation, p. 181

Step 1

Get into groups and collect ideas.
What's your dream for a better future?
Think about communities, rights, the environment, school life, industry/products, …

peace, no racism or discrimination, fair trade, protecting animals, …

Step 2

Choose one idea from step 1. Make an outline.
Think of three aspects of your dream.

- What examples can you think of?
- What should people do, or how should they try to change what they usually do?

Protecting animals

1. *Farm animals must have better lives. Example: cows that are kept outside and eat grass*
2. *People should eat less meat. Example: a famous influencer who became a vegetarian*
3. *People must treat their pets well. Example: …*

S

Skills

If you want to make people excited about something and motivate them to change what they usually do, you should show examples of role models who have already done this. Think of success stories and positive results.

Step 3

Choose different media for your presentation. Illustrate each aspect of your dream with a link to an audio or video on the internet, a photo, a diagram or a cartoon.

► S16 How to use photos, films and texts, p. 198

Media tip

Audios, videos and photos can create feelings. Diagrams and cartoons can illustrate facts and make people think about a topic in a new way.

Step 4

Write a short introduction and a conclusion. Say what your dream is, what you want to change and why this is important to you.

You won't need to comment on the media that you'll show in your presentation.

Step 5

Prepare your presentation and try it out. If a link doesn't work any more, you need to change it.

Media tip

Links on the internet can change at any time.

Step 6

Give your presentation.
Ask for and give feedback.

► S8 Giving and asking for feedback, p. 190

A 56

Music from the South

1 What kinds of music do you think these musicians play or played?

1

2

3

1 Louis Armstrong (1901–1971) sang and played the cornet[1] as a young boy in New Orleans. In the 1920s he moved to Chicago and became one of the top trumpeters[2] there. Later Louis became famous for his singing, with hits like "What a Wonderful World".

2 Sister Rosetta Tharpe (1915–1973) was born in Arkansas. Her music combined[3] gospel with the electric guitar. Rosetta's songs, including "Didn't It Rain", influenced Elvis Presley, and she was called 'the godmother[4] of rock and roll'.

3 Elvis Presley (1935–1977), or 'the king of rock and roll', was born in Mississippi. Elvis had many hits in the 1950s, including "Jailhouse[5] Rock". In the 1960s he appeared[6] in more than 25 movies. Elvis returned to music in 1968, nine years before he died.

1 cornet – *das Kornett (Musikinstrument)*; 2 trumpeter – *der Trompeter / die Trompeterin*; 3 to combine – *kombinieren, verbinden*; 4 godmother – *die Patin, die Patentante*; 5 jailhouse – *das Gefängnis*; 6 to appear – *erscheinen*

2 Listen online to one of the songs in the text. Talk about the song.

A What do you think of …? How does it make you feel?
B I really like / don't like … because it's … . It makes me feel … .

4

5

6

4 Tina Turner (1939–2023) was born in Tennessee. In the first part of her career[7] she performed with her husband, Ike Turner. But in 1976 Tina left Ike. In the 1980s she was hugely successful as a solo artist with hits like "What's Love Got To Do With It".

5 André 3000 (born 1975) is a rapper, musician, and producer from Georgia. He was one half of the hip-hop duo Outkast, who had a huge hit with "Hey Ya!" in 2003. Later André made an instrumental album and played the flute[8], which surprised many of his fans.

6 Taylor Swift (born 1989) is from Pennsylvania, but she moved to Nashville with her family as a teenager. Taylor started her career as a country singer, but in later songs like "Shake It Off" her music is more influenced by pop and dance.

7 career – *die Karriere, die Laufbahn*; 8 flute – *die Flöte, die Querflöte*

D 182 Support

1 Find the words and phrases that mean the same.

teaches | didn't listen to | get around ✓ | the people who you work with | not clever | what happened | very angry | say awful things to

1. Some people use a wheelchair to go from place to place.
   get around
2. I'm sorry to hear about your experience.
3. You should never insult people.
4. Jin's mother educates people about discrimination.
5. Some students thought that Ricarda was stupid because of her Mexican accent.
6. Jamar ignored the people who called him names.
7. Macy got mad when she was discriminated against.
8. Talk to your team and try to find a solution.

2 At a workshop about discrimination.

Complete what they said. Use can, can't, may, must, mustn't, or needn't.

1. You *mustn't* feel helpless when you have a bad experience.
2. I — do this activity. I don't understand it!
3. We — stop now. It's time for the next activity.
4. — I open the window, please? – Yes, of course.
5. Discrimination — happen everywhere – at work, on the bus, in shops …
6. You — do this activity if it's hard for you to talk about this.
7. Let's talk about strategies that — help.
8. It's important to remember that you — give up!

3 Jamar's job

a) Complete the sentences about Jamar's job at a summer camp last month. Use substitute verbs in the simple past.

1. Jamar *had to* look after some teenagers. (must)
2. A boy and a girl called Jamar names, but he — cope with the problem. (can)
3. The volunteers — wear a uniform. (needn't)
4. The teenagers — use phones during the day. (may not)
5. One teenager was ill. She — go on a trip that day. (can't)
6. Jamar helped some teenagers who — swim. (can't)
7. The teenagers — play games after lunch. (may)
8. They were sad when the camp finished and they — go home. (must)

can → be able to
needn't → not have to
must → have to
may → be allowed to

b) Write five sentences about your last school trip.

We went to … | … was/wasn't allowed/able to … | … had/didn't have to …

4 The future

a) Match the words and phrases to make pairs.

eat ✓ | explore | meet | use | establish | travel | solve

the world's problems | natural resources | in driverless cars | artificial meat ✓ | in virtual reality | a colony on Mars | other planets

1. eat artificial meat

b) What's your opinion? Write a sentence about the future with each pair.

1. I think / don't think we will eat artificial meat in the future.

5 Put in the opposites.

1. If we had a colony on Mars, it would be very *expensive*. (cheap)
2. Maybe we should try to build a — future on Earth. (worse)
3. You can ask questions at the — of the presentation. (start)
4. The extreme temperatures on Mars would make life there —. (easy)
5. Maybe people will try to — natural resources on other planets in the future. (lose)
6. A — colony with four or five astronauts might be possible on Mars one day. (large)
7. — intelligence in computers can help to solve some problems. (natural)
8. Astronauts who have been in space never — the experience. (remember)

6 People and things

a) Choose the right relative pronouns to complete the sentences.

1. It's a national park **who** | *that* is in Florida.
2. It's an astronaut **who** | **whose** walked on the Moon in 1969.
3. It's a planet **which** | **who** is red.
4. It's a person **which** | **who** repairs cars.
5. It's a name for a person **that** | **whose** home is the South.
6. It's someone **who** | **which** does experiments.
7. It's an American city **that** | **who** has a famous carnival.
8. It's an American state **who** | **whose** biggest city is Atlanta.

b) What are the people and things in a)?

1. It's the Everglades.

7 An email to a friend

Write an email to an American friend about a nice day in the school holidays.

1. Ask if your friend is OK.
2. Say what you did.
3. Say why it was a nice day.
4. Add one more piece of information or question.

Don't forget to start and finish the email correctly. You should use the simple past when you write about the day.

Unit 1, p.11

○ 3 Words for parts of a building ► W1 Parts of a building, p.232

Match the words with the parts of the building (A–H).

basement | entrance | balcony | story | elevator | solar panels | ground level ✓ | staircase

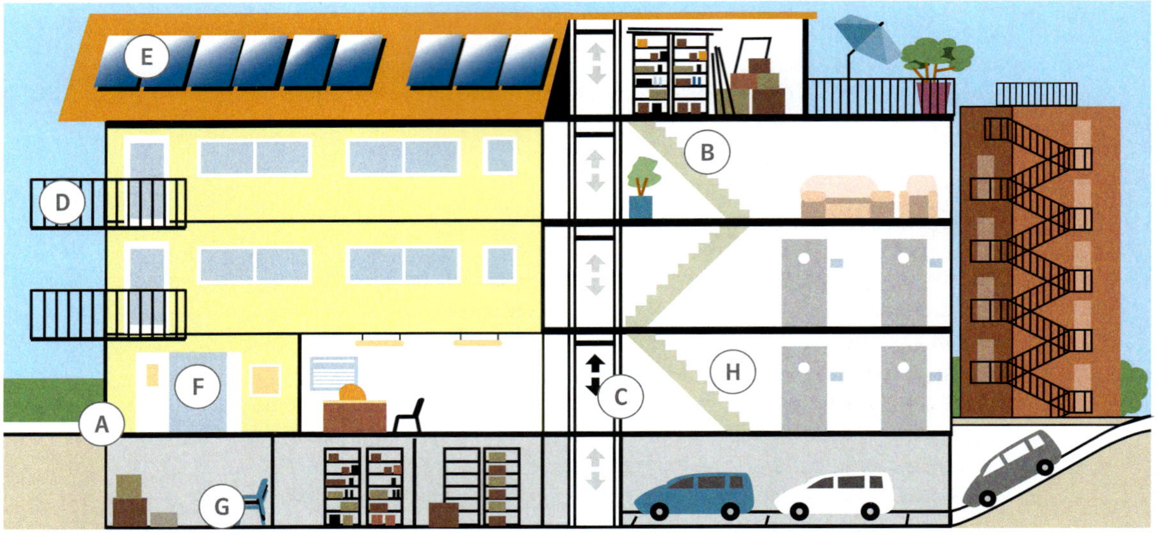

A. *ground level* B. s___ C. e___ D. b___ E. s___ F. e___ G. b___ H. s___

Unit 1, p.12

○ 4 New York City's tallest buildings ► S14 Using the internet, p.196

Find the missing information. Complete the notes and the sentences.

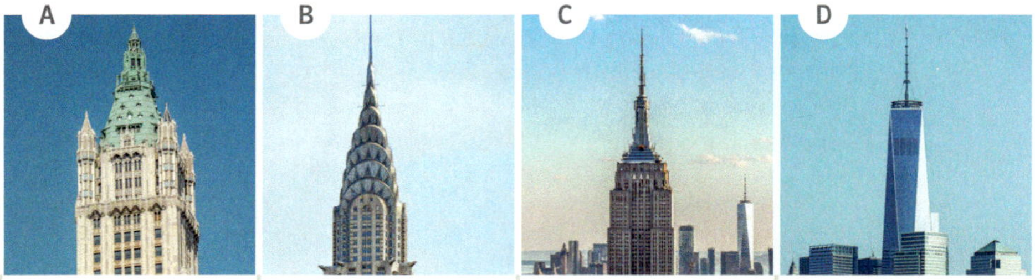

	A	B	C	D
Name	Woolworth Building	Chrysler Building	Empire State Building	One World Trade Center
Opened	1913	1930	1931	…
Metres	…	319 m	…	546 m
Floors	60	…	…	94
Lifts	…	32	73	…
Tallest building in NYC	1913–1930	…	1931–1970 2001–2012	since 2012

►►

A. *241* m, — lifts; The Woolworth Building is *241* metres tall and has — lifts.
B. — floors, tallest building —; The Chrysler Building has — floors and was the tallest building from — to —.
C. — m, — floors; The Empire State Building is — metres tall and has — floors.
D. opened in —, — lifts; The One World Trade Center opened in — and has — lifts.

Unit 1, p.13

7 How was New York?

Put the parts in the right order. Act the dialogue with a partner. Then change roles.

You Hi, (was | how | to New York? | your trip) (1)
Hi, *how was your trip to New York?*
Aya Hi. My trip to New York was great.
You (return? | you | did | When) (2)
Aya We returned yesterday.
You (with | Who | you? | was) (3)
Aya Leo was with me.
You (Edge? | Did | visit | you) (4)
Aya Yes, we visited Edge.
You (highlight? | was | What | your) (5)
Aya My highlight was the Intrepid Museum.
You (take | you | a taxi? | Did) (6)
Aya No, we didn't take a taxi.

Unit 1, p.17

4 That's interesting! ► W2 Adjectives, p. 233 ► S13 Looking up words, p. 194

Make five groups with the adjectives.

1. good, *great*, f—
2. bad, a—, t—
3. sad, m—, u—
4. unusual, s—, w—
5. interesting, e—, f—

awful | great ✓ | strange | exciting | terrible | fantastic | miserable | fascinating | weird | unhappy

Unit 1, p.17

5 Saying it differently ► W2 Adjectives, p.233

Replace the underlined adjectives with adjectives that have a similar meaning.

You can use words like: awful, great, strange, exciting, terrible, fantastic, miserable, fascinating, weird, unhappy.

1. The clubs at our school are nice. I'm in two clubs.
   The clubs at our school are *fantastic*. I'm in two clubs.
2. I'm sad that I couldn't join the basketball club too.
3. The tea that we had at school yesterday was bad. I won't drink it again!
4. Some people think that the Magic Gardens are very unusual. But I like them.
5. The people at church talked about a good plan this morning. I liked it a lot.
6. The film that we saw last week was interesting.

Unit 1, p.18

7 Life in an Amish community

A 6

Listen to Bridget and choose the right answers.

You just have to decide between two answers.

1. Where does Bridget live?
   A ~~She lives near a lake with her parents.~~
   B She lives in a flat with her mother.
   C She lives on a farm with her parents and brothers.

2. When did Bridget leave the Amish school?
   A She left when she was 16.
   B She left when she was 15.
   C ~~She left when she was 18.~~

3. What does Bridget do most mornings?
   A She helps with the animals and in the kitchen.
   B She looks after her two younger brothers.
   C ~~She stays in bed until 8:30 a.m.~~

4. Why does she enjoy her job at the store?
   A She can be on her own, and it isn't busy.
   B She meets people there and finds out what's new.
   C ~~She can choose what the store sells.~~

5. When do most Amish people use a machine?
   A They use one when they work in the garden.
   B ~~They use one when they wash the plates after a meal.~~
   C They use one when they wash their clothes.

6. What does Bridget say about social media?
   A Her group doesn't use it.
   B Most Amish use it.
   C ~~She often posts videos.~~

Unit 1, p. 19

○ 9 **Boston or Waitsfield – which place do you like better?**

Use these adjectives to compare the places.

large small

noisy busy

colourful interesting exciting modern

A

B

A I think Boston is better. The city is larger and … .
B I prefer Waitsfield. It's … .

A I think Waitsfield is better. The city is smaller and … .
B I prefer Boston. It's larger and … .

large – larger
small – smaller
noisy – noisier
colourful – more colourful
interesting – more interesting
modern – more modern

Unit 2, p. 33

2 Lena's blog

A 16

Internet

11/05/2024

Hey, it's Lena, welcome to my blog! I'm an exchange student at a high school in Columbus, Ohio. I started school here at the beginning of September. Let me tell you all what it's really like!

I get up at 6:30 and get ready for school. You know, there's a dress code, and students aren't allowed to wear baseball caps or crop tops, for example! I usually wear jeans and a sweater. I also check the school's online portal every morning. Then I walk to the end of the road with Paisley, my host sister. We meet our friends where the yellow school bus stops and ride to school together.

The bus arrives at school at about 7:45. We have to walk through a metal detector. That felt a bit strange at first. Then I put my bag in my locker and hang out with my friends in the hallway. At 7:55 the school gates close. If you're late three times, you have to go to detention.

We start the day with homeroom at 8:00. It's like a class meeting with our homeroom teacher. I love my homeroom group. We get information and news about school events, and we can talk if we have any problems. Students also take the Pledge of Allegiance every day. They say that they're loyal to their country.

Each student has a schedule. It has classes which everyone does, like math, English, and science, but there are also electives. These are classes which students can choose. I wanted to try out some new things, so I chose film production, creative writing, and drama. How cool is that?

The school cafeteria is where everyone eats. The food isn't as good as it is at home with my host family, but it's OK. The cafeteria is also a good place to hang out with friends. Paisley has really helped me make friends. She's awesome, and because of her I feel totally at home here.

There are clubs after school every day, so the school days are longer than they are in Germany. I go to a foreign language club on Mondays and Wednesdays and our yearbook club on Thursdays. Paisley plays volleyball and she's a member of the student council. She's organizing the prom, the dance that takes place once a year. It's a highlight for most students. I can't wait to go there in March! On Friday afternoons everyone goes to watch a big American football game at the school. It's an amazing event, and they also live stream the games on the school's social media channel.

I'm loving my time here at high school. Do you have any questions? Please post them in the comments. Maybe I can answer them for you.
Bye!

Language tip ► G5, p. 154

We meet our friends **where** the bus stops.

Culture

The most popular foreign languages at school in the USA are Spanish, French and German.

Complete the sentences with information from the text. Use one or more words.

1. Lena started school in the USA in *September*.
2. She and her host sister Paisley go to school by —.
3. Students must go through a — when they enter the school.
4. The school gates — at 7:55.
5. Students have to go to — if they are late too often.
6. Each student has different —, like film production or drama.
7. Students can go to — after school every day.
8. They can watch an — at school or on the school's social media channel.

Unit 2, p. 33

○ 4 High schools in the USA ► W3 School life in the USA, p. 234

Choose the right words.

1. some rules about what you can wear at school
   dress code | **registration**
2. a website with news and messages
   online portal | **blog**
3. a small cupboard where students keep their bags
   box | **locker**
4. when a student has broken the rules and must stay longer
   homeroom | **detention**
5. classes that students can choose themselves
   electives | **clubs**
6. an activity where students make a book about the school year
   homeroom | **yearbook club**
7. a group of students who meet regularly to organise things for other students
   yearbook club | **student council**

Unit 2, p. 35

○ 8 Lena's American family life

Write sentences.

A

Lena | talk to | every Sunday

B

she and Paisley | hang out | on Saturdays

C

her host parents | sometimes | cook | together

D

Lena and Paisely | not do | homework | together

E

Lena | not play | at school

F

she | often | write | in the evenings

A. Lena talks to her parents every Sunday.

Unit 2, p. 35

○ 9 How is life in Columbus? ► S18 Peer correction, p. 200

Complete the dialogue.

Todd How *do you like* (1 you – like) life in Columbus, Lena?
Lena It — (2 be) great!
Todd Cool. Where — (3 you – live)?
Lena In Logan Street.
Todd What — (4 you – do) in your free time?
Lena I often — (5 spend) time with my host sister.
Todd — (6 you – miss) anything?
Lena Yes, my family. I often — (7 think) about them.

Unit 2, p. 39

○ 4 Holidays and celebrations ► W4 Celebrating special days, p. 235

Match the words to make phrases.

A

light *candles*

B

prepare and eat a s…

C

give or receive p…

D

watch or take part in a p…

E

wear s…

F

put up d…

- presents
- decorations
- parade
- special clothes
- candles ✓
- special meal

Unit 2, p. 40

○ 8 A cartoon ► S5 Describing photos and pictures, p. 182

Describe the cartoon. These questions can help you:

- Who is in the picture?
- Where are they?
- Who says the sentence?
- Why does the turkey want to go somewhere else?

A turkey and a … .

…

TRAVEL AGENCY
"I'd like to spend November and December in a foreign country."

Unit 2, p. 41

9 What's happening?

Complete the phone call.

Alice	How *are* you *enjoying* (1 enjoy) Thanksgiving, Regan?
Regan	We — (2 have) a lot of fun. I — (3 play) a game with Brad and Moira at the moment. How about you? — you — (4 visit) Pedro's family?
Alice	Yes, we — (5 stay) with Pedro's parents. It's cold here, but it — (6 not rain) at the moment!
Brad	Hey Regan, who — you — (7 talk) to?
Regan	Aunt Alice.
Brad	Oh, say hi from me. But we need you here, Regan. Moira — (8 win) the game, and we have to stop her!
Regan	OK, Aunt Alice, I have to go. They — (9 wait) for me. Would you like to speak to Mom? She — (10 not play).
Alice	Sure, speak soon, Regan!

am/are/is + -ing
Be careful with the spellings:
have → ha**v**ing
win → wi**nn**ing

Unit 2, p. 41

10 Photos from a Midwest carnival

Put in the verbs in the simple present or the present progressive.

Moira	The Saint Paul Winter Carnival last February was fun. This is a photo of the parade. Look, the people *are wearing* (1 wear) cool costumes.
Brad	Wow! There's snow too.
Moira	Yes, it — (2 not snow) every year, but we had a lot this time! The carnival king — (3 ride) in the parade in this photo.
Brad	Cool. What about the people in this one?
Moira	They — (4 take part) in the Fire & Ice Run. It's a special race.
Brad	Is the food good too?
Moira	Yes, they always — (5 sell) awesome burgers. Look, my friend Ben — (6 eat) one in this photo.

The underlined signal words will help you.

Unit 3, p. 57

5 What do they do?

► W5 Life cycle of a product, p. 236 ► S18 Peer correction, p. 200

Match the phrases with the pictures.

program devices | process metal | produce packaging | transport products | manufacture devices ✓ | mine raw materials

A

m ___

B
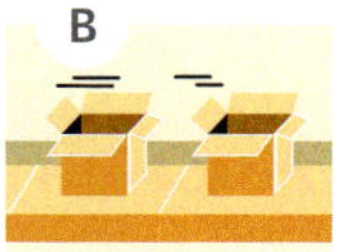
p ___

C
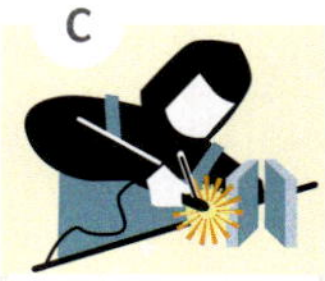
p ___

D
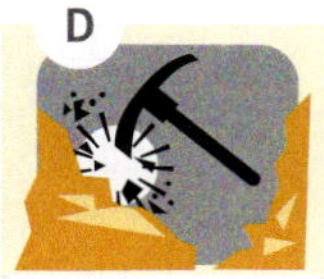
m ___

E
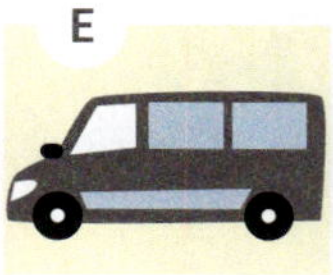
t ___

F

p ___

A. manufacture devices

Unit 3, p. 58

7 How a robot is made

Complete the sentences.

1. The school robot *is designed* (design).
2. The raw materials ___ (process) into parts in a factory.
3. The parts ___ (transport) to other factories.
4. The robots ___ (put together).
5. Then each robot ___ (program).
6. The robots ___ (check).
7. The robots ___ (deliver) to schools around the country.
8. I ___ (ask) to try the robot at my school.

am/are/is + -ed
The verb put is irregular
(see page 172).

Unit 3, p. 59

10 From apples to apple jam

Write sentences. The verbs with * are irregular. You can look up the past participles (third forms) on page 172.

A

apples | grow*

B

the apples | choose*

C
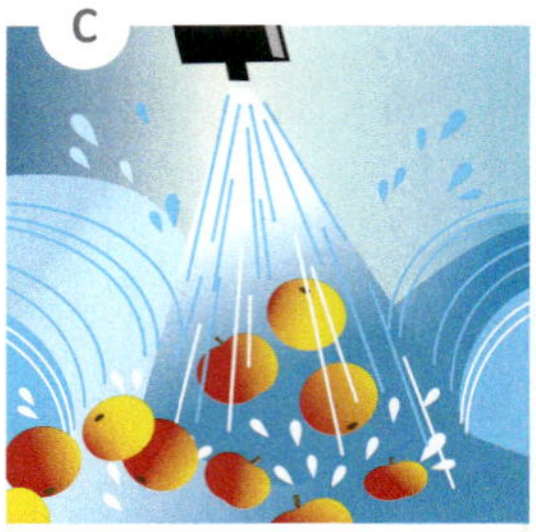
they | wash

D
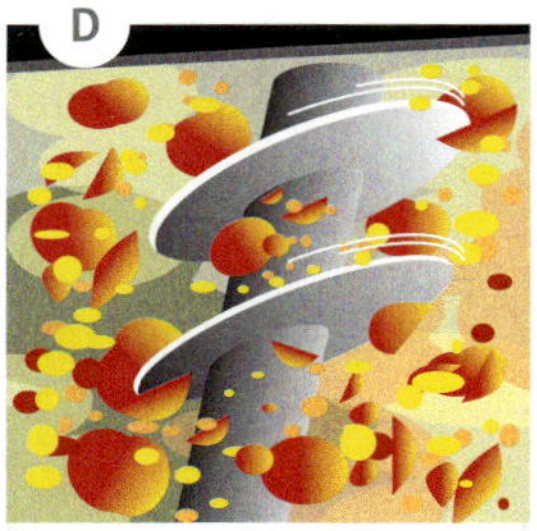
they | cut*

E

they | cook

F

sugar | add

G
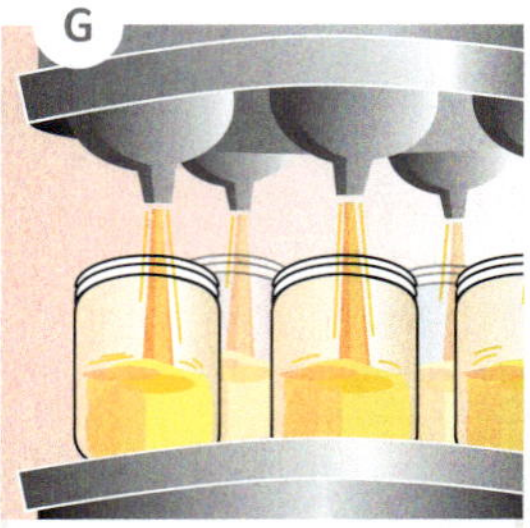
the jam | put* into jars

H

it | sell* in shops

A. Apples are grown on a large farm.

Unit 3, p. 63

4 Social work ► W6 Social work, p. 237

Choose the right words.

1. people without a place to live
   homeless people | **volunteers**
2. another word for 'to help'
   to cope | **to support**
3. another word for 'workers'
   staff | **respect**
4. advice about a problem
   counseling | **health**
5. having no work
   jobless | **in debt**
6. not being able to stop doing something
   addicted | **in debt**
7. another word for 'very bad'
   amazing | **serious**
8. another word for 'very sad'
   heartbreaking | **forever**

Unit 3, p. 63

○ 5 Lois' diary entries ► S7 Planning, writing and checking texts, p. 184

Write Lois' diary entry after her conversation with Bob.

May 26
Today I met Bob, a very special person from Room to Hope. We talked about his work …

You can use these notes: told me about Room to Hope, told me how people become homeless, interesting, want to work as a volunteer

Unit 3, p. 65

○ 8 Being a volunteer ► S18 Peer correction, p. 200

Complete the description by a volunteer.

Tessa I'm a volunteer in a local second-hand store that supports people who need help in Seattle.
I started last summer and I love *working* (1 work) here.
I really enjoy — (2 help) these people.
— (3 sell) clothes is fun, but — (4 talk) to the people in the store is what I like best. I think I'm quite good at — (5 make) customers feel welcome. I've made so many friends.
I'm really interested in — (6 get) a job in social work later. I'm looking forward to — (7 learn) more about the work this place does. I can say that — (8 be) a volunteer is great, both for yourself and for the community.

We form the gerund like this:
work → working
Be careful with the spellings:
make → ma**k**ing
get → ge**tt**ing

Unit 4, p. 79

○ 4 Character traits ► W7 Describing a role model, p. 237

Match the adjectives with the sentences.

ambitious | modest ✓ | confident | positive | patient | determined

1. What I did wasn't special, anyone could do it.
   modest
2. I know exactly what I want and I'm going to follow my dream.
3. I always stay calm when I have to wait for something.
4. I believe that I'm good enough to do this.
5. One day I'd like to start my own company.
6. I always try and remember what's good in my life.

Unit 4, p. 80

8 Interview with a role model

Complete the interview with the right forms of the verbs.

Julie Hi Coach. I*'ve* just *had* (1 have) an idea. I'd like to write a blog about my role models. You're one of them! Can I ask you some questions?
Coach That's awesome! Sure.
Julie — you always — (2 be) a track and field coach?
Coach No, I — (3). I worked in a small company after college.
Julie — you ever — (4 lose) a really important competition with a team?
Coach Yes, I — (5). It was a year ago. I was angry because the other team wasn't good.
Julie That sounds awful. — you ever — (6 run) a race in another country?
Coach Yes, I — (7). We went to Australia two years ago. It was really exciting!
Julie Thanks for talking to me, Mr. Morales.
Coach You're welcome.

You can find the irregular verbs have, be, lose and run in the list on page 172.
We form short answers in the present perfect like this:
Yes, I have.
No, I haven't.

Unit 4, p. 81

9 Since or for?

Write sentences about Becky. Use since or for.

A

Becky | have | her dog | six months

B

Becky | read | a lot of books | September

G **Grammar** ► G9, p. 160
I've had these shoes **for** two years.
I've been a member of the basketball team **since** March.

C

Becky | know | Julie | middle school

D

Becky | play | the guitar | two months

E

Becky | make | pottery | one year

A. Becky has had her dog for six months.

Unit 4, p. 85

4 In a town or a city

► W8 Infrastructure and services, p. 238

Copy the mind map. Add the words to your mind map. Add your own words too.

library | train station | cinema | basketball court | hospital | youth club | supermarket | cycle lane | swimming pool

Unit 4, p. 86

6 A letter to a mayor

► S18 Peer correction, p. 200

Replace the underlined parts of the letter with these words and phrases.

talk | children | great | thank you | mother and father | dear ✓ | friends

Hi Dear (1) Mayor Wilson,
I am writing to you because we need better sports facilities for kids (2) and young people in our town. The sports facilities that we have are very old. Some were there when my mom and dad (3) were my age!
Sports are important to help people have healthy lives.
Every town should have awesome (4), modern facilities where young people can do their favorite sports.
I understand that new facilities are expensive, but I believe that they will help the town in the future.
Could my BFFs (5) and I have a meeting with you about this?
I hope that we can chat (6) about the problem soon.
Thanks (7) and kind regards,
Mona Abbadi

S Skills

It's important to use more formal language when you write to someone like the mayor of a town. This shows that you respect the person.

Unit 4, p. 87

○ 10 How long?

Ask a partner. ► S18 Double circle, p. 201

How long have you +	been taking	the bus to school?
	been living	where you live?
	been using	the local skate park?
	been listening to +	...?
	been going to	...?
	been playing	...?
	been watching	...?

A How long have you been taking the bus to school?
B I've been doing that since I was ten. How long have you ...?

Unit 5, p. 101

○ 3 What you can do ► W9 Attitudes and behaviour, p. 239

Complete the flyer.

behave | strategies | choices | discrimination ✓ | danger | tolerant | discriminated against

Be strong – Training for young people

In our training sessions we talk about all kinds of *discrimination* (1). We want to talk about why, when, where, and how people are d— (2). We want to work together to learn about s— (3) for coping with discrimination in your daily life.
We will show you what c— (4) you have.
We will also talk about how you can b— (5) in different situations without putting yourself in d— (6).
Help us to live in a more t— (7) world.
Visit our website for more information.

Unit 5, p.102

7 You really must do it!

Complete the sentences. Use each modal auxiliary only once.

must | may ✓ | can | mustn't | can't | needn't

A

People *may* ride bikes here.

B

He — play the guitar very well yet.

C

You — use phones in this building.

D

Students — wear a uniform.

E

He — run very fast.

F

They — study hard for their exams.

Unit 5, p.103

9 Your future

Complete Jin's diary entry.
Use will be able to, will be allowed to, and will have to.

G Grammar ► G11, p.164
I'**ll be able to** make new friends.

June 24
I'll go to college in Charlotte, North Carolina soon. I'll live in my own apartment. *I'll have to* (1 must) cook and clean for myself. I — (2 can) cook my favorite food every day and eat when I want to. I — (3 may) go out and meet my friends whenever I want. I — (4 must) get a job to pay for my car and my rent. I — (5 can) buy my own things and travel around. My parents — (6 can) come and visit me every year. I'm really excited about the future!

can → be able to
may → be allowed to
must → have to

Unit 5, p.107

3 Future directions

A 48

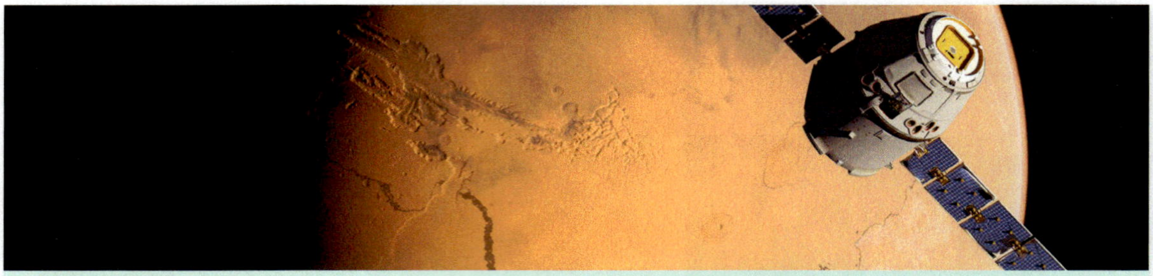

FUTURE DIRECTIONS

How will technology change our lives in the future? *The Miami News* is looking at this question during May. We've written about developments in food and farming, communication, transportation, and artificial intelligence so far. But Florida has always been important for space travel, and last week we wrote about the topic 'Our future is on Mars'. Today we're publishing some of the letters and emails which we received.

Dear Editor,

I'm writing about the topic 'Our future is on Mars'. In my opinion, having a human colony on Mars would be a good idea. There are many reasons for this.

For one thing, it's possible that war or another disaster could destroy life on Earth in the future. If we have a second home on Mars, we can survive.

Moreover, a human colony on Mars would also give us the chance to find natural resources, like rare metals. These may help us solve the problems that we have on Earth.

Finally, I wouldn't worry about leaving Earth. I think that humans could start again on Mars. There would be no countries and no wars. We could build a better, happier, and more peaceful future for everyone.

For all these reasons, I'm definitely in favor of having a colony on Mars.

Sincerely,

Delvon Andrews

Orlando, Florida

Dear Editor,

I'd like to join the discussion about our future. As a high school student who worries about the future of our planet, I don't think it's a good idea to live on Mars.

Firstly, Mars is a planet whose atmosphere is not suitable for human life. It has more extreme temperatures than Earth. It would be highly expensive to build just a small colony which could support life, with air, water, and food for the people who live there.

Secondly, Mars is a long way away. It might be possible to send four or five astronauts there in the future. But it would be too difficult to send enough people to establish a colony.

To sum up, I believe it's wrong to use resources to move to Mars instead of solving problems here. We should try to save our planet and build a better future on Earth.

Sincerely,

Cassidy Rogers

Tampa, Florida

Answer the questions in full sentences.

1. Who is for the idea and who is against it?
   Delvon is for the idea and … .
2. What could destroy life on Earth, in Delvon's opinion?
3. What could people find on Mars?
4. What does Cassidy say about the atmosphere on Mars?
5. Why would it be difficult to establish a colony?
6. What should we try to do, in her opinion?

Unit 5, p.107

○ 6 Future developments ► W11 In the future, p.240

Copy and complete the table. Put the words in the right groups.

virtual reality (VR) ✓ | the Moon ✓ | face-to-face | insects ✓ | air taxis ✓ | the solar system | artificial meat | to explore | driverless cars | robot doctors and nurses | to connect | drones

A	B	C	D
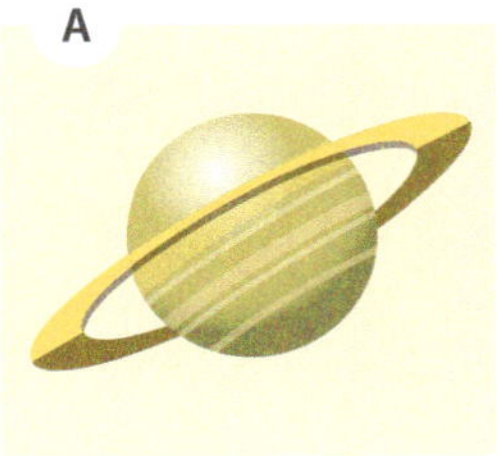	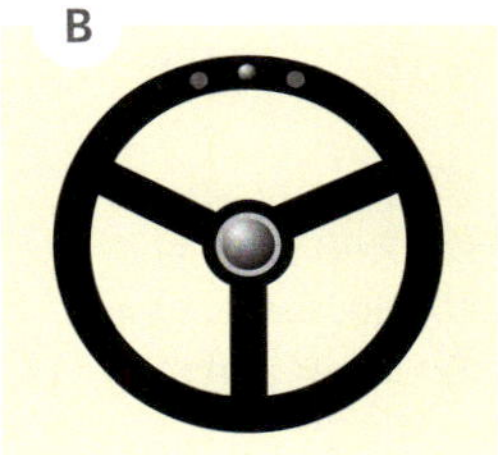		
Space	Transport	Communication	Food and health
the Moon	*air taxis*	*virtual reality (VR)*	*insects*
…	…	…	…

Unit 5, p.109

○ 10 Landmarks in science and technology

Put in <u>who</u> or <u>which</u>.

1. Johannes Kepler was a scientist *who* found out how planets move around the sun.
2. The Vostok 3KA was a spacecraft ___ took the first human into space.
3. The DynaTAC 8000x was the phone ___ made the first mobile phone call.
4. Neil Armstrong was the astronaut ___ first stood on the Moon.
5. The Model T was a machine ___ was one of the first modern cars.
6. Ada Lovelace was a scientist ___ wrote a kind of computer program.

Teenage life

A chart

An American teenager's day*

*Aged 15–17, September–June

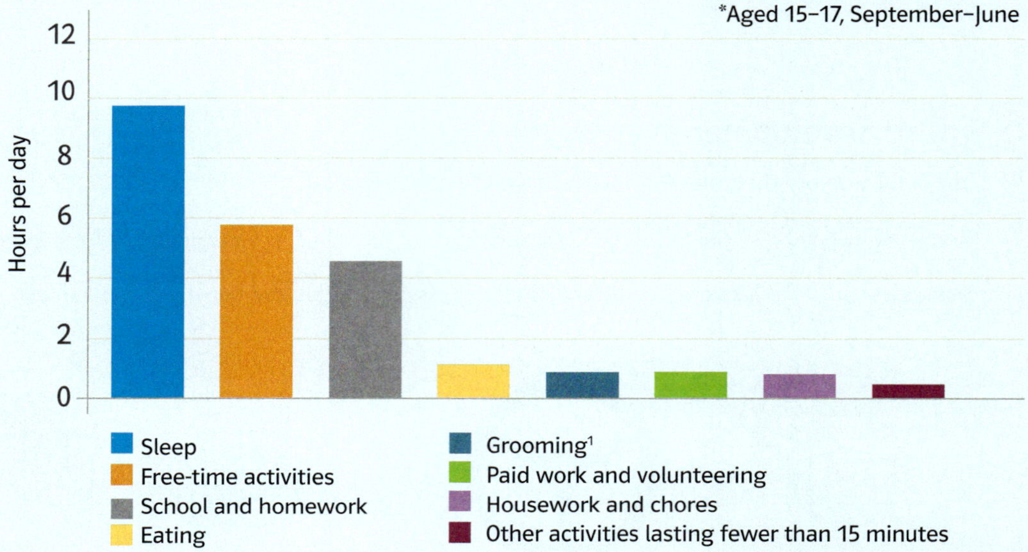

(Source: Pew Research Center, 2014 – 2017)

1 How does the information compare with your day? ► S6 Describing charts, p. 183

A poem

A 57

Leisure

What is this life if, full of care[2],
We have no time to stand and stare[3]?
[...]

No time to see, when woods we pass[4],
Where squirrels hide[5] their nuts in grass.

No time to see, in broad daylight[6],
Streams[7] full of stars, like skies[8] at night.
[...]

A poor[9] life this if, full of care,
We have no time to stand and stare.

W. H. Davies

2 What's the message of the poem?

1 grooming – *die Pflege*; 2 care – *die Sorge*; 3 to stare – *starren*; 4 to pass – *vorbeigehen*; 5 to hide – *verstecken*; 6 in broad daylight – *am helllichten Tag*; 7 stream – *der Bach*; 8 sky – *der Himmel*; 9 poor – *arm, armselig*

A play

A 58

The Last Days of High School

Characters: Lara, Ben, Farah
Lara is sitting in the corner of a classroom.
Ben enters from the right.

Ben Hey Lara. How are you?

Lara *(Very upset)* Not great.

Ben Yeah, I understand. I heard about the graffiti about you in the girls' bathrooms. I want you to know that I don't believe it. My friends don't believe it either.

Lara Thanks, Ben. But why would anyone do that? *(Starts crying.)*

Ben *(Sits down next to Lara and puts his arm on her shoulder.)* Some people are just cruel[10]. But in a few days the school will be talking about something else. *(Phone pings.)*

Lara What's this? *(Looks in shock.)* Oh no! I can't believe it. *(Shows Ben.)*

Ben What is it? Don't look at the photo, Lara. You'll just feel worse.

Lara *(More stressed and upset)* Look at the reflection in the mirror. The girl holding a pen. It's Farah!

Ben What?

Lara Look! I can't believe one of my best friends would write that about me.

Ben You don't know that she wrote it.

Lara *(Angry)* Ben, she's holding a pen and laughing! This is awful! I wouldn't care if it was someone else. But not Farah!

Ben It doesn't make sense[11]. But maybe you can ask her.

Lara She's the last person I want to talk to. *(Farah enters from the right.)*

Farah *(Happy and cheerful[12])* Who's the last person you want to talk to? Not me, I hope!

Lara *(Gets up quickly.)* Do you think this is funny?

Farah Funny? What are you talking about?

Lara *(Angry)* You know what I'm talking about.

Farah *(Confused)* Can someone please tell me what's going on here?

Ben Have you seen the new photo of the graffiti?

Farah No. *(Ben shows his phone to Farah.)*

Lara Not so funny now, is it?

Farah *(Very confused)* Lara, do you really think that I wrote that about you? You're my best friend.

Lara Well, can you explain it then?

Farah *(Looks again.)* That's not me.

Lara What?

Farah I mean, it's my face, but that's not my body. Someone digitally added my face to the photo. And look, those aren't my hands! Look at the rings on her fingers. Wait a minute. I've seen those rings before.

Ben Me too!

Lara I don't believe it! *(They all look at one another.)*

10 cruel – *grausam*; 11 to make sense – *Sinn ergeben*; 12 cheerful – *fröhlich*

3 Act the play. Decide who can play which part and learn your lines.

4 How can the play continue? Share ideas in your group.

Jackson's Island

A 59

The Adventures of Huckleberry Finn is a novel by the American Mark Twain. It tells a story about people and places along the Mississippi River in the 19th century.
The main character is 13-year-old Huckleberry Finn. Huck and his best friend, Tom Sawyer, have a gang. At the end of one of their adventures Huck finds some money. Huck's father finds out about it and wants the money, so he keeps his son prisoner[1] in a cabin. Huck escapes[2]. He wants everybody to believe that he is dead so that people will stop looking for him. Then he takes a canoe and goes to Jackson's Island, in the middle of the Mississippi River.

When I woke up the next morning the sun was high in the sky; it was probably after eight o'clock. I could see parts of the sky through the branches[3] of the tall trees, but it was still dark in the woods. I was happy because I escaped from my father – I was free! Suddenly I heard a loud boom. Then I heard it again – *boom*!

"What's that boom?" I asked myself. I wanted to find out.

I got up and looked at the river through the branches. There was a lot of smoke near the water and a steamboat[4] full of people looking at the river.

"I know what's happening," I thought. "Everybody thinks I'm dead and they're shooting cannon balls[5] into the river to make my dead body come up. My plan's perfect and nobody will know the truth!"

I was hungry but I couldn't start a fire to cook breakfast because the people on the steamboat might see the smoke. So I just watched the cannon smoke and listened to the booms.

The river was pretty at this time of year and I liked watching the people who were looking for my dead body.

The steamboat soon came close to the island and I could see my father, Joe, Tom, his old Aunt Polly and many others. They were all standing together looking at the river and they seemed worried.

Suddenly the captain shouted, "Look carefully now! The current[6] comes close to the island here; maybe we can find his body."

The steamboat went all around Jackson's Island and then went back to St Petersburg. I knew I was safe now so I went back to the canoe to get my things.

I made a tent with some branches and then I caught some fish. In the woods I found lots of strawberries and other fruit. That evening I made a small fire to cook the fish I caught and had dinner. I slept under the stars and enjoyed myself on Jackson's Island, but after three days and three nights I wished I could talk to someone again.

On the fourth day I thought, "This is my island and I want to find out what's on it. I've got a lot of time to do it. Who knows what's on the other side?"

I took my gun and started walking. As I walked through the woods I thought I was the only person on the island, but that was wrong. Suddenly my heart jumped when I saw a big man near some trees. He was sleeping with a shirt over his head.

1 prisoner – *der Gefangene / die Gefangene*; 2 to escape – *entkommen, fliehen*; 3 branch – *der Zweig, der Ast*; 4 steamboat – *das Dampfschiff*; 5 cannon ball – *die Kanonenkugel*; 6 current – *die Strömung*

I was very surprised and I was a bit scared. Soon the man woke up and threw the shirt off his head. It was Jim, Miss Watson's slave, and I was so happy to see him!

A 60

"Hello Jim!" I shouted happily and jumped out from behind the trees.

Jim stood up and said, "Please, don't hurt me! I've never hurt anyone! I like dead people!" He was scared because he thought I was a ghost[7].

I explained to Jim that I wasn't dead and he understood. I was so happy to see Jim and talked and talked to him, but he never said a word. After I told him how I escaped, we had breakfast together.

"What a great plan!" said Jim. "Even Tom Sawyer couldn't think of a better one."

Now Jim knew what happened to me, but I still didn't know what happened to him. I had to ask.

"Why are you here, Jim?" I asked.

He looked at me with his big eyes and said, "You won't tell anybody, will you, Huck?"

"Of course not, Jim," I said. "I promise[8]!"

Jim said, "Well, Huck, I … I ran away."

"You ran away?" I said excitedly.

"You said you won't tell anybody, Huck," said Jim nervously.

"I promised you, Jim," I answered. "I'll never tell anybody. But when did you run away?"

"I ran away the night after you did," said Jim.

I was surprised and asked, "Why did you run away?"

"You know, old Miss Watson wasn't nice to me, but at least she didn't want to sell me to anyone worse than her," said Jim. "Last week a slave trader[9] from New Orleans came to her house three or four times, and I was worried. I found out that he wanted to pay Miss Watson $800 for me! She really didn't want to sell me, but $800 is a lot of money for her, so she agreed. After that I decided to run away; I couldn't wait. So I swam across the river to this island and I stayed here until you found me."

"Well, don't worry now; I'm here and we can do things together," I said.

While Jim and I were exploring[10] the island, we found a big cave. We decided to make it our home. That night there was an awful storm. Then it rained for more than a week and we had to stay in our cave.

7 ghost – *der Geist*; 8 to promise – *versprechen*; 9 slave trader – *der Sklavenhändler / die Sklavenhändlerin*; 10 to explore – *erkunden*

1 About the story

a) What do you learn about Huckleberry Finn?

Culture

Mark Twain published *The Adventures of Huckleberry Finn* in 1876, eleven years after slavery was abolished in the USA. The novel criticises slavery and the racism of the time. However, readers today should see some of its ideas and language critically. Many stereotypes about Black people can be found in the novel, for example.

b) Do you like the story? Say why.

G

Grammar

G7 Das Passiv

Mit **G** sind alle Grammatikthemen gekennzeichnet und durchnummeriert.
Eine Übersicht über alle Themen in diesem Band findest du auf der nächsten Seite.
Direkt zu jedem Grammatikthema gibt es Übungen, mit denen du das neu Gelernte festigen kannst.

G6 Bestätigungsfragen

Graue Überschriften haben die Grammatikthemen der Language tips.
Du kannst dir die neuen Formen dort wie neue Vokabeln merken oder – wenn du es genauer wissen willst – ein paar Regeln dazu lernen. Auch hierzu gibt es Übungen.

G1 Die einfache Vergangenheit – Aussagen, Verneinung, Fragen

Grammatikthemen, die du bereits kennst, haben eine dunkelgrüne Überschrift.
Die wichtigsten Regeln und Formen werden wiederholt und du kannst dein Wissen bei den Übungen festigen.

Du kannst deine Ergebnisse zu allen Übungen ab S. 168 überprüfen.

! Hier stehen Tipps, Besonderheiten oder Ausnahmen.

Hier findest du einen Zusatz oder ein anspruchsvolles Extra zum Thema.

Tipp zum Lernen mit dem Grammatikanhang

So lernst du mit dem Grammatikanhang: Lies dir die Regeln und die Beispielsätze zunächst aufmerksam durch. Achte auf **fett** gedruckte Wörter und auf ! . Löse dann die Aufgaben zum Thema. Kontrolliere deine Ergebnisse in den Lösungen.

Inhalt

		Deutsch	Englisch	Beispiel	
Unit 1	G1	einfache Vergangenheit • Aussagen • Verneinung • Fragen	simple past • statements • negatives • questions	Leo went to New York last week. He didn't visit Ellis Island. Did you meet him? No, I didn't. How long did he stay?	146
	G2	Adjektive 1. und 2. Steigerungsform	adjectives comparative and superlative forms	New York is bigger than Boston. Italy has the most fantastic pizza in the world.	148
Unit 2	G3	einfache Gegenwart • Aussagen • Verneinung • Fragen	simple present • statements • negatives • questions	Lena goes to school by bus. She doesn't break the rules. Does Paisley organise events? Yes, she does.	150
	G4	Verlaufsform der Gegenwart • Aussagen • Verneinung • Fragen	present progressive • statements • negatives • questions	I'm making fruit punch now. Brad isn't preparing the turkey. Is Grandma baking a cake? No, she isn't. What are you doing?	152
	G5	Adverbialsätze	adverbial clauses	Let's meet where we always meet. We use a locker so that our things are safe.	154
	G6	Bestätigungsfragen	question tags	Your recipe is a secret, isn't it? Regan lives in Texas, doesn't she?	155
Unit 3	G7	Passiv • einfache Gegenwart	passive voice • simple present	A lot of plastic is recycled. Many old phones aren't repaired.	156
	G8	Gerundium	gerund	Being a volunteer is great. I like helping other people. I'm good at playing with children.	158
Unit 4	G9	Perfekt • Aussagen • Verneinung • Fragen • seit	present perfect • statements • negatives • questions • for and since	Julie has become very confident. I haven't tried horse riding yet. Have you ever played baseball? No, I haven't. Why haven't you told me? We've been friends for years.	160
	G10	Verlaufsform des Perfekts • Aussagen • Verneinung • Fragen	present perfect progressive • statements • negatives • questions	How long have you been learning English? I've been learning English since I was six.	162
Unit 5	G11	modale Hilfsverben und ihre Ersatzformen	modal auxiliaries and their substitutes	We mustn't wear baseball caps. I wasn't allowed to work at the café after 10 p.m. I'll have to cook for myself today.	164
	G12	notwendige Relativsätze	defining relative clauses	Mars is a planet which has extreme temperatures. We need people who want to build a better future on Earth.	166

G1 Die einfache Vergangenheit – Aussagen, Verneinung, Fragen

V 4
How to

The simple past
– statements, negatives, questions

We bought a nice game yesterday. What a great idea!

Um über Dinge zu sprechen, die in der **Vergangenheit** passiert und **vorbei** sind, verwendest du im Englischen die **einfache Vergangenheit** (simple past).
Bei den meisten Verben hängst du für das **simple past** die Endung **-ed** an das Verb. Sie ist für alle Personen gleich, z. B. walk – walk**ed**, like – lik**ed**.

Signalwörter

yesterday	gestern
last Friday	letzten Freitag
three years ago	vor drei Jahren
in 2023	(im Jahr) 2023

!

Einige Verben haben unregelmäßige Formen. Diese Formen musst du auswendig lernen, z. B. see → **saw**, buy → **bought** etc.

Eine Liste mit unregelmäßigen Verben findest du ab Seite 172.

Im Deutschen gibt es oft zwei Möglichkeiten, Vergangenes auszudrücken.

We **visited** New York.	Wir **besuchten** New York. / Wir **haben** New York **besucht**.
They **went** for a walk.	Sie **gingen** spazieren. / Sie **sind** spazieren **gegangen**.

Für die **Verneinung** in der **einfachen Vergangenheit** (simple past) setzt du bei Vollverben für **alle Personen** **didn't** (kurz für: **did not**) vor das Verb in der **Grundform** (infinitive).

I	**didn't see** the river.	Ich **sah** den Fluss **nicht**. / Ich **habe** den Fluss **nicht gesehen**.
Leo	**didn't use** the stairs.	Leo **benutzte** die Treppe **nicht**. / Leo **hat** … **nicht benutzt**.
They	**didn't have** a ticket.	Sie **hatten kein** Ticket. / Sie **haben kein** Ticket gehabt.

Bei **Fragen** in der **einfachen Vergangenheit** (simple past), auf die man mit **Ja** oder **Nein** antworten kann, steht **did** am Satzanfang. Nach **did** folgt das Verb in der **Grundform** (infinitive). Darauf kannst du mit Kurzantworten reagieren. Bei **Fragen** mit **Fragewörtern** steht das Fragewort am **Satzanfang**.

Did Aya **go** up the stairs?	**Ging** Aya die Treppe nach oben? **Ist** Aya … **gegangen**?
Yes, she **did**. / No, she **didn't**.	Ja. / Nein.
What did you **see** in New York?	**Was sahst** du in New York? / **Was hast** du … **gesehen**?

In der **einfachen Vergangenheit** (simple past) hat **be** zwei verschiedene Formen: **was** und **were**.
Bei der **Verneinung** hängst du einfach **n't** (kurz für: **not**) an.
Bei **Fragen** mit **be** steht **was** oder **were** oder ein **Fragewort** am Anfang.

I / He / She / It **was (wasn't)** in New York.	Ich / Er / Sie / Es **war (war nicht)** in New York.
We / They **were (weren't)** in New York.	Wir / Sie **waren (waren nicht)** in New York.
You **were (weren't)** there.	Du **warst (warst nicht)** / Ihr **wart (wart nicht)** da.
Was the weather nice?	**War** das Wetter schön?
Yes, it **was**. / No, it **wasn't**.	Ja. / Nein.
Where were you last year?	**Wo warst** du letztes Jahr? / **Wo bist** du … **gewesen**?

1 Sophia and Nathan visited New York. Use the verbs in the simple past.

Last month Sophia and Nathan *spent* (1 spend) a few days in New York City. They — (2 start) their tour at Edge, a platform on the 100th floor of a skyscraper in Hudson Yards, Manhattan. Sophia — (3 climb) the world's highest outdoor stairs to get to the top, but Nathan — (4 use) the lift. Sophia — (5 take) lots of photos there.
The following day they — (6 go) to the Intrepid Museum. They — (7 like) the fantastic exhibitions there.
In the afternoon they — (8 visit) Fifth Avenue. It's famous for its shops. They — (9 love) the place, but they — (10 not buy) anything. After that they — (11 rent) bikes and — (12 ride) around Central Park. They — (13 meet) some New Yorkers who — (14 tell) them about a good place to eat pizza. Sophia and Nathan — (15 enjoy) the meal. The pizza — (16 be) fantastic.
On their last day Sophia and Nathan — (17 want) to watch a Broadway show, but they — (18 not get) any tickets. They — (19 not be) sad because they will come back next year.

2 Ask questions for the interview with Sophia. Read the answers first.

You	Sophia
1. *Hi. How was your trip to New York?*	Hi. The trip was fantastic.
2. —?	We got back yesterday.
3. —?	We saw lots of famous places and Fifth Avenue.
4. —?	My highlight was Central Park.
5. —?	No, we didn't use the bus. We walked or took the subway.
6. —?	We ate lots of pizza.
7. —?	We stayed for four days.
Thanks for the interview.	You're welcome.

3 Talk about the last holidays. Use the keywords. Then take turns.

stay at home? or **go away?**

meet friends or family?

where go?
where stay?
with family or friends?

weather?
what do?
try new food?
highlight?

A Did you go away in the last holidays or did you stay at home?

stay at home
B I stayed … .
A Did you meet your …?
B …

or:

go away
B I/We went … .
A Where did …?
B …
A Did you …?
B …

A How was …?
B It was … .
A …

G2 Steigerung von Adjektiven

Comparison of adjectives

V 9 How to

V 10 How to

I'm younger than you,
but I'm more famous.

Zum Vergleichen von Personen, Tieren oder Dingen brauchst du Steigerungsformen.
Bei **einsilbigen** und **zweisilbigen** Adjektiven auf **-y** hängst du für die **1. Steigerungsform** (**comparative form**) ein **-er** und für die **2. Steigerungsform** (**superlative form**) ein **-est** an.

Grundform	1. Steigerungsform	2. Steigerungsform	
old	old**er**	the old**est**	alt, ält**er**, der/die/das ält**este**
small	small**er**	the small**est**	klein, klein**er**, der/die/das klein**ste**
quiet	quiet**er**	the quiet**est**	ruhig ruhig**er**, der/die/das ruhig**ste**
cold	cold**er**	the cold**est**	kalt, kält**er**, der/die/das kält**este**

Achtung Schreibweise! large – large**r** – the large**st**, earl**y** – earl**ier** – the earl**iest**, hot – hot**ter** – the hot**test**, big – big**ger** – the big**gest**

Vor alle anderen Adjektive mit **zwei und mehr Silben** setzt du **more** und the **most**.

famous	**more** famous	the **most** famous	berühmt, berühmt**er**, der/die/das berühmt**este**
beautiful	**more** beautiful	the **most** beautiful	schön, schön**er**, der/die/das schön**ste**

Einige Adjektive werden unregelmäßig gesteigert.

good	**better**	the **best**	gut, **besser**, der/die/das **beste**
bad	**worse**	the **worst**	schlecht, schlecht**er**, der/die/das schlecht**este**
little	**less**	the **least**	wenig, wenig**er**, der/die/das wenig**ste**

Für Vergleiche benutzt du **than**.

Waitsfield is quieter **than** Boston.	Waitsfield ist ruhiger **als** Boston.
Country life is more relaxing **than** city life.	Das Landleben ist erholsamer **als** das Stadtleben.
Waitsfield is less crowded **than** Boston.	Waitsfield ist weniger überfüllt **als** Boston.

Die Steigerung der **Adverbien** funktioniert ähnlich wie die Steigerung der Adjektive.

My sister **swims more quickly** than I do.	Meine Schwester **schwimmt schneller** als ich.
Alice **sings** the **most beautifully** of all.	Alice **singt** von allen **am schönsten**.
Nick's dog **runs faster** than our dog.	Nicks Hund **rennt schneller** als unser Hund.
Do you have to **work harder** than last year?	Musst du **härter arbeiten** als letztes Jahr?

Die Adverbien **well** und **badly** werden so gesteigert: well – **better** – the **best**, badly – **worse** – the **worst**

I can **read better** with my new glasses.	Ich kann mit meiner neuen Brille **besser lesen**.
Our team **played worse** last week.	Unser Team hat letzte Woche **schlechter gespielt**.

1 Look at the table. Compare the facts.

Complete the sentences. Use the comparative or the superlative forms.

	the Northeast of the USA	England	Germany
population	about 57 million	about 56 million	about 84 million
area	about 470,000 km²	about 130,300 km²	about 357,000 km²
biggest city	New York City (NYC), about 7.6 million people	London, about 9.6 million people	Berlin, more than 3.85 million people
highest mountain	Mount Washington, 1,917 metres	Scafell Pike, 978 metres	the Zugspitze, 2,962 metres

population	Germany has the *largest* (1 large) population of the three places. The Northeast of the USA has a — (2 small) population than Germany, but its population is — (3 large) than England's.
area	England has the — (4 small) area. The area of the Northeast of the USA is the — (5 big) of all three places. Germany's area is — (6 big) than England's but — (7 small) than that of the Northeast of the USA.
cities	When you compare the populations of the three biggest cities, you can see that New York City is — (8 small) than London. London has the — (9 large) number of people compared to the other cities. Berlin has the — (10 small) population of the three cities.
mountains	Mount Washington is — (11 high) than Scafell Pike – England's — (12 high) mountain. But the Zugspitze in Germany is the — (13 high) mountain in this list.

2 Complete this ad. Use the comparative or the superlative forms.

Come to the Northeast and get to know some of the *most beautiful* (1 beautiful) landscapes in the United States. The North Atlantic coast is one of the — (2 unusual) coasts in the country.
It's — (3 exciting) to watch whales from May to October than during the other months of the year. This is one of the — (4 fantastic) parts of the USA for sea life. And don't forget! The famous Niagara Falls are a lot — (5 interesting) than a shopping tour in New York City.
Farming and fishing are — (6 important) in the Northeast than in some other parts of the USA. So why not spend your next holiday here on a farm?

3 Say what you think about these topics.

Compare your opinions about different topics. Use adjectives in the comparative and the superlative forms. You can use some of these ideas or your own ideas.

Topics

- Italian/Chinese/vegetarian/... food
- black/colourful/... clothes
- dogs/cats/...
- reading books / travelling / playing ... / kayaking / ...
- films about animals / the news on TV / love stories / ...

good · cheap · easy · nice · interesting · cool · boring · exciting · ...

A Dancing is **the best** activity. What do you think?
B I think playing football is **more exciting than** dancing. What do you think about ...?
A ...

V 15
How to

G3 Die einfache Gegenwart – Aussagen, Verneinung, Fragen

The simple present
– statements, negatives, questions

I often listen to music. I don't do sport at the weekend.

Wenn du über **Gewohnheiten** sprichst oder über Dinge, die **allgemein gültig** sind, verwendest du die **einfache Gegenwart** (simple present).

Signalwörter

every day	jeden Tag	usually	normalerweise
often	oft	sometimes	manchmal
always	immer	never	nie

I work, you work	ich arbeite, du arbeitest / ihr arbeitet / Sie arbeiten
he/she/it work**s**	er/sie/es arbeitet
we/they work	wir/sie arbeiten

He, she, it,
das **s** muss mit!

! Achtung Schreibweise! I **go** → he **goes**; I **do** → she **does**; I **have** → it **has**

Mit **don't** (= do not) oder **doesn't** (= does not) vor einem Verb sagst du, was man **nicht tut**.

I **don't** work	ich arbeite **nicht**
you **don't** work	du arbeitest **nicht** / ihr arbeitet **nicht** / Sie arbeiten **nicht**
he/she/it **doesn't** work	er/sie/es arbeitet **nicht**
we/they **don't** work	wir/sie arbeiten **nicht**

Bei **Fragen** mit **Vollverben**, auf die man mit **Ja** oder **Nein** antworten kann, steht immer **do** oder **does** am **Satzanfang**. Darauf kannst du mit Kurzantworten reagieren. **Fragewörter** stellst du nach vorne.

Do you/we/they **work** …?	Yes, I/we/they **do**.	No, I/we/they **don't**.
Does he/she/it **work** …?	Yes, he/she/it **does**.	No, he/she/it **doesn't**.
What do you **do** after school?	**Was machst** du nach der Schule?	
When does Lena **call** her parents?	**Wann ruft** Lena ihre Eltern **an**?	
Who do you **help**? But: **Who helps** you?	**Wem hilfst** du? Aber: **Wer hilft** dir?	

Das Verb **be** hat im **simple present** verschiedene Formen: **am**, **are** und **is**.

I'**m** (= I **am**) Olivia.	He'**s** (= He **is**) American.	We'**re** (= We **are**) 15.
You'**re** (= You **are**) OK.	It'**s** (= It **is**) a good place.	They'**re** (= They **are**) at home.

Verneinungen, **Fragen** und **Kurzantworten** bildest du so:

I'**m not** Olivia.	**Are** you her sister?	Yes, I **am**. / No, I'**m not**.
Joe **isn't** American.	**Is** he English?	Yes, he **is**. / No, he **isn't**.
	Where are my shoes?	**They're** over there.

! Man verwendet das **simple present** auch, wenn **ein Ereignis zu einem bestimmten Zeitpunkt in der Zukunft** bereits festgelegt ist, z. B. durch einen Stundenplan oder Fahrplan.

The train **leaves** at 6 p.m. tomorrow.	Der Zug **fährt** morgen um 18 Uhr.

1 Put in the verbs in the simple present.

1. Every day of the week Lena *gets* (get) up at 6:30 and — (check) the school's online portal.
2. Then she and Paisley — (catch) the school bus at the end of the road.
3. The bus usually — (arrive) at school at about 7:45.
4. When they — (come) to the school building, they — (have to) walk through a metal detector.
5. Lena always — (carry) her bag to the first floor and — (put) it in her locker.
6. Then she — (hang) out with her friends for a few minutes.
7. The school gates — (close) at 7:55.
8. Students who — (be) late three times — (get) a detention.
9. At 8:00 Mrs Martinez — (give) the class information and news about events in the homeroom.
10. Each student — (have) a schedule with classes and electives.

2 Write negative sentences with the verbs.

think | stay | speak | be | feel | think ✓ | hang out

1. Lena: I *don't think* school in the USA is harder than in Germany.
2. She — late after class because she has to catch the school bus home.
3. Her classmates — it's difficult to understand her German accent.
4. Some teachers — very slowly, so it's difficult for Lena to understand them.
5. Lena and Paisley — with the same friends all the time.
6. Paisley's parents — always there to solve the girls' problems.
7. Because of Paisley, Lena — lonely.

3 Complete the sentences with positive (+) or negative (–) forms.

1. Students *don't wear* (wear –) baseball caps at this high school in Columbus, Ohio.
2. The food in the school cafeteria — (be –) as good as it — (be +) at home.
3. Lena — (go –) to the volleyball club; she — (go +) to the foreign language club.
4. Paisley — (be +) a member of the student council, and she — (organise +) events.
5. They — (live stream –) every school event, but they — (live stream +) the football games.
6. Because of all the clubs after school, the school days — (be –) shorter than in Germany.
7. Lena — (call –) her parents on Mondays. She usually — (talk +) to them on Sundays.

4 Ask an American friend.

Frage euren amerikanischen Austauschschüler Jason, der zurzeit in Deutschland ist, …

you

1. … wie er normalerweise zur Schule kommt, ob er mit dem Bus fährt oder zu Fuß geht.
2. … ob es an seiner Schule einen Dresscode gibt.
3. … ob viele Menschen in den USA vegetarisches Essen kochen.
4. … was seine Lieblingsfächer sind.
5. … ob er nach der Schule zu einer AG geht.
6. … was er am Wochenende macht.

G4 Die Verlaufsform der Gegenwart – Aussagen, Verneinung, Fragen

V 17
How to

V 18
How to

The present progressive
– statements, negatives, questions

Quiet, please. I'm talking to my friends!

Mit dem **present progressive** kannst du sagen, dass jemand gerade dabei ist, etwas zu tun.
Du verwendest es auch, um ein Bild zu beschreiben.
So bildest du Aussagen im present progressive:
am/**are**/**is** + **Verb** + **-ing**.
Es gibt Langformen und Kurzformen.

Signalwörter

(right) now	(gerade) jetzt, nun
at the moment	im Moment
today	heute
Look!	Schau!
this evening	heute Abend

Langform	Kurzform	
I **am** wait**ing**.	I'**m** wait**ing**.	Ich **warte** (gerade).
You **are** wait**ing**.	You'**re** wait**ing**.	Du **wartest** / Ihr **wartet** (gerade).
He/She/It **is** wait**ing**.	He'**s**/She'**s**/It'**s** wait**ing**.	Er/Sie/Es **wartet** (gerade).
We/They **are** wait**ing**.	We'**re**/They'**re** wait**ing**.	Wir/Sie **warten** (gerade).

!

Achtung Schreibweise! writ**e** → writ**ing**, hav**e** → hav**ing**, cha**t** → chatt**ing**, ru**n** → runn**ing**

Sätze im **present progressive verneinst** du, indem du nach **am**/**are**/**is** ein **not** einfügst.

I **am not** wait**ing**.	I'**m not** wait**ing**.	Ich **warte** (gerade) **nicht**.
You **are not** wait**ing**.	You **aren't** wait**ing**.	Du **wartest** / Ihr **wartet** (gerade) **nicht**.
He/She/It **is not** wait**ing**.	He/She/It **isn't** wait**ing**.	Er/Sie/Es **wartet** (gerade) **nicht**.
We/They **are not** wait**ing**.	We/They **aren't** wait**ing**.	Wir/Sie **warten** (gerade) **nicht**.

Mit dem **present progressive** kannst du auch **fragen**, was jemand gerade macht.
Dafür stellst du **am**/**are**/**is** an den **Satzanfang**.
Bei **Fragen mit Fragewort** stellst du das Fragewort an den **Anfang**.

Are you hav**ing** fun?	Yes, I **am**. / No, I'**m not**.	**Hast** du (gerade) Spaß? Ja. / Nein.
	Yes, we **are**. / No, we **aren't**.	**Habt** ihr (gerade) Spaß? Ja. / Nein.
Is she bak**ing**?	Yes, she **is**. / No, she **isn't**.	**Backt** sie (gerade)? Ja. / Nein.
Are they tidy**ing** the kitchen?	Yes, they **are**. / No, they **aren't**.	**Räumen** sie (gerade) die Küche **auf**? Ja. / Nein.
What are you do**ing**?		**Was machst** du / **macht** ihr (gerade)?
Who is help**ing** in the café?		**Wer hilft** (gerade) im Café?
Why aren't they work**ing**?		**Warum arbeiten** sie (gerade) **nicht**?

!

Man kann das **present progressive** auch für **Ereignisse in der Zukunft** verwenden, die **fest verabredet** sind.
Dies wird z. B. durch Zeitangaben deutlich.

Brad **is** hav**ing** a party tomorrow.	Brad **feiert** morgen eine Party.

1 Make positive (+) or negative (–) statements in the present progressive.

1. Look out of the window. It*'s snowing* (snow +).
2. Brad's dad — (prepare +) the turkey and his mother — (bake +) the pumpkin pie at the moment.
3. Lincoln — (help –) in the kitchen this year. "I — (tidy +) the living room now."
4. Brad — (make +) his famous Thanksgiving fruit punch right now.
5. Aunt Alice and Pedro — (visit +) Pedro's family today.
6. They — (take part –) in the Thanksgiving party at Brad's home.
7. Regan — (bake +) some cinnamon cookies at the moment. They're still in the oven.
8. Grandma — (share +) her famous pecan pie recipe with everyone.
9. Uncle Peter and Aunt Susan: "We — (have +) a great time!"

2 Write questions about Thanksgiving. Give short answers.

1. Brad, | you | make | your famous punch | at the moment → +
   Brad, are you making your famous punch at the moment? – Yes, I am.
2. your neighbours | have | a party | now? → –
3. your aunt | make | a pie | at the moment? → +
4. Lincoln | help | in the kitchen? → –
5. a lot of people | watch | the Thanksgiving parade on TV today? → +
6. you | prepare | the turkey for Thanksgiving | right now? → –
7. you and your family | walk | in the park | now? → –

3 Ask for the missing information.

Use the present progressive and what, where or who.

1. We are planning a ϟ. *What are you planning?*
2. We are having ϟ.
3. ϟ is helping his parents to prepare Thanksgiving.
4. Look, Grandma is putting the hot pies on ϟ.
5. Dad is preparing the ϟ.
   He's going to put it in the oven soon.
6. ϟ is waiting for the bus to the airport.
7. Grandma is sharing ϟ with everyone.

4 Match the answers with your questions from ex. 3. Write sentences.

a) the table near the window
b) Regan
c) her recipe
d) Thanksgiving party
e) turkey
f) a lot of fun
g) Brad

1. *d) We are planning a Thanksgiving party.*

5 Imagine it's Thanksgiving. Chat with a partner.

Fragt euch gegenseitig, …

1. … ob ihr gerade den Truthahn vorbereitet. A *Are you preparing …?* B *Yes, I am. / No, I'm not.* Or: *Yes, we are. / No, we aren't.*
2. … ob ihr im Moment Spiele spielt. A *Are …?* B …
3. … ob ihr jetzt zu Abend esst. A *…?* B …
4. … wer mit euch Fernsehen schaut. A *Who is …?* B …

G5 Adverbialsätze

Adverbial clauses

Adverbialsätze sind Nebensätze. Sie ergänzen den Hauptteil des Satzes (Hauptsatz) mit weiteren Informationen. Dadurch können Aussagen interessanter und vollständiger werden. Diese Nebensätze können etwas darüber aussagen, wo (**where**), wo (auch) immer (**wherever**), wenn (**when**), wann (auch) immer (**whenever**), so dass (**so that**), als ob (**as if / as though**), warum (**because**) usw. etwas passiert.

Yesterday Lena went for a walk **where** she lives.	Gestern hat Lena einen Spaziergang (da) gemacht, **wo** sie wohnt.
Lena takes her phone **wherever** she goes.	Lena nimmt ihr Handy mit, **wo immer** sie hingeht.
She'll call me **when** she gets home.	Sie ruft mich an, **wenn** sie nach Hause kommt.
Ask me **whenever** you need help.	Frag mich, **wann immer** du Hilfe brauchst.
We left early **so that** we had enough time.	Wir gingen früh los, **so dass** wir genug Zeit hatten.
She looked **as if** she wasn't sure.	Sie sah aus, **als ob** sie nicht sicher wäre.
Most of us stay longer after school **because** there are good clubs every day.	Die meisten von uns bleiben nach der Schule länger da, **weil** es jeden Tag gute AGs gibt.

! Adverbialsätze mit **where**, **wherever**, **when** und **whenever** können auch am Satzanfang stehen. Vor dem Hauptsatz steht dann ein Komma.

When we have lunch, the cafeteria gets noisy.	**Wenn** wir zu Mittag essen, wird es in der Mensa laut.
Whenever the teacher leaves the classroom, we all start talking.	**Wann immer** die Lehrperson den Klassenraum verlässt, fangen wir alle an zu reden.

1 Put the sentence parts in the right order. Make sentences.

1. has helped me make friends | here in Ohio | I feel at home | **because** Paisley
   I feel at home here in Ohio because Paisley has helped me make friends.
2. in different rooms | Students talk about | their projects | **when** they have group work
3. the metal detectors | met her friend | are | Paisley | **where**
4. a dress code at American high schools | **so that** | There's | students know what clothes aren't allowed
5. left his scarf | had lunch | **where** | Luke | he
6. after a long day at school | **when** | very tired | You can feel | you get home

2 Choose the right word to make sentences about school life in the USA.

1. Many students eat lunch in the cafeteria *so that* | **because** they get a warm meal every day.
2. After school, **when** | **where** classes have finished, many students take part in clubs.
3. Schools have different clubs **so that** | **when** there's something for everyone.
4. The teams will meet **so that** | **where** they always play against each other.
5. Students and teachers will choose next Friday **so that** | **where** they want to go to a science fair.
6. Most students have lockers **so that** | **because** they have a safe place for their books and phones.
7. School trips are exciting **because** | **when** they let students learn outside the classroom.
8. Students can play basketball in the afternoon **where** | **because** they have sports classes in the morning.
9. **Because** | **When** there's a break, most of the students enjoy the fresh air outside.

G6 Bestätigungsfragen

Question tags

Um ein Gespräch nicht abreißen zu lassen, kannst du eine **Bestätigungsfrage** (**question tag**) benutzen.
Im Deutschen sagt man oft dafür **nicht wahr**?, **nicht**?, **oder**?
Alle **question tags** werden mit einem **Komma** vom Aussagesatz abgetrennt.

Ist der **Aussagesatz positiv +**, wird die **Bestätigungsfrage negativ –**.
Bei **negativen Bestätigungsfragen** benutzt du immer **Kurzformen**.
Ist der **Aussagesatz negativ –**, wird die **Bestätigungsfrage positiv +**.

Aussagesatz +	question tag –	Aussagesatz –	question tag +
It **is** (It'**s**) funny,	**isn't** it?	Your uncle **isn't** at the party,	**is** he?
They **are** (They'**re**) at school,	**aren't** they?	You **aren't** at home,	**are** you?
She **was** in Austin,	**wasn't** she?	They **weren't** surprised,	**were** they?

Besteht das **Verb aus mehreren Wörtern**, ist das **erste Verb** für die **question tag** entscheidend.

They'**re baking** a cake,	**aren't** they?	We **haven't been** late,	**have** we?
You **can call** him,	**can't** you?	Noah **won't bake** a cake,	**will** he?

Für **question tags** mit **Vollverben** im **simple present** und **simple past** musst du **don't**, **doesn't**, **didn't** oder **do**, **does**, **did** einsetzen.

You **like** fruit punch,	**don't** you?	They **don't speak** French,	**do** they?
Regan **wants** to fly home,	**doesn't** she?	It **doesn't happen** often,	**does** it?
You **met** Aunt Susan,	**didn't** you?	Matt **didn't call** his aunt,	**did** he?

1 Complete the sentences with the correct question tags.

1. Regan is still in Austin, *isn't she?*
2. She can't come earlier, —
3. We can pick her up at the airport, —
4. Regan, you're baking cinnamon cookies, —
5. Aunt Alice and Pedro aren't coming this year, —
6. Brad's mum isn't preparing the turkey this year, —
7. Lincoln isn't happy to tidy the living room, —
8. The punch recipe is different from last year, —

aren't you? | is she? | isn't it? | can't we? | is he? | are they? | isn't she? ✓ | can she?

2 Look at the verbs in the sentences. Then add the correct question tags.

1. Regan always flies to the local airport when she comes home, *doesn't she?*
2. She doesn't need an umbrella, —
3. They want to pick her up from the airport, —
4. Lincoln doesn't help in the kitchen, —
5. You don't know how to make fruit punch, —
6. The recipe is a secret. Brad won't tell us, —
7. Regan and Brad don't see their cousin Moira very often, —
8. Dad loves to prepare the turkey, —

You **know** what to do here, **don't** you?
!

G7 Das Passiv (einfache Gegenwart)

V 22
How to

The passive voice (simple present)

English is used all over the world.

Die meisten Sätze sind **Aktiv**sätze. Mit dem **Passiv** kannst du über eine Handlung Auskunft geben, ohne zu sagen, **wer** die Handlung ausführt. Im Vordergrund steht die **Handlung**.

So bildest du das **Passiv** im **simple present**:
am/are/is + **dritte Form** des Verbs
(past participle)

Eine Liste mit unregelmäßigen Verben findest du ab Seite 172.

A lot of energy **is used** to produce phones.	Viel Energie **wird gebraucht**, um Handys herzustellen.
Many phones **are produced** in China.	Viele Handys **werden** in China **hergestellt**.
Let's look at how this **is done**.	Schauen wir, wie dies **gemacht wird**.
A lot of phones **aren't repaired**.	Viele Handys **werden nicht repariert**.

Und so bildest du im **Passiv Fragen** im **simple present**:

Is plastic **recycled**?	**Wird** Plastik **recycelt**?
Where **are** these phones **produced**?	Wo **werden** diese Handys **hergestellt**?
Why **aren't** phones **repaired**?	Warum **werden** Handys **nicht repariert**?

Auch eine **Person** kann Subjekt eines englischen Passivsatzes sein („persönliches Passiv“).
Achte auf die unterschiedlichen Übersetzungsmöglichkeiten.

We are told that robots work faster.	**Uns wird gesagt**, dass Roboter schneller arbeiten. Oder: **Man sagt uns**, dass Roboter schneller arbeiten.

Willst du in einem Passivsatz doch sagen, **wer** die Handlung ausführt, kannst du sie oder ihn mit **by** ergänzen.

Most phones **are put together by** robots.	Die meisten Handys **werden von** Robotern **zusammengebaut**.
The phones **are packaged by** workers.	Die Handys **werden von** Arbeiterinnen und Arbeitern **verpackt**.

So bildest du das **Passiv** im **simple past**: **was/were** + **dritte Form** des Verbs (past participle)

The new robot **was bought** in the USA.	Der neue Roboter **wurde** in den USA **gekauft**.
The parts **were put together** later.	Die Teile **wurden** später **zusammengesetzt**.
How many phones **were sold** last year?	Wie viele Handys **wurden** letztes Jahr **verkauft**?

Und so bildest du das **Passiv** im **present perfect: have/has been** + **dritte Form** des Verbs (past participle)

I **haven't been asked**.	Ich **bin nicht gefragt worden**.
Have you **been invited** too?	**Bist** du / **Seid** ihr auch **eingeladen worden**?

1 Are these sentences in the active or the passive voice?

1. The raw materials for phones come from the earth. → *active voice*
2. Metals, plastics and other materials are used in phones.
3. In most factories in China, robots put the phones together.
4. A lot of energy is needed to make phones.
5. Phones are transported around the world by ship and road.
6. People use their phones for a few hours every day.
7. Old phones are sometimes recycled to save materials.
8. You can save a lot of energy if you recycle.

2 Use the passive voice in its positive (+) or negative (–) form.

1. A lot of phones *are thrown* (throw +) away.
2. It's a problem that most phones — (repair –).
3. A lot of energy — (need +) to produce phones every day.
4. They — (package +) in paper, card and plastic.
5. In most factories, phones — (put +) together by robots.
6. The workers in these factories — (pay –) well.
7. Sustainable phones — (make +) from recycled materials.
8. They — (make –) to be thrown away after two years. You can repair them.
9. Phones — (transport +) around the world by ship and road every day.
10. Phones — (use +) for three to four hours each day.

Phones for raccoons are recycled. That's great, isn't it?

3 Ask questions. Use the passive voice in the simple present.

1. Where *are* most phones *put* (put) together?
2. Where — the raw materials for phones — (take) from?
3. What — (need) to produce sustainable phones?
4. What materials — (use) to package new products?
5. How — the products — (transport) around the world?
6. How long — phones usually — (use) for every day?
7. How often — most phones — (charge)?
8. How many phones — (recycle)?

4 Answer the questions in ex. 3. Make sentences. Use the passive voice in the simple present.

fewer than 20 %	paper, card and plastic	in China ✓	for three to four hours per day
by ship and road	old recycled metals	every day	under the ground

1. *Most phones are put together in China.*
2. *The raw materials are taken from ... .*
3. *... are needed to ... .*
4. *...*

G8 Das Gerundium

The gerund

V 24
How to

Das **Gerundium** (**gerund**) entsteht, wenn ein Verb als Nomen verwendet wird. Im Deutschen erkennst du ein Gerundium an der Großschreibung: (das) Lernen, (das) Schreiben usw.

Im Englischen wird **-ing** an das Verb angehängt: learn**ing**, play**ing**, writ**ing** etc.

! Achtung Schreibweise! Ein nicht gesprochenes '**e**' am Ende eines Verbs entfällt bei der **ing**-Form, z. B.: mak**ing**. Das '**t**', '**m**', '**n**' am Ende eines Verbs **verdoppelt sich**, z. B.: sit**ting**, swim**ming**, run**ning**.

Ein **Gerundium** wird im Deutschen auch mit „zu" umschrieben.

Das **Gerundium** als **Subjekt** (Satzgegenstand) steht zu Beginn eines Satzes.

Help**ing** homeless people is Bob's job.	Obdachlosen Menschen **zu helfen**, ist Bobs Beruf.
Talk**ing** to them is important.	**Die Unterhaltung** mit ihnen ist wichtig./ **Sich** mit ihnen **zu unterhalten**, ist wichtig.
Swimm**ing** is his favourite sport.	**Schwimmen** ist sein Lieblingssport.

Das **Gerundium** als **Objekt** (Satzergänzung) steht oft nach Verben der **Vorliebe** oder **Abneigung**.

I **like** help**ing** people.	Ich **helfe** Menschen **gerne**.
I **don't like** work**ing** in the garden.	Ich **arbeite nicht gerne** im Garten.
You'**ll enjoy** cook**ing** for others.	**Es wird** dir **gefallen**, für andere **zu kochen**.
I **love** be**ing** part of the community.	Ich **liebe es**, Teil der Gemeinschaft **zu sein**.

Das **Gerundium** kann auch nach bestimmten Wendungen stehen, z. B. **be good at**, **be interested in**, **look forward to**, **instead of**, **What about** ...? etc.

He **is good at** work**ing** with children.	Er **ist gut darin**, mit Kindern **zu arbeiten**.
Everyone **looks forward to** celebrat**ing** Thanksgiving.	Alle **freuen sich darauf**, Thanksgiving **zu feiern**.
Instead of go**ing** out, we stayed at home yesterday.	**Anstatt** aus**zugehen**, sind wir gestern Abend zu Hause geblieben.
What about volunteer**ing**?	**Wie wär's mit Freiwilligenarbeit**?

! Verwechsle ein **Gerundium** nicht mit **present progressive** oder **going to-future**. Vergleiche.

Working in the garden is fun. (gerund)	Es macht Spaß, im Garten **zu arbeiten**.
I **like working** in the garden. (gerund)	Ich **arbeite gerne** im Garten.
I'**m working** in the garden. (present progressive)	Ich **arbeite gerade** im Garten.
I'**m going to work** in the garden. (going to-future)	Ich **habe vor**, im Garten **zu arbeiten**.

1 Start each sentence with a gerund.

give | help | try ✓ | get | find | spend | cook | be | make

1. *Trying* to support homeless people is a good thing to do.
2. — places for homeless people to live is part of Bob's job.
3. — meals for homeless people is a good way to support them.
4. — your old clothes or games away can help kids who don't have much.
5. — old people feel happy for an hour is wonderful.
6. — someone find a job is the best thing you can do.
7. — time with kids is a perfect free-time activity.
8. — part of the community feels really good.
9. — a job in social work after school would be great.

2 Complete what James and Linda said. Use gerunds.

James
I like *collecting* (1 collect) money for homeless people and — (2 give) out warm clothes in winter. I hate — (3 see) people in trouble. — (4 talk) to them can be an important first step. I love — (5 be) part of the community and — (6 meet) people who think like I do.

Linda
I enjoy — (7 teach) maths to younger children and — (8 help) them with their homework. I think I'm good at — (9 explain) things to others. Some of my friends like — (10 cook) meals for homeless people. They are really good at — (11 organise) things. They love — (12 work) in a team.

A

B

3 Talk about what you like or don't like doing.

Use different sentences and gerunds.
Here are some ideas. You can use your own ideas too.

Playing football is fun.

What do you think? / What do you like doing?

Or: I like playing football at the weekend.

What about you?

Or: I'm good at playing football.

I'm good at playing football, but I don't like being the captain of the team.

What about you?

play … | dance | listen to music
go for a walk with a dog | go shopping
go to … | help other people
hang out with friends | cook | bake
my favourite activity/sport
great | boring | cool | …
love | don't like | enjoy | …
I'm (not) good at
I always/never look forward to | …

G9 Das Perfekt – Aussagen, Verneinung, Fragen

V 27 How to
V 28 How to

The present perfect – statements, negatives, questions

The film has just started.
But Mia hasn't arrived yet.
RACCOONS IN SPACE

Wenn eine Handlung in der Vergangenheit beginnt und in der Gegenwart zu einem Ergebnis führt, verwendest du das **present perfect**.
So bildest du das present perfect:
have/has + **dritte Form** des Verbs (past participle).
Bei den meisten Verben hängst du für die dritte Form ein **-ed** an das Verb: help → help**ed**

Signalwörter

already, yet	schon, bereits
just	gerade
not … yet	noch nicht
ever (in Fragen)	jemals
since	seit (Zeitpunkt)
for	seit (Zeitspanne)

Einige Verben haben unregelmäßige dritte Formen, z. B. do → did → **done**, teach → taught → **taught**, be → was/were → **been**, put → put → **put**.

Eine Liste mit unregelmäßigen Verben findest du ab Seite 172.

I **have** just talk**ed** to Lena.	Ich **habe** gerade mit Lena **gesprochen**.
You **have done** the shopping.	Du **hast** / Ihr **habt eingekauft**.
He/She **has taught** baseball.	Er/Sie **hat** Baseball **unterrichtet**.
We/They **have been** very busy.	Wir / Sie **sind** sehr beschäftigt **gewesen**.

Vergleiche die Lang- und Kurzformen. I **have seen** (= I**'ve seen**) … . He **has been** (= He**'s been**) … .

Für die **Verneinung** setzt du **haven't** (= have not) oder **hasn't** (= has not) vor die dritte Form des Verbs.

I **haven't seen** the new film yet.	Ich **habe** den neuen Film noch **nicht gesehen**.
She **hasn't tried** horse riding yet.	Sie **hat** das Reiten noch **nicht** (aus-)**probiert**.

So bildest du **Fragen** und **Kurzantworten**. **Fragewörter** stehen am **Satzanfang**.

Have you ever **written** a blog?	Yes, I/we **have.** / No, I/we **haven't**.
Has he/she ever **lost** a competition?	Yes, he/she **has.** / No, he/she **hasn't**.
Have they **met** Emma Stone?	Yes, they **have.** / No, they **haven't**.
What has happened? **Where have** you **been**?	**Was ist passiert**? **Wo bist** du **gewesen**?

Present perfect mit **for** und **since**
For (seit) verwendest du vor einer **Zeitspanne**, z. B. **for** three hours, **for** two months, **for** a long time.
Since (seit) verwendest du vor einem **Zeitpunkt**, z. B. **since** 7 o'clock, **since** July, **since** 2023.

I haven't seen Tom **for** three days.	Ich habe Tom **seit** drei Tagen nicht gesehen.
I haven't seen Tom **since** Friday.	Ich habe Tom **seit** Freitag nicht gesehen.

! Seit wann oder wie lange etwas schon andauert, sagt man im Deutschen oft mit der **Gegenwart**.

I**'ve had** these shoes **for** two years.	Ich **habe** diese Schuhe **seit** zwei Jahren.
I**'ve been** a member of the team **since** March.	Ich **bin seit** März Mitglied der Mannschaft.

1 Make positive (+) or negative (–) sentences in the present perfect.

1. Dave *has acted* (act +) with some famous people, but he — (make –) a film yet.
2. I — (have –) any problems with my new phone yet.
3. Our neighbour — never — (teach +) maths, but he — (help +) me a lot.
4. Mr Smith — (write +) some important articles on the Southwest of the USA.
5. Alex — (try –) dancing yet.
6. Mr Lee's students — (show +) that they like his lessons.
7. Sarah — (be +) to five American states, but she — (visit –) Arizona yet.
8. My best friend is ill, but she — (speak –) to the doctor yet.

2 Do these words go with <u>for</u> or <u>since</u>? Write two lists.

for	since
five years	…
…	…

3:30 p.m. | five years ✓ | an hour | last month | 2023 | January | three weeks | a long time | I was ten | two days

3 Choose <u>for</u> or <u>since</u>.

1. Jane has played football *since* she was twelve years old.
2. Scarlett and Emma have been friends — their first year of school.
3. Roman has been part of the high school baseball team — January.
4. Mia has had her horse — one year.
5. Mr Finn has lived in the flat next door — seven months.
6. My aunt and uncle haven't visited us — last Christmas.

4 Ask questions. Use the present perfect.

1. *Have* you ever *helped* (help) a person who had a problem? – Yes, I have. / No, I haven't.
2. — you — (read) Julie's blog post in class yet? – Yes, we have. / No, we haven't.
3. — Julie always — (be) a good athlete? – No, she hasn't.
4. Who — (show) Julie that life is what you choose to make it? – Becky.
5. How long — Julie and Becky — (be) good friends? – Since they started at their new school.
6. How many years — Julie — (know) Becky? – About four years.

5 Interview a partner. He or she answers your questions.

Frage, …

1. … ob er/sie jemals einen Hund gehabt hat.
   Have you ever had a dog?
2. … ob er/sie schon mal in den USA war.
3. … ob er/sie jemals im Krankenhaus war.
4. … ob er/sie jemals zu viel Eis gegessen hat.
5. … wie oft er/sie ein Treffen vergessen hat.
6. … wie viele Filme er/sie dieses Jahr schon im Kino angeschaut hat.

G10 Die Verlaufsform des Perfekts – Aussagen, Verneinung, Fragen

V 30
How to

The present perfect progressive – statements, negatives, questions

This is my new home. I've been living here for ten days.
HOME SWEET HOME

Du kennst schon das **present perfect**. Auch von dieser Zeitform gibt es eine **Verlaufsform**.
Du kannst sie verwenden, wenn ein Vorgang oder ein Zustand bis in die Gegenwart und darüber hinaus weiterhin andauert und du die **Dauer des Vorgangs** besonders betonen möchtest.

So bildest du Aussagen im **present perfect progressive**:
have been (kurz: **'ve been**) / **has been** (kurz: **'s been**) + **Verb** + **-ing**
Im Deutschen benutzt man dafür oft die Gegenwart mit **schon**.

I**'ve been waiting** for the bus for an hour.	Ich **warte** schon seit einer Stunde auf den Bus.
You**'ve been** work**ing** all day. Take a break.	Du **arbeitest** schon den ganzen Tag. Mach eine Pause.
He**'s**/She**'s been** try**ing** to call Mayor Sanchez.	Er/Sie **versucht** (die ganze Zeit), Bürgermeisterin Sanchez anzurufen.
We**'ve**/They**'ve been** check**ing** the air quality since 2023.	Wir/Sie **überprüfen** die Luftqualität seit 2023 (ständig).

Um auszudrücken, wie lange ein Vorgang schon andauert, verwendest du **for** (für einen Zeitraum) und **since** (für einen Zeitpunkt).

He/She **has been** us**ing** the skate park **for** years.	Er/Sie **benutzt** den Skatepark schon **seit** Jahren.
They **have been** plant**ing** trees **since** last September.	Sie **pflanzen** **seit** letztem September Bäume.

So verneinst du Aussagen im **present perfect progressive**:
have not been (kurz: **haven't been**) / **has not been** (kurz: **hasn't been**) + **Verb** + **-ing**

I **haven't been** work**ing** the whole time.	Ich **habe nicht** die ganze Zeit **gearbeitet**.
She **hasn't been** watch**ing** TV all day.	Sie **hat nicht** den ganzen Tag **ferngesehen**.

Bei Fragen stellst du **have**/**has** oder ein **Fragewort** an den **Satzanfang**.

Have you **been** tak**ing** the bus to school every day in the last few weeks?	**Hast** du in den letzten paar Wochen immer den Bus zur Schule **genommen**?
Has it **been** rain**ing** all day?	**Regnet** es schon den ganzen Tag?
How long have you **been** liv**ing** in Texas?	**Wie lange lebst** du / **lebt** ihr / **leben** Sie schon in Texas?
Since when have you **been** learn**ing** English at school?	**Seit wann lernst** du / **lernt** ihr schon in der Schule Englisch?

1 Write what they have been doing.

1. The students *have been studying* (study) for their exams since early this morning.
2. They — (do) a project about the history of the town.
3. Some people — (complain) about graffiti at the bus station for months.
4. The workers — (plant) trees for five hours.
5. Our town — (plan) to build more parks for months.
6. The supermarket in our town — (try) to reduce waste.

2 Complete the sentences about a project.

Use positive (+) or negative (−) forms of the present perfect progressive.

1. We*'ve been planning* (plan +) a project to make the air better in our town.
2. Our team — (talk +) to a lot of people in the town since the project started.
3. We — (meet −) for the last two days.
4. Roman: It's a lot of work. I — (sleep −) well for a few days.
5. Tommy — (do +) research on financial support.
6. Scarlett — (look +) at projects in other towns.
7. A lot of local people — (send +) us their ideas by email.

3 Ask for the missing information. Use the present perfect progressive.

1. We've been planning ↯ to encourage cycling. *What have you been planning* to encourage cycling?
2. ↯ have been working on some new gardens since last spring. *Who has been …*
3. We've been planting trees in our town because ↯.
4. Some local people have been ↯ near the station, with the town's help.
5. Two community groups have been organising ↯.
6. My school has been planting flowers in ↯ this year.

4 Match the answers with the questions from ex. 3. Write sentences.

a) we want to improve the air quality
b) the school playground
c) more bike lanes
d) picking up waste
e) tours in the park
f) some volunteers

1. *c) We've been planning more bike lanes to encourage cycling.*
2. *…*

G11 Modale Hilfsverben und ihre Ersatzformen

V 33
How to

Modal auxiliaries and their substitutes

You mustn't eat this. It's the cat's food. We can find something else.
Kitty

Modale Hilfsverben kannst du nur im **simple present** verwenden. Mit ihren **Ersatzformen** kannst du **alle Zeiten** bilden. Ausnahme: Für **can** kannst du im **simple past** auch **could** verwenden.

Mit **can/could** und der Ersatzform **be able to** sagst du, was du tun kannst. (ability = **Fähigkeit**)

simple present	simple past	will-future
I **can/'m able to** speak English. Ich **kann** Englisch sprechen. He **can't/isn't able to** read. Er **kann nicht** lesen.	I **could/was able to** run fast. Ich **konnte** schnell rennen. I **couldn't/wasn't able to** … . Ich **konnte nicht** … .	He**'ll be able to** help us. Er **wird** uns helfen **können**. She **won't be able to** walk. Sie **wird nicht** laufen **können**.

Mit **can/could**, **may** und der Ersatzform **be allowed to** sagst du, was du tun darfst. (permission = **Erlaubnis**)

You **can/may/are allowed to** use my tablet. Du **darfst** mein Tablet benutzen. You **can't/may not/aren't allowed to/mustn't** use it. Du **darfst** es **nicht** benutzen.	She **could/was allowed to** use my tablet. Sie **durfte** … benutzen. We **couldn't/weren't allowed to** use our phones. Wir **durften** unsere Handys **nicht** benutzen.	You**'ll be allowed to** use my tablet. Du **wirst** … benutzen **dürfen**. They **won't be allowed to** use their phones. Sie **werden** ihre Handys **nicht** benutzen **dürfen**.

Mit **must** und der Ersatzform **have to** sagst du, was du tun musst. (obligation = **Verpflichtung**)
Bei **must** musst du die Ersatzform schon in **verneinten Sätzen** im **simple present** benutzen.
Statt **don't/doesn't have to** kannst du auch **needn't** sagen.

I **must/have to** go now. Ich **muss** jetzt gehen. We **don't have to** wait long./ We **needn't** wait long. Wir **müssen nicht** … .	She **had to** work yesterday. Sie **musste** gestern arbeiten. He **didn't have to** wait long. Er **musste nicht** … .	I**'ll have to** wait. Ich **werde** warten **müssen**. You **won't have to** wait long. Du **wirst nicht** … **müssen**.

Aufgepasst bei **mustn't** und **needn't/don't have to/doesn't have to**:

I **mustn't** eat fruit.	Ich **darf kein** Obst essen.
I **don't have to** eat fruit./I **needn't** eat fruit.	Ich **muss kein** Obst essen.

Should/shouldn't drückt eine **Empfehlung** aus, **would/wouldn't** oder **might** eine **Möglichkeit**.

I think we **should** help Clara.	Ich denke, wir **sollten** Clara helfen.
I **would** help her if I knew her.	Ich **würde** ihr helfen, wenn ich sie kennen würde.
It **might** rain tomorrow.	Es **könnte** morgen regnen.

1 Use must (4x), mustn't (2x) or needn't (2x).

There are a lot of rules at our school. For example, ...

1. ... we *mustn't* use our phones in class.
2. ... we — bring our books every day; the school has some which we can use.
3. ... we — leave the school site during break.
4. ... we — do our homework every day. The teachers often check it.
5. ... we — wear a uniform, but our clothes — look tidy.
6. ... we — put our waste in the bin to keep the playground and the school building clean.
7. ... we — respect everyone.

2 Choose the best modal verb.

1. The warm climate in the South means that people *can* | **must** spend a lot of time outside.
2. People **should** | **mustn't** visit the national parks without a ticket.
3. Tourists **must** | **may** follow the rules when they go on a boat tour in the Everglades.
4. Visitors **can't** | **must** let the police officers at Cape Canaveral check their bags.
5. Hurricanes **mustn't** | **can** be a problem in the South.
6. We still **have to** | **needn't** fight against racism.
7. You **needn't** | **mustn't** worry about food in the South. The people there love their barbecues.

3 Complete the sentences.

Use (not) have to, (not) be able to or (not) be allowed to in the simple past.

1. My mum sometimes has to work at weekends, but she *didn't have to* (not have to) work last Christmas.
2. We can go to the beach today. We — (not can) go there yesterday because the weather was bad.
3. We were late. We — (not can) get tickets for the jazz festival in New Orleans.
4. You may swim in the Mississippi River now, but we — (not may) swim in it last year.
5. We — (needn't) wait in a long queue to visit the launch site at Cape Canaveral yesterday.
6. We tried some dishes at a local food festival, but I — (not can) try everything because I'm a vegetarian.

4 Make sentences with modals in the will-future.

Stell dir vor, dass du am nächsten Sonntag alleine zu Hause sein wirst. Erzähle einem Freund oder einer Freundin, was an dem Tag möglich sein wird und was nicht.

1. Du wirst bis 13 Uhr schlafen können.
2. Du wirst kein Frühstück für deine Familie machen müssen.
3. Du wirst über etwas zum Mittagessen nachdenken müssen.
4. Du wirst mit deinen Freunden Filme anschauen dürfen.
5. Ihr werdet alle Chips und Nüsse im Schrank essen dürfen.
6. Du wirst die Küche und das Wohnzimmer danach aufräumen müssen.
7. Du wirst nicht mit deinem Abendessen warten müssen, bis deine Familie nach Hause kommt.
8. Du wirst ins Bett gehen können, wann du willst.

1. *I'll be able to sleep until 1 p.m.*
2. *...*

G12 Notwendige Relativsätze

Defining relative clauses

V 36
How to

I'm looking for someone who can play rugby with me.

Wenn du eine **Person** oder eine **Sache** genauer beschreiben möchtest, verwendest du die Relativpronomen **who**, **which** oder **that**.

! **who** → Personen **which** → Dinge **that** → Personen und Dinge
Bei Tieren verwendet man meistens **which** / **that**, wenn man das Tier bzw. den Namen nicht kennt!
Einen Ort kannst du mit **where** näher beschreiben.

This is the woman **who** / **that** won the race.	Dies ist die Frau, **die** das Rennen gewann.
Mars is a planet **which** / **that** is very cold.	Mars ist ein Planet, **der** sehr kalt ist.
This is the first dog **which** / **that** went to space.	Das ist der erste Hund, **der** im Weltraum war.
I like the area **where** I live.	Ich mag die Gegend, **in der** / **wo** ich wohne.

Um **Zugehörigkeit** oder **Besitz** auszudrücken, verwendest du **whose**.

Ana is the girl **whose** grandpa lives in the USA.	Ana ist das Mädchen, **dessen** Opa in den USA lebt.
I know a woman **whose** dog can swim well.	Ich kenne eine Frau, **deren** Hund gut schwimmen kann.

! Wenn **who** im Relativsatz als **Objekt** gebraucht wird, kann auch **whom** stehen. Es gilt nur für Personen, wird vorwiegend in der Schriftsprache gebraucht und klingt sehr formell.

The scientist **who** / **whom** we met in Cape Canaveral was from the USA.	Der Wissenschaftler, **den** wir in Cape Canaveral trafen, war aus den USA.

Achte auf die Satzstellung in **Relativsätzen mit Verb** + **Präposition**. Die Präposition bleibt beim Verb! Achte auch auf die deutsche Entsprechung.

This is the book **which** I **looked for** yesterday.	..., **nach dem** ich gestern **gesucht habe**.
There were a lot of topics **which** we **talked about**.	..., **über die** wir **gesprochen haben**.

Das **Relativpronomen** kann **weggelassen** werden, wenn es sich auf das **Objekt** des Relativsatzes bezieht. Auf **who**, **which** oder **that** folgt dann ein Personalpronomen wie **I**, **you**, **he**, **she**, **it**, **we**, **they** oder eine Person. Diesen Satz nennt man **contact clause**.

We like **the books** (**which**) Asimov wrote. → We like **the books** Asimov wrote.	Wir mögen **die Bücher**, **die** Asimov schrieb.
We'll meet **a scientist** (**who**) we can interview. → We'll meet **a scientist** we can interview.	Wir werden **eine Wissenschaftlerin** treffen, **die** wir interviewen können.

! Im Englischen steht bei all diesen Relativsätzen vor dem Relativpronomen **kein Komma**, während im Deutschen ein Komma stehen muss!

1 Choose who or which.

In 50 years maybe …
1. … scientists *who* | **which** study planets will travel through space a lot.
2. … there will be schools on other planets **who** | **which** will offer lessons in different subjects.
3. … people **who** | **which** live on Mars will grow their food in special houses.
4. … buildings on Mars will have roofs **who** | **which** will protect us against the extreme temperatures.
5. … everyone **who** | **which** works on Mars will have to wear special clothes.
6. … tourists **who** | **which** want to travel between Earth and Mars will use special spacecraft.
7. … clothes will have materials **who** | **which** will be able to keep our bodies at the same temperature.
8. … children will learn at schools **who** | **which** will use the most modern technologies.

2 Make sentences with whose.

1. These | astronauts || flight to Moon | was | very successful.
   These are the astronauts whose flight to the Moon was very successful.
2. Mars | planet || temperatures | are sometimes | too cold for human life.
   Mars is a planet …
3. This | international team || project | could take us | to Mars one day.
4. Kashvi M. | engineer || plans | are used | in new spacecraft.
5. That | new robot || reports | will tell us more | about life on Mars.
6. These | scientists || experiments | will help us to build | space colonies in the future.

3 Complete the dialogue. Use who, which or whose.

Liam Did you read the report *which* (1) was in the local newspaper last week?

Maya Yes, I did, but I didn't want to use the information from it in my presentation. The author wrote about a lot of facts — (2) were difficult to understand.

Liam I see. Where did you get your information for your presentation from, then?

Maya I went to the library and asked a woman — (3) works there. She gave me some books and showed me some interesting websites.

Liam Great. What's that on your tablet?

Maya These are some photos of Mars — (4) I want to show in my presentation.

Liam Wow! And who's that?

Maya Neil Armstrong. He was the first man — (5) walked on the Moon. That was in July 1969. He was a great astronaut — (6) stay on the Moon became famous.

Liam Are you going to talk about people — (7) want to fly to the Moon as tourists?

Maya No, I'm not. That's a topic — (8) would need an extra presentation.

Unit 1

G1 1 Sophia and Nathan visited New York. Use the verbs in the simple past.

2. started | 3. climbed | 4. used | 5. took | 6. went | 7. liked | 8. visited | 9. loved | 10. didn't / did not buy | 11. rented | 12. rode | 13. met | 14. told | 15. enjoyed | 16. was | 17. wanted | 18. didn't / did not get | 19. weren't / were not

2 Ask questions for the interview with Sophia. Read the answers first.

2. When did you get back? | 3. What did you see in New York? | 4. What was your highlight in New York? | 5. Did you use the bus to get around the city? | 6. What did you eat? | 7. How long did you stay in New York?

3 Talk about the last holidays. Use the keywords. Then take turns.

Dialog 1 Lösungsvorschlag

A Did you go away in the last holidays or did you stay at home?
B I stayed at home.
A Did you meet your friends or family?
B Yes, I did. I often visited my cousins.
A How was the weather?
B It was warm and sunny, but it also rained on some days.
A What did you do?
B I sometimes helped our neighbours in their garden. I took their dog for a walk every day.
A Did you try any new food?
B Oh yes, I tried something new. My neighbours invited me to eat a cherry cake with them.
A What was your highlight?
B My highlight was a free concert in the park two weeks ago. The music was great.

Dialog 2 Lösungsvorschlag

A Did you go away in the last holidays or did you stay at home?
B We went to Spain.
A Where did you stay?
B We stayed at a youth hostel in Barcelona.
A Did you go with your family or friends?
B I went with some of my best friends.
A How was the weather?
B It was perfect: warm and sunny.
A What did you do there?
B Well, we went shopping and visited museums.
A Did you try any new food?
B Oh yes. We tried some paella.
A What was your highlight?
B My highlight was the Sagrada Família in Barcelona.

G2 1 Look at the table. Compare the facts.

2. smaller | 3. larger | 4. smallest | 5. biggest | 6. bigger | 7. smaller | 8. smaller | 9. largest | 10. smallest | 11. higher | 12. highest | 13. highest

2 Complete this ad. Use the comparative or the superlative forms.

2. most unusual | 3. more exciting | 4. most fantastic | 5. more interesting | 6. more important

3 Say what you think about these topics.

Individuelle Lösungen

Unit 2

G3 1 Put in the verbs in the simple present.

1. checks | 2. catch | 3. arrives | 4. come; have to | 5. carries; puts | 6. hangs | 7. close | 8. are; get | 9. gives | 10. has

2 Write negative sentences with the verbs.

2. doesn't / does not stay | 3. don't / do not think | 4. don't / do not speak | 5. don't / do not hang out | 6. aren't / are not | 7. doesn't / does not feel

3 Complete the sentences with positive (+) or negative (–) forms.

2. isn't / is not; is | 3. doesn't / does not go; goes | 4. is; organises | 5. don't / do not live stream; live stream | 6. aren't / are not | 7. doesn't / does not call; talks

4 Ask an American friend.

1. How do you usually go to school? Do you take the bus or do you walk? | 2. Is there a dress code at your school? | 3. Do a lot of people cook vegetarian food in the USA? | 4. What are your favourite subjects? | 5. Do you go to a club after school? | 6. What do you do at the weekend?

G4 1 Make positive (+) or negative (–) statements in the present progressive.

2. is preparing; is baking | 3. isn't / is not helping; 'm / am tidying | 4. is making | 5. are visiting | 6. aren't / are not taking part | 7. is baking | 8. is sharing | 9. 're / are having

2 Write questions about Thanksgiving. Give short answers.

2. Are your neighbours having a party now? – No, they aren't.
3. Is your aunt making a pie at the moment? – Yes, she is.
4. Is Lincoln helping in the kitchen? – No, he isn't.
5. Are a lot of people watching the Thanksgiving parade on TV today? – Yes, they are.
6. Are you preparing the turkey for Thanksgiving right now? – No, I'm not.
7. Are you and your family walking in the park now? – No, we aren't.

3 Ask for the missing information.

2. What are you having? | 3. Who is helping his parents to prepare Thanksgiving? | 4. Where is Grandma putting the hot pies? | 5. What is Dad preparing? | 6. Who is waiting for the bus to the airport? | 7. What is Grandma sharing with everyone?

4 Match the answers with your questions from ex. 3. Write sentences.

2. f) We are having a lot of fun. | 3. g) Brad is helping his parents to prepare Thanksgiving. | 4. a) Look, Grandma is putting the hot pies on the table near the window. | 5. e) Dad is preparing the turkey. He's going to put it in the oven soon. | 6. b) Regan is waiting for the bus to the airport. | 7. c) Grandma is sharing her recipe with everyone.

5 Imagine it's Thanksgiving. Chat with a partner.

1. … the turkey at the moment? – …
2. … you playing games at the moment? – Yes, I am. / No, I'm not. / Yes, we are. / No, we aren't.
3. Are you having dinner now? – Yes, I am. / No, I'm not. / Yes, we are. / No, we aren't.
4. … watching TV with you? – My aunt/uncle/grandparents/… .

G5 1 Put the sentence parts in the right order. Make sentences.

2. Students talk about their projects in different rooms **when** they have group work. | 3. Paisley met her friend **where** the metal detectors are. | 4. There's a dress code at American high schools **so that** students know what clothes aren't allowed. | 5. Luke left his scarf **where** he had lunch. | 6. You can feel very tired **when** you get home after a long day at school.

2 Choose the right word to make sentences about school life in the USA.

2. when | 3. so that | 4. where | 5. where | 6. so that | 7. because | 8. where | 9. When

G6 1 Complete the sentences with the correct question tags.

2. can she? | 3. can't we? | 4. aren't you? | 5. are they? | 6. is she? | 7. is he? | 8. isn't it?

2 Look at the verbs in the sentences. Then add the correct question tags.

2. does she? | 3. don't they? | 4. does he? | 5. do you? | 6. will he? | 7. do they? | 8. doesn't he?

Unit 3

G7 1 Are these sentences in the active or the passive voice?

2. passive voice | 3. active voice | 4. passive voice | 5. passive voice | 6. active voice | 7. passive voice | 8. active voice

2 Use the passive voice in its positive (+) or negative (–) form.

2. aren't / are not repaired | 3. is needed | 4. are packaged | 5. are put | 6. aren't / are not paid | 7. are made | 8. aren't / are not made | 9. are transported | 10. are used

3 Ask questions. Use the passive voice in the simple present.

2. are … taken | 3. is needed | 4. are used | 5. are … transported | 6. are … used | 7. are … charged | 8. are recycled

4 Answer the questions in ex. 3. Make sentences. Use the passive voice in the simple present.
2. ... under the ground. | 3. Old recycled metals ... produce sustainable phones. | 4. Paper, card and plastic are used to package new products. | 5. The products are transported around the world by ship and road. | 6. Phones are usually used for three to four hours every day. | 7. Most phones are charged every day. | 8. Fewer than 20 % are recycled.

G8 1 Start each sentence with a gerund.
2. Finding | 3. Cooking | 4. Giving | 5. Making | 6. Helping | 7. Spending | 8. Being | 9. Getting

2 Complete what James and Linda said. Use gerunds.
2. giving | 3. seeing | 4. Talking | 5. being | 6. meeting | 7. teaching | 8. helping | 9. explaining | 10. cooking | 11. organising | 12. working

3 Talk about what you like or don't like doing.
Individuelle Lösungen

Unit 4

G9 1 Make positive (+) or negative (–) sentences in the present perfect.
1. ...; hasn't / has not made | 2. haven't / have not had | 3. has ... taught; has helped | 4. has written | 5. hasn't / has not tried | 6. have shown | 7. has been; hasn't / has not visited | 8. hasn't / has not spoken

2 Do these words go with for or since? Write two lists.

for	since
five years	3:30 p.m.
an hour	last month
three weeks	2023
a long time	January
two days	I was ten

3 Choose for or since.
2. since | 3. since | 4. for | 5. for | 6. since

4 Ask questions. Use the present perfect.
2. Have ... read | 3. Has ... been | 4. has shown | 5. have ... been | 6. has ... known

5 Interview a partner. He or she answers your questions.
Individuelle Antworten / Lösungsvorschlag
2. Have you ever been to the USA? – Yes, I have. / No, I haven't.
3. Have you ever been in hospital? – Yes, I have. / No, I haven't.
4. Have you ever eaten too much ice cream? – Yes, I have. / No, I haven't.
5. How often have you forgotten a meeting? – Never.
6. How many films have you already watched in the cinema this year? – Two.

G10 1 Write what they have been doing.
2. have been doing | 3. have been complaining | 4. have been planting | 5. has been planning | 6. has been trying

2 Complete the sentences about a project.
2. has been talking | 3. haven't / have not been meeting | 4. haven't / have not been sleeping | 5. has been doing | 6. has been looking | 7. have been sending

3 Ask for the missing information. Use the present perfect progressive.
2. ... working on some new gardens since last spring? | 3. Why have you been planting trees in your town? | 4. What have some local people been doing near the station, with the town's help? | 5. What have two community groups been organising? | 6. Where has your school been planting flowers this year?

4 Match the answers with the questions from ex. 3. Write sentences.
2. f) Some volunteers have been working on some new gardens since last spring. | 3. a) We've been planting trees in our town because we want to improve the air quality. | 4. d) Some local people have been picking up waste near the station, with the town's help. | 5. e) Two community groups have been organising tours in the park. | 6. b) My school has been planting flowers in the school playground this year.

Unit 5

G11 1 Use must (4x), mustn't (2x) or needn't (2x).

2. needn't | 3. mustn't | 4. must | 5. needn't; must | 6. must | 7. must

2 Choose the best modal verb.

2. mustn't | 3. must | 4. must | 5. can | 6. have to | 7. needn't

3 Complete the sentences.

2. weren't able to | 3. weren't able to | 4. weren't allowed to | 5. didn't have to | 6. wasn't able to

4 Make sentences with modals in the will-future.

2. I won't have to make breakfast for my family.
3. I'll have to think about something for lunch.
4. I'll be allowed to watch films with my friends.
5. We'll be allowed to eat all the crisps and the nuts in the cupboard.
6. I'll have to clean / tidy (up) the kitchen and the living room after that.
7. I won't have to wait with my dinner until my family comes home.
8. I'll be able to / I'll be allowed to go to bed when I want.

G12 1 Choose who or which.

2. which | 3. who | 4. which | 5. who | 6. who | 7. which | 8. which

2 Make sentences with whose.

2. … whose temperatures are sometimes too cold for human life. | 3. This is the international team whose project could take us to Mars one day. | 4. Kashvi M. is the engineer whose plans are used in new spacecraft. | 5. That is the new robot whose reports will tell us more about life on Mars. | 6. These are the scientists whose experiments will help us to build space colonies in the future.

3 Complete the dialogue. Use who, which or whose.

2. which | 3. who | 4. (which) | 5. who | 6. whose | 7. who | 8. which

Manche unregelmäßigen Verben folgen einem bestimmten Muster:

chicken verbs: put – put – put
echo verbs: have – had – had
sandwich verbs: come – came – come
cat verbs: sing – sang – sung

Die Zuordnung zu einer dieser Gruppen kann dir helfen, dir die Verben gut zu merken.

infinitive	simple past	past participle	German
be [biː]	was, were [wɒz, wɜː]	been [biːn]	sein
become [bɪ'kʌm]	became [bɪ'keɪm]	become [bɪ'kʌm]	werden
begin [bɪ'gɪn]	began [bɪ'gæn]	begun [bɪ'gʌn]	beginnen; anfangen
break [breɪk]	broke [brəʊk]	broken ['brəʊkn]	brechen; zerbrechen
bring [brɪŋ]	brought [brɔːt]	brought [brɔːt]	bringen; mitbringen
build [bɪld]	built [bɪlt]	built [bɪlt]	bauen
burn [bɜːn]	burnt, burned [bɜːnt, bɜːnd]	burnt, burned [bɜːnt, bɜːnd]	brennen; verbrennen
buy [baɪ]	bought [bɔːt]	bought [bɔːt]	kaufen
catch [kætʃ]	caught [kɔːt]	caught [kɔːt]	fangen; einfangen
choose [tʃuːz]	chose [tʃəʊz]	chosen ['tʃəʊzn]	auswählen; wählen
come [kʌm]	came [keɪm]	come [kʌm]	kommen
cut [kʌt]	cut [kʌt]	cut [kʌt]	schneiden
dig [dɪg]	dug [dʌg]	dug [dʌg]	graben; schürfen
do [duː]	did [dɪd]	done [dʌn]	machen; tun
draw [drɔː]	drew [druː]	drawn [drɔːn]	zeichnen
dream [driːm]	dreamt, dreamed [dremt, driːmd]	dreamt, dreamed [dremt, driːmd]	träumen
drink [drɪŋk]	drank [dræŋk]	drunk [drʌŋk]	trinken
drive [draɪv]	drove [drəʊv]	driven ['drɪvn]	fahren
eat [iːt]	ate [eɪt]	eaten ['iːtn]	essen
fall [fɔːl]	fell [fel]	fallen ['fɔːln]	fallen
feed [fiːd]	fed [fed]	fed [fed]	füttern
feel [fiːl]	felt [felt]	felt [felt]	(sich) fühlen

infinitive	simple past	past participle	German
fight [faɪt]	fought [fɔ:t]	fought [fɔ:t]	kämpfen; (sich) streiten
find [faɪnd]	found [faʊnd]	found [faʊnd]	finden; herausfinden
fly [flaɪ]	flew [flu:]	flown [fləʊn]	fliegen
forbid [fə'bɪd]	forbade [fə'bæd]	forbidden [fə'bɪdn]	verbieten
forget [fə'get]	forgot [fə'gɒt]	forgotten [fə'gɒtn]	vergessen
freeze [fri:z]	froze [frəʊz]	frozen ['frəʊzn]	einfrieren; frieren
get [get]	got [gɒt]	got [gɒt]	bekommen; werden
get up [ˌget‿'ʌp]	got up [ˌgɒt‿'ʌp]	got up [ˌgɒt‿'ʌp]	aufstehen
give [gɪv]	gave [geɪv]	given ['gɪvn]	geben
go [gəʊ]	went [went]	gone [gɒn]	gehen; fahren
grow [grəʊ]	grew [gru:]	grown [grəʊn]	wachsen; anbauen; züchten
hang out (with) [ˌhæŋ‿'aʊt]	hung out (with) [ˌhʌŋ‿'aʊt]	hung out (with) [ˌhʌŋ‿'aʊt]	rumhängen (mit); sich treffen (mit); sich herumtreiben (mit)
hang up [ˌhæŋ‿'ʌp]	hung up [ˌhʌŋ‿'ʌp]	hung up [ˌhʌŋ‿'ʌp]	auflegen; aufhängen
have [hæv]	had [hæd]	had [hæd]	haben; essen
hear [hɪə]	heard [hɜ:d]	heard [hɜ:d]	hören
hit [hɪt]	hit [hɪt]	hit [hɪt]	stoßen; schlagen; treffen
hold [həʊld]	held [held]	held [held]	halten; festhalten; tragen
hurt [hɜ:t]	hurt [hɜ:t]	hurt [hɜ:t]	weh tun; verletzen
keep [ki:p]	kept [kept]	kept [kept]	behalten; halten; aufbewahren
know [nəʊ]	knew [nju:]	known [nəʊn]	wissen; kennen
lead [li:d]	led [led]	led [led]	leiten; führen; anführen
learn [lɜ:n]	learnt, learned [lɜ:nt, lɜ:nd]	learnt, learned [lɜ:nt, lɜ:nd]	lernen
leave [li:v]	left [left]	left [left]	abfahren; verlassen; lassen
let [let]	let [let]	let [let]	lassen
lie [laɪ]	lay [leɪ]	lain [leɪn]	liegen

infinitive	simple past	past participle	German
light [laɪt]	lit [lɪt]	lit [lɪt]	anzünden; erhellen; beleuchten
lose [lu:z]	lost [lɒst]	lost [lɒst]	verlieren
make [meɪk]	made [meɪd]	made [meɪd]	machen; tun; bilden
mean [mi:n]	meant [ment]	meant [ment]	bedeuten; meinen
meet [mi:t]	met [met]	met [met]	treffen; kennenlernen
pay [peɪ]	paid [peɪd]	paid [peɪd]	bezahlen
put [pʊt]	put [pʊt]	put [pʊt]	stellen; setzen; legen; werfen
read [ri:d]	read [red]	read [red]	lesen
ride [raɪd]	rode [rəʊd]	ridden ['rɪdn]	fahren; reiten
run [rʌn]	ran [ræn]	run [rʌn]	rennen; laufen
say [seɪ]	said [sed]	said [sed]	sagen; sprechen
see [si:]	saw [sɔ:]	seen [si:n]	sehen
sell [sel]	sold [səʊld]	sold [səʊld]	verkaufen
send [send]	sent [sent]	sent [sent]	schicken; senden
shake [ʃeɪk]	shook [ʃʊk]	shaken ['ʃeɪkn]	schütteln
shoot [ʃu:t]	shot [ʃɒt]	shot [ʃɒt]	schießen
show [ʃəʊ]	showed [ʃəʊd]	shown [ʃəʊn]	zeigen
shut [ʃʌt]	shut [ʃʌt]	shut [ʃʌt]	zumachen; schließen
sing [sɪŋ]	sang [sæŋ]	sung [sʌŋ]	singen
sink [sɪŋk]	sank [sæŋk]	sunk [sʌŋk]	untergehen; sinken
sit down [ˌsɪt 'daʊn]	sat down [ˌsæt 'daʊn]	sat down [ˌsæt 'daʊn]	sich hinsetzen; sich setzen
sleep [sli:p]	slept [slept]	slept [slept]	schlafen
smell [smel]	smelt, smelled [smelt, smeld]	smelt, smelled [smelt, smeld]	riechen
speak [spi:k]	spoke [spəʊk]	spoken ['spəʊkn]	sprechen
spell [spel]	spelt, spelled [spelt, speld]	spelt, spelled [spelt, speld]	buchstabieren

infinitive	simple past	past participle	German
spend [spend]	spent [spent]	spent [spent]	(Zeit) verbringen; (Geld) ausgeben
stand [stænd]	stood [stʊd]	stood [stʊd]	stehen
steal [stiːl]	stole [stəʊl]	stolen ['stəʊln]	stehlen
stick [stɪk]	stuck [stʌk]	stuck [stʌk]	kleben
sting [stɪŋ]	stung [stʌŋ]	stung [stʌŋ]	stechen
swim [swɪm]	swam [swæm]	swum [swʌm]	schwimmen
swing [swɪŋ]	swung [swʌŋ]	swung [swʌŋ]	schwingen; schwenken
take [teɪk]	took [tʊk]	taken ['teɪkn]	nehmen; mitnehmen; dauern
teach [tiːtʃ]	taught [tɔːt]	taught [tɔːt]	beibringen; unterrichten; lehren
tear down [ˌteə 'daʊn]	tore down [ˌtɔː 'daʊn]	torn down [ˌtɔːn 'daʊn]	abreißen; zerstören; abbrechen
tell [tel]	told [təʊld]	told [təʊld]	sagen; erzählen
think [θɪŋk]	thought [θɔːt]	thought [θɔːt]	finden; denken; glauben
throw [θrəʊ]	threw [θruː]	thrown [θrəʊn]	werfen
understand [ˌʌndə'stænd]	understood [ˌʌndə'stʊd]	understood [ˌʌndə'stʊd]	verstehen
wake up [ˌweɪk‿'ʌp]	woke up [ˌwəʊk‿'ʌp]	woken up [ˌwəʊkn‿'ʌp]	aufwachen; wecken
wear [weə]	wore [wɔː]	worn [wɔːn]	(Kleidung) tragen; anhaben
win [wɪn]	won [wʌn]	won [wʌn]	gewinnen; siegen
write [raɪt]	wrote [rəʊt]	written ['rɪtn]	schreiben

S

Skills and methods

Ein Skill beschreibt, wie du beim Lernen vorgehst. Wenn du weißt, was bei bestimmten Aufgaben zu tun ist, fällt dir das Lernen leichter. Denn vieles läuft immer gleich ab. Folgende Skills kannst du hier nachschlagen.

! Hier stehen Tipps, Besonderheiten oder Ausnahmen.

Inhalt

S1 Hörtexte verstehen

V 12
How to

Understanding listening texts

Ein Hörtext kann manchmal knifflig sein, je nachdem, wie deutlich oder in welchem Tempo gesprochen wird. Die folgenden Schritte helfen dir, mit Hörtexten besser zurechtzukommen.

Keep cool. You needn't understand everything!

Vor dem Hören

1. Sieh dir die **Bilder** an und lies die **Überschrift**. Überlege, **worum es in dem Text gehen könnte**.
2. Weißt du schon etwas über das Thema? Welche Wörter könnten vorkommen?
3. Was für ein Text ist es (Dialog, Radiosendung, Interview, Werbung …)? Wer spricht mit wem?

Während des Hörens

Normalerweise wird der Hörtext im Unterricht **zweimal** nacheinander abgespielt.
Wenn du dir beim Zuhören Notizen machst, achte darauf, dass sie kurz sind (ein Wort, Abkürzungen …).

Erstes Hören: Den Text grob verstehen

1. Beantworte die **W-Fragen**: *Who? Where? When? What? Why?*
2. Sieh dir die Aufgaben an. Löse schon die Aufgaben, bei denen du die Antwort sicher weißt.

Zweites Hören: Einzelheiten verstehen

Konzentriere dich auf das, was in den **Aufgaben** von dir verlangt wird. Die Antworten im Hörtext sind meistens in der gleichen Reihenfolge wie in den Aufgaben.

Nach dem Hören

Überprüfe deine Antworten. Hast du nichts vergessen?

! Höre oder sieh dir so oft wie möglich englische Inhalte an (Radio, Fernsehen, Internet …). Du wirst sehen, mit der Zeit verstehst du immer mehr und es fällt dir leichter. So kannst du das Hörverstehen ganz nebenbei trainieren.

S2 Lesetexte verstehen

V 13
How to

Understanding texts

Es gibt viele unterschiedliche Lesetexte, z. B. E-Mails, Geschichten, Dialoge usw. Sie können kurz oder auch länger sein. Du erfährst hier ein paar Tricks, wie du Lesetexte knacken kannst, egal was für ein Text es ist.

Vor dem Lesen

1. Sieh dir die **Bilder** an und lies die **Überschrift**. Überlege, **worum es in dem Text gehen könnte**.
2. Weißt du schon etwas über das Thema?

Während des Lesens

Es ist gut, einen Stift zur Hand zu haben, wenn du einen Text liest. Du kannst wichtige Wörter (*key words*) oder Sätze im Text markieren. Allerdings nur, wenn du ein Arbeitsblatt bearbeitest oder dir das Buch oder Arbeitsheft gehört.
Einen längeren Text kannst du in **Sinnabschnitte** gliedern und z. B. am Rand Notizen zum Inhalt des jeweiligen Abschnitts machen.

Erstes Lesen: Verschaffe dir einen Überblick (*Skimming*)

1. Lies den Text. Du musst nicht jedes Wort verstehen, um herauszufinden, worum es darin geht.
2. Beantworte die **W-Fragen** zum Text: *Who? Where? When? What? Why?*

Zweites Lesen: Konzentriere dich auf Einzelheiten (*Scanning*)

1. Lies dir die **Aufgaben** zum Text genau durch.
2. Lies den Text dann ein weiteres Mal und suche gezielt nach den Informationen, die du zur Bearbeitung der Aufgaben benötigst.

Nach dem Lesen

Überprüfe deine Antworten. Hast du alle Fragen beantwortet? Ist alles richtig geschrieben?

!

Du musst nicht alle Wörter in einem Text verstehen. Wörter, die zur Beantwortung der Fragen wichtig sind, kannst du im (Online-)Wörterbuch nachschlagen. Du kannst aber auch selbst versuchen, die Bedeutung herauszufinden. Das geht oft schneller.
1. Ist das Wort mit einem Wort verwandt, das du schon gelernt hast? Kennst du z. B. das Wort *teacher*, dann weißt du auch, was *to teach* bedeutet.
2. Gibt es das Wort vielleicht in einer anderen Sprache auch? *moment* 🇬🇧 → Moment 🇩🇪, *cinema* 🇬🇧 → sinema 🇹🇷.

Kannst du das Wort mithilfe der Bilder, der Überschrift oder des Satzes, in dem es vorkommt, erschließen?

Überlege, wenn du einen Text liest, um was für eine Art von Text es sich handelt.
Es fällt dir leichter, Texte zu verstehen, wenn du weißt, was dich erwartet.

Text	Wichtige Merkmale
story	– kürzer als ein Roman – meistens in der Ich- oder Er-/Sie-Perspektive – häufig im *simple past* – Einleitung, Hauptteil, Schluss – mit einem Höhepunkt – Adjektive, Erzählwörter (*suddenly*, *at first*, …) und wörtliche Rede
short story	– kürzer als eine Geschichte – Beginn mitten in der Handlung – spielt meist an einem Ort in einem kurzen Zeitraum – sehr oft ein offenes Ende – chronologische Handlung – ein zentrales Thema und eine Hauptfigur
letter	– Briefkopf: Adresse – rechts: Datum – links unterhalb des Datums: Anrede – Hauptteil – unten links: Verabschiedung/Unterschrift
diary entry	– Datum am Anfang – in der Ich-Perspektive – berichtet über persönliche Erlebnisse im *simple past* – Gedanken und Gefühle
flyer	– Schriftart und -größe so, dass der Flyer gut lesbar ist – alle wichtigen Informationen in kurzen Sätzen oder Stichpunkten – übersichtlich und gut strukturiert (Nummerierung, Aufzählungen, Zwischenüberschriften usw.) – Bilder und Fotos zur Veranschaulichung – Überschriften und Slogans machen den Flyer interessant
dialogue	– zwei Sprecher oder Sprecherinnen, sie sprechen abwechselnd und beziehen sich aufeinander – oft Kurzformen und Umgangsspache
conversation	– mehrere Sprecher oder Sprecherinnen, sie sprechen abwechselnd und beziehen sich aufeinander – oft Kurzformen und Umgangsspache
factual text	– oft Fakten, Zahlen o.Ä. – informiert sachlich – beschreibt genau – keine Gefühle oder Gedanken

S3 Miteinander sprechen

Speaking with other people

Englisch zu sprechen, ist gar nicht so schwer. Trau dich, auch wenn es nicht perfekt ist. Je öfter du Englisch sprichst, umso sicherer wirst du dich dabei fühlen.

Allgemeine Tipps zu Gesprächen

1. Sprecht **langsam und deutlich**.
2. **Seht euch gegenseitig an** oder sprecht zur Klasse.
3. Versucht, **frei zu sprechen** und nicht abzulesen.

A Rollenspiel

1. Denkt euch in eure Rollen hinein: Wie ist die Person aufgelegt, z. B. munter, traurig?
2. Was möchtet ihr sagen? Schreibt eure Notizen oder Fragen und Antworten z. B. auf Kärtchen.
3. Übt das Rollenspiel gemeinsam ein.
4. Wählt passende Gesichtsausdrücke/Körpersprache, z. B. erstaunt schauen usw.
5. Drückt die Gefühle der Person(en) auch mit der Stimme aus, z. B. traurig, wütend.

B Umfrage/Interview

1. Bereitet die Fragen für die Umfrage/das Interview vor.
2. Achtet auf die richtige Wortstellung.
3. Fragt nach, wenn etwas unklar ist.
4. Bei Umfragen: Wertet das Ergebnis aus (z. B. in einem Diagramm).

Can you …? | Can I …? What's your …? | How old …? | Do you …? | Are you …? | …

Sorry, can you say that again, please? | Excuse me. What does that mean?

C Diskussion

Vorbereitung

1. Überlegt euch eure Meinung zum Thema der Diskussion.
2. Sammelt Argumente und Gegenargumente und überlegt euch Beispiele. So werden eure Argumente überzeugender.

Durchführung

1. Beginnt die Diskussion.
2. Lasst euch immer ausreden und geht aufeinander ein.
3. Seid höflich und fragt nach, wenn ihr etwas nicht verstanden habt.
4. Beendet die Diskussion.

Let's talk about … . | The topic today is … .

I think … . | You're right. | Sorry, I think you're wrong. | I don't think so. | I can understand you, but I think … .

Could …, please? | Sorry, I didn't understand. | Can you say it again, please?

Let's stop here. | Thank you everybody.

S4 Etwas präsentieren

V 19 How to

D 183 Support

Giving a presentation

Bei einer Präsentation kommt es nicht nur auf den Vortrag an, sondern auch auf eine gute Vorbereitung.

Eine Präsentation vorbereiten

1. Es gibt ganz kurze und auch längere Präsentationen. Kläre zunächst: Wie lange soll der Vortrag dauern?
2. **Sammle deine Ideen.**
3. **Plane deine Präsentation**: Was möchtest du in welcher Reihenfolge sagen?
4. Schreibe **Stichwörter** auf Kärtchen. Nummeriere die Kärtchen in der richtigen Reihenfolge.
5. Gestalte dann ein **Poster** mit Stichpunkten. Du kannst auch eine Computerpräsentation vorbereiten.
6. Mache eine Liste mit Vokabeln, die du deiner Klasse vor der Präsentation erklären willst. So kannst du sicher sein, dass sie alles verstehen, was du vorträgst.
7. **Übe die Präsentation** vor dem Spiegel, deinen Freunden oder deiner Familie. Du kannst dich auch selbst aufnehmen. Prüfe, wie lange deine Präsentation dauert.

Ein Poster oder eine Folie gestalten

1. Schreibe eine interessante Überschrift in großer Schrift. Hebe sie farbig hervor.
2. Schreibe nur Stichwörter auf das Poster. Verwende auch Zwischenüberschriften.
3. Schreibe sauber und so groß, dass man es auch hinten im Klassenzimmer lesen kann.
4. Gestalte dein Poster mit Zeichnungen oder Bildern mit Bildunterschrift.
   ► S16 Fotos, Filme und Texte richtig verwenden

Eine Präsentation halten

1. Begrüße deine Klasse.
2. Sprich langsam, deutlich und nicht zu leise.
3. Sprich möglichst frei und sieh die Klasse an.
4. Achte auf eine aufrechte Haltung.
5. Achte auf deine Aussprache.
6. Verweise beim Sprechen auf dein Poster oder deine Computerpräsentation.
7. Bedanke dich am Schluss. Beantworte dann Fragen.

Good morning. | Hello.

My presentation is about … .

My first point is … . | Then … . | Lastly … .

Thank you. | Do you have any questions?

Nach der Präsentation

Lass dir Feedback zu deinem Vortrag geben. ► S8 Feedback geben und bekommen

!

Beim Sprechen kommt es auf die Aussprache an.
Versuche, so oft es geht, Englisch zu sprechen. Du kannst dir die Hörtexte zum Buch immer wieder anhören und mitsprechen. Singe mit, wenn du englische Musik z. B. im Radio hörst.
Nimm dich auf, wenn du Englisch sprichst, und höre dir die Aufnahme an. Was war gut und was kannst du besser machen?

S5 Fotos und Bilder beschreiben

V 37
How to

Describing photos and pictures

Manchmal musst du ein Foto, ein Bild oder einen Cartoon beschreiben. Du kannst dabei immer gleich vorgehen. So vergisst du nichts und es kommt nichts durcheinander.

Beantworte die W-Fragen.

Sieh dir das Bild genau an und beantworte in ein bis zwei Sätzen die W-Fragen: **Was** und **wer** ist zu sehen? **Wo** ist es?

A family is sitting in front of their tent.
They are in the wood.

Beschreibe das Foto oder das Bild genauer.

1. Entscheide, wo deine Beschreibung starten soll. Du kannst z. B. von unten rechts nach oben links beschreiben.
2. Benutze diese Ausdrücke, um zu sagen, wo sich die Personen und Dinge im Bild befinden:

In the lower right corner you can see plates and cups.
On the right there is a man …

3. Sieh dir das Bild noch einmal an und sage noch genauer, wo die Personen und Dinge sind. Benutze dazu Präpositionen.

next to, between, behind, over, in, on, in front of, under, …

Beschreibe, was auf dem Foto oder Bild passiert.

Benutze dazu das *present progressive*.

A family is sitting … .
A man is playing … .

! Cartoons haben oft eine Bildunterschrift oder Sprechblasen. Erkläre auch deren Bedeutung, wenn du den Cartoon beschreibst.

S6 Diagramme beschreiben

D 184 Support

Describing charts

Informationen oder Ergebnisse (z. B. einer Umfrage in der Klasse) werden oft in Diagrammen dargestellt, weil das übersichtlich ist.

Verschiedene Diagramme

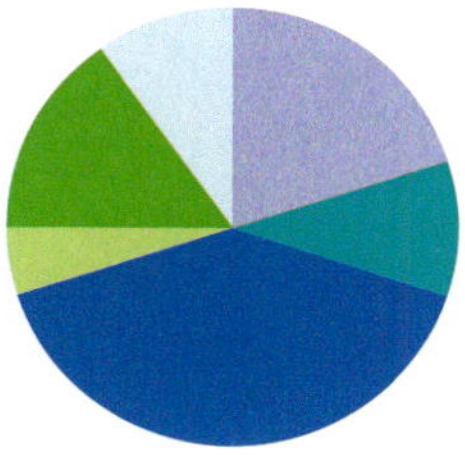

In einem Kuchen- oder Kreisdiagramm (*pie chart*) kannst du zeigen, wer oder was wie viele **Anteile** hat.

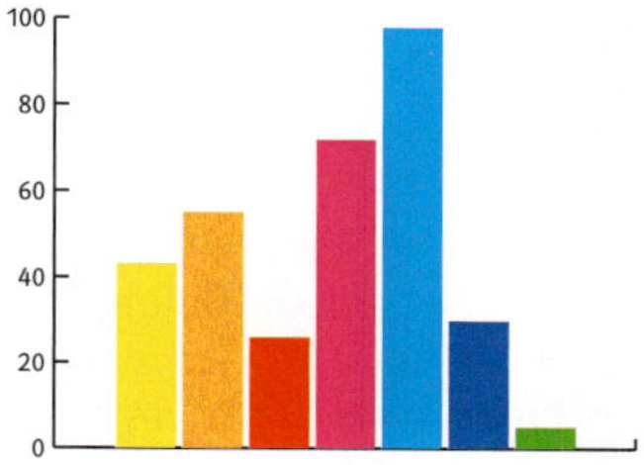

Ein Säulen- oder Balkendiagramm (*bar chart*) verwendet man, um Zahlen direkt miteinander zu **vergleichen**.

Wenn du einen Text zu einem Diagramm schreiben sollst, gehe schrittweise vor.

1. Allgemeine Information

Sage zunächst, um welche Art von Diagramm es sich handelt und was es darstellt. Vergiss nicht, die Quelle und das Jahr der Veröffentlichung zu nennen.

… published the bar chart / pie chart / … in … . | It's about … ./ The topic of the … is … . | www.dia12999999#l.co.uk, 02.11.2022

2. Beschreibung des Diagramms

Beschreibe, was du aus dem Diagramm ablesen kannst. Gehe schrittweise vor und finde eine sinnvolle Reihenfolge, z. B. im Uhrzeigersinn, vom größten Anteil bis zum kleinsten usw.

The largest part … | Only … | The smallest part … | Most of the … | Nobody …

3. Abschlusssatz

Fasse die wichtigsten Aussagen des Diagramms in ein bis zwei Sätzen zusammen.

The … shows that … . | In my opinion … . | You can say that … .

! Du kannst Diagramme in einem Textverarbeitungsprogramm selbst erstellen.

! Achte auf die richtige Schreibung der Zahlen im Englischen.

🇬🇧		🇩🇪
10,000	↔	10.000
1,000	↔	1.000
5.5%	↔	5,5%

S7 Texte planen, schreiben und überarbeiten

V 11
How to

Planning, writing and checking texts

Selbst einen Text auf Englisch zu schreiben, ist gar nicht so schwer. Wenn du ein paar Dinge beachtest, kannst du gute und interessante Texte schreiben.

Du kannst immer nach diesen Schritten vorgehen.

First Lucas opened the black door. Then he heard a terrible sound. He was so scared …

Plane deinen Text.

1. Was für einen Text sollst du schreiben, z. B. eine E-Mail, eine Geschichte, einen Steckbrief?
2. **Sammle deine Ideen** in einer Liste oder einer Mindmap.
3. Was möchtest du **in welcher Reihenfolge** schreiben?
4. Überlege dir einen Anfang und einen Schluss.
5. Sammle Wörter, die du für deinen Text brauchst. Schlage Wörter, die du nicht weißt, in deiner Wortliste oder einem (Online-) Wörterbuch nach.

Schreibe deinen Text.

1. Schreibe mithilfe deines Plans einen **ersten Entwurf**.
2. Suche Texte in deinem Englischbuch als Muster, wenn du Hilfe brauchst.
3. Achte beim Schreiben auf Grammatik und Rechtschreibung.
4. Achte auf einen guten Schreibstil, z. B. **abwechslungsreiche Satzanfänge** (*First …*, *Then …*), **Bindewörter** (*and*, *but …*), **Adjektive** (*black*, *terrible*, *scared …*) usw.

Überarbeite deinen Text.

1. Lies deinen Text zum Schluss noch einmal durch und **überprüfe** ihn auf Fehler.
2. Du kannst jemanden bitten, ihn durchzusehen. Nutze auch den Grammatik- und Vokabelanhang deines Schulbuchs.
3. Schreibe deinen Text ins Reine.
4. Wenn du am Computer oder auf dem Tablet geschrieben hast, kann dir die Rechtschreib- und Grammatikprüfung im Textverarbeitungsprogramm bei der Überprüfung deines Textes helfen. Stelle dazu die Sprache auf Englisch um.

Du findest hier Schreibanleitungen für die wichtigsten Textarten:

D 185
Support

A Einen Dialog erstellen

1. Schreibe den Namen der Person vor das Gesagte. — Lisa: | Ben: | …
2. Beginne beim Wechsel der Person eine neue Zeile.
3. Benutze echte mündliche Sprache, wie z. B. **Kurzformen** oder **Füllwörter** für Sprechpausen. — he's | she's | I've got | they've got | Err, … | Well, …
4. Achte darauf, dass sich die sprechenden Personen aufeinander beziehen, z. B. müssen die Antworten zu den Fragen passen usw.

D 122
Support

B Eine E-Mail schreiben

1. Fülle zunächst den **Kopf** der E-Mail aus:

email

To: Trage hier die Adresse der empfangenden Person ein, z. B. chris.school@ … .

Cc: Hier kannst du Adressen der Personen einfügen, die eine Kopie deiner Mail erhalten sollen.

Subject: Schreibe hier den Grund, warum du schreibst, z. B. *Homework today.*

2. Schreibe dann die **Begrüßung**. — Hi Sarah, | Hello Malik,
3. Beginne den ersten Satz deiner E-Mail immer mit einem **Großbuchstaben**. — Did you get …
4. Schreibe nun deine Nachricht.
5. Schreibe am Ende eine **Verabschiedung**. — Bye. | XOXO

D 186
Support

C Einen persönlichen Brief schreiben

1. Schreibe oben rechts deine **Adresse** und darunter das **Datum**. — Deine Adresse / 12th March 2022
2. Lass eine Zeile frei und schreibe dann die **Begrüßung** und den Namen. — Dear Ron, | Hi/Hello Yeliz,
3. Lass eine Zeile frei. Beginne den **ersten Satz** deines Briefs immer mit einem **Großbuchstaben**. — How are you? My …
4. Schreibe nun deine Nachricht. Bei einem längeren Brief kannst du vorab Ideen sammeln.
5. Schreibe am Ende eine **Verabschiedung**. — Bye, | Love,
6. Vergiss nicht, den Brief zu unterschreiben. — Tom/Lisa/…

D 187
Support

D Einen Tagebucheintrag schreiben

In einem Tagebuch kannst du aufschreiben, was du selbst erlebt hast, was du darüber denkst und wie du dich dabei gefühlt hast.

1. Schreibe das Datum.
2. Schreibe in der **Ich-Form**. — I'm … . | I was … . | My … .
3. Schreibe im *simple past* über das, was du erlebt hast und wie du dich dabei gefühlt hast. — Today I met … . | Yesterday I … . | Lisa's party was so … .
4. Schreibe im *simple present* über Gedanken und Gefühle, die du jetzt hast. — I'm so happy because … . | I'm so angry with Leo … .
5. Verwende **Adjektive**, um Gedanken und Gefühle auszudrücken. — boring | funny | exciting | terrible | …

D 188
Support

E Geschichten

So kannst du vorgehen, wenn du eine Geschichte schreibst:

1. Lass eine Zeile für die Überschrift frei.
2. Schreibe einen spannenden und interessanten Anfang. Schreibe, **wer** in der Geschichte vorkommt und **wo** und **wann** die Handlung spielt.
3. Schreibe nacheinander, **was passiert**. Benutze **Erzählwörter** und **verbinde** deine Sätze.
4. Achte darauf, dass du **unterschiedliche Satzanfänge** wählst.
5. Verwende **Adjektive und Adverbien**, um deinen Text interessant zu machen.
6. Füge **wörtliche Rede** ein. Das macht die Geschichte lebendiger. Achtung: Im Englischen sind beide Anführungszeichen oben. Anders als im Deutschen steht das Komma innerhalb der Anführungszeichen.
7. Schreibe ein gutes **Ende**. Du kannst z.B. auch mit einer Frage aufhören oder das Ende offen lassen.
8. Finde eine passende **Überschrift**.
9. Schreibe alles außer der wörtlichen Rede in der **Vergangenheit**.

"Oh, no!" Malik thought, when he .... | It was a very dark night, and Fatma felt the cold air in the forest .... | It was .... | Nobody knew that .... | Suddenly there was ....

First | Later | When | Suddenly | ...

big | boring | funny | exciting | walk slowly | speak calmly | ...

"You're right," Pete answered. | "Wait!" ... screamed. | "Why?" ... asked angrily. | Helin cried: "Wait!" | "Well," Ben whispered, "that's it."

He didn't know the answer. | Hylem was happy to be home again.

Eine Geschichte zu Bildern schreiben

Wenn du eine Geschichte zu Bildern schreiben sollst, kannst du so vorgehen:
Sieh dir die Bilder genau an und mache dir Notizen.

1. **Worum** geht es?
2. **Welche Personen** kommen vor?
3. **Wann** und **wo** spielt die Geschichte?
4. **Was passiert** nacheinander?

Schreibe nun die Geschichte und gehe so vor wie in E Geschichten beschrieben.

Eine Geschichte zu einem Text schreiben

Wenn du eine Geschichte zu einem Text schreiben sollst, musst du ihn aufmerksam lesen. Deine Geschichte muss nämlich genau dazu passen. Du kannst Dinge erfinden, aber sie dürfen nicht im Widerspruch zu dem Text stehen. Mache dir vor dem Schreiben Notizen zu diesen Punkten:

1. **Worum** geht es?
2. **Welche Personen** kommen vor und was erfährst du über sie?
3. **Wann** und **wo** spielt die Geschichte?
4. **Was passiert** nacheinander?
5. **Wer erzählt** die Geschichte, z.B. *I went to ...* oder *He/She went to ...*?

Sammle dann Ideen.
Schreibe nun die Geschichte und gehe so vor wie in E Geschichten beschrieben.

D 189 Support

F Einen Blogeintrag verfassen

Mit einem Blog kannst du online viele Menschen erreichen und sie z. B. an deinen Erlebnissen teilhaben lassen. Um einen guten Blogeintrag zu schreiben, kannst du so vorgehen:

1. Überlege, **für wen** du den Eintrag schreibst. Was weiß dein Publikum schon zu dem Thema? Wie alt sind die Interessierten? Usw.
2. Überlege dir einen **Titel**, der das Interesse am Thema weckt.
3. Denke dir einen **guten Anfang** aus, der Lust macht, weiterzulesen.
4. Sprich das Publikum an und stelle so einen **persönlichen Bezug** her, z. B. *Hi everybody. It's ...* .
5. Schreibe auch über **Gefühle** und benutze Emojis.

Sei dir bewusst, dass alles, was du im Internet veröffentlichst, von vielen Leuten gelesen wird und dass du es nicht zurücknehmen kannst. ► S14 Das Internet nutzen, S16 Fotos, Filme und Texte richtig verwenden

D 190 Support

G Eine Zusammenfassung schreiben

Wenn du eine Zusammenfassung von einem Text schreiben sollst, lies dir den Text zuerst ganz durch. Lies ihn dann ein zweites Mal Abschnitt für Abschnitt und mache dir Notizen zu den wichtigsten Informationen.

Schreibe nun mithilfe der Stichwörter eine Zusammenfassung.

1. Beginne mit der **Einleitung**. Nenne den Titel, den Autor / die Autorin, die Textsorte, woher der Text kommt und das Thema.
   ... wrote the text "..." on .... | The text/article/story is about .... .
2. Fasse den Text jetzt Abschnitt für Abschnitt in deinen **eigenen Worten** zusammen. Schreibe in der Gegenwart (*simple present*) und verbinde die Sätze mit Bindewörtern (*and*, *but*, *or* usw.).
   First/Second/Third ... | Then/After that ... | Finally/Last ...
3. Schreibe einen Abschlusssatz.
   To sum up I can say .... | In general the article explains .... .

Die Zusammenfassung sollte grob nur ein Drittel der Länge des Ausgangstexts haben. Sie kann auch kürzer sein.

D 191 Support

H Eine Textnachricht schreiben

Textnachrichten sind sehr kurze Texte mit oft unvollständigen Sätzen. Emojis und Abkürzungen werden verwendet, um Gefühle oder Informationen auszudrücken.

Beispiele für Abkürzungen:

brb = be right back	lol = laughing out loud	ttys = talk to you soon
btw = by the way	nbd = no big deal	u = you
cu = see you	pm = personal message	ur = your
idk = I don't know	tbc = to be continued	XOXO = hugs and kisses
irl = in real life	thx = thanks	2nite = tonight
lmk = let me know	tmi = too much information	4 = for

Achte bei Textnachrichten darauf, wem du sie schickst. Emojis und Abkürzungen sind nicht in jeder Situation angemessen.

D 170
Support

I Einen Kommentar schreiben

In einem Kommentar (*comment*) schreibst du deine **Meinung** zu einem vorgegebenen Thema.

1. Lies dir das Thema durch. Entscheide dich für eine Seite (dafür/dagegen). Sammle dann zuerst **Argumente**.
2. Ein gutes Argument besteht aus mindestens drei großen „B": **Behauptung**, **Begründung**, **B**eispiel. Anschauliche Beispiele und Fakten unterstützen deine Begründungen zusätzlich.
3. Nummeriere die Ideen. Beginne mit dem schwächsten Argument und ende mit dem stärksten. So wird dein Kommentar überzeugend.
4. Schreibe eine **Einleitung** und formuliere deine Meinung.
5. Schreibe jetzt den **Hauptteil**: Schreibe zwei bis drei Argumente mit Beispielen in deiner vorher festgelegten Reihenfolge. Jedes Argument mit Beispielen steht in einem eigenen **Absatz**. So wird es übersichtlicher.
6. Verwende Strukturwörter.
7. Schreibe nun einen **Schluss**.
8. Überprüfe deinen Entwurf und bitte jemanden um Feedback.

Robots will become more and more important. | I think it's true that .... | In my opinion .... | I don't think .... | I think there won't be ....

Firstly ... | Secondly ... | The next point is ... | Additionally ... | Lastly ...
To sum up ... | As a result ...

D 192
Support

J Eine Rezension schreiben

In einer Rezension (*review*) schreibst du deine Meinung z.B. zu einem Buch oder Film. Manchmal gehört auch eine Bewertung dazu ★★★☆☆. Die Sterne zeigen auf den ersten Blick, wie gut der Film oder das Buch bewertet wurde.

1. Sammle zuerst Ideen (Thema, Personen, Spannung, Wirkung auf dich usw.).
2. Schreibe deinen Text. Folge dabei dieser Struktur: Beginne mit der **Einleitung**: Titel, Autor/Autorin/Regisseur/Regisseurin, Erscheinungsjahr und Art des Buchs/Films (*comedy, romance, fantasy, action* usw.).
3. Schreibe dann kurz, worum es in dem Buch/Film geht.
4. Schreibe nun **deine Meinung** und vergib Sterne.
5. Gib zum Schluss eine **Empfehlung** dafür oder dagegen.
6. Schreibe in der Gegenwart (*simple present*) und verwende Adjektive (*good, fantastic, boring, surprising* usw.).

The title of the book/film is .... | ... wrote it/made it in the year .... | It's a romance/action story/fantasy film/comedy/....
The topic of the film/book is .... | The book/film is about .... | In my opinion .... | I think .... | ... is interesting/boring/funny/scary because .... | I liked .... | I really recommend this book/film. | Everybody should read this book/watch this film .... | The film is not worth watching./The book is a waste of time.

D 193 Support

K Einen Steckbrief schreiben

Ein Steckbrief enthält die wichtigsten Informationen zu einer Person, einem Tier oder einer Pflanze: z. B. Name, Farbe, was er/sie/es mag usw.

1. Schreibe **Stichwörter** (keine ganzen Sätze).
2. Schreibe jede neue Kategorie in eine neue Zeile.
3. Male ein Bild der Person/des Tiers/der Pflanze neben die Informationen oder klebe ein Foto auf. ► S16 Fotos, Filme und Texte richtig verwenden

D 194 Support

L Ein Poster gestalten

Für ein Poster brauchst du ein großes Blatt Papier, verschiedenfarbige Stifte, einen Klebestift, Bilder und eine Schere.

1. Wähle eine **Überschrift**, die gut zum Thema des Posters passt. Diese schreibst du am besten oben mittig auf dein Blatt (z. B. *School*).
2. Formuliere **kurze Texte** mit eigenen Überschriften, die zum Thema deines Posters passen (z. B. *Rules*, *Cafeteria*). Am besten schreibst du deine Texte erst auf ein anderes Blatt und überträgst sie später gut leserlich auf dein Poster.
3. Wähle passende **Bilder** aus. Sie sollten so groß sein, dass man sie auch aus etwas Entfernung gut sehen kann. Schneide sie aus und ordne sie zusammen mit deinen Texten auf dem Poster an, ehe du sie festklebst. Zu den Bildern kannst du kurze Bildunterschriften ergänzen, die das Bild beschreiben. ► S16 Fotos, Filme und Texte richtig verwenden

D 195 Support

M Einen Flyer gestalten

1. Ein Flyer sollte gut lesbar sein und alle wichtigen Informationen enthalten: *Who? Where? When? What? Why?*
2. Ordnet die Informationen in einer sinnvollen Reihenfolge an. Ihr könnt mit Zwischenüberschriften, Aufzählungen oder Nummerierungen arbeiten. So wird es übersichtlicher.
3. Fügt Bilder oder Fotos ein, um den Flyer ansprechender zu machen.
4. Wählt interessante Überschriften oder fügt aussagekräftige Slogans ein.

S8 Feedback geben und bekommen

D 196 Support

Giving and asking for feedback

Feedback bedeutet, Tipps und Rückmeldung z. B. zu einer Präsentation, einem Text, einem Rollenspiel oder einem Poster zu geben oder zu bekommen. Feedback von anderen ist wichtig und kann dabei helfen, dass ihr euch verbessert.

I really like the photos …

Feedback geben

1. Beginne immer mit den Dingen, die du **gut** oder **interessant** fandest.
2. **Begründe** deine Aussagen.
3. Wenn dir etwas nicht gefallen hat, kannst du vorsichtig Kritik üben.
   - Sage immer genau, was du meinst. Sage z. B. nicht einfach nur *I didn't like the presentation*.
   - Verbinde Kritik immer mit einem **Verbesserungsvorschlag**.
4. Sei höflich und beziehe dich auf den Inhalt und nicht auf die Person selbst.

I really liked … because … . | … was/were really good because … . | The information about … was very … . | Your examples were … .
The … part isn't/wasn't so good … . | In the first part there was too much/not enough information about … . | The photo on the left/right is too small/not so interesting/… . | The example in the third sentence is not so good. |
Next time you could … . | Sometimes I find … helpful.

Du kannst dir z. B. während einer Präsentation notieren, was dir gut/nicht so gut gefallen hat.

Feedback for a presentation	☺	😐	☹
The presentation was … easy to understand.	always	sometimes	not
The information was … .	interesting	OK	not so interesting
The examples were … .	good	OK	not so good
The photos were … .	great	OK	not so good
The presentation was … loud enough.	always	sometimes	not
You … looked at the class.	always	sometimes	never
…			

Feedback bekommen

1. Höre aufmerksam zu und lass die Person ausreden.
2. Frage nach, wenn du etwas nicht verstanden hast.
3. Bleibe freundlich, auch wenn du das Feedback nicht ganz nachvollziehen kannst.

Thank you. | I understand that. | That's a good idea.
Sorry, I didn't understand the last sentence/word/… . Can you say that again, please? | Can you give me an example?
Thank you. I'll think about it.

S9 Informationen in eine andere Sprache übertragen

V 3
How to

Mediation

Manchmal musst du Informationen für eine Person, die kein Englisch kann, auf Deutsch übermitteln. Oder du musst für jemanden etwas vom Deutschen ins Englische übertragen.

Allgemeine Tipps

Es handelt sich hier **nicht** um eine Übersetzungsaufgabe. Es ist viel wichtiger, den **Sinn wiederzugeben**. Das kannst du mit deinen **eigenen Worten** machen. Wenn du bestimmte Wörter nicht weißt, kannst du sie umschreiben (*paraphrasing*).

Informationen aus Texten übermitteln

1. Um was für einen Text handelt es sich? Gibt es eine **Überschrift** oder **Fotos**, die dir helfen kann/können?
2. Lies dir die **Aufgabenstellung** durch. **Wem** sollst du helfen? **Welche Fragen** sollst du beantworten?
3. Lies den Text.

Tipps für englische Texte:

4. Du musst nicht jedes Wort verstehen, um die gesuchten Informationen herauszufinden. Suche im Text gezielt nach den Antworten zu den Fragen. Du kannst dabei nach bestimmten Wörtern suchen, z. B. bei der Frage: „Welche Hobbys werden angeboten?". Suche im Text nach den englischen Wörtern für Hobbys, z. B. *football*, *cinema* … So kommst du schneller zur richtigen Textstelle.

Tipps für deutsche Texte:

5. Suche im Text nach den Antworten und übertrage sie mit deinen eigenen Worten ins Englische.
6. Verwende kurze, einfache Sätze.
7. Umschreibe Wörter, die du nicht weißt, z. B. Koch oder Köchin → *He/She works in a kitchen.*

In Gesprächen vermitteln

1. Höre gut zu und schaue die Person, die spricht, an.
2. Frage nach, wenn du etwas nicht verstanden hast.
3. Wende dich dann der zweiten Person zu und fasse mit deinen eigenen Worten zusammen, was die erste Person gesagt hat.
4. Übermittle dann das, was die zweite Person antwortet usw.
5. Verändere die Pronomen.
   Lucy **I** like chocolate.
   Tom Sie sagt, dass **sie** Schokolade mag.
6. Umschreibe Wörter oder Sätze, die du nicht weißt.
   Emma Meine Mutter arbeitet als **Erzieherin**.
   You Her mum **works with young kids**.

S10 Filme verstehen

V 6
How to

Understanding films

Es gibt unterschiedliche englische Filme, die dir im Unterricht und im Alltag begegnen können: Filme im Internet, im Fernsehen usw. Auf den *Viewing*-Seiten übst du den Umgang damit.

Vor dem Ansehen

1. Finde heraus, was für ein Film es ist: Doku, Spielfilm usw.
2. Was könnte die Handlung sein: Sieh dir **Fotos**, **Titel**, **Überschriften** usw. an.
3. Weißt du schon etwas zu diesem Thema?

Während des Ansehens

Du kannst dir Notizen machen, während du den Film ansiehst. Achte darauf, dass sie kurz sind.

Erstes Ansehen

1. Es ist wichtig, dass du den Inhalt des Films verstehst. Beantworte die **W-Fragen**:
   Who? Where? When? What?
2. Sieh dir die **Aufgaben** an. Löse die Aufgaben, bei denen du die Antwort schon sicher weißt. Die Antworten im Film sind in der gleichen Reihenfolge wie in den Aufgaben.

Zweites Ansehen

Konzentriere dich auf das, was in den restlichen Aufgaben von dir verlangt wird. Wichtig hierfür kann Folgendes sein:

1. Wie verhalten sich die Personen?
   Achte vor allem auf Sprache, Mimik und Gestik.
2. Wie werden Handlungsort und -zeit (*setting*) dargestellt?
   Achte auf Landschaften, Gebäude und Innenräume, Kleidung, Frisuren und Gegenstände.
3. Wie wird eine bestimmte Atmosphäre (*atmosphere*) geschaffen?
   Achte auf Licht, Farben, Musik, Geräusche.
4. Wie unterstützt die Musik (*music*) den Inhalt des Films?
   Beachte, wann welche Musik ertönt und wann sie wechselt.
5. Wie helfen bestimmte Kameraeinstellungen (*shots*), den Inhalt deutlicher darzustellen?
   Achte z. B. auf Nahaufnahmen (*close-ups*).
6. Wie wird Spannung (*suspense*) erzeugt?
   Achte auf Vorandeutungen, Musik, Licht, Geräusche sowie Gestik und Mimik.

Nach dem Ansehen

Wie hat dir der Film gefallen? Würdest du ihn weiterempfehlen?

! Bei vielen Filmen kann man die deutschen oder englischen Untertitel einschalten. Probiere es einmal aus! Schaue im Alltag Filme, die du bereits auf Deutsch kennst, ein zweites Mal auf Englisch an.

S11 Einen kurzen Film drehen

Making a short film

Eigene Filme zu drehen, ist eine Herausforderung, weil man auf viele Dinge achten muss. Die folgenden Tipps können euch helfen, einen guten Film zu drehen.

1. **Sammelt Ideen** zum Thema.
2. Wählt zwei bis drei Dinge aus, die im Film vorkommen sollen.
3. **Plant euren Film.**
   - Entscheidet, wer spricht und wer filmt.
   - Schreibt den Text und übt ihn ein.
   - Überlegt euch, wo ihr die Kamera platziert. Es ist leichter, sie an einem bestimmten Ort aufzustellen, als mit ihr herumzugehen.
4. **Fragt nach**, ob ihr an dem Ort drehen dürft. Alle Personen, die im Film vorkommen, müssen ihr Einverständnis geben. ► S16 Fotos, Filme und Texte richtig verwenden
5. Filmt eine Szene nach der anderen. Schaut jede Szene nach dem Aufnehmen genau an: Schärfe | Licht | Verwacklung | Kontrast | Lautstärke | Störgeräusche | Aussprache
   Wenn etwas nicht okay ist, dreht die Szene noch einmal.
6. Wenn ihr mehrere Filmsequenzen macht, könnt ihr diese einzeln abspielen oder mit einer App schneiden und zusammenfügen.

S12 Ein kurzes Audio aufnehmen

Making a short audio

Manchmal könnt ihr Informationen oder Geschichten auch als kurzes Audio für andere aufnehmen. Die Personen, die es nutzen, können den Text nur hören. Sie sind darauf angewiesen, dass der Hörtext gut verständlich ist.

1. Infotext: Beginnt mit der Begrüßung/Vorstellung und nennt das Thema. Verwendet gut strukturierte, einfache Sätze.
2. Geschichte: Um Spannung zu erzeugen, könnt ihr bestimmte Stellen lauter oder leiser lesen. Versucht, Gefühle oder Stimmungen auszudrücken (z. B. schluchzen, vor Schreck stottern usw.). Ihr könnt auch Geräusche machen.
3. Der Text kann von einer oder von mehreren Personen gesprochen werden.
4. Kontrolliert den Text vor der Aufnahme und übt die Aussprache.
5. Überprüft eure Aufnahme und wiederholt sie, wenn nötig.
6. Ihr könnt die Sequenzen mit einer App schneiden.

Hello. | Welcome to .... | I'm .... | We're .... | Do you want to know more about ...? | Did you know that ...? | First .... | Then .... | The next point .... | I also find ... interesting. | Lastly .... | The last point is ....

S13 Wörter nachschlagen

V 38
How to

Looking up words

Wenn du ein Wort nicht kennst, kannst du es in einem Wörterbuch nachschlagen. Hier lernst du, was du dabei beachten musst.

A Eintrag in einem Wörterbuch

Hier findest du das Stichwort *(headword)*. Die Stichwörter sind alphabetisch geordnet.

Diese Ziffern zeigen an, dass ein Stichwort unterschiedliche Bedeutungen hat.

Einem Stichwort sind häufig Redewendungen und typische *phrases* zugeordnet.

Unregelmäßige Formen stehen oft in Klammern.

show [ʃəʊ, AM ʃoʊ] **I.** *n* (1) *(showing)* Demonstration *f geh;* ~ **of solidarity** Solidaritätsbekundung *f geh* (2) *no pl (display, effect)* Schau *f;* **just for** ~ nur der Schau wegen (3) *(exhibition, event)* Schau *f,* Ausstellung *f;* **slide** ~ Diavortrag *m;* ■ **to be on** ~ ausgestellt sein (4) *(entertainment)* Show *f; (on TV a.)* Unterhaltungssendung *f; (at a theatre)* Vorstellung *f* ► PHRASES: **let's get this** ~ **on the road** *(fam)* lasst uns die Sache [endlich] in Angriff nehmen; **the** ~ **must go on** *(saying)* die Show muss weitergehen **II.** *vt* <showed, shown *or* showed> (1) *(display, project, express) film* zeigen; *(exhibit)* ausstellen; *(perform)* vorführen; *(produce) passport* vorzeigen; **to** ~ **sb respect** jdm Respekt erweisen (2) *(expose)* sehen lassen; ***this carpet*** **~s *all the dirt*** bei dem Teppich kann man jedes bisschen Schmutz sehen (3) *(reveal)* zeigen; ***he started to*** ~ ***his age*** man konnte ihm langsam sein Alter sehen; **to** ~ **common sense** gesunden Menschenverstand beweisen (4) *(explain)*

Die Lautschrift zeigt dir, wie das Wort ausgesprochen und betont wird.

Die kursiv gedruckten Hinweise helfen dir, die für deinen Text passende Bedeutung zu finden.

Die römischen Ziffern machen deutlich, dass ein Stichwort unterschiedlichen Wortarten angehört.

Beachte bei der Arbeit mit einem Wörterbuch folgende Punkte:

- Du findest meist mehrere Bedeutungen für ein Wort. Achte also auf den Zusammenhang, wenn du ein Wort nachschlägst:
  Take the second street on the right (rechts). *That's the right* (richtig) *way to the station.*
- Achte darauf, welche Wortart du suchst – Nomen, Verb, Adjektiv, ...?
- Lies auch immer die besonderen Ausdrücke, denn das Wort könnte Teil einer Redewendung sein: *to take place* bedeutet nicht 'Platz nehmen'; es bedeutet 'stattfinden'!

B Eintrag in einem Online-Wörterbuch

Du kannst unbekannte Wörter auch in einem Online-Wörterbuch nachschlagen. Lies immer den ganzen Eintrag und suche nach der passenden Bedeutung. Es passt nicht immer die erste Übersetzung.

Hier findest du Beispielsätze, in denen das Wort vorkommt.

Hier siehst du, welche Sprache eingestellt ist.

Hier siehst du, wie das Wort ausgesprochen wird. Zuerst die Aussprache im britischen Englisch, dann im amerikanischen Englisch.

Hier siehst du die Wortart des gesuchten Wortes: Substantiv, Verb, Adjektiv, Adverb usw.

Hier stehen die Übersetzungen.

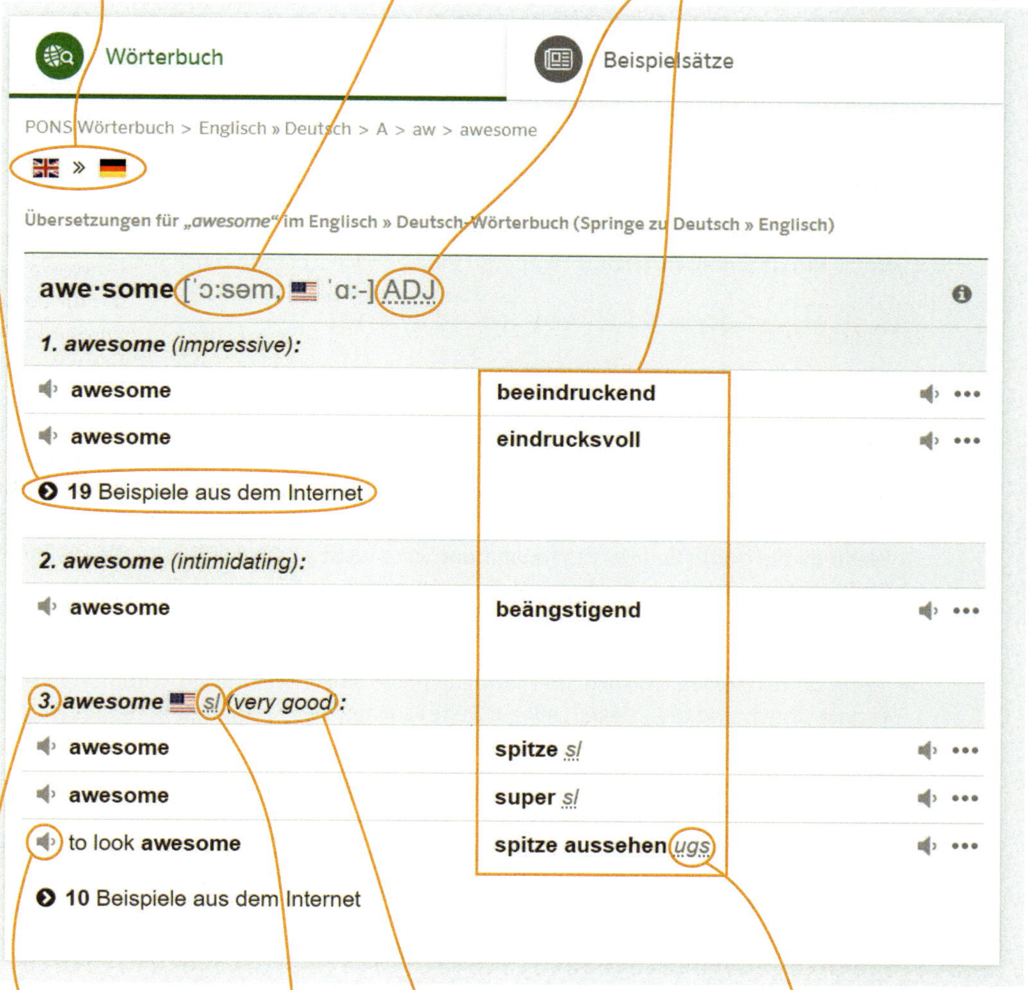

Hier kannst du die Aussprache anhören.

Slang

Hier wird die Bedeutung des Wortes auf Englisch beschrieben.

umgangssprachlich

Die Zahlen zeigen an, dass dieses Wort drei unterschiedliche Bedeutungen hat. Wähle sorgfältig aus, welche Bedeutung die richtige für dich ist.

S14 Das Internet nutzen

Using the internet

Wenn du im Internet nach Informationen suchst, musst du gezielt vorgehen. Mithilfe der folgenden Schritte kannst du passende Inhalte finden.

Suchmaschinen richtig nutzen

1. Überlege dir möglichst **genau, was du wissen möchtest.**
2. Gib möglichst genaue Suchbegriffe ein, z. B. *ticket boat tour Greenwich*. Mache den Gegentest: Welche Informationen erhältst du, wenn du nur nach *ticket boat tour* suchst?
3. Du kannst auch die ganze Frage auf Englisch eingeben.
4. Wenn du im Suchfeld zusätzlich *explained for kids* eingibst, kommst du automatisch auf weniger komplizierte Seiten.
5. Nutze ein (Online-)Wörterbuch, wenn du Wörter nachschlagen möchtest.

Inhalte aus dem Internet übernehmen

1. Schau dir die Adresse der Websites in der Suchergebnisliste an: Wie glaubwürdig ist die Website? Handelt es sich z. B. um einen Lexikon-Eintrag, die Website einer Tageszeitung oder eines bekannten Radio- oder Fernsehsenders, wurden die Inhalte überprüft. In Foren oder sozialen Netzwerken handelt es sich eher um persönliche Meinungen, die nicht unbedingt richtig sein müssen.
2. Rufe dann zwei bis drei Seiten auf und **vergleiche die Informationen**. Stimmen sie überein?
3. Wenn du die gesuchte Information auf der Seite nicht gleich findest, kannst du dort oft einen Suchbegriff eingeben.
4. Schreibe dir passende Informationen auf. Notiere dir immer den Link zur Seite und das Datum dazu.
5. Wenn du Textstellen wörtlich übernimmst, musst du sie als **Zitat** (in Anführungszeichen) kennzeichnen und die Quelle (Link zur Seite) sowie das Abfragedatum nennen.
   ► S16 Fotos, Filme und Texte richtig verwenden

Sicherheit im Internet

1. Sei extrem **vorsichtig** mit der Weitergabe deiner persönlichen Daten (Name, Geburtsdatum, Adresse usw.) im Internet. Die Daten können geklaut und für kriminelle Zwecke missbraucht werden.
2. Wenn du soziale Medien nutzt, **beschränke den Zugriff** (z. B. nur Freundinnen und Freunde und Familie haben Zugriff). Poste keine unangemessenen Kommentare oder Fotos. Du darfst auch keine Fotos von anderen ohne deren Einverständnis veröffentlichen. ► S16 Fotos, Filme und Texte richtig verwenden
3. Nicht jede Internetseite ist vertrauenswürdig. Prüfe deshalb auf anderen Seiten oder z. B. in einem Lexikon, ob die Information stimmt und noch aktuell ist.

S15 Gute Fotos machen

Taking good photos

Wenn du Texte ansprechend gestalten möchtest, benötigst du manchmal Fotos. Wenn du sie selbst machst, beachte die folgenden Dinge.

1. Überlege, was auf dem Foto zu sehen sein soll. Brauchst du ein Hoch- oder Querformat?
2. Um ein gutes, nicht verwackeltes Foto zu erhalten, nimm deine Oberarme eng an deinen Körper oder lehne dich gegen eine Wand.
3. Wähle eine **interessante Perspektive**.

A B C

4. Fotografiere nicht gegen das Licht.
5. Achte darauf, dass im Hintergrund nichts zu sehen ist, das dir oder anderen unangenehm sein oder das Gesamtbild stören könnte.
6. Wenn du **Einzelheiten** fotografieren möchtest, nutze die **Zoomfunktion** oder mache ein paar Schritte nach vorne. Einzelheiten sind oft interessanter als das ganze Bild.

D E F

7. Auf Smartphones, Kameras und PCs/Tablets gibt es normalerweise die Möglichkeit, Fotos zu bearbeiten. D.h., du kannst sie z.B. zurechtschneiden oder die Helligkeit verändern.
8. Wenn du Personen fotografieren möchtest, musst du vorher um Erlaubnis fragen.

► S16 Fotos, Filme und Texte richtig verwenden

S16 Fotos, Filme und Texte richtig verwenden

D 197 Support

How to use photos, films and texts

Im Internet kann man tolle Sachen finden. Weißt du, wann und wie du diese Dinge verwenden darfst? Das ist wichtig, damit du nicht gegen die Rechte von anderen verstößt.

Inhalte aus Büchern oder aus dem Internet übernehmen

1. Wenn du im Unterricht einen Text oder ein Foto aus dem Internet verwenden willst, musst du angeben, von wem der Text oder das Foto ist. Außerhalb des Unterrichts darfst du die Inhalte aber **niemals ohne das Einverständnis veröffentlichen**, z. B. in der Schulzeitung, in Textnachrichten oder im Internet.
2. Wenn du Textstellen wörtlich übernimmst, musst du sie als **Zitat** (in Anführungszeichen) kennzeichnen und die Quelle (Link zur Seite) sowie das Abfragedatum nennen.

Personen filmen oder fotografieren

1. Wenn du **Personen fotografieren** möchtest, musst du vorher fragen, ob es in Ordnung ist, sie zu fotografieren. Sag ihnen auch, wofür du das Bild brauchst. Nur wenn sie einverstanden sind, darfst du das Foto auch wirklich verwenden. Am besten ist eine **schriftliche Einverständniserklärung**. Handelt es sich dabei um Minderjährige, müssen auch deren Eltern zustimmen.
2. Wenn du **Personen filmen** möchtest, musst du diese vorher um Erlaubnis bitten, am besten schriftlich. Handelt es sich dabei um Minderjährige, müssen auch deren Eltern zustimmen. Bei der **Einverständniserklärung** muss auch angegeben werden, wo der Film gezeigt oder veröffentlicht werden soll.
3. Wenn du z. B. in deiner Schule filmen möchtest, musst du vorher um Erlaubnis fragen.

S17 Vokabeln lernen

V 39
How to

Learning vocabulary

Es gibt unterschiedliche Möglichkeiten, Vokabeln zu lernen und deinen Wortschatz zu erweitern. Jeder Mensch lernt ein bisschen anders. Finde heraus, wie du dir Vokabeln am besten einprägen kannst.

A Vokabeln schreiben

Wenn du neue Vokabeln schreibst, prägst du sie dir so schon ein.

1. Lege ein Vokabelheft, einen Vokabelordner oder einen Vokabelkasten mit Kärtchen an. Schreibe die Lernwörter mit deutscher Übersetzung und Beispielsatz (falls vorhanden) aus dem Vokabelanhang ab und sprich sie dabei vor dich hin.
2. Markiere schwierige Stellen.
3. Es ist einfacher Wörter zu lernen, die zusammengehören. Ordne sie z. B. in einer Mindmap an oder gestalte eine *word bank* mit Fotos oder Zeichnungen. Du kannst Wörter aus den Units oder eigene Wörter, die für dich wichtig sind, so sammeln.
4. Schreibe Gegensatzpaare auf, z. B. *good* ↔ *bad*; *loud* ↔ *quiet*.
   Schreibe Wörter zusammen auf, die zu einer Wortfamilie gehören: Kennst du z. B. schon das Wort *sun*, dann weißt du auch, was *sunny* bedeutet. Weitere Beispiele: *work* → *worker*; *friend* → *friendly*
   Das geht auch in digitaler Form auf dem Handy, Tablet oder PC. Aber manchmal ist es besser, die Wörter tatsächlich per Hand und Stift auf Papier zu schreiben.

B Vokabeln anhören und aufnehmen

Wenn du gut durch Zuhören lernst, kannst du die Lernwörter auch aufnehmen. Allerdings solltest du dir mit der Aussprache sicher sein.

1. Nimm zuerst das englische Wort auf.
2. Lass eine Pause und nimm dann die deutsche Übersetzung auf.
3. Höre dir die aufgenommenen Wörter ein paarmal an und sprich mit.
4. Sage in der Pause nach den englischen Wörtern die deutsche Übersetzung.

C Vokabeln durch Bewegung lernen

1. Vokabeln lernen mit Bewegung kann sehr effektiv sein. Du bringst so nicht nur deinen Körper und dein Gehirn in Schwung, sondern kannst dir die Vokabeln auch langfristig besser merken. Laufe z. B. mit deinem Vokabelheft im Zimmer herum.
2. Manche Wörter kann man mit Gesichtsausdrücken oder Bewegungen darstellen.
3. Die Aussprache von Wörtern prägt sich besser ein, wenn du dazu marschierst und laut zum Takt sprichst.

! Weniger ist mehr! Lerne Vokabeln immer in kleinen Portionen von 10 bis 15 Wörtern. Lerne lieber nur 5 bis 10 Minuten am Tag, aber dafür regelmäßig.

S18 Methoden

Methods

Freeze frame

1. Entscheidet, welche Szene oder Person ihr darstellen wollt. Verteilt die Rollen.
2. Probiert verschiedene Standbilder aus und entscheidet euch dann für eines. Denkt daran: Ihr müsst euer Standbild eine Minute lang durchhalten. Keiner darf sich bewegen oder etwas sagen.
3. Präsentiert der Klasse euer Standbild. Die anderen beschreiben, was sie sehen.

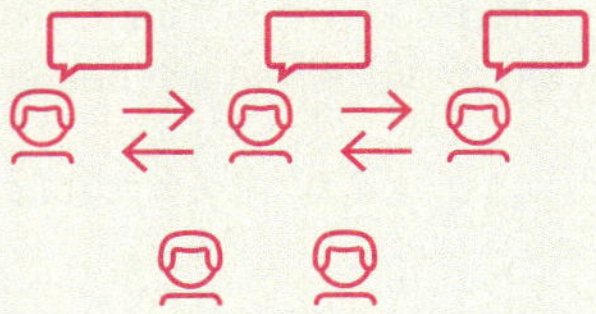

Peer correction

1. Bearbeite die Aufgabe zunächst allein.
2. Tausche deine Lösungen mit einer anderen Person. Kontrolliert eure Lösungen gegenseitig.
3. Vergleicht eure Lösungen.

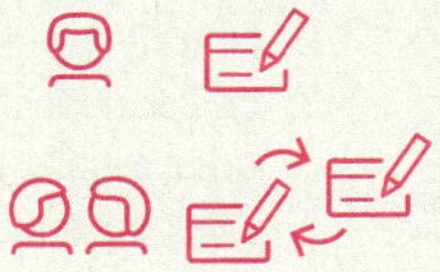

Read and look up

1. Schaue auf deinen Text und präge dir die erste Zeile oder den ersten Satz ein. Schaue hoch und sprich deine Zeile / deinen Satz leise vor dich hin. Nimm dir die nächste Zeile / den nächsten Satz vor.
2. Übt nun zu zweit. Sprich deinen Text Zeile für Zeile oder Satz für Satz. Dazwischen schaust du immer wieder nach unten auf deinen Text.
3. Wiederhole alles, bis es gut klappt.

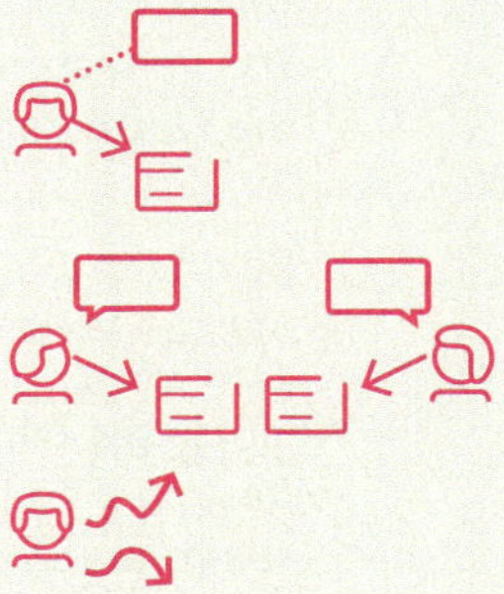

Think-pair-share

1. Schreibe deine Ideen, Gedanken oder Lösungen auf.
2. Tauscht euch aus und besprecht eure Notizen.
3. Präsentiert euer Ergebnis anderen Paaren oder der gesamten Klasse.

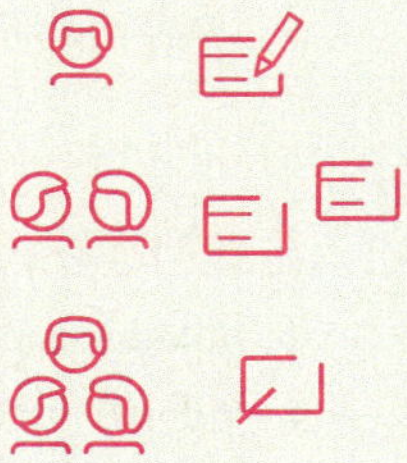

Double circle

1. Teilt euch in zwei Gruppen A und B auf. Gruppe A bildet den inneren Kreis. Gruppe B bildet den äußeren Kreis. Steht dabei so, dass ihr euch anseht.
2. Wenn ein Signal ertönt, sprecht ihr mit der Person, die euch gegenübersteht.
3. Beim nächsten Signal rückt der innere Kreis zwei Plätze weiter nach rechts. Wiederholt den Vorgang.

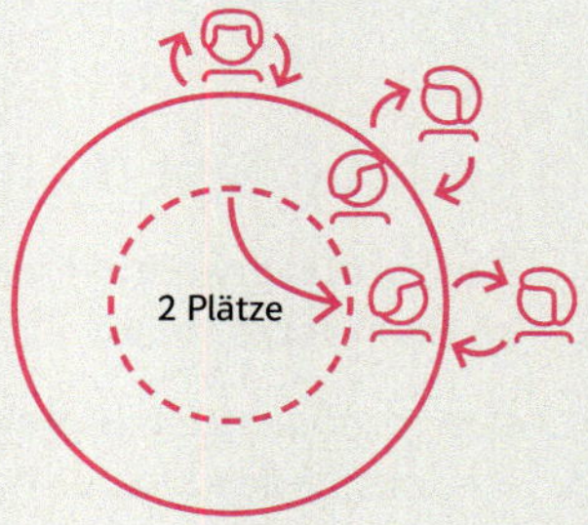

Gallery walk

1. Hängt nach eurer Gruppenarbeit euer Produkt gut sichtbar im Klassenzimmer auf.
2. Eine Expertin oder ein Experte aus eurer Gruppe bleibt bei eurem Produkt stehen und erklärt es den anderen. Die anderen gehen herum. Nach jedem Durchgang wechselt die Expertin oder der Experte.
3. Seht euch die Produkte der anderen an und bewertet sie.
4. Wertet im Anschluss eure Ergebnisse in der Klasse aus.

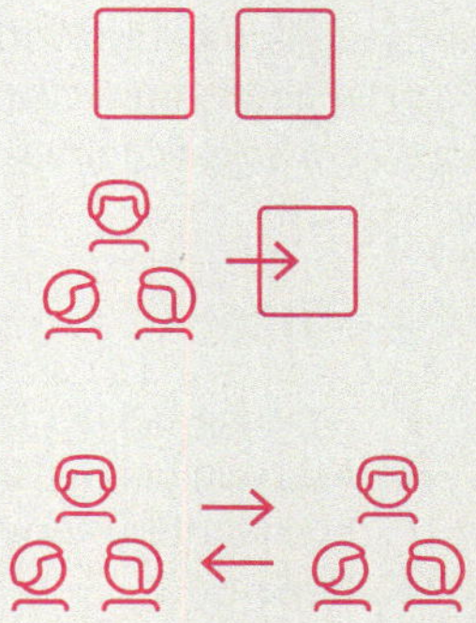

Milling around

1. Bearbeite die Aufgabe zunächst allein.
2. Auf ein Zeichen von eurer Lehrkraft steht ihr auf und geht durch den Raum. Vergesst nicht, die Aufgabe und einen Stift mitzunehmen.
3. Wenn ein Signal ertönt, bleibt ihr stehen. Besprecht die Aufgabe mit der Person, die euch am nächsten steht.
4. Beim nächsten Signal trennt ihr euch und geht weiter durch den Raum. Wiederholt den Vorgang.

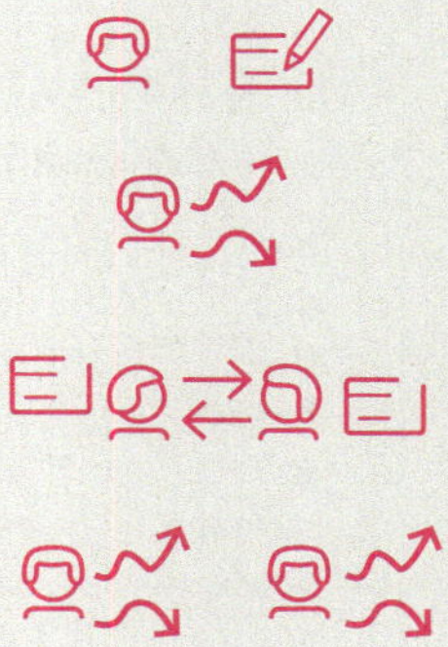

Round robin

1. Bildet Gruppen und setzt euch in einen Kreis.
2. Jedes Gruppenmitglied überlegt sich kurz einen Satz, der seine persönliche Meinung zum Thema ausdrückt.
3. Wenn alle bereit sind, sagen die Gruppenmitglieder der Reihe nach ihre Meinung.
4. Die anderen Gruppenmitglieder dürfen die Sätze nicht kommentieren.

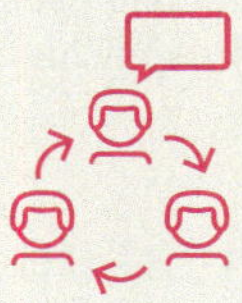

V 39
How to

Vocabulary

So arbeitest du mit dem *Vocabulary*:

Das *Vocabulary* enthält alle neuen Wörter und Wendungen. Sie stehen in der Reihenfolge, wie sie im Buch vorkommen.

Das *Vocabulary* ist in drei Spalten aufgeteilt:
- Links findest du das englische Wort aus der Unit. Die Lautschrift in eckigen Klammern zeigt dir, wie das Wort ausgesprochen wird.
- In der mittleren Spalte steht die deutsche Übersetzung.
- Rechts findest du Beispielsätze, Hinweise und Tipps, die dir beim Lernen helfen.

Die blau gedruckten Wörter musst du lernen.
Die grün gedruckten Wörter kannst du lernen, musst du aber nicht.
Tipps zum Vokabellernen findest du auf S.199 und im Erklärvideo dazu.

Beachte:

- ✎ Achtung bei der Schreibung!
- 👄 Achtung bei der Aussprache!
- ! Ausnahmen; Verwechslungsgefahr
- ↔ Gegensatz
- → ist verwandt mit

Word bank

Auf den *word bank*-Seiten ab S.232 kannst du gezielt Wörter zu einem bestimmten Thema nachschlagen und üben. Du kannst die *word banks* auch herunterladen und selber Wörter einfügen.

Englische Laute

Mitlaute (Konsonanten)

[b]	**b**ed	[k]	**c**an, mil**k**	[t]	**t**en
[d]	**d**ay	[l]	**l**etter	[tʃ]	**ch**air
[ð]	**th**e	[m]	**m**an	[v]	**v**ideo
[f]	**f**amily	[n]	**n**o	[w]	**w**e, **o**ne
[g]	**g**o	[p]	**p**icture	[z]	ea**s**y
[ŋ]	morni**ng**	[r]	**r**ed	[ʒ]	revi**s**ion
[h]	**h**ouse	[s]	**s**ix	[dʒ]	pa**g**e
[j]	**y**ou	[ʃ]	**sh**e	[θ]	**th**ank you

Selbstlaute (Vokale)

[ɑː]	c**ar**	[i]	happ**y**
[æ]	**a**pple	[iː]	t**ea**cher
[e]	p**e**n	[ɒ]	d**o**g
[ə]	**a**gain	[ɔː]	b**a**ll
[ɜː]	g**ir**l	[ʊ]	b**oo**k
[ʌ]	b**u**t	[u]	Jan**u**ary
[ɪ]	**i**t	[uː]	t**oo**, tw**o**

Doppellaute

[aɪ]	**I**, m**y**
[aʊ]	n**ow**, m**ou**se
[eɪ]	n**a**me, th**ey**
[eə]	th**ere**, p**air**
[ɪə]	h**ere**, id**ea**
[əʊ]	hell**o**
[ɔɪ]	b**oy**
[ʊə]	s**ure**

[ː] der vorangehende Laut ist lang, z.B. *you* [juː]
[‿] der Bindebogen zeigt, dass zwei Wörter in der Aussprache verbunden werden
[ˈ] die folgende Silbe trägt den Hauptakzent
[ˌ] die folgende Silbe trägt den Nebenakzent

So nutzt du Wissen über andere Sprachen zum Lernen:

Jede Sprache funktioniert anders. Welche Sprachen sprichst du? Überlege dir, was in diesen Sprachen vielleicht gleich oder anders funktioniert als im Englischen.

Gibt es …
- Wörter, die ähnlich gesprochen werden (sinema, cinéma, cinema),
- andere Buchstaben (ä, ö, ü, oder ñ, ó),
- andere Zeiten (я пишу, ich schreibe gerade)
- …?

So erkennst du amerikanisches Englisch

In den USA sprechen die Menschen amerikanisches Englisch (AE). Bisher hast du in der Schule meist britisches Englisch (BE) gelernt. Hier sind die wichtigsten Unterschiede im Überblick.

1. Amerikanische Wörter

Hier findest du Wörter, die sich im amerikanischen Englisch vom britischen Englisch unterscheiden.

British English (BE)	American English (AE)	German
autumn	fall	der Herbst
car park	parking lot	der Parkplatz
flat	apartment	die Wohnung
floor	story	das Stockwerk
holidays	vacation	die Ferien
lift	elevator	der Aufzug
mum	mom	die Mama
pavement	sidewalk	der Gehweg; der Bürgersteig
shop	store	der Laden
shopping centre	shopping mall	das Einkaufszentrum
underground	subway	die U-Bahn
waste	garbage	der Abfall

2. Die amerikanische Schreibweise

Unterschiede in der Schreibweise zwischen britischem und amerikanischem Englisch folgen meist bestimmten Mustern.

British English (BE)	American English (AE)
cent**re**, theat**re**	cent**er**, theat**er**
col**our**, fav**our**ite	col**or**, fav**or**ite
to organ**ise**, organ**is**ation	to organ**ize**, organ**iz**ation
I trave**ll**ed to Berlin.	I trave**l**ed to Berlin.
Mr/Mrs	**Mr./Mrs.**

3. Die amerikanische Aussprache

Amerikanisches Englisch klingt etwas anders als britisches Englisch. Hier findest du einige Beispiele.

[r] Das [r] ist in Wörtern wie *Thursday* oder *form* immer hörbar.

[ju:], [u:] In manchen Wörtern wie *new* oder *Tuesday* kann man nur ein [u:] und kein [ju:] hören.

[a:], [æ] Das [a:] (BE) wird zu [æ] in Wörtern wie *can't* und *dance*.

[t], [d] Das [t] wird zu [d] in Wörtern wie *water* oder *party*.

4. Maßeinheiten in den USA

In den USA benutzen die Menschen besondere Maßeinheiten, die auch in den Texten vorkommen.
► V Units of length, p. 204 ► V Temperature units, p. 214

Zoom in – Welcome to the USA

p. 6	**baseball** ['beɪsbɔ:l]	der Baseball	
	favorite *(AE)* ['feɪvrɪt]	Lieblings-	AE: **favorite** BE: favourite
	track and field [ˌtræk‿ən 'fi:ld]	die Leichtathletik	I really like **track and field** activities.
p. 7	**recipe** ['resɪpi]	das Rezept	Achtung Aussprache!
	sustainable [sə'steɪnəbl]	zukunftsfähig; nachhaltig	You have to use **sustainable** materials today.
	fashion ['fæʃn]	die Mode	Leo loves **fashion**.
	hot dog ['hɒt ˌdɒg]	der Hotdog (*Würstchen im Brötchen*)	
p. 6	**currency** ['kʌrnsi]	die Währung	The **currency** in Germany is the euro.
	US [ˌju:'es]	US-amerikanisch	The currency is the **US** dollar.
p. 7	**state** [steɪt]	der Bundesstaat; der Staat; das Land; der Zustand	There are 50 **states** in the USA.

Unit 1 Arriving in the Northeast

Check in

Units of length

In den USA verwenden die Menschen „feet" (Fuß) und „inches" (Zoll) für kürzere Längenangaben, und „miles" (Meilen) für größere Distanzen. In Großbritannien findet man sowohl Angaben in „miles" als auch in „kilometres". Du kannst die Maßeinheiten selbst umrechnen oder online in eine Suchmaschine eingeben.
1 cm = 0.39 inches
1 km = 0.62 miles

1 inch	one inch	ein Zoll	**2,54 cm**
6 inches	six inches	sechs Zoll	**15,24 cm**
1 foot (= 12 inches)	one foot (= twelve inches)	ein Fuß (= zwölf Zoll)	**30,48 cm**
6 feet	six feet	sechs Fuß	**182,88 cm**
1 mile	one mile	eine Meile	**1,61 km**

p. 8	**foot** [fʊt]	der Fuß (*Längenmaß: 30,48 cm*)	The building is 400 **feet** high.
	spectacular [spek'tækjələ]	spektakulär	Achtung Aussprache!
p. 9	**Native American** [ˌneɪtɪv‿ə'merɪkən]	zu der amerikanischen Urbevölkerung gehörig; der amerikanische Ureinwohner / die amerikanische Ureinwohnerin	**Native Americans** live in the USA.
	tribe [traɪb]	der Stamm; der Volksstamm	We're from a Native American **tribe**.

European [ˌjʊərəˈpiːən]	europäisch; aus Europa; der Europäer / die Europäerin	**European** → Europe
settler [ˈsetlə]	der Siedler / die Siedlerin	Many **settlers** came from England.
immigration [ˌɪmɪˈɡreɪʃn]	die Einwanderung; die Immigration; die Zuwanderung; die Einreise	Achtung Aussprache!
center *(AE)* [ˈsentə]	das Zentrum; die Mitte; das Center	AE: **center** BE: centre
immigrant [ˈɪmɪɡrənt]	der Immigrant / die Immigrantin; der Einwanderer / die Einwanderin	**immigrant** → immigration
whale watching [ˈweɪl ˌwɒtʃɪŋ]	das Walbeobachten; das Whale-watching	Let's go **whale watching** in the Northeast.
up and down [ˌʌp‿ən ˈdaʊn]	entlang	You can see whales **up and down** the coast.
percent (%) [pəˈsent]	das Prozent (%)	2**%** is not much.
economy [ɪˈkɒnəmi]	die Wirtschaft	23% of the USA's **economy** is in the Northeast.
financial [faɪˈnænʃl]	Finanz-; finanziell	Where is the **financial** centre of the world?
runner [ˈrʌnə]	der Läufer / die Läuferin	**runner** → to run
marathon [ˈmærəθn]	der Marathon	Achtung Aussprache!
to raise money [ˌreɪz ˈmʌni]	Geld sammeln; Geld aufbringen	We **raised money** for a charity.
historical [hɪˈstɒrɪkl]	historisch; geschichtlich	**historical** → history
government [ˈɡʌvnmənt]	die Regierung	Achtung Schreibweise: gover**n**ment

Station 1

p. 10 **attraction** [əˈtrækʃn]	die Attraktion; die Sehenswürdigkeit	Achtung Schreibweise: a**tt**ra**c**tion
viewing [ˈvjuːɪŋ]	Aussichts-	**viewing** → view
side [saɪd]	die Seite	The platform is on the **side** of the building.
story *(AE)* [ˈstɔːri]	die Etage; das Stockwerk	AE: **story** BE: storey, floor
steel [stiːl]	der Stahl	The North Tower is a glass and **steel** building.
skyscraper [ˈskaɪskreɪpə]	der Wolkenkratzer	
above [əˈbʌv]	über; oberhalb; oben	I can't read the sign **above** the shop.
best of all [ˈbest‿əv‿ɔːl]	am besten; das Beste	better than other things
outdoor [ˌaʊtˈdɔː]	Außen-; im Freien	Those are the world's highest **outdoor** stairs.
top [tɒp]	das Top; das Oberteil; das obere Ende; die Spitze	There's a restaurant on the **top** of the building.
elevator *(AE)* [ˈelɪveɪtə]	der Aufzug; der Lift	AE: **elevator** BE: lift
former [ˈfɔːmə]	ehemalige / ehemaliger / ehemaliges; frühere / früherer / früheres	He's a **former** student of my school.
railroad *(AE)* [ˈreɪlrəʊd]	die Eisenbahn	AE: **railroad** BE: railway
track [træk]	die Strecke; das Gleis	The High Line was an old railroad **track**.
half [hɑːf]	halb *(bei Uhrzeitangaben)*	Das **l** wird nicht gesprochen.

	subway *(AE)* ['sʌbweɪ]	die U-Bahn	AE: **subway** BE: underground
	aircraft carrier [ˌeəkrɑːft 'kæriə]	der Flugzeugträger	Planes can land on an **aircraft carrier**.
	submarine [ˌsʌbmr'iːn]	das U-Boot	
	space shuttle ['speɪs ˌʃʌtl]	die Raumfähre	We saw a **space shuttle** at the museum.
	brand [brænd]	die Marke	I don't like that fashion **brand**.
	designer [dɪ'zaɪnə]	der Designer / die Designerin; der Gestalter / die Gestalterin; der Entwickler / die Entwicklerin	Das **g** wird nicht gesprochen.
	store *(AE)* [stɔː]	der Laden; das Geschäft	AE: **store** BE: shop
	to **design** [dɪ'zaɪn]	entwerfen; gestalten; entwickeln	**to design** → designer
	not ... anything [ˌnɒt ... 'eniθɪŋ]	nichts	Leo did**n't** buy **anything**.
	oh well ['əʊ ˌwel]	was soll's	She thinks shopping is boring – **oh well**.
p. 11	**basement** *(AE)* ['beɪsmənt]	der Keller; das Untergeschoss; das Kellergeschoss	AE: **basement** BE: cellar
	balcony ['bælkəni]	der Balkon	Our flat has a **balcony**. 
	solar panel [ˌsəʊlə 'pænl]	der Sonnenkollektor; das Solarpaneel	
	ground level ['graʊnd ˌlevl]	das Erdgeschoss	The entrance is at **ground level**.
	staircase ['steəkeɪs]	die Treppe; das Treppenhaus	**staircase** = stairs
	parking lot *(AE)* ['pɑːkɪŋ ˌlɒt]	der Parkplatz	AE: **parking lot** BE: car park
	lobby ['lɒbi]	die Eingangshalle; die Empfangshalle; das Foyer	There is a **lobby** in most skyscrapers.
	terrace ['terɪs]	die Terrasse	The view from the roof **terrace** is awesome.
	loft [lɒft]	der Dachboden	**loft** = attic
	fire escape ['faɪər‿esˌkeɪp]	der Notausgang	You should know where the **fire escape** is.
	apartment [ə'pɑːtmənt]	die Wohnung; das Apartment	People in the USA say '**apartment**' and not 'flat'.
p. 13	**taxi** ['tæksi]	das Taxi	

Viewing

p. 15	**barbecue** ['bɑːbɪkjuː]	das Grillfest; der Grill	
	ceremony ['serɪməni]	die Zeremonie; die Feier	Achtung Schreibweise: c**e**remon**y**
	independence [ˌɪndɪ'pendəns]	die Unabhängigkeit	They celebrated 100 years of **independence**.
	parade [pə'reɪd]	die Parade; der Umzug	I watched the **parade** on Independence Day.
	freedom ['friːdəm]	die Freiheit; die Unabhängigkeit	'**freedom**' hat keine Mehrzahl.

citizen ['sɪtɪzn]	der Staatsbürger / die Staatsbürgerin; der Staatsangehörige / die Staatsangehörige	They're now **citizens** of the USA.
attack [ə'tæk]	der Anschlag; die Attacke; der Angriff; der Überfall	There were **attacks** on September 11, 2001.
memorial [mə'mɔ:riəl]	das Denkmal; die Gedenkstätte	There is a **memorial** for 9 / 11 in New York.
waterfall ['wɔ:təfɔ:l]	der Wasserfall	
to **collapse** [kə'læps]	einstürzen; zusammenbrechen; kollabieren	The two towers in New York **collapsed**.
terrorist ['terərɪst]	der Terrorist / die Terroristin; Terror-	Die Betonung liegt hier: **ter**rorist.
to **hijack** ['haɪdʒæk]	entführen; kapern	Terrorists **hijacked** four planes.
to **fly, flew, flown** [flaɪ, flu:, fləʊn]	fliegen	We **flew** on holiday from Stuttgart Airport.
emergency worker [ɪ,mɜ:dʒnsi 'wɜ:kə]	die Rettungskraft	I help in an emergency. I'm an **emergency worker**.
to **crash** [kræʃ]	abstürzen (*Flugzeug*); krachen; zusammenstoßen	Their plane **crashed** into the mountain.

Station 2

p. 16 **teenager** ['ti:n,eɪdʒə]	der Teenager; der Jugendliche / die Jugendliche	She's 15 years old. She's a **teenager**.
post [pəʊst]	der Post (*online gestellte Nachricht*); der Beitrag; der Eintrag	There are some interesting **posts** on this website.
suburb ['sʌbɜ:b]	der Vorort	Charlestown is a **suburb** of Boston.
harbor *(AE)* ['hɑ:bə]	der Hafen	AE: **harbor** BE: harbour
to **dream, dreamt, dreamt** [dri:m, dremt, dremt]	träumen	**to dream** → dream
foreign ['fɒrɪn]	fremd; ausländisch	**Foreign** things are from another country.
to **offer** ['ɒfə]	anbieten; bieten	My school **offers** some great clubs.
practice ['præktɪs]	die Probe; die Übung; das Training	band **practice** = band training
cozy *(AE)* ['kəʊzi]	gemütlich	AE: **cozy** BE: cosy
grounds [graʊndz]	die Anlage; das Gelände	! The sports **grounds** are amazing. Die Sportanlage ist unglaublich.
lacrosse [lə'krɒs]	das Lacrosse (*Ballsportart*)	**Lacrosse** is a new sport for me.
ice hockey ['aɪs ,hɒki]	das Eishockey	
fall *(AE)* [fɔ:l]	der Herbst	AE: **fall** BE: autumn
mall *(AE)* [mɔ:l]	das Einkaufszentrum	I love shopping in a big **mall**.
seafood ['si:fu:d]	die Meeresfrüchte	! The **seafood** is fresh. Die Meeresfrüchte sind frisch.
to **organize** *(AE)* ['ɔ:gənaɪz]	organisieren	Let's **organize** a big party.
northeastern [nɔ:ð'i:stən]	nordöstlich	I live in the **northeastern** part of the USA.

	apartment [ə'pɑ:tmənt]	die Wohnung; das Apartment	People in the USA say '**apartment**' and not 'flat'.
	private ['praɪvɪt]	Privat-; privat	There's not much **private** space in my room.
	nosy ['nəʊzi]	neugierig	My sister is very **nosy**.
	that's why ['ðæts ˌwaɪ]	deswegen	**That's why** I want to talk to you.
	possible ['pɒsəbl]	möglich	I'm outside as much as **possible**.
	left [left]	übrig	Sorry, I haven't got any money **left**.
p. 17	**strange** [streɪndʒ]	merkwürdig; seltsam	My parents are really **strange** sometimes.
	miserable ['mɪzrəbl]	elend; armselig; jämmerlich	**miserable** ↔ happy
	fascinating ['fæsɪneɪtɪŋ]	faszinierend	My dad told me a **fascinating** story.
	unusual [ʌn'ju:ʒl]	ungewöhnlich	The colour of her hair is very **unusual**.
	odd [ɒd]	seltsam; merkwürdig; komisch	**odd** = strange
	unpleasant [ʌn'pleznt]	unangenehm; unerfreulich	**unpleasant** = not very nice
	impressive [ɪm'presɪv]	beeindruckend	The view from the top was **impressive**.
	heartbroken ['hɑ:tˌbrəʊkn]	untröstlich	He was **heartbroken** when she left.
p. 18	**Amish** ['ɑ:mɪʃ]	amisch	Bridget is from an **Amish** family.
	on one's own [ˌɒn wʌnz‿'əʊn]	allein; für sich; ohne Hilfe	I can be **on my own** in my room.
	machine [mə'ʃi:n]	die Maschine; das Gerät	Careful! This **machine** can get very hot!
	the Amish [ði‿'ɑ:mɪʃ]	die Amischen	**The Amish** don't have tablets.

Listening

p. 21	**belief** [bɪ'li:f]	der Glaube; die Überzeugung	**belief** → to believe
	opportunity [ˌɒpə'tju:nəti]	die Möglichkeit; die Gelegenheit; die Chance	The USA is full of **opportunities**.
	to **achieve** [ə'tʃi:v]	erreichen; schaffen; leisten	I **achieved** the best level in the game.
	yourself [jɔ:'self]	dich selbst; selber	Did you make this cake **yourself**? – Yes, I did.
	success [sək'ses]	der Erfolg	**success** → successful
	to **matter** ['mætə]	von Bedeutung sein; etw. ausmachen	It doesn't **matter** where you're from.
	to **immigrate** ['ɪmɪgreɪt]	einwandern; immigrieren	**to immigrate** → immigrant, immigration
	chance [tʃɑ:ns]	die Chance; die Möglichkeit; die Gelegenheit	**chance** = opportunity

Reading

p. 22	**overwhelmed** [ˌəʊvə'welmd]	überwältigt; überfordert	I was **overwhelmed** by America.
	to **seem** [si:m]	scheinen	Paul **seems** to like his new school.
	except [ɪk'sept]	außer	We work every day **except** Sundays.
	to **stand in line** [ˌstænd‿ɪn 'laɪn]	anstehen	We had to **stand in line** and wait.

	Poland ['pəʊlənd]	Polen	**Poland** is a European country.
	to **succeed (in)** [sək'si:d (ɪn)]	Erfolg haben (mit / bei); nachfolgen	**to succeed** → success, successful
	extremely [ɪk'stri:mli]	äußerst; sehr	Climbing is **extremely** popular.
	exhausted [ɪg'zɔ:stɪd]	erschöpft	After the marathon I was **exhausted**.
	official [ə'fɪʃl]	der Beamte / die Beamtin; der Funktionär / die Funktionärin	The immigration **official** wasn't very nice.
	to **be terrified** [bi 'terəfaɪd]	schreckliche Angst haben	The child **was terrified** of the dog.
	head chef ['hed ˌʃef]	der Chefkoch / die Chefköchin	The **head chef** is the boss in the kitchen.
	fair [feə]	gerecht; fair	Most parents are **fair** to their children.
	ocean ['əʊʃn]	der Ozean; das Meer	There is an **ocean** between Europe and the USA.
	on board [ɒn 'bɔ:d]	an Bord	✎ Achtung Schreibweise: **o**n b**oa**rd
	seasick ['si:sɪk]	seekrank	We were all **seasick** on the ship.
	the rest [ðə 'rest]	der Rest	I spent **the rest** of the day in bed.
	deck [dek]	das Schiffsdeck	The **deck** of the ship was dirty.
	cabin ['kæbɪn]	die Kabine	The **cabins** on the ship were very small.
	natural ['nætʃrl]	natürlich; Natur-	**natural** → nature
	friendship ['frendʃɪp]	die Freundschaft	**friendship** → friend
	department store [dɪ'pɑ:tmənt ˌstɔ:]	das Kaufhaus	You can buy everything in a **department store**.
	scared [skeəd]	verängstigt	**scared** = to be afraid
	to **make sb feel better** [ˌmeɪk fi:l 'betə]	jmdm. helfen, sich besser zu fühlen	Her nice words **made me feel better**.
p. 23	**blouse** [blaʊz]	die Bluse	
	a pair of [ə 'peər‿əv]	ein Paar	I need **a pair of** black socks.
	sock [sɒk]	die Socke	
	underwear ['ʌndəweə]	die Unterwäsche	You wear **underwear** under your clothes.
	perfume ['pɜ:fju:m]	das Parfüm	**Perfume** makes you smell nice.
	papers ['peɪpəz]	die Papiere; die Dokumente; die Unterlagen	Don't forget your **papers** and your ticket.
	dried fruit [ˌdraɪd 'fru:t]	die Trockenfrüchte; das Trockenobst	You can use **dried fruit** in cakes.
	list [lɪst]	die Liste	Let's write a **list** of ideas.
	diary ['daɪəri]	das Tagebuch	No one is allowed to read my **diary**.
	wife, wives [waɪf, waɪvz]	die Ehefrau, die Ehefrauen	! I have one **wife**. I don't have two **wives**. Ich habe eine Ehefrau. Ich habe nicht zwei Ehefrauen.

Unit 2 Off to the Midwest

p. 30	**off to** ['ɒf tə]	ab in; auf zu / nach	**Off to** the airport and our holiday.

Check in

	time zone ['taɪm ˌzəʊn]	die Zeitzone	There are nine **time zones** in the USA.
	agriculture ['ægrɪkʌltʃə]	die Landwirtschaft; der Ackerbau	The Midwest is important for **agriculture**.
	manufacturing [ˌmænjə'fæktʃərɪŋ]	die Produktion; die Herstellung; die Fertigung	**Manufacturing** is making things in factories.
	endless ['endləs]	endlos	There are **endless** fields in the Midwest.
	wheat [wi:t]	der Weizen	
	corn [kɔ:n]	der Mais; das Korn; das Getreide	**Corn** is yellow and great in salads.
	soy [sɔɪ]	die Soja	The Midwest is famous for **soy**.
	dairy farming ['deəri ˌfɑ:mɪŋ]	der Milchbetrieb; die Milchproduktion	You need lots of cows for **dairy farming**.
p. 31	**bison** ['baɪsn]	der Bison	! One **bison**, three **bison**. Ein Bison, drei Bisons.
	to **learn about sth** [ˌlɜ:n ə'baʊt]	etwas erfahren über etw.	I'd like to **learn about the city**.
	living history village [ˌlɪvɪŋ hɪstri 'vɪlɪdʒ]	das Freilichtmuseum	We learned a lot at the **living history village**.
	to **settle (in)** ['setl (ɪn)]	sich niederlassen (in); besiedeln	**to settle (in)** → settler
	farmer ['fɑ:mə]	der Landwirt / die Landwirtin; der Bauer / die Bäuerin	
	craftspeople ['krɑ:ftsˌpi:pl]	die Handwerker / die Handwerkerinnen	**Craftspeople** make things with their hands.
	American football [əˌmerɪkən 'fʊtbɔ:l]	der American Football	
	won [wʌn]	simple past, past participle von *to win* (gewinnen)	I **won** = ich gewann / ich habe gewonnen
	shore [ʃɔ:]	das Ufer; die Küste	Chicago is on the **shores** of Lake Michigan.
	movie *(AE)* ['mu:vi]	der Film	AE: **movie** BE: film, movie 
	formation [fɔ:'meɪʃn]	die Formation; die Entstehung	Die Betonung liegt hier: for**ma**tion.
	fossil ['fɒsl]	das Fossil; die Versteinerung	We found **fossils** on the beach.
	plain [pleɪn]	die Ebene	The **plains** in the Midwest are huge.
	president ['prezɪdnt]	der Präsident / die Präsidentin	Die Betonung liegt hier: **pres**ident.
	crop [krɒp]	die Feldfrucht; die Ernte	**Crops** are grown in the fields.
	tornado [tɔ:'neɪdəʊ]	der Tornado; der Wirbelsturm	We could see the **tornado** a mile away.

Station 1

p. 32	**exchange** [ɪks'tʃeɪndʒ]	der Austausch	I'm an **exchange** student from Germany.
	beginning [bɪ'gɪnɪŋ]	der Anfang; der Beginn	**beginning** → to begin
	to **get ready** [ˌget 'redi]	sich fertig machen; sich vorbereiten	We have to **get ready** for school.
	dress code ['dres ˌkəʊd]	die Kleiderordnung	There isn't a **dress code** at my school.
	cap [kæp]	die Kappe; die Mütze	It's good to wear a **cap** in the sun.
	crop top ['krɒp ˌtɒp]	das bauchfreie Oberteil	We can't wear **crop tops** to school.
	portal ['pɔ:tl]	das Portal; der Zugang	Die Betonung liegt hier: **por**tal.
	host [həʊst]	der Gastgeber / die Gastgeberin; der Moderator / die Moderatorin	My parents were the **hosts** of the party.
	metal detector [ˌmetl dɪ'tektə]	der Metalldetektor; das Metallsuchgerät	We looked for metal on the beach with a **metal detector**.
	hallway ['hɔ:lweɪ]	der Flur	AE: **hallway** BE: corridor
	detention [dɪ'tenʃn]	das Nachsitzen	Sam was late again and got **detention**.
	homeroom *(AE)* ['həʊmru:m]	*Treffpunkt vor der ersten Stunde, u. a. zur Überprüfung der Anwesenheit*	We are in the same **homeroom** group.
	Pledge of Allegiance [ˌpledʒ‿əv‿ə'li:dʒns]	der Treueeid	Students in America take the **Pledge of Allegiance** every day.
	schedule *(AE)* ['skedʒu:l]	der Stundenplan; der Fahrplan	AE: **schedule** BE: timetable
	math *(AE)* [mæθ]	Mathematik; Mathe	AE: **math** BE: maths
	elective [ɪ'lektɪv]	das Wahlfach	You can choose your **electives**.
	production [prə'dʌkʃn]	die Produktion; die Herstellung	Die Betonung liegt hier: pro**duc**tion.
	writing ['raɪtɪŋ]	das Schreiben; Schreib-	**writing** → to write
	totally ['təʊtli]	total; völlig	I feel **totally** happy with my host family.
	yearbook ['jɪəbʊk]	das Jahrbuch	Most schools in the USA have a **yearbook**.
	volleyball ['vɒlibɔ:l]	der Volleyball	I play **volleyball** with my friends on Fridays.
	student council [ˌstju:dnt 'kaʊnsl]	der Schülerrat	The **student council** meets every Monday before school.
	prom [prɒm]	*Ball am Ende des Jahres in einer amerikanischen High School*	I still have to buy my dress for the **prom**.
	to **live stream** ['laɪv ˌstri:m]	live streamen; live übertragen	I **live streamed** the match yesterday.
	comment ['kɒment]	der Kommentar	I never post any **comments**.
p. 33	**orchestra** ['ɔ:kɪstrə]	das Orchester	Achtung Schreibweise: orches**tra**
	to **practice** *(AE)* ['præktɪs]	üben; trainieren; praktizieren	AE: **to practice** BE: to practise
	peer [pɪə]	der Gleichaltrige / die Gleichaltrige	My classmates are my **peers**.
	tutoring ['tju:tərɪŋ]	die Nachhilfe	I go to peer **tutoring** for maths.
	debate [dɪ'beɪt]	Debattier-; die Debatte; die Diskussion	Achtung Schreibweise: deba**te**
	cheerleading ['tʃɪəˌli:dɪŋ]	das Cheerleading	**cheerleading** → cheerleader

Listening

p. 37	**cherry** ['tʃeri]	die Kirsche	My dad makes a great **cherry** cake.
	grass [grɑ:s]	das Gras; der Rasen	
	cost [kɒst]	die Kosten; der Preis	The **costs** of the project are high.
	to **increase** [ɪn'kri:s]	wachsen; zunehmen; vergrößern; ansteigen	The prices are **increasing** every day.
	acre ['eɪkə]	der Acre (*Flächenmaß: 4.050 m²*)	The farm is 20 **acres**.
	to **produce** [prə'dju:s]	herstellen; produzieren; erzeugen; anbauen	**to produce** → production

Station 2

p. 38	**Thanksgiving** [ˌθæŋks'gɪvɪŋ]	das Erntedankfest	**Thanksgiving** is on the fourth Thursday in November.
	turkey ['tɜ:ki]	der Truthahn; die Pute	
	oven ['ʌvn]	der Backofen	There is a big **oven** in our kitchen.
	pumpkin ['pʌmpkɪn]	der Kürbis	Mum always makes the **pumpkin** pie.
	to **snow** [snəʊ]	schneien	**to snow** → snow
	Good job! [ˌgʊd 'dʒɒb]	Gut gemacht!	Diese Wörter am besten als Einheit lernen.
	homemade [ˌhəʊm'meɪd]	selbst gemacht	I love **homemade** cakes and bread.
	cornbread ['kɔ:nbred]	das Maisbrot	You need corn to make **cornbread**.
	pecan ['pi:kæn]	die Pekannuss	**Pecan** pie is my favourite pie.
	punch [pʌnʃ]	der Punsch; die Bowle	You can use lots of fruit and juice in **punch**.
	secret ['si:krət]	das Geheimnis	I can't tell you, it's a **secret**.
	Safe flight! [ˌseɪf 'flaɪt]	Guten Flug!	Diese Wörter am besten als Einheit lernen.
	suitcase ['su:tkeɪs]	der Koffer	
	cinnamon ['sɪnəmən]	der Zimt	We have **cinnamon** cookies at Thanksgiving.
	to **finish doing sth** [ˌfɪnɪʃ 'du:ɪŋ]	etw. fertig gemacht haben	I have to wait for the pie to **finish baking**.
p. 39	to **light, lit, lit** [laɪt, lɪt, lɪt]	anzünden; erhellen; beleuchten	**to light** → light
	to **put up** [ˌpʊt_'ʌp]	aufhängen; aufstellen; hochhalten; errichten	I can help you **put up** the lights.
	decoration [ˌdek'reɪʃn]	die Dekoration; der Schmuck	**decoration** → to decorate
	to **donate** [də'neɪt]	spenden; stiften	We **donated** money to the charity.
	resolution [ˌrezl'u:ʃn]	der Vorsatz; der Entschluss	I always make a New Year's **resolution**.
	display [dɪ'spleɪ]	die Vorführung; die Ausstellung; der Schaukasten; die Anzeige	The fireworks **display** was awesome.
	no longer [ˌnəʊ 'lɒŋgə]	nicht mehr; nicht länger	The park is closed. It's **no longer** open.

	alive [ə'laɪv]	am Leben	**alive** ↔ dead
p. 40	**travel agency** ['trævl‿ˌeɪdʒnsi]	das Reisebüro	We booked our holiday at a **travel agency**.
p. 41	**carnival** ['kɑːnɪvl]	der Karneval; der Fasching	Achtung Schreibweise: carnival

Viewing

p. 43	**storm** [stɔːm]	der Sturm; das Unwetter	Achtung Schreibweise: storm
	chaser ['tʃeɪsə]	der Jäger / die Jägerin; der Verfolger / die Verfolgerin	Warren is a storm **chaser**.
	to **chase** [tʃeɪs]	jagen; verfolgen	**to chase** → chaser
	shot [ʃɒt]	die Aufnahme; die Einstellung; der Schuss	That is a great **shot** of the mountain.
	television ['telɪvɪʒn]	der Fernseher; das Fernsehen	
	hailstone ['heɪlstəʊn]	das Hagelkorn	The **hailstones** in the storm were huge.
	to **shut, shut, shut** [ʃʌt, ʃʌt, ʃʌt]	zumachen; schließen	**to shut** = to close
	atmosphere ['ætməsfɪə]	die Atmosphäre; die Stimmung	There was a strange **atmosphere** at the party.
	feeling ['fiːlɪŋ]	das Gefühl	**feeling** → to feel
	to **get hurt** [ˌget 'hɜːt]	sich verletzen; verletzt werden	We **got hurt** in the storm.

Reading

p. 44	**fancy dancer** ['fænsi ˌdɑːnsə]	*Person, die einen traditionellen Tanz der amerikanischen Ureinwohner / Ureinwohnerinnen vorführt*	A **fancy dancer** dances a traditional Native American dance.
	Cree [kriː]	Cree-; der Cree / die Cree; das Cree	Rory's mum is a **Cree** Native American.
	light [laɪt]	leicht; hell	The dancer was **light** on her feet.
	well [wel]	na ja	I was really happy, **well**, I was quite happy.
	stepdad ['stepdæd]	der Stiefvater	I live with my mum and my **stepdad**.
	step- [step]	Stief-	**step-** + dad = stepdad
	ever ['evə]	*hier:* niemals	He never phoned me. **Ever**.
	probably ['prɒbəbli]	wahrscheinlich	They **probably** thought I was strange.
	to **forbid, forbade, forbidden** [fə'bɪd, fə'bæd, fə'bɪdn]	verbieten	My dad **forbade** me to go to the party.
	thirsty ['θɜːsti]	durstig	I'm so **thirsty**! I need a drink now.
	beat [biːt]	der Takt; der Rhythmus; der Schlag	The **beat** of the music was new to me.
	powerful ['paʊəfl]	stark; mächtig; bedeutend; beeindruckend	The beat of the music was **powerful**.
	drum [drʌm]	die Trommel	

	feather ['feðə]	die Feder	Birds have **feathers**.
	to **be ashamed of** [bi‿ə'ʃeɪmd‿əv]	sich schämen für / wegen	I **was ashamed of** my clothes.
p. 45	**proud (of)** [praʊd (əv)]	stolz (auf)	**proud (of)** ↔ ashamed (of)
	both [bəʊθ]	beide	We are **both** happy.
	librarian [laɪ'breəriən]	der Bibliothekar / die Bibliothekarin	**librarian** → library
	sibling ['sɪblɪŋ]	das Geschwister	**siblings** = brothers and sisters
	heart [hɑ:t]	das Herz	
	powwow ['paʊwaʊ]	die Versammlung (*der indigenen Völker Nordamerikas*)	A **powwow** is what Native Americans call a meeting.
	salt [sɔ:lt]	das Salz	I like **salt** on my chips.
p. 46	**seat** [si:t]	der Sitz; der Sitzplatz	Don't put your feet on the bus **seats**!
	brain [breɪn]	das Gehirn	Your **brain** is in your head.
	hope [həʊp]	die Hoffnung	**hope** → to hope
	fancy dancing ['fænsi ˌdɑ:nsɪŋ]	*traditioneller Tanzstil amerikanischer Ureinwohner / Ureinwohnerinnen*	**fancy dancing** → fancy dancer
	strength [streŋθ]	die Stärke; die Kraft	**strength** → strong
	to **turn to sb** ['tɜ:n tə]	sich jmdm. zuwenden	He **turned to me** and laughed.
	to **define** [dɪ'faɪn]	definieren	Don't let what people say **define** you.

Unit 3 Going to the West

Check in

Temperature units

Die Temperaturangaben werden in den USA in der Einheit „Fahrenheit“ (°F) angegeben. In Europa benutzt man die Einheit „Celsius“ (°C). Benutze einen Online-Rechner, um die Temperaturangaben umzurechnen. Du kannst dir leicht merken: 100°F entsprechen ungefähr der menschlichen Körpertemperatur von 37°C!

0°F	zero degrees Fahrenheit (minus seventeen point seven eight degrees Celsius)	null Grad Fahrenheit (minus siebzehn Komma sieben acht Grad Celsius)	−17,78°C
32°F	thirty-two degrees Fahrenheit (zero degrees Celsius)	zweiunddreißig Grad Fahrenheit (null Grad Celsius)	0°C
100°F	one hundred degrees Fahrenheit (thirty-seven point seven eight degrees Celsius)	einhundert Grad Fahrenheit (siebenunddreißig Komma sieben acht Grad Celsius)	37,78°C
212°F	two hundred and twelve degrees Fahrenheit (one hundred degrees Celsius)	zweihundertzwölf Grad Fahrenheit (einhundert Grad Celsius)	100°C

p. 54	**degree Fahrenheit (°F)** [ˌdɪgriː ˈfærnhaɪt]	das Grad Fahrenheit	134°F = 57°C
	degree Celsius (°C) [ˌdɪgriː ˈselsiəs]	das Grad Celsius	It's 28 **degrees Celsius (°C)** outside.
	volcano, volcanoes [vɒlˈkeɪnəʊ, vɒlˈkeɪnəʊz]	der Vulkan, die Vulkane	
	Hawaiian [həˈwaɪən]	hawaiianisch; das Hawaiianisch; aus Hawaii; der Hawaiianer / die Hawaiianerin	There are volcanoes on the **Hawaiian** islands.
	desert [ˈdezət]	die Wüste	
	canyon [ˈkænjən]	die Schlucht; der Canyon	You can see **canyons** in Arizona.
p. 55	**multicultural** [ˌmʌltiˈkʌltʃrl]	multikulturell	The south is a **multicultural** area.
	Hispanic [hɪˈspænɪk]	lateinamerikanisch; hispanisch; aus Lateinamerika; der Lateinamerikaner / die Lateinamerikanerin	Almost 40% of the population of California is **Hispanic**.
	Asian [ˈeɪʒn]	asiatisch; aus Asien; der Asiate / die Asiatin	**Asian** → Asia
	start-up [ˈstɑːtˌʌp]	das Start-up	A new company is a **start-up**.
	leading [ˈliːdɪŋ]	führend	Lots of **leading** brands come from Germany.
	producer [prəˈdjuːsə]	der Erzeuger / die Erzeugerin; der Hersteller / die Herstellerin; der Produzent / die Produzentin	**producer** → to produce, product
	pear [peə]	die Birne	**Pears** can be green or yellow.
	grape [greɪp]	die Traube	
	seasonal [ˈsiːznl]	Saison-; saisonal	**seasonal** → season
	reservoir [ˈrezəvwɑː]	der Stausee	There should be water in a **reservoir**.
	wildfire [ˈwaɪldfaɪə]	das Lauffeuer; der Flächenbrand	When it is dry, there are more **wildfires**.
	sunrise [ˈsʌnraɪz]	der Sonnenaufgang	You can see the **sunrise** in the morning.
	sunset [ˈsʌnset]	der Sonnenuntergang	**sunset** ↔ sunrise
	daylight [ˈdeɪlaɪt]	das Tageslicht	There is **daylight** during the day.
	peninsula [ˌpəˈnɪnsjələ]	die Halbinsel	There is water on three sides of a **peninsula**.
	fog [fɒg]	der Nebel	

Station 1

p. 56	**average** [ˈævrɪdʒ]	durchschnittlich	I'm an **average** American teenager.
	to **take** [teɪk]	*hier:* brauchen; benötigen	It **takes** a lot of energy to make a phone.
	raw material [ˌrɔː məˈtɪəriəl]	der Rohstoff; das Rohmaterial	You need **raw materials** to produce things.
	rare [reə]	selten; rar	This book is **rare**, there aren't many of it.

to **replace** [rɪ'pleɪs]	ersetzen	We **replaced** our old dishwasher.
every ['evri]	alle	My mum calls me **every** ten minutes.
life cycle ['laɪf ˌsaɪkl]	der Lebenszyklus; die Lebensdauer; die Laufzeit	Some products have a long **life cycle**.
packaging ['pækɪdʒɪŋ]	die Verpackung; das Verpackungsmaterial	There is too much **packaging** on this phone.
transportation *(AE)* [ˌtrænspɔː'teɪʃn]	das Verkehrsmittel; der Transport; die Beförderung	AE: **transportation** BE: transport
use [juːs]	die Verwendung; der Gebrauch; der Nutzen	**use** → to use
disposal [dɪ'spəʊsl]	die Entsorgung	The **disposal** of a lot of products isn't easy.
to **be made of** [bi 'meɪd‿əv]	hergestellt sein aus	This house **is made of** stone.
ceramic [sə'ræmɪk]	die Keramik	Achtung Aussprache!
to **put together** [ˌpʊt tə'geðə]	zusammensetzen; zusammenbauen	My phone was **put together** in China.
amount (of) [ə'maʊnt (əv)]	die Menge; die Summe	Look at the **amount of** waste!
chemical ['kemɪkl]	die Chemikalie	The rain washes the **chemicals** into the sea.
to **package** ['pækɪdʒ]	verpacken	**to package** → packaging
card [kɑːd]	die Pappe; der Karton; die Karte	Boxes made from **card** are very strong.
to **transport** [træn'spɔːt]	transportieren; befördern	**to transport** → transportation
to **charge** [tʃɑːdʒ]	aufladen; berechnen; verlangen; erheben	I can **charge** my phone in an hour.
either … or … ['aɪðə … ɔː …]	entweder … oder …	I'll **either** go to high school **or** get a job.
recycled [ˌriː'saɪkld]	recycelt; wiederverwertet	**recycled** → to recycle
to **reduce** [rɪ'djuːs]	reduzieren; verringern; vermindern	**to reduce** ↔ to increase
pollution [pə'luːʃn]	die Verschmutzung	**pollution** → to pollute
p. 57 to **work** [wɜːk]	*hier:* funktionieren	Oh no, my computer doesn't **work**.
to **need to** ['niːd tə]	müssen	A company **needs to** make money.
to **program** ['prəʊgræm]	programmieren	Die Betonung liegt hier: **pro**gram.
to **process** ['prəʊsəs]	verarbeiten; aufbereiten; verstehen	They **process** things in the factory.
to **manufacture** [ˌmænjə'fæktʃə]	herstellen; fertigen	**to manufacture** → manufacturer, manufacturing
to **mine** [maɪn]	abbauen; graben nach	Workers **mine** raw materials.
van [væn]	der Lieferwagen; der Transporter	
to **distribute** [dɪ'strɪbjuːt]	verteilen; liefern	The teacher **distributed** the books.
finished ['fɪnɪʃt]	fertig	The **finished** products are in the shops.
to **extract** [ɪk'strækt]	entnehmen; herausnehmen; gewinnen	The raw materials are **extracted** from the ground.
to **treat** [triːt]	verarbeiten; bearbeiten	The material has to be **treated** first.

	to **assemble** [ə'sembl]	zusammenbauen; montieren	The model took a long time to **assemble**.
	to **dispose (of)** [dɪs'pəʊz (əv)]	entsorgen	**to dispose (of)** → disposal
p. 58	**passive voice** ['pæsɪv ˌvɔɪs]	das Passiv	Write the sentence in the **passive voice**.
	active voice ['æktɪv ˌvɔɪs]	das Aktiv	That sentence is in the **active voice**.

Viewing

p. 61	**climate** ['klaɪmət]	das Klima	The **climate** is mostly dry in the desert.
	global ['gləʊbl]	weltweit; global	
	to **install** [ɪn'stɔ:l]	installieren; einrichten; anschließen	The town is **installing** new traffic lights.
	solution [sə'lu:ʃn]	die Lösung	**solution** → to solve
	engineer [ˌendʒɪ'nɪə]	der Ingenieur / die Ingenieurin; der Techniker / die Technikerin	She wants to be an **engineer**.
	to **detect** [dɪ'tekt]	entdecken; aufdecken; ermitteln	**to detect** → detective
	screensaver ['skri:nseɪvə]	der Bildschirmschoner	My **screensaver** is a holiday photo.
	connection [kə'nekʃn]	die Verbindung	**connection** → to connect
	program *(AE)* ['prəʊgræm]	das Programm; die Sendung	AE: **program** = das Programm; die Sendung BE: program = das Computerprogramm
	Mexico ['meksɪkəʊ]	Mexiko	**Mexico** is south of the USA.

Station 2

p. 62	**outreach center** *(AE)* [ˌaʊtri:tʃ 'sentə]	die Beratungsstelle	AE: **outreach center** BE: outreach centre
	homeless ['həʊmləs]	obdachlos; wohnungslos	when you don't have a home to live in
	may [meɪ]	dürfen; können	**May** I open the window, please?
	to **support** [sə'pɔ:t]	unterstützen	My parents **supported** my idea.
	medical ['medɪkl]	medizinisch; ärztlich	Die Betonung liegt hier: **med**ical.
	counseling *(AE)* ['kaʊnslɪŋ]	die Beratung; die psychologische Betreuung	AE: **counseling** BE: counselling
	mental ['mentl]	mental; geistig; psychisch	**Mental** is about in your head.
	health [helθ]	die Gesundheit	Some people have mental **health** problems.
	practical ['præktɪkl]	praktisch	I like making things, I'm **practical**.
	first responder [ˌfɜ:st rɪ'spɒndə]	der Ersthelfer / die Ersthelferin; *hier:* der Notfallbegleiter / die Notfall-begleiterin	The **first responder** was the first person who helped me.
	to **cope with** ['kəʊp ˌwɪð]	bewältigen; fertig werden mit	It's hard to **cope with** the new situation.
	main [meɪn]	Haupt-	My **main** idea is to help people in our town.
	support [sə'pɔ:t]	die Unterstützung; die Hilfe	**support** → to support
	jobless ['dʒɒbləs]	arbeitslos	without a job

	to **get into debt** [ˌget ɪntə 'det]	sich verschulden	It's easy to **get into debt** when you lose your job.
	to **afford** [ə'fɔ:d]	sich leisten	Sorry, I can't **afford** to give you the money.
	rent [rent]	die Miete	**rent** → to rent
	serious ['sɪəriəs]	schwer; ernsthaft	My friend was **seriously** ill, but she's OK now.
	sick [sɪk]	krank	**sick** = ill
	addicted (to) [ə'dɪktɪd (tə)]	süchtig (nach)	Life is hard when you are **addicted to** drugs.
	pregnant ['pregnənt]	schwanger	She was surprised when she got **pregnant**.
	social work ['səʊʃl ˌwɜ:k]	die Sozialarbeit	**Social work** is all about helping people.
	self-respect [ˌselfrɪ'spekt]	die Selbstachtung	Some people have no **self-respect**.
	single ['sɪŋgl]	alleinerziehend; alleinstehend; einzeln; einzige / einziger / einziges	My mum is a **single** mum, my dad doesn't live with us.
	forever [fə'revə]	für immer; ewig	I want to live here **forever**.
	heartbreaking ['hɑ:tbreɪkɪŋ]	herzzerreißend	**heartbreaking** → heart
p. 63	to **encourage** [ɪn'kʌrɪdʒ]	ermutigen; unterstützen	My parents **encouraged** me to get help.
	to **recommend** [ˌrekə'mend]	empfehlen	I can **recommend** the new restaurant in town.
	to **advise sb** [əd'vaɪz]	jmdn. beraten; jmdm. raten	**to advise sb** → advice
	therapy ['θerəpi]	die Therapie; die Behandlung	I advise you to get some **therapy**.

Listening

p. 67	**gold rush** ['gəʊld ˌrʌʃ]	der Goldrausch	Everyone wanted gold in the **gold rush**.
	ghost town ['gəʊst ˌtaʊn]	die Geisterstadt	Das **h** wird nicht gesprochen.
	creek *(AE)* [kri:k]	der Bach	a small river
	luck [lʌk]	das Glück	I never have any **luck**.
	gold-mining ['gəʊldˌmaɪnɪŋ]	das Goldschürfen	There are **gold-mining** places in Oregon.
	tool [tu:l]	das Werkzeug; das Tool; das Hilfsmittel; das Gerät	You need special **tools** for different jobs.

Reading

p. 68	**natural** ['nætʃrl]	Natur-; natürlich	There were no windows or **natural** light.
	treasure ['treʒə]	der Schatz	You have to find the box of **treasure**.
	precious ['preʃəs]	wertvoll; kostbar	The time we have is very **precious** to us.
	glacier ['glæsiə]	der Gletscher	Achtung Aussprache! 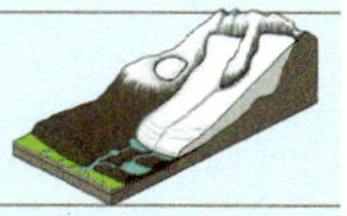
	variety [və'raɪəti]	die Vielfalt; die Auswahl	There's a **variety** of landscapes in the USA.
	to **spot** [spɒt]	entdecken; sehen; erkennen	I **spotted** a wolf in the forest.
	grizzly bear ['grɪzli ˌbeə]	der Grizzlybär	We wanted to see a **grizzly bear**.

alligator ['ælɪgeɪtə]	der Alligator	
unique [ju:'ni:k]	einzigartig	This plant is **unique** in this area.
ecosystem ['i:kəʊˌsɪstəm]	das Ökosystem	This **ecosystem** is home to lots of fish.
ancient ['eɪnʃnt]	alt; altertümlich	**ancient** = very old
cactus, cacti ['kæktəs, 'kæktaɪ]	der Kaktus, die Kakteen	
writer ['raɪtə]	der Schriftsteller / die Schriftstellerin	**writer** → to write
convinced [kən'vɪnst]	überzeugt	I was **convinced** that I was right.
wilderness ['wɪldənəs]	die Wildnis	Our camp was in the **wilderness**.
future ['fju:tʃə]	zukünftig; Zukunfts-	Forests are important for **future** generations.
generation [ˌdʒenə'reɪʃn]	die Generation	Achtung Aussprache!
to pass a law [ˌpɑ:s_ə 'lɔ:]	ein Gesetz beschließen; ein Gesetz verabschieden	It isn't easy to **pass a law**.
to establish [ɪ'stæblɪʃ]	gründen; einrichten; eröffnen	The newspaper was **established** in 2001.
to manage ['mænɪdʒ]	verwalten	NPS **manages** the national parks in the USA.
to employ [ɪm'plɔɪ]	beschäftigen; einstellen; anstellen	There are 1,000 people **employed** here.
facility [fə'sɪləti]	die Einrichtung	What **facilities** are there in the park?
scientific [ˌsaɪən'tɪfɪk]	wissenschaftlich; naturwissenschaftlich	**scientific** → science
research [rɪ'sɜ:tʃ]	die Forschung; die Recherche; die Untersuchung	The NPS does a lot of **research**.
by law [baɪ 'lɔ:]	gesetzlich	The national parks are protected **by law**.
development [dɪ'veləpmənt]	die Erschließung; die Entwicklung	There is a new **development** in our town.
responsible [rɪ'spɒnsəbl]	verantwortungsvoll; verantwortlich	He is a **responsible** person.
to leave [li:v]	zurücklassen	Visitors should only **leave** footprints.
footprint ['fʊtprɪnt]	der Fußabdruck	**footprint** → foot
garbage *(AE)* ['gɑ:bɪdʒ]	der Müll; der Abfall	AE: **garbage** BE: rubbish
to avoid [ə'vɔɪd]	vermeiden; meiden; aus dem Weg gehen; ausweichen	We have to **avoid** damaging the trees.
strict [strɪkt]	streng; strikt	Achtung Schreibweise: stri**ct**
Switzerland ['swɪtzlənd]	die Schweiz	**Switzerland** is smaller than Germany.
p. 69 to publish ['pʌblɪʃ]	veröffentlichen; publizieren; verlegen	This book was **published** last year.

Unit 4 Around the Southwest

Check in

p. 76	**stunning** ['stʌnɪŋ]	sensationell; fantastisch; überwältigend	The view from the tower is **stunning**.
	at night [ət 'naɪt]	nachts	I can't sleep well **at night**.
p. 77	**Navajo** ['nævəhəʊ]	der Navajo / die Navajo; Navajo-	Where do the **Navajo** live?
	lifestyle ['laɪfstaɪl]	der Lebensstil; der Lifestyle	We have a very modern **lifestyle**.
	alive [ə'laɪv]	am Leben	**alive** ↔ dead
	to **migrate** [maɪ'greɪt]	abwandern; wandern; umherziehen	Lots of people have **migrated** to the USA.
	Latin America [ˌlætɪn‿ə'merɪkə]	Lateinamerika	Hispanic people are from **Latin America**.
	to **form** [fɔ:m]	bilden	How was the canyon **formed**?
	dam [dæm]	die Talsperre; die Staumauer; der Damm	The **dam** is very important for the region.
	to **provide** [prə'vaɪd]	liefern; bereitstellen; bieten; versorgen	The dam **provides** energy to Nevada.
	power ['paʊə]	die Energie; der Strom; die Kraft; die Macht	The **power** comes from the dam.
	copper ['kɒpə]	das Kupfer	**Copper** mining is important in the Southwest.
	cowboy ['kaʊbɔɪ]	der Cowboy	**Cowboys** ride horses and work with animals.
	cattle ['kætl]	die Rinder; das Vieh	! 500 cattle died in the fire. 500 Rinder starben bei dem Feuer.
	rodeo [rəʊ'diəʊ]	das Rodeo	Die Betonung liegt hier: ro**deo**.
	horn [hɔ:n]	das Horn	There is a rope around the cow's **horns**.
	to **recommend** [ˌrekə'mend]	empfehlen	I can **recommend** the new restaurant in town.
	Pueblo ['pwebləʊ]	Pueblo-; der Angehörige / die Angehörige der Pueblovölker	The **Pueblo** people have lived here for over a thousand years.
	bean [bi:n]	die Bohne	
	plateau ['plætəʊ]	die Hochebene; das Plateau	There are plains and **plateaus** in the region.
	rug [rʌg]	der Teppich; der Vorleger	I have a **rug** next to my bed.

Station 1

p. 78	**role model** ['rəʊl ˌmɒdl]	das Vorbild	Who are your **role models**?
	to **inspire** [ɪn'spaɪə]	inspirieren; anregen	My older brother **inspires** me.
	talented ['tæləntɪd]	talentiert; begabt	Maja is a very **talented** dancer.
	modest ['mɒdɪst]	bescheiden	Don't be **modest**! You're really good at this!
	determined [dɪ'tɜ:mɪnd]	(fest) entschlossen; entschieden; zielstrebig	I'm **determined** to get a good job.
	theater *(AE)* ['θɪətə]	das Theater	AE: **theater** BE: theatre

	to **apply (for)** [ə'plaɪ (fə)]	sich bewerben (für / um)	He **applied for** the student job.
	part-time [ˌpɑ:t'taɪm]	die Teilzeit	I work **part-time** while I study.
	award [ə'wɔ:d]	der Preis; die Auszeichnung	
	to **give up** [ˌgɪv‿'ʌp]	aufgeben	You can't **give up** now!
	influence ['ɪnfluəns]	der Einfluss	He is a bad **influence** on her.
	to **encourage** [ɪn'kʌrɪdʒ]	ermutigen; unterstützen	My parents **encouraged** me to get help.
	for [fɔ:]	seit	I've played football **for** two years now.
	fit [fɪt]	fit; in Form	I must be **fit** for football.
	patient ['peɪʃnt]	geduldig	Just be **patient**! We'll be there soon.
	to **finish** ['fɪnɪʃ]	*hier:* absolvieren	I **finished** my first big race yesterday.
	myself [maɪ'self]	mich selbst; mich; mir; selbst; selber	I suddenly started believing in **myself**.
	ambitious [æm'bɪʃəs]	ehrgeizig	Peter is very **ambitious**. He studies a lot.
	to **be a little person** [bi‿ə ˌlɪtl 'pɜ:sn]	kleinwüchsig sein	Becky **is a litte person**.
	genetic [dʒə'netɪk]	genetisch	Becky was born with a **genetic** condition.
	condition [kən'dɪʃn]	die Bedingung; der Zustand; *hier:* die Erkrankung	I have a medical **condition** and need help.
	to **stop** [stɒp]	*hier:* aufhalten; verhindern	**to stop** ↔ to start
	known [nəʊn]	past participle von *to know* (kennen; wissen)	I've **known** her for three years now.
	middle school ['mɪdl ˌsku:l]	die Mittelschule (*weiterführende Schule in den USA, Mittelstufe*)	Children at **middle school** in the US are usually 11 to 14 years old.
	to **stand up to sb** [ˌstænd‿'ʌp tə]	jmdm. die Stirn bieten; jmdm. gewachsen sein; sich gegen jmdn. behaupten	Let's **stand up to all those mean people**!
	bully ['bʊli]	der Mobber / die Mobberin; der Tyrann / die Tyrannin	**bully** → bullying
p. 79	**determination** [dɪˌtɜ:mɪ'neɪʃn]	die Entschlossenheit; die Entschiedenheit	**determination** → determined
	influential [ˌɪnflu'enʃl]	einflussreich	**influential** → influence, to influence, influencer
	modesty ['mɒdɪsti]	die Bescheidenheit	**modesty** → modest
	talent ['tælənt]	das Talent	**talent** → talented
	ambition [æm'bɪʃn]	der Ehrgeiz; das Ziel	**ambition** → ambitious
	patience ['peɪʃns]	die Geduld	**patience** → patient
p. 80	**accident** ['æksɪdnt]	der Unfall	The man has had an **accident**.

Viewing

p. 83	**right** [raɪt]	das Recht	Everyone wants the same **rights**.
	slave [sleɪv]	der Sklave / die Sklavin	**Slaves** had to work very hard.

racism ['reɪsɪzm]	der Rassismus	How can we stop **racism**?
plantation [plæn'teɪʃn]	die Plantage	People worked on the **plantations**.
reservation [ˌrezə'veɪʃn]	das Reservat	Some Native Americans live on **reservations**.
slavery ['sleɪvri]	die Sklaverei	**slavery** → slave
as [æz]	wie	That's the same bag **as** mine.
Africa ['æfrɪkə]	Afrika	**Africa** → African
to end [end]	enden; beenden; aufhören	Classes **ended** at 3:30 p.m.

Station 2

p. 84	town hall [ˌtaʊn 'hɔ:l]	das Rathaus	The meeting took place at the **town hall**.
	mayor / mayoress [meə / ˌmeə'res]	der Bürgermeister / die Bürgermeisterin	Achtung Aussprache!
	graffiti [grə'fi:ti]	das Graffiti	Achtung Aussprache!
	unfortunately [ʌn'fɔ:tʃnətli]	leider; unglücklicherweise	**Unfortunately**, I can't come to your party.
	to ask sb to do sth [ˌɑ:sk tə 'du:]	jmdn. bitten, etw. zu tun	He **asked her to close the window**.
	frozen ['frəʊzn]	gefroren; tiefgefroren	I love **frozen** yoghurt. It's yummy!
	bank [bæŋk]	die Bank; die Böschung; das Ufer	Help! My **bank** has closed my account!
	shape [ʃeɪp]	die Form	Did you see that sign in the **shape** of a cow?
	sidewalk *(AE)* ['saɪdwɔ:k]	der Gehweg; der Bürgersteig	AE: **sidewalk** BE: pavement
	to be happy to do sth [bi ˌhæpi tə 'du:]	etw. gerne tun; etw. tun können	We**'re** always **happy to help** others.
	business ['bɪznɪs]	das Geschäft; das Unternehmen; die Branche	The mayor is happy to support new **businesses**.
	speaker ['spi:kə]	der Sprecher / die Sprecherin; der Redner / die Rednerin	**speaker** → to speak
	to improve [ɪm'pru:v]	verbessern	**to improve** → improvement
	quality ['kwɒləti]	die Qualität; die Eigenschaft	I only buy good **quality** products.
p. 85	transport ['trænspɔ:t]	das Verkehrsmittel; der Transport; die Beförderung	**transport** → to transport
	hairdresser's ['heəˌdresəz]	der Friseursalon	Achtung Schreibweise: hairdresser**'s**
	hall [hɔ:l]	die Halle; der Saal	Have you been to the new concert **hall** yet?
	police station [pə'li:s ˌsteɪʃn]	das Polizeirevier; die Polizeiwache	We all had to go to the **police station**.
	athletics track [æθˌletɪks 'træk]	die Leichtathletikbahn	The new **athletics track** is blue.
	low-emission [ˌləʊ_ɪ'mɪʃn]	emissionsarm; schadstoffarm	These **low-emission** buses are awesome.
	optician's [ɒp'tɪʃnz]	das Optikfachgeschäft	Achtung Schreibweise: optician**'s**
	sculpture ['skʌlptʃə]	die Skulptur	Achtung Schreibweise: **sc**ulpture
	law court ['lɔ: ˌkɔ:t]	der Gerichtshof; das Gericht *(juristisch)*	Where's the **law court**? – Next to the town hall.

	charging point [ˈtʃɑːdʒɪŋ ˌpɔɪnt]	die Ladestation	Our town needs more **charging points**.
	butcher's [ˈbʊtʃəz]	die Metzgerei; die Fleischerei	✎ Achtung Schreibweise: butcher**'s**
p. 86	**BFF** [ˌbiː‿efˈef]	der BFF / die BFF; bester Freund / beste Freundin für immer	**BFF** is short for best friend forever.
	Kind regards, [ˌkaɪnd rɪˈgɑːdz]	Viele Grüße	So kann man in englischsprachigen Ländern Briefe und E-Mails beenden: **Kind regards,**
	dude [duːd]	der Typ; der Kerl	There was a cool **dude** at the party.
	big deal [ˌbɪg ˈdiːl]	große Sache	It's no **big deal** if we're late.
	broke [brəʊk]	pleite	I've got no money. I'm **broke**.
	buck *(AE)* [bʌk]	der Dollar	ten **bucks** = ten dollars
	to **roll up** [ˌrəʊl‿ˈʌp]	zusammenrollen; aufrollen; aufkrempeln	We **rolled up** our clothes.
	sharp [ʃɑːp]	pünktlich; scharf; schneidend	You need to be at home at 9 p.m. **sharp**.
	to **miss** [mɪs]	übersehen; verfehlen	You can't **miss** me. I'm wearing a red hat.
p. 87	**start** [stɑːt]	der Anfang; der Beginn; der Start	**start** → to start

Listening

p. 89	**working hours** [ˈwɜːkɪŋ‿ˌaʊəz]	die Arbeitszeiten; die Arbeitszeit	Long **working hours** are not good for you.
	degree [dɪˈgriː]	der Hochschulabschluss; der akademische Grad	I have a **degree** in maths.
	apprenticeship [əˈprentɪʃɪp]	die Ausbildung; die Lehre	Cathy did her **apprenticeship** here.
	salary [ˈsælri]	das Gehalt	Your **salary** is what you earn.
	programming [ˈprəʊgræmɪŋ]	Programmier-	**programming** → to program
	emergency medical technician (EMT) [ɪˌmɜːdʒnsi ˌmedɪkl tekˈnɪʃn (ˌiːemˈtiː)]	der Rettungssanitäter / die Rettungssanitäterin	Ricardo is an **emergency medical technician**.
	software [ˈsɒftweə]	die Software	Jenna is a **software** engineer.
	electrician [ˌelɪkˈtrɪʃn]	der Elektriker / die Elektrikerin	There was no power and the **electrician** came.
	carpenter [ˈkɑːpəntə]	der Zimmermann / die Zimmerin; der Tischler / die Tischlerin	**Carpenters** make things from wood.
	social worker [ˈsəʊʃl ˌwɜːkə]	der Sozialarbeiter / die Sozialarbeiterin	**social worker** → social work

Reading

p. 90	**alarm** [əˈlɑːm]	der Wecker; der Alarm; die Angst	
	to **reach out** [ˌriːtʃ‿ˈaʊt]	die Hand ausstrecken	He **reached out** to his phone.
	slim [slɪm]	dünn; schlank; schmal; gering	My mum has very **slim** fingers.
	to **sit up** [ˌsɪt‿ˈʌp]	sich aufrichten; aufrecht sitzen	I **sat up** in bed and looked around.

to **pull up** [ˌpʊl‿ˈʌp]	hochhalten; hochziehen; heranziehen	I **pulled up** the blanket on my bed.
covers [ˈkʌvəz]	das Bettzeug	The **covers** on my bed are green.
shocked [ʃɒkt]	schockiert; geschockt	We were all **shocked** to hear the news.
woken up [ˌwəʊkn‿ˈʌp]	past participle von *to wake up* (aufwachen)	He was **woken up** by a loud noise.
panic [ˈpænɪk]	die Panik	Achtung Schreibweise: pani**c**
wardrobe [ˈwɔːdrəʊb]	der Kleiderschrank	
empty [ˈemti]	leer	**empty** ↔ full
front door [ˌfrʌnt ˈdɔː]	die Eingangstür; die Haustür; die Wohnungstür	She went out the **front door** into the street.
make-up [ˈmeɪkʌp]	das Make-up; die Schminke	
look [lʊk]	der Look; das Aussehen	He loved her new colourful **look**.
confused [kənˈfjuːzd]	verwirrt; wirr	I'm quite **confused** now. Where are we going?
appearance [əˈpɪərns]	das Aussehen; die Erscheinung; der Auftritt	Why are you all so interested in my **appearance**?
to **invite** [ɪnˈvaɪt]	auffordern	Sara **invited** Robert to sit next to her.
to **realize** *(AE)* [ˈrɪəlaɪz]	sich bewusst werden; erkennen; realisieren	AE: **to realize** BE to realise
even so [ˌiːvn ˈsəʊ]	und doch; trotzdem; selbst dann	**Even so**, Robert felt quite happy.
towards [təˈwɔːdz]	gegenüber	Everyone was **friendly** towards him.
to ask sb on a date [ˌɑːsk‿ɒn‿ə ˈdeɪt]	jmdn. um eine Verabredung bitten	How exciting! He **asked me on a date**!
shy [ʃaɪ]	schüchtern	She's very **shy** and almost never talks.
to **kiss** [kɪs]	küssen	I would never **kiss** a spider.
honest [ˈɒnɪst]	ehrlich	Das **h** wird nicht gesprochen.
forward [ˈfɔːwəd]	nach vorne; vorwärts	Sam moved his head **forward** and kissed me.

Unit 5 Settling in the South

Check in

p. 98 **fertile** [ˈfɜːtaɪl]	fruchtbar	The South is a **fertile** region.
farmland [ˈfɑːmlænd]	das Ackerland; der Ackerboden; die Landwirtschaftsflächen	You can see corn on **farmland** in the Midwest.
to **flow** [fləʊ]	fließen; strömen	The river **flows** into the sea over there.
launch site [ˈlɔːnʃ ˌsaɪt]	die Raketenabschussbasis	We went to the **launch site** at Cape Canaveral.

	mission ['mɪʃn]	die Mission; der Auftrag; der Einsatz	Are there still US space **missions**? – I think so.
p. 99	smoked [sməʊkt]	geräuchert	**smoked** → smoking
	rib [rɪb]	die Rippe; *hier:* das Rippchen	**Ribs** and spicy sauce are my favourite.
	Southerner ['sʌðnə]	der Südstaatler / die Südstaatlerin	**Southerner** → south
	unique [juː'niːk]	einzigartig	This plant is **unique** in this area.
	the French [ðə 'frenʃ]	die Franzosen	The city was founded by **the French**.
	civil rights [ˌsɪvl 'raɪts]	die Bürgerrechte	**civil rights** → right
	movement ['muːvmənt]	die Bewegung	The Civil Rights **Movement** started in the 1950s.
	to protest [prə'test]	protestieren	**to protest** → protest
	segregation [ˌsegrɪ'geɪʃn]	die Rassentrennung; die Trennung	Not everyone believed in **segregation**.
	hurricane ['hʌrɪkən]	der Orkan; der Wirbelsturm; der Hurrikan	There are powerful **hurricanes** in the South.
	to cause [kɔːz]	verursachen	The driver **caused** the accident.
	flood [flʌd]	die Überschwemmung; die Flut; das Hochwasser	
	Creole ['kriːəʊl]	kreolisch; das Kreolisch; der Kreole / die Kreolin	**Creole** food is yummy.
	ingredient [ɪn'griːdiənt]	die Zutat	Here are the **ingredients** for the cake.
	shrimp [ʃrɪmp]	die Krabbe; die Garnele	You need fresh **shrimps** for jambalaya.
	coral reef [ˌkɒrəl 'riːf]	das Korallenriff	There are many **coral reefs** in Australia.
	wetland ['wetlænd]	das Sumpfgebiet; das Feuchtgebiet	The Everglades is a big **wetland** area.

Station 1

p. 100	man [mæn]	der Mensch	**man** = person
	equal ['iːkwəl]	gleich; gleichberechtigt	Everyone is **equal**.
	equal ['iːkwəl]	der Gleichgestellte / die Gleichgestellte	We should all treat each other as **equals**.
	again and again [ə'gen‿ən‿ə'gen]	immer wieder	He calls me **again and again** and I don't know why.
	access ['ækses]	der Zugang; der Zutritt	**Access** for people with disabilities is hard.
	to ask for ['ɑːsk fɔː]	bitten um; fragen nach	I **asked for** help with my homework.
	to push [pʊʃ]	schubsen; drängeln; schieben; drücken	Don't **push** other people!
	to insult [ɪn'sʌlt]	beleidigen	People pushed and **insulted** me.
	mad [mæd]	wütend; verrückt	I was **mad** with everyone.
	person of color (POC) *(AE)* [ˌpɜːsn‿əv 'kʌlə (ˌpiːəʊ'siː)]	die Person of Color (*Person mit dunkler Hautfarbe*)	Barack Obama is a **person of color**.
	to call sb names [ˌkɔːl 'neɪmz]	jmdn. beschimpfen	There were people at school who **called me names**.
	(the) public [(ðə) 'pʌblɪk]	die Öffentlichkeit	I don't like to go out in **public**.

	whenever [wen'evə]	jedes Mal, wenn; wann immer; immer, wenn; jederzeit	I enjoy the food **whenever** I'm in London.
	helpless ['helpləs]	hilflos; machtlos	**helpless** → help
	to **prove** [pru:v]	beweisen	He has to **prove** that he owns the land.
	to **ignore** [ɪg'nɔ:]	ignorieren; außer Acht lassen	I **ignored** the comments that people made.
	interest ['ɪntrəst]	das Interesse	**interest** → to be interested in
	Mexican ['meksɪkn]	mexikanisch; aus Mexiko; der Mexikaner / die Mexikanerin	**Mexican** → Mexico
	to **take sb / sth seriously** [ˌteɪk 'sɪəriəsli]	jmdn. / etw. ernst nehmen	**to take sb / sth seriously** → serious
	to **raise awareness** [ˌreɪz‿ə'weənəs]	das Bewusstsein schärfen; jmdn. sensibilisieren	It is important to **raise awareness** of discrimination.
	to **educate** ['edʒʊkeɪt]	aufklären; bilden; erziehen	**to educate** → education
p. 101	to **behave** [bɪ'heɪv]	sich verhalten; sich benehmen	I don't know how to **behave** sometimes.
	strategy ['strætədʒi]	die Strategie; die Vorgehensweise	Achtung Aussprache und Schreibweise: **strategy**
	choice [tʃɔɪs]	die Auswahl; die Wahl	**choice** → to choose
	danger ['deɪndʒə]	die Gefahr	**danger** → dangerous
	tolerant ['tɒlrnt]	tolerant	My parents are **tolerant** of others.
	to **discriminate against** [dɪ'skrɪmɪneɪt‿əˌgenst]	diskriminieren; benachteiligen	Black people are still **discriminated against** today.
	to **put oneself in danger** [ˌpʊt‿ɪn 'deɪndʒə]	sich in Gefahr bringen	Don't **put yourself in danger**!
	to **reflect** [rɪ'flekt]	nachdenken; reflektieren	We **reflected** in class about the school year.
	rude [ru:d]	unhöflich; unverschämt	Don't be **rude** to other people!
	to **put oneself in other people's shoes** [ˌpʊt‿ɪn‿ʌðə pi:plz 'ʃu:z]	sich in jmdn. hineinversetzen	**Put yourself in his shoes**, then you'll know what it feels like.
	stubborn ['stʌbən]	eigensinnig; störrisch	He won't change his mind, he's **stubborn**.
	to **imagine (sth)** [ɪ'mædʒɪn]	sich (etw.) vorstellen	I **imagined** I was on a beach far away.
	to **present** [prɪ'zent]	präsentieren; vorstellen	**to present** → presentation
	poster ['pəʊstə]	das Poster	The **posters** on the wall are colourful.

Viewing

p. 105	**bug** [bʌg]	das Insekt; der Käfer	
	sleeve [sli:v]	der Ärmel	My shirt has short **sleeves**.
	to **release** [rɪ'li:s]	freilassen; loslassen; freigeben; entlassen; herausgeben	**Release** the fish after you have caught it.
	snook [snu:k]	der Barsch	I caught a **snook** in the Everglades.
	minnow ['mɪnəʊ]	die Elritze; der Bitterfisch (*kleiner, schlanker Beutefisch*)	**Minnows** are very small fish.

	food chain ['fu:d ˌtʃeɪn]	die Nahrungskette	The **food chain** is important in an ecosystem.
	shark [ʃɑ:k]	der Hai	
	license *(AE)* ['laɪsns]	die Lizenz; die Erlaubnis	AE: **license** BE: licence

Station 2

p. 106	**artificial intelligence (AI)** [ˌɑ:tɪfɪʃl‿ɪn'telɪdʒənts (ˌeɪ'aɪ)]	die künstliche Intelligenz (KI)	Everyone is talking about **artificial intelligence**.
	space travel ['speɪs ˌtrævl]	die Raumfahrt	Florida is important for **space travel**.
	topic ['tɒpɪk]	das Thema	I like the **topic** of the story.
	Mars [mɑ:z]	der Mars	**Mars** is a planet in space.
	editor ['edɪtə]	der Redakteur / die Redakteurin; der Herausgeber / die Herausgeberin; der Lektor / die Lektorin	Do you know the **editor** of this book? – No, I don't.
	in my opinion [ɪn 'maɪ‿əˌpɪnjən]	meiner Meinung nach	**In my opinion**, she's right.
	for one thing [ˌfə 'wʌn θɪŋ]	zum einen; einerseits; erstens	**For one thing**, I really like it here.
	disaster [dɪ'zɑ:stə]	die Katastrophe; das Desaster; das Unglück	My holiday was a **disaster**.
	to **destroy** [dɪ'strɔɪ]	zerstören	The storm **destroyed** the forest.
	to **survive** [sə'vaɪv]	überleben	**to survive** ↔ to die
	moreover [mɔ:r'əʊvə]	außerdem; ferner; zudem	**Moreover**, I have found lots of friends here.
	natural resource [ˌnætʃrl rɪ'zɔ:s]	der Rohstoff; der Bodenschatz; die Ressource	There are lots of **natural resources** in the US.
	in favor of *(AE)* [ɪn 'feɪvər‿əv]	für; zugunsten von	**in favor of** ↔ against
	Sincerely, [sɪn'sɪəli]	Mit freundlichen Grüßen	So kann man in englischsprachigen Ländern Briefe und E-Mails beenden: **Sincerely,**
	discussion [dɪ'skʌʃn]	die Diskussion	Achtung Aussprache!
	firstly ['fɜ:stli]	erstens; zuerst	**Firstly**, we need to think about this idea.
	suitable ['su:təbl]	geeignet; passend	Mars isn't **suitable** for human life.
	extreme [ɪk'stri:m]	extrem; radikal	Achtung Schreibweise: extrem**e**
	secondly ['sekndli]	zweitens	Firstly, … and **secondly**, …
	might [maɪt]	könnte / könnten	I **might** be late so start without me.
	to sum up [ˌtə sʌm‿'ʌp]	zusammengefasst	**To sum up**, you can say this food is better.
	instead of [ɪn'sted‿əv]	statt; anstatt; anstelle von	Let's walk **instead of** using the car.
p. 107	**virtual reality (VR)** [ˌvɜ:tʃuəl ri'æləti (ˌvi:'ɑ:)]	die virtuelle Realität (VR)	This isn't real, it's **virtual reality**.
	Moon [mu:n]	der Mond	
	face-to-face [ˌfeɪstə'feɪs]	persönlich; von Angesicht zu Angesicht	Let's talk **face-to-face** about the problem.

	drone [drəʊn]	die Drohne	Achtung Schreibweise: **drone**
	to **explore** [ɪk'splɔ:]	erkunden; erforschen	Let's **explore** the Everglades together.
	driverless ['draɪvələs]	führerlos	I don't think **driverless** cars are safe.
	nurse [nɜ:s]	der Krankenpfleger / die Krankenpflegerin	
	solar system ['səʊlə ˌsɪstəm]	das Sonnensystem	The planets make the **solar system**.
	seaweed ['si:wi:d]	der Seetang	
	transfer ['trænsfɜ:]	die Übertragung; der Transfer	Can you tell me about thought **transfer**?
	zero gravity [ˌzɪərəʊ 'grævəti]	die Schwerelosigkeit	There is **zero gravity** in space.
	hyperloop ['haɪpəˌlu:p]	der Hyperloop	Things move very fast in a **hyperloop**.
	network ['netwɜ:k]	das Netzwerk	I have a large **network** of friends.
p. 109	**close** [kləʊs]	nahe; eng	The sun is the **closest** star to Earth.
	mobile phone [ˌməʊbaɪl 'fəʊn]	das Handy; das Mobiltelefon	People usually call **mobile phones** 'mobiles' or 'phones'.

Listening

p. 111	**coffin** ['kɒfɪn]	der Sarg	Dead people are buried in **coffins**.
	musician [mju:'zɪʃn]	der Musiker / die Musikerin	
	cemetery ['semətri]	der Friedhof	We visited a famous **cemetery** in Paris.
	to **march** [mɑ:tʃ]	marschieren	The people **marched** behind the coffin.
	funeral ['fju:nrəl]	die Beerdigung; das Begräbnis	I cried at my grandpa's **funeral**.
	jazz [dʒæz]	der Jazz (*Musikrichtung*)	My brother likes **jazz**.

Reading

p. 112	**introduction** [ˌɪntrə'dʌkʃn]	die Einleitung; die Einführung	The **introduction** is at the start of a text.
	to **abolish** [ə'bɒlɪʃ]	abschaffen	It took a long time to **abolish** slavery.
	case [keɪs]	der Fall; die Angelegenheit	In your **case**, this is true.
	to **vote** [vəʊt]	wählen; abstimmen	Black people couldn't **vote**.
	racist ['reɪsɪst]	rassistisch; der Rassist / die Rassistin	**racist** → racism
	to **exist** [ɪg'zɪst]	existieren; bestehen	The laws still **existed** in the 1950s.
	activist ['æktɪvɪst]	der Aktivist / die Aktivistin	There were lots of **activists** at the protest.
	to **refuse** [rɪ'fju:z]	sich weigern; ablehnen	Rosa **refused** to move.
	to **arrest** [ə'rest]	festnehmen; verhaften	She was **arrested** by the police.

	response [rɪ'spɒns]	die Reaktion; die Antwort; die Erwiderung	I was surprised by his **response** to the news.
	boycott ['bɔɪkɒt]	der Boykott	Achtung Schreibweise: **boycott**
	to **last** [lɑ:st]	dauern; andauern; anhalten	The boycott **lasted** a year.
	attention [ə'tenʃn]	die Aufmerksamkeit	The news caused a lot of **attention**.
p. 113	**location** [ləʊ'keɪʃn]	der Ort; der Standort; die Lage; der Drehort	There are three **locations** in town where there are parks.
	to **decide** [dɪ'saɪd]	(sich) entscheiden	My parents **decide** what we should do.
	segregated ['segrɪgeɪtɪd]	getrennt	**segregated** → segregation
	not ... anymore *(AE)* [ˌnɒt ... ˌeni'mɔ:]	nicht mehr	AE: **not ... anymore** BE: not ... any more
	protesting [prə'testɪŋ]	protestierend	**protesting** → to protest
	protestor [prə'testə]	der Demonstrant / die Demonstrantin	**protestor** → protest
	inside [ˌɪn'saɪd]	in ... hinein	Let's go **inside** the room.
	to **order** ['ɔ:də]	befehlen	The president **ordered** the police to do it.
	to **defend** [dɪ'fend]	verteidigen	The man **defended** himself against the dog.
	to **attend** [ə'tend]	besuchen; teilnehmen (an)	Do you want to **attend** school?
	shocking ['ʃɒkɪŋ]	schockierend	**shocking** → shocked
	divided [dɪ'vaɪdɪd]	geteilt; getrennt	**divided** → to divide
	to **face** [feɪs]	sich gegenübersehen; sich gegenüberstehen; entgegentreten	Black people **faced** discrimination everywhere.
	campaign [kæm'peɪn]	die Kampagne; die Aktion	Das **g** wird nicht gesprochen.
	elementary school *(AE)* [elɪ'mentri ˌsku:l]	die Grundschule	AE: **elementary school** BE: primary school
	image ['ɪmɪdʒ]	das Bild; das Image	There were lots of bad **images** in the news.
	to **shock** [ʃɒk]	schockieren	**to shock** → shocked, shocking
p. 114	**strike** [straɪk]	der Streik	The workers went on **strike**.
	speech [spi:tʃ]	die Rede; die Sprache	Martin Luther King's **speech** is famous.
	to **shoot, shot, shot** [ʃu:t, ʃɒt, ʃɒt]	schießen	King was **shot** on the balcony.
	riot [raɪət]	die Ausschreitung; der Aufruhr; die Unruhe	There were **riots** across the country.

Instructions

(Arbeitsanweisungen mit Operatoren)

Act the phone call • the role play.	**Spielt** das Telefongespräch • das Rollenspiel.
Add one detail • more information • photos.	**Ergänze** ein Detail • weitere Informationen • Fotos.
Answer the email • the questions.	**Beantworte** die E-Mail • die Fragen.
Are these sentences true or false?	**Sind diese Sätze richtig oder falsch?**
Arrange your photos.	**Ordne** deine Fotos **(an).**
Ask questions.	**Stelle** Fragen.
Ask for feedback.	**Bitte um** Rückmeldung.
Choose the right forms • the sentence with the same meaning.	**Wähle** die richtigen Formen • den Satz mit der gleichen Bedeutung **aus.**
Collect ideas • reasons from the text.	**Sammle** Ideen • Gründe aus dem Text.
Compare the information • with your partner.	**Vergleicht** die Informationen • zu zweit.
Complete the email • the sentences • the table.	**Vervollständige** die E-Mail • die Sätze • die Tabelle.
Copy the notes • the table.	**Schreibe** die Notizen • die Tabelle **ab.**
Correct the false statements • the mistakes.	**Korrigiere** die falschen Sätze • die Fehler.
Describe the cartoon • the chart • the picture.	**Beschreibe** den Cartoon • das Diagramm • das Bild.
Discuss your ideas.	**Diskutiert** eure Ideen.
Do the quiz • a survey.	**Macht** das Quiz. • **Führt** eine Umfrage **durch.**
Explain.	**Erkläre.**
Find the differences • more information • the passage • the words • phrases in the text.	**Finde** die Unterschiede • mehr Informationen • den Abschnitt • die Wörter • Satzteile im Text.
Find a word from the same word family.	**Finde** ein Wort aus derselben Wortfamilie.
Give examples • the lines.	**Nenne** Beispiele • die Zeilenzahlen.
Give feedback • a presentation • your opinion.	**Gib** Rückmeldung. • **Halte** einen Vortrag. • **Äußere** deine Meinung.
Listen and **say.**	**Höre zu** und **sprich nach.**
Listen to the interview • the podcast.	**Höre dir** das Interview • den Podcast **an.**
Look at the photos (again).	**Schau** dir die Fotos (noch einmal) **an.**
Make dialogues • a list • a mind map • notes.	**Erstelle** Dialoge • eine Liste • eine Mindmap • Notizen.
Make phrases • questions • sentences.	**Bilde** Satzteile • Fragen • Sätze.
Match the words **with** the definitions • the photos.	**Ordne** die Wörter den Definitionen • den Fotos **zu.**
Name the rule.	**Benenne** die Regel.
Organise your information.	**Ordne** deine Informationen.
Practise your presentation.	**Übe** deine Präsentation.
Prepare an interview • a statement.	**Bereite** ein Interview • eine Aussage **vor.**
Present your photos • your poster.	**Präsentiere** deine Fotos • dein Poster.
Put the photos • words in the right order.	**Bringe** die Fotos • Wörter in die richtige Reihenfolge.
Put in the right forms.	**Setze** die richtigen Formen **ein.**
Read the story • the text.	**Lies** die Geschichte • den Text.
Record your interview • your text.	**Nimm** dein Interview • deinen Text **auf.**
Replace the underlined words.	**Ersetze** die unterstrichenen Wörter.
Rewrite the sentences • the text.	**Schreibe** die Sätze • den Text **um.**
Search the internet for more information.	**Suche** im Internet nach mehr Informationen.
Share your ideas.	**Teilt** eure Ideen.
Structure your notes.	**Ordne** deine Notizen.
Swap roles.	**Tauscht die Rollen.**
Take notes • photos • turns.	**Mache** dir Notizen • Fotos. • **Wechselt** euch **ab.**
Talk about the picture • to a partner.	**Rede** über das Bild. • **Sprecht** zu zweit.
Tell your partner about it.	**Erzählt** es euch gegenseitig.
Think of more details.	**Denke dir** mehr Einzelheiten **aus.**

Turn the legend • the story • **into** a comic.	**Mache** einen Comic **aus** der Geschichte • der Legende.
Use a dictionary • your phone • short forms • these words.	**Benutze** ein Wörterbuch • dein Handy • Kurzformen • diese Wörter.
Watch the film (again).	**Schau** dir den Film (noch einmal) **an.**
Work in groups • in pairs.	**Arbeitet** in Gruppen • zu zweit.
Write a comment • your own definitions • a paragraph • the questions • sentences • short answers • a summary.	**Schreibe** einen Kommentar • eigene Definitionen • einen Absatz • die Fragen • Sätze • Kurzantworten • eine Zusammenfassung.
Write keywords.	**Notiere** Schlüsselwörter.

Classroom phrases

(Redemittel für den Unterricht)

Before or after the lesson

Good morning Mr … • Mrs/Ms … .	Guten Morgen, Herr … • Frau … .
I'm sorry I'm late.	Tut mir leid, dass ich mich verspätet habe.
I'm sorry, I don't have my exercise book • my homework with me.	Tut mir leid, ich habe mein Heft • meine Hausaufgaben nicht dabei.
What's the homework?	Was haben wir als Hausaufgabe auf?

Asking for help

Can you help me, please?	Können Sie / Kannst du mir bitte helfen?
What page is it, please?	Auf welcher Seite ist das?
Can you say that again, please?	Können Sie / Kannst du das bitte wiederholen?
What's the German • English word for …?	Was ist das deutsche • englische Wort für …?
How do you spell …?	Wie schreibt man …?
Sorry, I don't understand • don't know.	Tut mir leid, ich verstehe • weiß das nicht.
Sorry, I can't find the homepage • program.	Tut mir leid, ich finde die Homepage • das Programm nicht.
Sorry, the link doesn't work.	Tut mir leid, der Link funktioniert nicht.
What's the password?	Wie ist das Passwort?
Can I go to the toilet, please?	Kann ich bitte auf Toilette gehen?
Mr… • Mrs / Ms …, I don't feel well.	Herr … • Frau …, mir geht es nicht gut.

Working together

Can we work in pairs • groups?	Können wir zu zweit • in Gruppen arbeiten?
Do you want to work with me • us?	Willst du / Wollt ihr mit mir • uns arbeiten?
Let's make / draw a … .	Lass(t) uns ein … machen / zeichnen.
I (don't) agree.	Ich stimme (nicht) zu.
Whose turn is it? – It's my • your turn.	Wer ist dran? – Ich bin • Du bist dran.

Your teacher can say

Turn to page …, please.	Schlagt bitte Seite … auf.
Look at the board, please.	Schaut bitte an die Tafel.
Switch on/off your smartphones • tablets, please.	Schaltet bitte eure Smartphones • Tablets ein/aus.
Turn on/off the microphones • cameras, please.	Schaltet bitte eure Mikros • Kameras an/aus.

Word banks

W1 Parts of a building

A 61

D 198 Support

1	balcony	Balkon
2	basement (AE)	Keller; Untergeschoss
3	corridor	Gang; Flur
4	door	Tür
5	elevator (AE); lift (BE)	Aufzug; Lift
6	entrance	Eingang
7	exit	Ausgang
8	fire escape	Notausgang
9	floor	Fußboden
10	ground level	Erdgeschoss
11	lobby	Eingangshalle; Empfangshalle; Foyer
12	loft	Dachboden
13	roof	Dach
14	roof terrace	Dachterrasse
15	room	Zimmer; Raum
16	solar panel	Sonnenkollektor
17	stairs; staircase	Treppe; Treppenhaus
18	story (AE); floor (BE)	Etage; Stockwerk
19	underground parking lot (AE); underground car park (BE)	Tiefgarage
20	wall	Wand; Mauer
21	window	Fenster

W2 Adjectives

A 62

D 199 Support

1 **awesome**	super; spitze
2 **awful**	schrecklich; furchtbar
3 **bad**	schlecht; schlimm
4 **beautiful**	schön; hübsch
5 **cool**	cool; super
6 **cozy (AE); cosy (BE)**	gemütlich
7 **crazy**	verrückt
8 **creative**	kreativ
9 **exciting**	spannend; aufregend
10 **fantastic**	fantastisch; großartig
11 **fascinating**	faszinierend
12 **foreign**	fremd
13 **friendly**	freundlich
14 **good**	gut
15 **great**	gut; toll; großartig
16 **happy**	glücklich
17 **heartbroken**	untröstlich
18 **impressive**	beeindruckend
19 **interesting**	interessant
20 **miserable**	elend; armselig
21 **nice**	schön; nett
22 **nosy**	neugierig
23 **odd**	seltsam; merkwürdig; komisch
24 **private**	Privat-; privat
25 **sad**	traurig
26 **strange**	seltsam; merkwürdig
27 **terrible**	schrecklich; schlimm; furchtbar
28 **unhappy**	unglücklich; traurig
29 **unpleasant**	unangenehm; unerfreulich
30 **unusual**	ungewöhnlich
31 **weird**	merkwürdig; seltsam; sonderbar
32 **wonderful**	wunderbar

W3 School life in the USA

A 63

D 200 Support

1

2

3

6

10

11

12 14

15

17

18

19

21

1	cafeteria	Cafeteria; Mensa
2	cheerleading	Cheerleading
3	creative writing	kreatives Schreiben
4	debate	Debatte; Diskussion
5	detention	Nachsitzen
6	drama	Theater; Schauspiel
7	dress code	Kleiderordnung
8	elective	Wahlfach
9	exchange student	Austauschschüler/ Austauschschülerin
10	film production	Filmproduktion
11	football game	Footballspiel
12	hallway	Flur
13	homeroom (AE)	Treffpunkt vor der ersten Stunde, u.a. zur Überprüfung der Anwesenheit
14	locker	Schließfach; Spind
15	metal detector	Metalldetektor
16	online portal	Onlineportal
17	Pledge of Allegiance	Treueeid
18	practice	Probe; Übung; Training
19	prom	Ball am Ende des Jahres in einer amerikanischen High School
20	schedule (AE)	Stundenplan
21	school bus	Schulbus
22	school club	Schulklub; Schul-AG
23	school gate	Schultor
24	student council	Schülerrat
25	tutoring	Nachhilfe
26	yearbook	Jahrbuch

W4 Celebrating special days

A 64
D 201 Support

1

3

4 14

6

11

12

13

19

20

1	to dance	tanzen
2	to donate money to charity	Geld für wohltätige Zwecke spenden
3	to eat homemade cookies	selbstgemachte Kekse essen
4	to give presents	Geschenke geben
5	to have a special meal	eine besondere Mahlzeit essen
6	to light a candle	eine Kerze anzünden
7	to make a resolution	einen Vorsatz/Entschluss fassen
8	to make a video call	einen Videoanruf machen
9	to pick someone up	jemanden abholen
10	to play games	Spiele spielen
11	to prepare a meal	eine Mahlzeit vorbereiten
12	to put up decorations	Dekoration anbringen/aufbauen/aufstellen
13	to read a recipe	ein Rezept lesen
14	to receive presents	Geschenke erhalten
15	to remember people who are no longer alive	sich an Menschen erinnern, die nicht mehr leben
16	to take part in a parade	an einer Parade/einem Umzug teilnehmen
17	to visit the family	die Familie besuchen
18	to watch a fireworks display	eine Feuerwerks-vorführung ansehen
19	to watch a parade	eine Parade/einen Umzug anschauen
20	to wear special clothes	besondere Kleidung tragen

W5 Life cycle of a product

A 65

D 202 Support

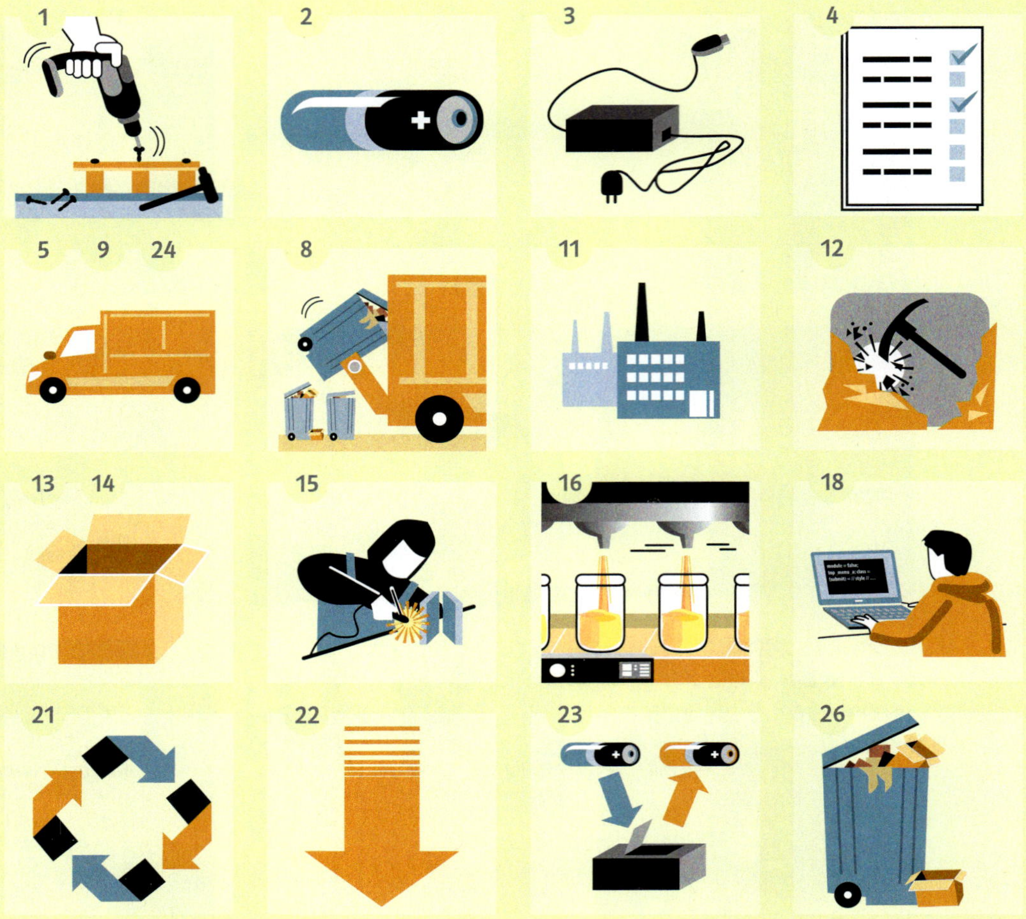

1	to assemble	zusammenbauen
2	battery	Akku; Batterie
3	to charge	aufladen
4	to check	überprüfen; kontrollieren
5	to deliver	liefern
6	to design	entwerfen; entwickeln
7	device	Gerät; Vorrichtung
8	to dispose of	entsorgen
9	to distribute	liefern; verteilen; vertreiben
10	to extract	entnehmen; gewinnen; herausnehmen
11	to manufacture	fertigen; herstellen
12	to mine	abbauen
13	to package	verpacken
14	packaging	Verpackung; Verpackungsmaterial
15	to process metal	Metall verarbeiten; aufbereiten
16	to produce	herstellen; produzieren; erzeugen
17	product	Produkt
18	to program	programmieren
19	rare metals	seltene Metalle
20	raw material	Rohstoff; Rohmaterial
21	to recycle	wiederverwenden; recyceln
22	to reduce	reduzieren; verringern
23	to replace	ersetzen
24	to transport	transportieren; befördern
25	to treat	verarbeiten/bearbeiten
26	waste	Abfall

W6 Social work

A 66
D 203 Support

1 6 8 12 29 31
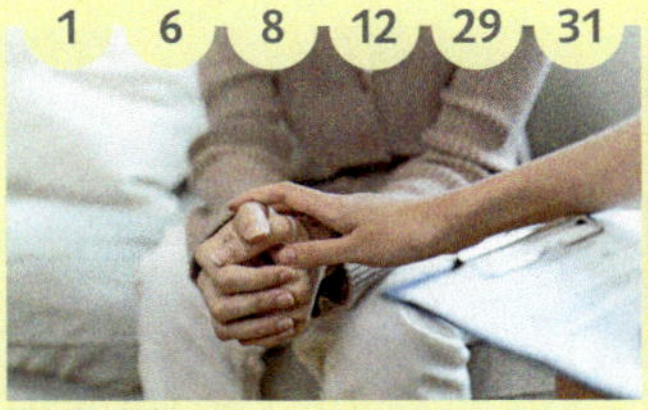

9

17

1 advice	Rat; Ratschlag
2 to advise	beraten; raten
3 to afford	sich leisten
4 alcohol	Alkohol
5 to be addicted to	süchtig sein nach
6 to cope with a situation	eine Situation bewältigen
7 counseling (AE)	Beratung
8 drug	Droge
9 to encourage	ermutigen; unterstützen
10 first responder	Ersthelfer/Ersthelferin; Notfallbegleiter/Notfallbegleiterin
11 to get into debt	sich verschulden
12 heartbreaking	herzzerreißend
13 to help	helfen
14 homeless	obdachlos; wohnungslos
15 ill	krank
16 jobless	arbeitslos
17 medical	medizinisch; ärztlich
18 medicine	Medizin; Medikamente
19 mental health	mentale/geistige/psychische Gesundheit
20 to offer	anbieten
21 outreach centre	Beratungsstelle
22 to pay the rent	Miete zahlen
23 practical help	praktische Hilfe
24 to recommend	empfehlen
25 to run away	weglaufen
26 self-respect	Selbstachtung
27 solution	Lösung
28 support	Unterstützung; Hilfe
29 to support	unterstützen; helfen
30 therapy	Therapie; Behandlung

W7 Describing a role model

A 67
D 204 Support

1 to achieve one's goals	seine Ziele erreichen
2 ambition	Ehrgeiz; Ziel
3 ambitious	ehrgeizig
4 to believe in oneself	an sich glauben
5 brave	mutig
6 confident	selbstsicher; selbstbewusst
7 determination	Entschlossenheit; Entschiedenheit; Zielstrebigkeit
8 determined	entschlossen; entschieden; zielstrebig
9 to encourage	ermutigen; unterstützen
10 fit	fit; in Form
11 to never give up	nie aufgeben
12 honest	ehrlich
13 influence	Einfluss
14 influential	einflussreich
15 modest	bescheiden
16 modesty	Bescheidenheit
17 patience	Geduld
18 patient	geduldig
19 strength	Stärke
20 strong	stark
21 success	Erfolg
22 successful	erfolgreich
23 talent	Talent; Begabung
24 talented	talentiert; begabt

W8 Infrastructure and services

A 68

D 205 Support

2
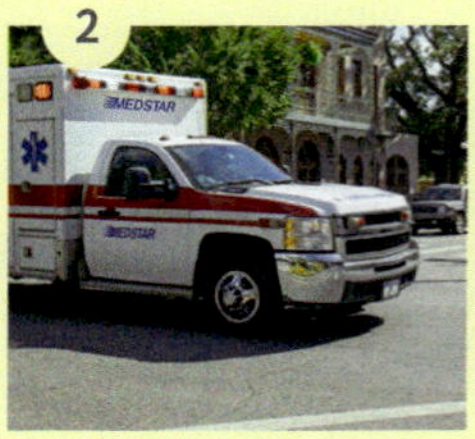
3

4

8

10

14

19

20

22

25

27

30

1	airport	Flughafen
2	ambulance	Krankenwagen
3	athletics track	Leichtathletikbahn
4	baker's	Bäckerei
5	bank	Bank
6	business	Geschäft; Unternehmen
7	bus station	Bushaltestelle; Busbahnhof
8	butcher's	Metzgerei; Fleischerei
9	café	Café
10	charging point	Ladestation
11	emergency service	Notdienst; Rettungsdienst
12	facilities	Einrichtungen
13	gym	Turnhalle
14	hairdresser's	Friseursalon
15	hall	Halle; Saal
16	harbor (AE); harbour (BE)	Hafen
17	hospital	Krankenhaus
18	hotel	Hotel
19	law court	Gerichtshof; Gericht (juristisch)
20	library	Bibliothek; Bücherei
21	museum	Museum
22	optician's	Optikfachgeschäft
23	park	Park
24	parking lot (AE); car park (BE)	Parkplatz
25	playground	Spielplatz
26	police station	Polizeirevier; Polizeiwache
27	post box	Briefkasten
28	restaurant	Restaurant
29	school	Schule
30	shopping mall (AE); shopping centre (BE)	Einkaufszentrum
31	sidewalk (AE); pavement (BE)	Gehweg; Bürgersteig
32	sports centre	Sportzentrum
33	store (AE); shop (BE)	Laden; Geschäft
34	subway (AE); underground (BE)	U-Bahn
35	supermarket	Supermarkt
36	town hall	Rathaus
37	train station	Bahnhof
38	tranportation (AE); transport (BE)	Verkehrsmittel; Beförderung
39	youth hostel	Jugendherberge

W9 Attitudes and behaviour

A 69
D 206 Support

1	to accept	akzeptieren; annehmen; hinnehmen
2	to agree	zustimmen
3	to be allowed to	dürfen
4	to behave	sich benehmen; sich verhalten
5	choice	Auswahl; Wahl
6	civil rights	Bürgerrechte
7	to cope with	bewältigen; fertig werden mit
8	danger	Gefahr
9	to discriminate against	diskriminieren; benachteiligen
10	discrimination	Diskriminierung
11	to educate	aufklären; bilden; erziehen
12	education	Ausbildung; Erziehung; Bildung
13	equal	gleich; gleichberechtigt
14	experience	Erlebnis; Erfahrung
15	fair	gerecht; fair
16	to ignore	ignorieren; außer Acht lassen
17	to listen to	zuhören; anhören
18	to organize (AE); to organise (BE)	organisieren
19	to protest	protestieren
20	to put yourself in other people's shoes	sich in die Lage einer anderen Person hineinversetzen
21	racism	Rassismus
22	to raise awareness	Bewusstsein schärfen; sensibilisieren
23	to reflect	nachdenken; reflektieren
24	to respect	respektieren
25	rude	unhöflich; unverschämt
26	to stop	aufhalten; verhindern
27	strategy	Strategie; Vorgehensweise
28	stubborn	eigensinnig; störrisch
29	to take seriously	ernst nehmen
30	tolerant	tolerant
31	to treat	behandeln
32	to understand	verstehen

W10 Giving opinions

A 70
D 207 Support

Introducing opinions

1	as I see it	wie ich das sehe
2	I agree	ich stimme zu
3	I believe	ich glaube
4	I'd say	ich würde sagen
5	I feel	ich habe das Gefühl
6	I imagine	ich stelle mir vor
7	I'm convinced	ich bin überzeugt
8	I'm in favor of (AE); I'm in favour of (BE)	ich bin für
9	I'm sure	ich bin sicher
10	in my eyes	in meinen Augen
11	in my opinion	meiner Meinung nach
12	I think	ich denke
13	it seems to me	es scheint mir
14	for me	für mich
15	my opinion is	meine Meinung ist
16	to be honest	um ehrlich zu sein
17	what I think is	was ich denke, ist

Structuring what you say

18	again	noch einmal; wieder
19	also	auch
20	although	obwohl
21	because of	wegen
22	finally	schließlich; endlich; zum Schluss
23	firstly, secondly	erstens, zweitens
24	for all these reasons	aus all diesen Gründen
25	for example	zum Beispiel
26	for one thing	zum einen; einerseits
27	however	jedoch
28	moreover	außerdem; ferner; zudem
29	next	als Nächstes
30	that's why	deshalb
31	then	danach; dann
32	to sum up	zusammengefasst

W11 In the future

A 71

D 208 Support

1	air taxi	Lufttaxi
2	artificial intelligence	künstliche Intelligenz
3	artificial meat	künstliches Fleisch
4	astronaut	Astronaut/Astronautin
5	to connect	verbinden
6	to destroy	zerstören
7	to develop	entwickeln
8	disaster	Katastrophe; Desaster; Unglück
9	disease	Krankheit
10	driverless	führerlos
11	drone	Drohne
12	Earth	Erde
13	environment	Umwelt; Umgebung
14	to explore	erkunden; erforschen
15	face-to-face	persönlich; von Angesicht zu Angesicht
16	hyperloop network	Hyperloop Netzwerk
17	insect	Insekt
18	to look for	suchen nach
19	low-emission	emissionsarm; schadstoffarm
20	Mars	Mars
21	Moon	Mond
22	peace	Frieden
23	planet	Planet
24	to protect	schützen; beschützen
25	robot	Roboter
26	to save	sparen; retten; speichern
27	science	Wissenschaft
28	scientist	Wissenschaftler/ Wissenschaftlerin
29	seaweed	Seegras
30	solar panel	Sonnenkollektor
31	solar system	Sonnensystem
32	solution	Lösung
33	space	Weltraum
34	spacecraft	Raumschiff
35	space walk	Weltraumspaziergang
36	to survive	überleben
37	sustainable	nachhaltig
38	technology	Technik; Technologie
39	thought transfer	Gedankenübertragung
40	virtual reality (VR)	virtuelle Realität (VR)
41	war	Krieg
42	wind energy	Windenergie
43	zero gravity	Schwerelosigkeit

Dictionary

Im *Dictionary* sind alle wichtigen Wörter aus deinem Buch enthalten.
Die Wörter stehen in alphabetischer Reihenfolge.
Englische Wörter schlägst du auf S. 241 – S. 263 nach, deutsche Wörter auf S. 264 – S. 285.

Die Abkürzungen geben die Fundstellen an, wo das Wort zum ersten Mal im Buch erscheint, z. B.:
book Buch; Heft I: kommt zum ersten Mal vor in Band 1.
Blaue Fundstellen = Lernwortschatz, z. B. **activist** Aktivist / Aktivistin IV U5, 112
Grüne Fundstellen = Differenzierungswortschatz, z. B. **ambition** Ehrgeiz; Ziel IV U4, 79
Graue Fundstellen = kein Lernwortschatz, z. B. **ability** Fähigkeit IV U5, 116
ZI = Zoom in, * = unregelmäßiges Verb → *List of irregular verbs*, S. 172 – S. 175

Manche Wörter haben verschiedene Bedeutungen. Am besten liest du dir alle durch, bevor du dich für eine entscheidest.

*to **get** werden; bekommen I; hinkommen II
to **get** around herumkommen I; sich bewegen III
to **get** dressed sich anziehen I
to **get** hurt sich verletzen; verletzt werden IV U2, 43
to **get** into bilden I; hineingelangen; hineinkommen IV U3, 62
to **get** into debt sich verschulden IV U3, 62
to **get** lost sich verlaufen; sich verirren II
to **get** married heiraten II
to **get** off aussteigen; absteigen II
to **get** on einsteigen II
to **get** out herausholen; herauskommen III
to **get** ready sich fertig machen; sich vorbereiten IV U2, 32
to **get** scared Angst bekommen III
to **get** up aufstehen I
to **get** used to (sth) sich an (etw.) gewöhnen III

A

a ein / eine I
a / one hundred einhundert; hundert I
a / one thousand eintausend; tausend II
a bit ein bisschen; ein wenig II
a few ein paar; wenige; einige II
a little ein bisschen II
a lot viel I
a lot of viel(e); eine Menge I
a piece of ein Stück; eine Scheibe; ein Blatt II
a week pro Woche; in der Woche II
a year pro Jahr III
a.m. vormittags (*Uhrzeit*) II
ability Fähigkeit IV U5, 116
*to be **able** to (do sth) (etw.) können; (etw.) dürfen; (zu etw.) fähig sein II
to **abolish** abschaffen IV U5, 112
about über; ungefähr; circa; etwa I
to care **about** wichtig nehmen; sich kümmern um; sich interessieren für III
out and **about** unterwegs I
above über; oberhalb; oben IV U1, 10
accent Akzent III
to **accept** akzeptieren; annehmen; hinnehmen III
access Zugang; Zutritt IV U5, 100
accident Unfall IV U4, 80
account Konto III
ache Schmerz; Schmerzen II
to **achieve** erreichen; schaffen; leisten IV U1, 21
acorn Eichel III
acre Acre (*Flächenmaß: 4.050 m²*) IV U2, 37
across über; quer durch; hinüber; herüber III
to **act** spielen; sich verhalten; handeln II
action Bewegung; Aktion; Handlung II
active aktiv IV U3, 58
active voice Aktiv IV U3, 58
activist Aktivist / Aktivistin IV U5, 112
activity Aktivität I
actor Schauspieler / Schauspielerin II
ad (= advertisement) Werbespot; Anzeige; Annonce II
AD (= Anno Domini) nach Christus III
to **add** hinzufügen; ergänzen; addieren III
addicted (to) süchtig (nach) IV U3, 62
address Adresse; Anschrift III
to **address** ansprechen; adressieren IV U3, 66
adjective Adjektiv; Eigenschaftswort I
administration Verwaltung IV U4, 88
adventure Abenteuer I
adverb Adverb II
to **advertise** werben; Werbung machen (für) III
advice Rat; Ratschlag III
to **advise** sb jmdn. beraten; jmdm. raten IV U3, 63
to **affect** beeinträchtigen; beeinflussen; betreffen IV U5, 110
to **afford** sich leisten IV U3, 62
afraid ängstlich II
to be **afraid** Angst haben; sich fürchten I
Africa Afrika IV U4, 83
African afrikanisch; aus Afrika; Afrikaner / Afrikanerin III
African American Afroamerikaner / Afroamerikanerin; afroamerikanisch IV U1, 25
after nach I; danach; nachdem; später III
after that danach I
to look **after** aufpassen auf; hüten II
afternoon Nachmittag I
afterwards danach; hinterher III
again wieder; noch einmal I
again and again immer wieder IV U5, 100
against gegen II
age Zeitalter; Alter II
in **ages** seit Ewigkeiten; seit einer Ewigkeit III
aged im Alter von III
ago vor (*zeitlich*) I
to **agree** zustimmen II
to **agree** (on) sich einigen (auf) III
agreement Vereinbarung; Vertrag; Einigung; Zustimmung III
agriculture Landwirtschaft; Ackerbau IV U2, 30
aim Ziel; Absicht IV U2, 34; IV U3, 66
air Luft II
air conditioning unit Klimaanlage II
aircraft Flugzeug IV U1, 10
aircraft carrier Flugzeugträger IV U1, 10
airport Flughafen III
alarm Wecker; Alarm; Angst IV U4, 90
alcohol Alkohol III
alive am Leben IV U4, 77
all alle; ganz; alles; all; ganz I
all of alle III
all of a sudden plötzlich; auf einmal III

all over überall III
all the way to bis ganz hinunter zu III
allegiance Treue IV U2, 32
allergic to allergisch gegen I
allergy Allergie IV U2, 49
alligator Alligator IV U3, 68
allotment Schrebergarten II
to **allow** erlauben; gestatten III
to be **allowed** to (do sth) (etw. tun) dürfen II
almost fast; beinahe II
alone allein II
along entlang I
aloud laut III
alphabet Alphabet I
already schon; bereits II
also auch I
although obwohl III
always immer I
am bin I
amazed erstaunt; verblüfft II
amazing unglaublich; toll; erstaunlich II
ambition Ehrgeiz; Ziel IV U4, 79
ambitious ehrgeizig IV U4, 78
ambulance Krankenwagen; Rettungswagen III
America Amerika II
American amerikanisch; Amerikanisch; aus Amerika; Amerikaner / Amerikanerin II
American football American Football IV U2, 31
the **Amish** Amischen IV U1, 18
Amish amisch IV U1, 18
amount (of) Menge; Summe IV U3, 56
an ein / eine I
ancestor Vorfahre / Vorfahrin III
ancient alt; altertümlich IV U3, 68
and und I
angle Winkel IV U1, 20
Anglo-Saxon Angelsachse / Angelsächsin; angelsächsisch III
angry wütend; zornig; verärgert; böse I
animal Tier I
animal home Tierheim II
animation Animation IV U3, 60
ankle Fußgelenk; Fußknöchel II
announcement Durchsage; Ankündigung III
annoyed verärgert III
to feel **annoyed** verärgert sein III
another ein anderer / eine andere; noch ein I; weitere III
one **another** einander; gegenseitig I
answer Antwort I
to **answer** beantworten; antworten II
ant-eater Ameisenbär II
anti- Anti-; Nicht- IV U5, 104
any irgendwas; etwas; irgendein I; irgendwelche II; jegliche / jeglicher / jegliches III
not … **any** kein / keine II
anyone irgendjemand; jeder (beliebige) III
anything irgendetwas I; alles IV U1, 10
not … **anything** nichts IV U1, 10
Anything else? Darf es sonst noch etwas sein? I
anyway wie auch immer; trotzdem; jedenfalls II; sowieso III
apartment Wohnung; Apartment IV U1, 16
app App; Anwendung III
to **appear** auftauchen; erscheinen III
appearance Aussehen; Erscheinung; Auftritt IV U4, 90
apple Apfel I
apple pie gedeckter Apfelkuchen II
to **apply** auftragen III
to **apply** (for) sich bewerben (für / um) IV U4, 78
apprenticeship Ausbildung; Lehre IV U4, 89
April April I
aquarium Aquarium II
Arabic Arabisch; arabisch III
archway Torbogen; Bogengang III
are sind; bist I
area Gegend; Gebiet; Areal II; Fläche III
arena Stadion I
argument Streit; Auseinandersetzung III; Argument IV U3, 57
arm Arm II
army Armee; Heer IV U3, 71
around rund um; um … herum I; ungefähr; gegen III
to get **around** herumkommen I; sich bewegen III
to show sb **around** (a place) jmdn. (an einem Ort) herumführen II
to **arrange** arrangieren; organisieren; ausmachen III
to **arrest** festnehmen; verhaften IV U5, 112
to **arrive** ankommen I
art Kunst I
arts Kunst III
article Artikel; Bericht III
artificial künstlich IV U5, 106
artificial intelligence (AI) künstliche Intelligenz (KI) IV U5, 106
artist Künstler / Künstlerin III
arts and crafts Kunsthandwerk III
as als III; da; weil II; wie IV U4, 83
as … **as** so … wie III
as soon **as** sobald III
as well auch III
… **as** well as … sowohl … als auch … IV U2, 37
*to be **ashamed** of sich schämen für / wegen IV U2, 44
Asia Asien III
Asian asiatisch; aus Asien; Asiate / Asiatin IV U3, 55
to **ask** fragen I
to **ask** for bitten um; fragen nach IV U5, 100
to **ask** sb on a date jmdn. um eine Verabredung bitten IV U4, 90
to **ask** sb to do sth jmdn. bitten, etw. zu tun IV U4, 84
to **ask** for bitten um; fragen nach I
aspect Aspekt; Gesichtspunkt; Blickwinkel II
to **assemble** zusammenbauen; montieren IV U3, 57
assistant Verkäufer / Verkäuferin; Assistent / Assistentin I
astronaut Astronaut / Astronautin I
at in; an; um; bei; auf I
at first zuerst; zunächst II
at home zu Hause I
at least mindestens; wenigstens; immerhin III
at night nachts IV U4, 76
at the moment im Moment; gerade; momentan; derzeit III
at the top oben II
ate simple past von *to eat* II
athlete Athlet / Athletin; Leichtathlet / Leichtathletin III
athletics Leichtathletik IV U4, 85
athletics track Leichtathletikbahn IV U4, 85
atmosphere Atmosphäre; Stimmung IV U2, 43
attack Anschlag; Attacke; Angriff; Überfall IV U1, 15
to **attend** teilnehmen (an); besuchen IV U5, 113
attention Aufmerksamkeit IV U5, 112
to catch sb's **attention** jmdn. auf sich aufmerksam machen III
attic Dachboden I
attitude Einstellung; Haltung IV U5, 101
attraction Attraktion; Sehenswürdigkeit IV U1, 10
attractive attraktiv II
au pair Au-pair IV U1, 19
audience Publikum; Zuschauer IV U2, 42
audio Audio; Hör-; Audio- III
audio guide Audioguide I
audiobook Hörbuch III
August August I
aunt Tante I
Australia Australien III
author Autor / Autorin III
autumn Herbst I
available erhältlich; verfügbar III
average durchschnittlich IV U3, 56
to **avoid** vermeiden; meiden; aus dem Weg gehen; ausweichen IV U3, 68
awake bei Bewusstsein; wach III
award Preis; Auszeichnung IV U4, 78
awareness Bewusstsein; Interesse IV U5, 100
to raise **awareness** das Bewusstsein schärfen; jmdn. sensibilisieren IV U5, 100
away weg; entfernt I
straight **away** sofort; gleich III
awesome super; spitze II
awful schrecklich; furchtbar II

B

B&B (bed and breakfast) Frühstückspension III
babysitting Babysitten III
back Rücken; Rückseite II
back zurück I
background Herkunft; Hintergrund II
bacon Speck II
bad schlecht; schlimm I

badminton Badminton I
bag Tasche; Tüte I; Sack III
bagpipes Dudelsack III
to **bake** backen I
baker's Bäckerei I
balcony Balkon IV U1, 11
ball Ball; Kugel II
banana Banane I
band Band; Musikgruppe II
bandage Verband III
bank Bank; Böschung; Ufer IV U4, 84
bar Tafel; Riegel; Stange I
barbecue Grillfest; Grill IV U1, 15
to **bark** bellen III
baseball Baseball IV ZI, 6
based on basierend auf; angelehnt an IV U3, 67
basement *(AE)* Keller; Untergeschoss; Kellergeschoss IV U1, 11
basketball Basketball III
bathroom Badezimmer; Bad I
battery Akku; Batterie II
BC (= before Christ) vor Christus III
*to **be** sein I
to **be** a little person kleinwüchsig sein IV U4, 78
to **be** able to (do sth) (etw.) können; (etw.) dürfen; (zu etw.) fähig sein II
to **be** afraid Angst haben; sich fürchten I
to **be** allowed to (do sth) (etw. tun) dürfen II
to **be** ashamed of sich schämen für / wegen IV U2, 44
to **be** born geboren werden III
to **be** called heißen; genannt werden III
to **be** cold frieren I
to **be** fun Spaß machen; witzig sein I
to **be** going on los sein III
to **be** good at gut sein in I
to **be** happy to do sth etw. gern tun; etw. tun können IV U4, 84
to **be** homesick Heimweh haben II
to **be** in charge (of) verantwortlich sein (für); zuständig sein (für) IV U2, 34
to **be** in pain Schmerzen haben III
to **be** late Verspätung haben; zu spät sein I
to **be** lucky Glück haben II
to **be** made of hergestellt sein aus IV U3, 56
to **be** missing fehlen I
to **be** on stattfinden; laufen (Veranstaltung) III
to **be** prepared bereit sein; vorbereitet sein III
to **be** right recht haben III
to **be** scared Angst haben; erschrocken sein III
to **be** set (in) spielen (in) IV U4, 79
to **be** sorry leidtun III
to **be** terrified schreckliche Angst haben IV U1, 22
to **be** used for verwendet werden für III
to **be** wrong nicht stimmen; unrecht haben; sich irren III
beach Strand I
beam Balken; Strahl IV U1, 12
bean Bohne IV U4, 77
beanie Mütze III
bear Bär IV U3, 68
beat Takt; Rhythmus; Schlag IV U2, 44
beautiful schön; hübsch I
became simple past von *to become* I
because weil; da I
because of wegen III
*to **become** werden I
become past participle von *to become* III
bed Bett I
bedroom Schlafzimmer; Kinderzimmer I
bee Biene II
beef Rindfleisch II
been past participle von *to be* II
before bevor; vor; vorher; zuvor I
began simple past von *to begin* I
*to **begin** beginnen; anfangen I
beginning Anfang; Beginn IV U2, 32
to **behave** sich verhalten; sich benehmen IV U5, 101
behaviour Verhalten IV U5, 101
behind hinter I
belief Glaube; Überzeugung IV U1, 21
to **believe** glauben III
bell Glocke II
below unter; unterhalb; unten II
belt Gürtel II
bench Bank; Sitzbank II
berry Beere II
best beste / bester / bestes I; am besten; am liebsten II
best of all am besten; das Beste IV U1, 10
better besser II
between zwischen I
BFF BFF / BFF; bester Freund / beste Freundin für immer IV U4, 86
big groß I
big deal große Sache IV U4, 86
bike Fahrrad I
biker Fahrradfahrer / Fahrradfahrerin; Motorradfahrer / Motorradfahrerin II
bin Mülleimer I
biology Biologie I
bionic bionisch II
birch Birke II
bird Vogel I
birthday Geburtstag I
biscuit Keks II
bison Bison IV U2, 31
a **bit** ein bisschen; ein wenig II
black schwarz I
Black schwarz *(soziale Kategorie)* IV U4, 83
blanket Decke; Bettdecke; Wolldecke III
blog Blog; Internettagebuch II
to **blog** bloggen; ein Internettagebuch führen III
blonde blond III
blood Blut III
blouse Bluse IV U1, 23
blue blau I
blue whale Blauwal II
blues Blues *(Musikrichtung)* IV U5, 111
board Tafel I
on **board** an Bord IV U1, 22
board game Brettspiel III
boarding Einsteigen; Anbordgehen III
boat Boot I
body Körper II
body language Körpersprache IV U2, 47
bonfire Freudenfeuer; Feuer *(im Freien)* I
book Buch; Heft I
print **books** gedruckte Bücher III
to **book** buchen; reservieren II
boot Stiefel II; Kofferraum; Gepäckraum III
border Grenze III
bored gelangweilt II
boring langweilig I
*to be **born** geboren werden III
to **borrow** ausleihen I
both beide II; beide IV U2, 45
both … and … sowohl … als auch … III
bottle Flasche I
bought simple past von *to buy* I
box Box; Kiste; Schachtel I
boy Junge I
boycott Boykott IV U5, 112
brain Gehirn IV U2, 46
brand Marke IV U1, 10
brave mutig; tapfer III
bread Brot I
break Pause II
*to **break** brechen; zerbrechen III
breakfast Frühstück I
to have **breakfast** frühstücken I
to **breathe** atmen II
bridge Brücke II
brilliant toll; brillant II
*to **bring** bringen; mitbringen II
Britain Großbritannien I
British britisch I
the **British** die Briten III
the **British Isles** die Britischen Inseln III
broke simple past von *to break* III
broke pleite IV U4, 86
broken gebrochen; kaputt II; past participle von *to break* III
brother Bruder I
brought simple past von *to bring* I
brown braun I
brush Bürste III
to **brush** putzen; bürsten II
to **brush** one's teeth sich die Zähne putzen II
buck *(AE)* Dollar IV U4, 86
bug Insekt; Käfer IV U5, 105
*to **build** bauen I
building Gebäude II; Bau- III
built simple past von *to build* I
bully Mobber / Mobberin; Tyrann / Tyrannin IV U4, 78
bullying Mobbing; Schikanieren; Tyrannisieren III
burger Hamburger II
*to **burn** verbrennen; brennen III
burnt simple past, past participle von *to burn* III
to **bury** begraben; beerdigen III
bus Bus I
bus stop Bushaltestelle II
business Geschäft; Unternehmen; Branche IV U4, 84

busy beschäftigt; belebt; arbeitsreich I; voller Menschen III
but aber I
butcher's Metzgerei; Fleischerei IV U4, 85
butter Butter I
butterfly Schmetterling II
button Knopf; Taste II
*to **buy** kaufen I
by von II; an; neben; um III
  by *(+ -ing)* indem III
  by (bike) mit (dem Fahrrad) I
  by law gesetzlich IV U3, 68
Bye. Tschüss. I

C

cabbage Kohl; Kraut II
caber Baumstamm III
caber toss Baumstammwerfen III
cabin Kabine IV U1, 22
cable car Seilbahn I
cactus Kaktus IV U3, 68
café Café II
cafeteria Cafeteria; Mensa I
cake Kuchen I
calf Kalb II
call Anruf; Ruf II; Aufforderung; Aufruf III
to **call** rufen; anrufen I; nennen II
  to be **called** heißen; genannt werden III
  to **call** sb names jmdn. beschimpfen IV U5, 100
to **calm** down sich beruhigen III
calm ruhig; friedlich II
came simple past von *to come* I
camera Kamera; Fotoapparat III
cameraperson Kameramann / Kamerafrau I
camp Lager; Camp I
campaign Kampagne; Aktion IV U5, 113
campervan Wohnmobil III
camping Camping; Zelten III
campsite Campingplatz; Zeltplatz III
can Dose I
can können I
  Can you help me? Können Sie mir helfen?; Kannst du mir helfen? I
  can't (= cannot) nicht können I
  I **can't** wait. Ich kann es kaum erwarten. III
Canada Kanada III
canal Kanal III
to **cancel** absagen; stornieren III
cancelled annulliert; gestrichen; abgesagt III
candle Kerze III
canoeing Kanufahren III
canyon Schlucht; Canyon IV U3, 54
cap Kappe; Mütze IV U2, 32
capital (city) Hauptstadt III
captain Kapitän / Kapitänin II
caption Bildunterschrift; Untertitel I
car Auto I
car boot sale Flohmarkt (*Verkauf aus dem Kofferraum*) III
car park Parkplatz I
caravan Wohnwagen III
card Pappe; Karton; Karte IV U3, 56
to **care** about wichtig nehmen; sich kümmern um; sich interessieren für III
  to **care** (for) sich kümmern (um) I
careful vorsichtig; sorgfältig II
caretaker Hausmeister / Hausmeisterin I
carnival Karneval; Fasching IV U2, 41
carpenter Zimmermann / Zimmerin; Tischler / Tischlerin IV U4, 89
carpet Teppich I
carrier Träger; Spediteur IV U1, 10
carrot Karotte II
to **carry** tragen; befördern I
carton Karton I
cartoon Cartoon; Zeichentrickfilm II
to **carve** schnitzen III
case Schaukasten; Gehäuse III; Fall; Angelegenheit IV U5, 112
castle Schloss; Burg I
cat Katze I
catastrophe Katastrophe; Unglück IV U1, 15
catch Fang III
*to **catch** fangen; einfangen III
  to **catch** sb's attention jmdn. auf sich aufmerksam machen III
catchy eingängig; einprägsam III
cathedral Dom; Kathedrale III
Catholic Katholik / Katholikin; katholisch III
cattle Rinder; Vieh IV U4, 77
caught simple past, past participle von *to catch* III
to **cause** verursachen IV U5, 99
cave Höhle I
to **celebrate** feiern II
celebration Feier; Fest III
Celt Kelte / Keltin III
cemetery Friedhof IV U5, 111
center *(AE)* Zentrum; Mitte; Center IV U1, 9
centimetre (cm) Zentimeter II
central zentral III
Central Europe Mitteleuropa III
centre Zentrum; Mitte; Center I
century Jahrhundert III
ceramic Keramik IV U3, 56
cereal Müsli II
ceremony Zeremonie; Feier IV U1, 15
certain bestimmte III
chain Kette IV U5, 105
chair Stuhl I
chairperson Vorsitzender / Vorsitzende III
challenge Herausforderung III
chance Chance; Möglichkeit; Gelegenheit IV U1, 21
change Wechselgeld; Restgeld; Münzgeld I; Veränderung; Änderung; Wechsel II
to **change** (sich) verändern; (sich) ändern; umsteigen; wechseln II
  to **change** one's mind seine Meinung ändern III
changing im Wandel; wechselnd; sich verändernd II
channel Kanal; Programm II
chant Sprechgesang I
chapter Kapitel III
character Charakter; Figur III
character trait Charakterzug IV U4, 79
characteristic Eigenschaft; Merkmal IV U1, 23
*to be in **charge** (of) verantwortlich sein (für); zuständig sein (für) IV U2, 34
to **charge** aufladen; berechnen; verlangen; erheben IV U3, 56
charging point Ladestation IV U4, 85
charity Wohltätigkeitsorganisation; Stiftung I
chart Diagramm; Tabelle III
to **chase** jagen; verfolgen IV U2, 43
chaser Jäger / Jägerin; Verfolger / Verfolgerin IV U2, 43
chat Chat; Unterhaltung III
to **chat** chatten; plaudern II
cheap billig II
to **check** überprüfen; kontrollieren; anschauen II; checken III
check in Einchecken I
check out Auschecken I
checklist Checkliste I
cheeky frech I
cheerleader Cheerleader / Cheerleaderin (*jmd., der in einer Gruppe eine Sportmannschaft anfeuert*) II
cheerleading Cheerleading IV U2, 33
cheese Käse I
chef Koch / Köchin I
chemical Chemikalie IV U3, 56
chemistry Chemie IV U1, 25
cherry Kirsche IV U2, 37
chest Brust; Brustkorb II
chewing gum Kaugummi III
chicken Hähnchen; Huhn II
child Kind II
children Kinder II
China China II
Chinese chinesisch; Chinesisch; aus China; Chinese / Chinesin II
chips Pommes frites I
chocolate Schokolade I; Praline II
choice Auswahl; Wahl IV U5, 101
choir Chor III
*to **choose** auswählen; wählen I
chore Aufgabe; Arbeit I
chose simple past von *to choose* I
Christmas Weihnachten I
church Kirche I
cinema Kino I
cinnamon Zimt IV U2, 38
circle Kreis III
citizen Staatsbürger / Staatsbürgerin; Staatsangehöriger / Staatsangehörige IV U1, 15
city Stadt; Großstadt I
city break Städtereise III
city hall Rathaus IV U4, 84
civil rights Bürgerrechte IV U5, 99
to **clap** klatschen II
class Klasse; Unterricht; Kurs; Unterrichtsstunde I
classmate Klassenkamerad / Klassenkameradin; Mitschüler / Mitschülerin II
classroom Klassenzimmer I
to **clean** sauber machen; putzen I
  to **clean** up sauber machen; aufräumen; beseitigen II
clean sauber I

cleaning Saubermachen; Reinigung I
clear scharf; klar; deutlich; eindeutig II
clever schlau; klug; intelligent III
to **click** klicken II
cliff Klippe; Kliff III
climate Klima IV U3, 61
to **climb** besteigen; klettern; steigen II
climbing Klettern I
climbing wall Kletterwand I
clip Clip; Ausschnitt; Kurzfilm III
clock Uhr II
clock tower Uhrenturm II
clog Holzschuh; Clog III
to **close** schließen; zumachen I
close nahe; eng IV U5, 109
closed geschlossen; gesperrt I
closing Schluss-; abschließend IV U4, 82
clothes Kleider; Kleidung I
cloud Wolke I
cloudy wolkig I
clove Nelke III
club Klub; Schul-AG I; Verein III
clubhouse Vereinsheim; Klubhaus III
clumsy ungeschickt; unbeholfen II
coach Trainer / Trainerin III
coast Küste I
coastal Küsten- III
coastal path Küstenweg; Küstenpfad III
coastguard Küstenwache III
coastline Küste III
coat Mantel; Jacke II
coffin Sarg IV U5, 111
cola Cola I
cold Erkältung; Schnupfen; Kälte II
cold kalt I
to be **cold** frieren I
collage Collage III
to **collapse** einstürzen; zusammenbrechen; kollabieren IV U1, 15
to **collect** einsammeln; sammeln I
college College; Hochschule; Fachhochschule III
colony Kolonie III
color *(AE)* Farbe IV U5, 100
colour Farbe I
colourful bunt; farbig; farbenfroh II
*to **come** kommen; geben; erhältlich sein I
to **come** true wahr werden; in Erfüllung gehen IV U5, 115
come past participle von *to come* II
comfortable bequem; angenehm II
to feel **comfortable** sich wohlfühlen II
comic Comic; Comicheft II
comic strip Comicstreifen III
comical komisch IV U4, 79
comma Komma III
comment Kommentar IV U2, 32
common häufig; verbreitet III
to have sth in **common** etw. gemeinsam haben III
communication Kommunikation II
community Gemeinde; Gemeinschaft II
company Firma; Unternehmen; Gesellschaft III
comparative Komparativ II
to **compare** vergleichen III
comparison Vergleich IV U1, 19
compass Kompass III
to **compete** (in) antreten (bei); teilnehmen (an); konkurrieren; sich messen III; IV U5, 101
competition Wettbewerb; Wettkampf; Turnier III
compilation Sammel-; Zusammenstellung; Sammlung III
to **complain** sich beschweren; sich beklagen III
to **complete** vervollständigen I
complete vollständig I
completely völlig IV ZI, 7
complex komplex III
compliment Kompliment II
computer Computer I
concert Konzert I
conclusion Schluss; Schlussfolgerung IV U3, 66
condition Bedingung; Zustand; Erkrankung IV U4, 78
confident selbstsicher; selbstbewusst II
conflict Konflikt; Auseinandersetzung III
confused verwirrt; wirr IV U4, 90
to **connect** verbinden; sich verbinden III
connection Verbindung IV U3, 61
consequence Folge; Konsequenz; Auswirkung III
conspiracy theory Verschwörungstheorie IV U4, 82
construction Bau; Konstruktion; Aufbau IV U1, 12
to **contact** sich in Verbindung setzen mit; kontaktieren III
container Behälter; Behältnis; Container I
content Inhalt III; Gehalt IV U5, 115
context Kontext; Zusammenhang IV U4, 79
continent Kontinent; Erdteil III
to **continue** fortfahren; weitergehen; weitermachen; fortführen III
to **contradict** widersprechen IV U4, 91
contribution Beitrag; Beteiligung IV U4, 83
conversation Gespräch; Unterhaltung; Konversation III
convinced überzeugt IV U3, 68
to **cook** kochen I
cooker Herd II
cookie *(AE)* Keks I
to **cool** kühlen II
cool cool; super; kühl I
to **cope** with bewältigen; fertig werden mit IV U3, 62
copper Kupfer IV U4, 77
to **copy** kopieren; abschreiben I
coral Koralle IV U5, 99
coral reef Korallenriff IV U5, 99
corn Mais; Korn; Getreide IV U2, 30
cornbread Maisbrot IV U2, 38
corner Ecke I
to **correct** korrigieren; verbessern; berichtigen I
correct richtig; korrekt II
correction Korrektur; Verbesserung II
corridor Gang; Flur III
cost Kosten; Preis IV U2, 37
costume Kostüm II
cottage Häuschen III
could konnte II; könnte III
council Rat IV U2, 32
counseling *(AE)* Beratung; psychologische Betreuung IV U3, 62
to **count** zählen II
country Land; ländliche Gegend I
in the **country** auf dem Land II
countryside Landschaft; Land III
county Landkreis; Grafschaft; Bezirk III
course Kurs III
of **course** natürlich; selbstverständlich I
court Spielfeld III; Gericht *(juristisch)* IV U4, 85
cousin Cousin / Cousine I
cover Titelblatt; Umschlag III
covers Bettzeug IV U4, 90
cow Kuh I
cowboy Cowboy IV U4, 77
cozy gemütlich IV U1, 16
cradle Wiege III
craft Handwerk III
craftspeople Kunsthandwerker / Kunsthandwerkerin; Handwerker / Handwerkerin III; Handwerker / Handwerkerinnen IV U2, 31
to **crash** abstürzen *(Flugzeug)*; krachen; zusammenstoßen IV U1, 15
crazy verrückt I
cream Sahne; Rahm; Creme I
cream cheese Frischkäse I
to **create** machen; schaffen; erschaffen II
creative kreativ II
credit card Kreditkarte III
Cree Cree-; Cree / Cree; Cree IV U2, 44
creek *(AE)* Bach IV U3, 67
Creole kreolisch; Kreolisch; Kreole / Kreolin IV U5, 99
crew Crew; Besatzung; Mannschaft II
crime Verbrechen II
criminal Krimineller / Kriminelle; Verbrecher / Verbrecherin I
crisp Kartoffelchip I
crop Feldfrucht; Ernte IV U2, 31
crop top bauchfreies Oberteil IV U2, 32
to **cross** überqueren I; wechseln; kreuzen IV U2, 40
crossing Kreuzung I
crowd Menschenmenge II
crowded überfüllt III
cruel grausam IV U4, 79
to **cry** schreien; weinen; rufen III
cucumber Gurke I
culture Kultur III
cupboard Schrank I
currency Währung IV ZI, 6
curry Curry II
curtain Vorhang I
customer Kunde / Kundin III
*to **cut** (sich) schneiden II
cut simple past, past participle von *to cut* II
cycle Fahrrad III; Zyklus; Kreislauf IV U3, 56
to **cycle** Fahrrad fahren II
cycle lane Radweg III
cycling Radfahren I
to go **cycling** Fahrrad fahren I

D

dad Papa I
daily täglich; Alltags- I
dairy Milch-; Molkerei IV U2, 30
dairy farming Milchbetrieb; Milchproduktion IV U2, 30
dam Talsperre; Staumauer; Damm IV U4, 77
to **damage** beschädigen; schaden III
dance Tanz I
to **dance** tanzen II
dancer Tänzer / Tänzerin II
dancing Tanzen; Tanz- I
danger Gefahr IV U5, 101
to put oneself in **danger** sich in Gefahr bringen IV U5, 101
dangerous gefährlich I
dark Dunkelheit III
dark dunkel I
database Datenbank III
date Datum I; Verabredung; Date IV U4, 90
to ask sb on a **date** jmdn. um eine Verabredung bitten IV U4, 90
daughter Tochter II
day Tag I
one **day** eines Tages II
some **day** eines Tages III
these **days** heutzutage III
daylight Tageslicht IV U3, 55
dead tot; leer II
*to **deal** with umgehen mit; sich befassen mit III
Dear …, Liebe / Lieber …, *(Anrede in Briefen, E-Mails, …)* III
debate Debattier-; Debatte; Diskussion IV U2, 33
debt Schulden IV U3, 62
*to get into **debt** sich verschulden IV U3, 62
December Dezember I
to **decide** (sich) entscheiden IV U5, 113
deck Schiffsdeck IV U1, 22
to **decorate** dekorieren; tapezieren; verzieren; schmücken III
decoration Dekoration; Schmuck IV U2, 39
deep tief III
deer Hirsch; Reh; Rotwild III
to **defeat** besiegen III
to **defend** verteidigen IV U5, 113
to **define** definieren IV U2, 46
defining relative clause notwendiger Relativsatz IV U5, 109
definitely auf jeden Fall; definitiv; eindeutig III
definition Definition I
degree Grad I; Hochschulabschluss; akademischer Grad IV U4, 89
degree Celsius (°C) Grad Celsius IV U3, 54
degree Fahrenheit (°F) Grad Fahrenheit IV U3, 54
delayed verspätet III
to **deliver** liefern II
democracy Demokratie IV U5, 100
Denmark Dänemark III
department store Kaufhaus IV U1, 22
to **describe** beschreiben III
description Beschreibung IV U2, 42
desert Wüste IV U3, 54
design Design; Gestaltung; Entwurf IV U1, 10
to **design** entwerfen; gestalten; entwickeln IV U1, 10
designer Designer / Designerin; Gestalter / Gestalterin; Entwickler / Entwicklerin IV U1, 10
desk Schreibtisch; Schalter III
dessert Nachspeise II
destination Ziel; Reiseziel III
to **destroy** zerstören IV U5, 106
detail Detail; Einzelheit II
to **detect** entdecken; aufdecken; ermitteln IV U3, 61
detective Detektiv / Detektivin; Kriminalbeamter / Kriminalbeamtin II
detention Nachsitzen IV U2, 32
determination Entschlossenheit; Entschiedenheit IV U4, 79
determined (fest) entschlossen; entschieden; zielstrebig IV U4, 78
to **develop** erschließen; (sich) entwickeln III
development Erschließung; Entwicklung IV U3, 68
device Gerät; Vorrichtung II
diagram Diagramm III
to **dial** wählen *(Nummer)* II
dialect Dialekt IV U1, 18
dialogue Dialog; Gespräch I
diary Tagebuch IV U1, 23
dictionary Wörterbuch III
did simple past von *to do* I
to **die** sterben III
difference Unterschied III
different anders; unterschiedlich; verschieden I
difficult schwierig I
*to **dig** graben; schürfen III
to **dig** up aufreißen *(Straße)*; umgraben III
digital digital III
diner *(AE)* Diner *(amerikanisches Schnellrestaurant)* II
dining room Esszimmer I
dinner Abendessen I
to have **dinner** zu Abend essen I
dinosaur Dinosaurier II
to **direct** Regie führen bei; anweisen; leiten II
direction Richtung II
directions Anweisungen; Wegbeschreibung III
dirty dreckig; schmutzig I
disability Behinderung; Unfähigkeit III
disagreement Meinungsverschiedenheit; Streit III
to **disappear** verschwinden III
disaster Katastrophe; Desaster; Unglück IV U5, 106
discipline Disziplin III
to **discriminate** unterscheiden IV U5, 101
to **discriminate** against diskriminieren; benachteiligen IV U5, 101
discrimination Diskriminierung III
to **discuss** diskutieren II
discussion Diskussion IV U5, 106
disease Krankheit; Erkrankung III
dish Gericht; Speise II
dishwasher Spülmaschine II
to load the **dishwasher** die Spülmaschine einräumen II
display Vorführung; Ausstellung; Schaukasten; Anzeige IV U2, 39
disposal Entsorgung IV U3, 56
to **dispose** (of) entsorgen IV U3, 57
to **distribute** verteilen; liefern IV U3, 57
divide Kluft III
to **divide** teilen; aufteilen III; unterteilen IV U3, 60
divided geteilt; getrennt IV U5, 113
*to **do** machen; tun I
to **do** handicrafts basteln I
to **do** sport Sport treiben I
doctor Arzt / Ärztin II
documentary Dokumentarfilm III
dog Hund I
dog tag Hundemarke II
dollar ($) Dollar *(Währungseinheit)* II
dolphin Delfin I
to **donate** spenden; stiften IV U2, 39
done past participle von *to do* II
door Tür I
double-decker bus Doppeldeckerbus II
down hinunter; herunter; entlang I; nach unten III
up and **down** entlang IV U1, 9
to **download** herunterladen III
downstairs unten; im Untergeschoss; nach unten II
draft Entwurf I
dragon Drache III
drama Theater; Drama; Schauspiel III
drank simple past von *to drink* I
*to **draw** zeichnen I
drawer Schublade I
drawing Zeichnung; Bild I
dream Traum II
*to **dream** träumen IV U1, 16
dreamt simple past, past participle von *to dream* IV U1, 16
dress Kleid II
dress code Kleiderordnung IV U2, 32
*to get **dressed** sich anziehen I
dried Trocken-; getrocknet IV U1, 23
dried fruit Trockenfrüchte; Trockenobst IV U1, 23
drink Getränk I
*to **drink** trinken I
to **drip** tropfen III
*to **drive** fahren; treiben I
driver Fahrer / Fahrerin II
driverless führerlos IV U5, 107
drone Drohne IV U5, 107
drug Droge III
drum Trommel IV U2, 44
drunk past participle von *to drink* II
to **dry** trocknen II
dry trocken I
dude Typ; Kerl IV U4, 86
dug simple past, past participle von *to dig* III
dug up simple past, past participle von *to dig up* III

dungeon Verlies; Kerker III
duration Dauer IV U4, 87
during während II
dwarf Zwerg III

E

each jede / jeder / jedes I
each other sich gegenseitig; sich; einander III
ear Ohr II
early früh I
to **earn** verdienen III
earth Erde; Boden; Erdboden I
east Osten; östlich; Ost- II
easy einfach; leicht I
*to **eat** essen I
eaten past participle von *to eat* II
eater Esser / Esserin II
e-book E-Book III
economy Wirtschaft IV U1, 9
ecosystem Ökosystem IV U3, 68
to **edit** bearbeiten; editieren III
editing Bearbeitung; Redaktion III
editing tool Bearbeitungstool; Bearbeitungswerkzeug III
editor Redakteur / Redakteurin; Herausgeber / Herausgeberin; Lektor / Lektorin IV U5, 106
to **educate** aufklären; bilden; erziehen IV U5, 100
education Ausbildung; Erziehung; Bildung IV U5, 101
egg Ei I
eight acht I
eighteen achtzehn I
eighteenth achtzehnte I
eighth achte I
eightieth achtzigste I
eighty achtzig I
not ... **either** auch nicht I
either ... or ... entweder ... oder ... IV U3, 56
elective Wahlfach IV U2, 32
electrician Elektriker / Elektrikerin IV U4, 89
elementary school *(AE)* Grundschule IV U5, 113
elevator *(AE)* Aufzug; Lift IV U1, 10
eleven elf I
eleventh elfte I
else andere; sonst I
email E-Mail II
to **email** mailen; E-Mails schreiben III
embarrassed verlegen II
embarrassing peinlich III
emerald smaragdgrün III
emergency Notfall III; Rettungs-; Behelfs-; Not- IV U1, 15
emergency call Notruf III
emergency medical technician (EMT) Rettungssanitäter / Rettungssanitäterin IV U4, 89
emergency service Notdienst; Rettungsdienst II
emergency worker Rettungskraft IV U1, 15
emission Emission; Ausstoß IV U4, 85
to **employ** beschäftigen; einstellen; anstellen IV U3, 68
empty leer IV U4, 90
to **encourage** ermutigen; unterstützen IV U4, 78
encyclopedia Enzyklopädie; Lexikon III
end Ende; Schluss III
to **end** enden; beenden; aufhören IV U4, 83
ending Schluss II; Endung IV U4, 79
endless endlos IV U2, 30
energy Energie; Kraft II
engineer Ingenieur / Ingenieurin; Techniker / Technikerin IV U3, 61
engineering Technik; Maschinenbau II
England England I
English Englisch; englisch; aus England I
the **English** die Engländer III
English-speaking englischsprachig; Englisch sprechend III
to **enjoy** genießen; mögen II
enormous riesig; gewaltig; enorm III
enough genug; genügend II
to **enter** hineingehen; hereinkommen; eintreten; betreten II; sich anmelden bei; teilnehmen an III
to **entertain** unterhalten II
entertainment Unterhaltung III
entrance Eingang; Eintritt II
entry Eintrag; Eintritt; Einlass III
environment Umwelt; Umgebung II
episode Folge; Episode III
equal Gleichgestellter / Gleichgestellte IV U5, 100
equal gleich; gleichberechtigt IV U5, 100
equal rights Rechtsgleichheit; gleiche Rechte; Gleichberechtigung IV U5, 115
equality Gleichberechtigung; Gleichheit; Gleichstellung IV U5, 100
equipment Ausrüstung; Ausstattung III
escape Flucht; Entkommen IV U1, 11
to **establish** gründen; einrichten; eröffnen IV U3, 68
euro (€) Euro *(Währungseinheit)* III
Europe Europa II
European europäisch; aus Europa; Europäer / Europäerin IV U1, 9
even sogar; noch III
even so und doch; trotzdem; selbst dann IV U4, 90
evening Abend I
in the **evening(s)** abends I
event Ereignis; Veranstaltung III
eventually schließlich; endlich; irgendwann III
ever jemals II; niemals IV U2, 44
every jede / jeder / jedes I
every alle IV U3, 56
everybody alle (zusammen); jeder II
everyone jeder I
everything alles II
everywhere überall III
exactly genau III
exam Prüfung; Examen I
example Beispiel I
for **example** zum Beispiel I
excellent exzellent; hervorragend II
except außer IV U1, 22
exchange Austausch IV U2, 32
to **exchange** tauschen; austauschen; umtauschen II
excited aufgeregt; begeistert I
excitement Aufregung III
exciting spannend; aufregend II
Excuse me! Entschuldigung. I
exercise (Ex.) Übung I; II
exercise book Übungsheft I
exhausted erschöpft IV U1, 22
exhibition Ausstellung II
to **exist** existieren; bestehen IV U5, 112
exit Ausgang; Abgang; Ausfahrt II
expensive teuer II
experience Erlebnis; Erfahrung III
experiment Versuch; Experiment I
expert Experten-; Experte / Expertin II
to **explain** erklären; erläutern III
to **explore** erkunden; erforschen IV U5, 107
to **express** ausdrücken IV U3, 57
expression Wendung; Ausdruck; Äußerung III
to **extinguish** ausmachen; löschen III
extra zusätzlich; Zusatz- I
extract Auszug; Extrakt III
to **extract** entnehmen; herausnehmen; gewinnen IV U3, 57
extreme extrem; radikal IV U5, 106
extremely äußerst; sehr IV U1, 22
eye Auge I

F

face Gesicht III
to **face** sich gegenübersehen; sich gegenüberstehen; entgegentreten IV U5, 113
face-to-face persönlich; von Angesicht zu Angesicht IV U5, 107
facility Einrichtung IV U3, 68
fact Fakt; Tatsache III
in **fact** genau genommen; eigentlich; tatsächlich III
factory Fabrik; Werk III
fair Messe; Jahrmarkt II
fair gerecht; fair IV U1, 22
fairground Rummelplatz I
fairy Fee III
fall *(AE)* Herbst IV U1, 16
*to **fall** fallen I
to **fall** off herunterfallen; fallen III
fallen past participle von *to fall* III
false falsch I
family Familie I
family tree Familienstammbaum I
famine Hungersnot III
famous berühmt I
fan Fan I
fancy ausgefallen; modisch IV U2, 44
fancy dancer *Person, die einen traditionellen Tanz der amerikanischen Ureinwohner / Ureinwohnerinnen vorführt* IV U2, 44
fancy dancing *traditioneller Tanzstil amerikanischer Ureinwohner / Ureinwohnerinnen* IV U2, 46
fantastic fantastisch; großartig III
fantasy Fantasy; Fantasie III

far weit I
farm Bauernhof I
farmer Landwirt / Landwirtin; Bauer / Bäuerin IV U2, 31
farming Landwirtschaft; Ackerbau III
farmland Ackerland; Ackerboden; Landwirtschaftsflächen IV U5, 98
fascinating faszinierend IV U1, 17
fashion Mode IV ZI, 7
fast schnell I
fast paced temporeich; flott IV U3, 71
father Vater I
in **favor** of *(AE)* für; zugunsten von IV U5, 106
favorite *(AE)* Lieblings- IV ZI, 6
favourite Lieblings- I
feather Feder IV U2, 44
feature Artikel; Merkmal IV U4, 82; Reportage; Feature IV U5, 98
to **feature** aufweisen IV U4, 79
February Februar I
fee Beitrag; Gebühr III
*to **feed** füttern I
feedback Feedback; Rückmeldung I
*to **feel** (sich) fühlen I
to **feel** annoyed verärgert sein III
to **feel** comfortable sich wohlfühlen II
to make sb **feel** better jmdm. helfen, sich besser zu fühlen IV U1, 22
I don't **feel** well. Mir geht es nicht gut. II
feeling Gefühl IV U2, 43
feet Füße I
fell simple past von *to fall* I
felt simple past von *to feel* I
female weiblich IV U1, 25
fence Zaun I
ferret Frettchen II
ferry Fähre III
fertile fruchtbar IV U5, 98
festival Festival; Fest III
fever Fieber II
few wenige III
a **few** ein paar; wenige; einige II
field Feld; Wiese; Weide II
fifteen fünfzehn I
fifteenth fünfzehnte I
fifth fünfte I
fiftieth fünfzigste I
fifty fünfzig I
*to **fight** kämpfen; (sich) streiten I
figure Figur; Gestalt; Persönlichkeit II; Zahl; Ziffer III
file Datei; Akte; Mappe; Ordner III
to **fill** in ausfüllen III
film Film I
to **film** filmen; drehen II
final letzte / letzter / letztes; endgültig III
final call letzter Aufruf; letzte Aufforderung III
finally schließlich; zum Schluss; endlich II
financial Finanz-; finanziell IV U1, 9
*to **find** finden; herausfinden I
to **find** out herausfinden II
finger Finger III
to **finish** aufhören; enden; beenden II; etw. fertig trinken / essen; etw. zu Ende trinken / essen III; absolvieren IV U4, 78
to **finish** doing sth etw. fertig gemacht haben IV U2, 38
finished fertig IV U3, 57
fire Feuer III
fire escape Notausgang IV U1, 11
fireworks Feuerwerk I
first zuerst; als Erstes III; erste / erster / erstes I
at **first** zuerst; zunächst II
first aid Erste Hilfe III
first-aid kit Erste-Hilfe-Kasten; Verbandskasten III
firstly erstens; zuerst IV U5, 106
first-person narrator Ich-Erzähler / Ich-Erzählerin IV U2, 46
first responder Ersthelfer / Ersthelferin; Notfallbegleiter / Notfallbegleiterin IV U3, 62
fish Fisch I
fishbone diagram Fischgräten-Diagramm (*Ursache-Wirkungs-Diagramm*) III
fishing Angeln; Fischen; Fischerei III
to **fit** passen II
fit fit; in Form IV U4, 78
five fünf I
to **fix** fixieren; befestigen II
fizzy sprudelnd I
flag Flagge; Fahne III
flat Wohnung I
flat flach; platt III
flatbread Fladenbrot II
flew simple past von *to fly* IV U1, 15
flight Flug III
flip-flop Flipflop III
flood Überschwemmung; Flut; Hochwasser IV U5, 99
floor Fußboden; Stockwerk; Etage II
flour Mehl II
to **flow** fließen; strömen IV U5, 98
flower Blume II
flown past participle von *to fly* IV U1, 15
fluent fließend; flüssig III
*to **fly** fliegen IV U1, 15
flyer Flyer; Faltblatt III
fog Nebel IV U3, 55
foggy neblig I
folder Ordner; Mappe I
to **follow** folgen; befolgen II
follower Follower / Followerin; Anhänger / Anhängerin IV U4, 82
food Essen; Nahrung; Lebensmittel I
food chain Nahrungskette IV U5, 105
foot Fuß I; Fuß (*Längenmaß: 30,48 cm*) IV U1, 8
on **foot** zu Fuß I
football Fußball I
football *(AE)* American Football II
footprint Fußabdruck IV U3, 68
for für I; seit IV U4, 78
for one thing zum einen; einerseits; erstens IV U5, 106
forbade simple past von *to forbid* IV U2, 44
*to **forbid** verbieten IV U2, 44
forbidden past participle von *to forbid* IV U2, 44
foreground Vordergrund II
foreign fremd; ausländisch IV U1, 16
forest Wald I
forever für immer; ewig IV U3, 62
*to **forget** vergessen I
forgot simple past von *to forget* II
forgotten past participle von *to forget* II
form Form I; Formular III
to **form** bilden IV U4, 77
formal formell; förmlich; formal IV U4, 86
formation Formation; Entstehung IV U2, 31
former ehemalige / ehemaliger / ehemaliges; frühere / früherer / früheres IV U1, 10
fortieth vierzigste I
forty vierzig I
forum Forum III
forward nach vorne; vorwärts IV U4, 90
to look **forward** to (+ -ing) sich freuen auf II
fossil Fossil; Versteinerung IV U2, 31
fought simple past, past participle von *to fight* III
to **found** gründen III
found simple past von *to find* I; past participle von *to find* II
fountain Brunnen; Springbrunnen II
four vier I
fourteen vierzehn I
fourteenth vierzehnte I
fourth vierte I
fox Fuchs III
France Frankreich II
to **free** befreien I
free kostenlos; frei I
for **free** umsonst; kostenlos; gratis II
free time Freizeit I
free-time Freizeit- I
freedom Freiheit; Unabhängigkeit IV U1, 15
*to **freeze** einfrieren; frieren; gefrieren II
freeze frame Standbild IV U2, 47
freezer Tiefkühlschrank; Tiefkühltruhe II
freight Fracht; Güter III
French Französisch; französisch; aus Frankreich III
the **French** die Franzosen IV U5, 99
frequent häufig IV U3, 61
fresh frisch II
Friday Freitag I
fridge Kühlschrank I
fried egg Spiegelei II
friend Freund / Freundin I
to make **friends** Freundschaften schließen II
friendly freundlich; nett I
friendship Freundschaft IV U1, 22
frightening furchterregend IV U1, 15
from von; aus I
front Vorder-; Vorderseite II
in **front** of vor; davor I
front door Eingangstür; Haustür; Wohnungstür IV U4, 90
froze simple past von *to freeze* II
frozen past participle von *to freeze* II
frozen gefroren; tiefgefroren IV U4, 84
fruit Frucht; Obst I
full voll; ganz III; vollständig; komplett IV U3, 69

full of voller III
fun Spaß; Freude I
to be **fun** Spaß machen; witzig sein I
Have **fun**! Viel Spaß! III
fun spaßig; lustig; amüsant III
function Funktion III
fundraising Spenden-; Geldbeschaffung III
funeral Beerdigung; Begräbnis IV U5, 111
funny lustig; witzig; komisch; merkwürdig; seltsam I
furniture Möbel I
furry pelzig II
future Zukunft; Zukunfts-; zukünftig IV U3, 68

G

gallery Galerie II
game Spiel I
gap Lücke; Abstand; Spalt II
Mind the **gap**. Vorsicht beim Ein- und Aussteigen. I
garbage *(AE)* Müll; Abfall IV U3, 68
garden Garten I
gas Gas III
gate Tor; Flugsteig; Gate; Ausgang III
gave simple past von *to give* I
gender Geschlecht IV U5, 104
general allgemein II
generation Generation IV U3, 68
genetic genetisch IV U4, 78
geography Erdkunde; Geografie I
germ Keim II
German Deutsch; deutsch; aus Deutschland I
Germany Deutschland I
gerund Gerundium IV U3, 65
*to **get** werden; bekommen I; hinkommen II
to **get** around herumkommen I; sich bewegen III
to **get** dressed sich anziehen I
to **get** hurt sich verletzen; verletzt werden IV U2, 43
to **get** into bilden; hineingelangen; hineinkommen IV U3, 62
to **get** into debt sich verschulden IV U3, 62
to **get** lost sich verlaufen; sich verirren II
to **get** married heiraten II
to **get** off aussteigen; absteigen II
to **get** on einsteigen II
to **get** out herausholen; herauskommen III
to **get** ready sich fertig machen; sich vorbereiten IV U2, 32
to **get** scared Angst bekommen III
to **get** up aufstehen I
to **get** used to (sth) sich an (etw.) gewöhnen III
ghost Geist II
ghost town Geisterstadt IV U3, 67
giant riesig; Riesen- II
ginger Ingwer III
giraffe Giraffe II
girl Mädchen I
girlfriend Freundin II
*to **give** geben; halten *(Vortrag)* II
to **give** up aufgeben IV U4, 78
glacier Gletscher IV U3, 68
glad froh III
glass Glas II
glasses Brille III
global weltweit; global IV U3, 61
glove Handschuh II
to **glue** kleben I
*to **go** gehen; fahren I
to be **going** on los sein III
to be **going** to do sth etw. tun werden II
to **go** cycling Fahrrad fahren I
to **go** for a walk spazieren gehen II
to **go** hunting auf die Jagd gehen; jagen gehen III
to **go** jogging joggen gehen II
to **go** mad ausrasten; überschnappen; verrückt werden III
to **go** out ausgehen I
to **go** shopping einkaufen gehen I
to **go** sightseeing eine Besichtigungstour machen II
to **go** swimming schwimmen gehen I
to **go** well gut laufen III
goal Tor; Ziel I
goat Ziege II
goggles Schwimmbrille; Skibrille; Schutzbrille III
gold Gold I
gold rush Goldrausch IV U3, 67
gold-mining Goldschürfen IV U3, 67
good gut I
to be **good** at gut sein in I
Good job! Gut gemacht! IV U2, 38
Good luck! Viel Glück! II
Good morning. Guten Morgen. I
We're **good**. Uns geht es gut. II
Goodbye. Auf Wiedersehen. I
gospel Gospel *(Musikrichtung)* IV U5, 111
got simple past von *to get* I; past participle von *to get* II
to have **got** haben; besitzen II
government Regierung IV U1, 9
to **graduate** einen akademischen Abschluss erwerben IV U1, 25
graffiti Graffiti IV U4, 84
gram (g) Gramm III
grammar Grammatik I
grandma Oma I
grandpa Opa I
grandparents Großeltern I
grape Traube IV U3, 55
grass Gras; Rasen IV U2, 37
grave Grab III
gravity Schwerkraft; Schwere IV U5, 107
great gut; toll; großartig; groß; riesig I
Great Britain Großbritannien III
great-grandparents Urgroßeltern I
Greece Griechenland II
Greek Griechisch; griechisch; aus Griechenland; Grieche / Griechin III
green grün I
greeting Begrüßung IV U4, 82
grew simple past von *to grow* II
grey grau I
grid Gitter; Raster I
grizzly bear Grizzlybär IV U3, 68
ground Boden; Erdboden II
ground floor Erdgeschoss II
ground level Erdgeschoss IV U1, 11
grounds Anlage; Gelände IV U1, 16
group Gruppe II
*to **grow** wachsen; anbauen; züchten; ziehen II
to **guess** erraten; raten; überlegen I
guest Gast II
guide Führer / Führerin II
guided tour Führung III
guitar Gitarre I
guy Typ; Kerl III
guys Leute II
gym Turnhalle; Fitnessstudio I

H

had simple past von *to have* I; past participle von *to have* II
hailstone Hagelkorn IV U2, 43
hair Haar; Haare III
hairbrush Haarbürste III
hairdresser's Friseursalon IV U4, 85
hairdryer Föhn III
half halb *(bei Uhrzeitangaben)* IV U1, 10
half past (six) halb (sieben) I
hall Flur; Korridor; Diele I; Halle; Saal IV U4, 85
Halloween Halloween II
hallway Flur IV U2, 32
ham Schinken I
hamburger Hamburger II
hammer Hammer III
hammer throw Hammerwerfen III
hand Hand I
to **hand** over abgeben; übergeben III
handicraft Handarbeit I
to do **handicrafts** basteln I
handmade handgefertigt III
handout Handout; Informationsblatt II
handwritten handgeschrieben III
*to **hang** out (with) rumhängen (mit); sich treffen (mit); sich herumtreiben (mit) I
*to **hang** up auflegen; aufhängen III
to **happen** geschehen; passieren II
happy glücklich I
to be **happy** to do sth etw. gern tun; etw. tun können IV U4, 84
harbor *(AE)* Hafen IV U1, 16
hard schwer; schwierig; hart II
hard-working fleißig II
has hat I
hashtag Hashtag; Rautezeichen IV U1, 14
hat Hut I
hate Hass III
to **hate** hassen; nicht mögen II
*to **have** haben; essen I
to **have** a shower duschen; eine Dusche nehmen II
to **have** breakfast frühstücken I
to **have** dinner zu Abend essen I
to **have** got haben; besitzen II
to **have** sth in common etw. gemeinsam haben III

to **have** to müssen II
Have fun! Viel Spaß! III
Hawaiian hawaiianisch; Hawaiianisch; aus Hawaii; Hawaiianer / Hawaiianerin IV U3, 54
he er I
head Kopf II
head chef Chefkoch / Chefköchin IV U1, 22
headache Kopfschmerzen; Kopfweh II
heading Überschrift; Titel I
headphones *(pl)* Kopfhörer II
to **heal** heilen III
health Gesundheit IV U3, 62
health gesundheitlich; Gesundheits- II
healthy gesund II
*to **hear** hören II
heard simple past von *to hear* II; past participle von *to hear* III
heart Herz IV U2, 45
heartbreaking herzzerreißend IV U3, 62
heartbroken untröstlich IV U1, 17
to **heat** erhitzen; heizen; aufwärmen II
heavy schwer; stark I
heavy cream *(AE) Sahne mit sehr hohem Fettgehalt* I
hedge Hecke II
hedgehog Igel II
held simple past von *to hold* II
helicopter Helikopter; Hubschrauber II
Hello. Hallo. I
help Hilfe I
to **help** helfen I
helpful hilfreich; nützlich III
helpless hilflos; machtlos IV U5, 100
her ihr / ihre; sie I
here hier I
Here you are. Bitte schön. I
heritage Erbe III
hero Held III
hers ihre / ihrer / ihrs III
Hi. Hi.; Hallo. I
high hoch; groß II
high school *(AE)* Highschool (*weiterführende Schule, Oberstufe*) II
highland Hochland III
highlight Highlight; Höhepunkt III
to **highlight** hervorheben; markieren III
highly sehr III
to **hijack** entführen; kapern IV U1, 15
to **hike** wandern II
hiking Wandern II
to go **hiking** wandern gehen II
hill Hügel; Berg II
him ihm / ihn I
himself sich; selbst; sich (selbst); er selbst III
hip-hop Hip-Hop III
to **hire** mieten; anheuern; einstellen II
his sein / seine I
Hispanic lateinamerikanisch; hispanisch; aus Lateinamerika; Lateinamerikaner / Lateinamerikanerin IV U3, 55
historical geschichtlich; historisch IV U1, 9
history Geschichte I
*to **hit** treffen; schlagen III
hit simple past, past participle von *to hit* III
hobby Hobby I
hockey Hockey III
Hogmanay Silvesternacht (*in Schottland*) III
*to **hold** halten; festhalten II
hole Loch I
holiday Ferien; Urlaub; Feiertag I
holiday cottage Ferienhäuschen III
holiday flat Ferienwohnung III
home Zuhause; Heim I; nach Hause III
at **home** zu Hause I
home town Heimatstadt I
homeless obdachlos; wohnungslos IV U3, 62
homemade selbst gemacht IV U2, 38
homeroom *(AE) Treffpunkt vor der ersten Stunde, u. a. zur Überprüfung der Anwesenheit* IV U2, 32
*to be **homesick** Heimweh haben II
homework Hausaufgabe I
honest ehrlich IV U4, 90
honey *(AE)* Schatz; Schätzchen II
hope Hoffnung IV U2, 46
to **hope** hoffen II
horn Horn IV U4, 77
horse Pferd I
horse riding Reiten III
hospital Krankenhaus; Hospital III
host Gastgeber / Gastgeberin; Moderator / Moderatorin IV U2, 32
to **host** ausrichten III
host family Gastfamilie III
hostel Herberge III
hot heiß I
hot dog Hotdog (*Würstchen im Brötchen*) IV ZI, 7
hotel Hotel III
hour Stunde I
kilometres per **hour** Kilometer pro Stunde; Stundenkilometer II
hours Zeiten; Zeit IV U4, 89
house Haus I
houseboat Hausboot III
household Haushalt II
how wie I
How are you? Wie geht es dir? I
How much (is / are) …? Wie viel (kostet / kosten) …? I
How old are you? Wie alt bist du? I
how to … wie man … I
however jedoch III
hug Umarmung III
huge riesig; riesengroß III
human Mensch III
human Menschen-; menschlich III
a / one **hundred** einhundert; hundert I
hundredth hundertste I
hung out (with) simple past von *to hang out (with)* II
hung up simple past, past participle von *to hang up* III
hungry hungrig I
hunt Jagd III
to **hunt** jagen III
hunter Jäger / Jägerin III
hunting Jagen; Jagd III
to go **hunting** auf die Jagd gehen; jagen gehen III
hurricane Orkan; Wirbelsturm; Hurrikan IV U5, 99
to **hurry** sich beeilen II
*to **hurt** weh tun; simple past, past participle von *to hurt*; verletzen II
to get **hurt** sich verletzen; verletzt werden IV U2, 43
husband Ehemann III
hyperloop Hyperloop IV U5, 107

I

I ich I
I can't wait. Ich kann es kaum erwarten. III
I don't feel well. Mir geht es nicht gut. II
I don't like … Ich mag … nicht; … gefällt mir nicht. I
I wish you were here. Ich wünschte, du wärst hier. III
I'd like (to) … (= I would like to) Ich möchte gerne …; Ich hätte gerne …; Ich würde gerne … I
I'd love to … (= I would love to) Ich würde sehr gern … II
I'll take … ich nehme … II
I'm from … Ich komme aus … I
I'm sorry. Es tut mir leid.; Entschuldigung. I
ice Eis IV U1, 16
ice cream Eiscreme; Eis I
ice hockey Eishockey IV U1, 16
ice pack Eisbeutel; Kühlakku III
ice skating Schlittschuhlaufen I
icon Icon; Symbol; Ikone IV U3, 71
icy eisig I
idea Idee; Ahnung I
to **identify** identifizieren; erkennen IV U1, 14
if falls; wenn I; ob II
if-clause if-Satz; Bedingungssatz III
to **ignore** ignorieren; außer Acht lassen IV U5, 100
ill krank; schlecht II
to **illustrate** veranschaulichen; darstellen; illustrieren IV U5, 117
image Bild; Image IV U1, 12; IV U1, 15; IV U5, 113
to **imagine** (sth) sich (etw.) vorstellen IV U5, 101
immediately sofort; gleich III
immigrant Immigrant / Immigrantin; Einwanderer / Einwanderin IV U1, 9
to **immigrate** einwandern; immigrieren IV U1, 21
immigration Einwanderung; Immigration; Zuwanderung; Einreise IV U1, 9
important wichtig; einflussreich I
impressed beeindruckt III
impressive beeindruckend IV U1, 17
to **improve** verbessern IV U4, 84
improvement Verbesserung III
in in; auf I
in addition zusätzlich; darüber hinaus; außerdem IV U3, 59
in ages seit Ewigkeiten; seit einer Ewigkeit III

in fact genau genommen; eigentlich; tatsächlich III
in favor of *(AE)* für; zugunsten von IV U5, 106
in front of vor; davor I
in my opinion meiner Meinung nach IV U5, 106
in pairs zu zweit II
in term time während der Schulzeit III
in the country auf dem Land II
in the evening(s) abends I
in the world der Welt; weltweit III
to **include** einbeziehen; beinhalten; einschließen; aufnehmen; einbinden II
including einschließlich II
to **increase** wachsen; zunehmen; vergrößern; ansteigen IV U2, 37
incredible unglaublich II
independence Unabhängigkeit IV U1, 15
independent unabhängig III
India Indien II
Indian indisch; Indisch; aus Indien; Inder / Inderin II
industrial Industrie-; industriell III
industry Industrie III
influence Einfluss IV U4, 78
to **influence** beeinflussen III
influencer Influencer / Influencerin II
influential einflussreich IV U4, 79
info (= information) Info (= Informationen) III
infographic Infografik IV U3, 71
information Information II
information desk Information; Auskunft III
infrastructure Infrastruktur IV U4, 85
ingredient Zutat IV U5, 99
inhabited bewohnt III
injury Verletzung III
inline skating Inlineskaten III
insect Insekt II
to **insert** einfügen IV U3, 60
inside in; innen in; im Innern III; in … hinein IV U5, 113
to **inspire** inspirieren; anregen IV U4, 78
to **install** installieren; einrichten; anschließen IV U3, 61
instead stattdessen II
instead of statt; anstatt; anstelle von IV U5, 106
instruction Anleitung II
instrument Instrument I
to **insult** beleidigen IV U5, 100
intelligence Intelligenz; Klugheit; Einsicht IV U5, 106
interest Interesse IV U5, 100
*to be **interested** in sich interessieren für; interessiert sein an II
interesting interessant I
international international II
internet Internet II
internship Praktikum; Berufspraktikum III
interview Interview; Befragung I
to **interview** interviewen; befragen IV U1, 23
into in; hinein I
intonation Betonung; Intonation III

to **introduce** einführen; zeigen; vorstellen III
to **introduce** oneself sich vorstellen I
introduction Einleitung; Einführung IV U5, 112
to **invent** erfinden III
invention Erfindung II
inventor Erfinder / Erfinderin III
invitation Einladung IV U2, 49
to **invite** einladen II; auffordern IV U4, 90
to **involve** einbeziehen; involvieren; beinhalten; beteiligen III
Iran Iran II
Ireland Irland III
Irish irisch; Irisch; aus Irland III
irregular unregelmäßig I
is ist I
island Insel III
isle Insel III
issue Angelegenheit; Frage; Problem; Thema IV U4, 76
it er / sie / es I
IT (= Information Technology) Informatik; Computerunterricht I
Italian italienisch; Italienisch; aus Italien; Italiener / Italienerin II
Italy Italien II
item Ding; Artikel III
its ihr / ihre; sein / seine I
itself (sich) selbst IV U4, 89

J

jacket Jacke II
jam Marmelade; Konfitüre I
Jamaica Jamaika II
January Januar I
Japan Japan II
jar Glas I
jazz Jazz (*Musikrichtung*) IV U5, 111
jealous eifersüchtig; neidisch II
jeans Jeans I
jewellery Schmuck I
Jewish jüdisch IV U1, 21
job Aufgabe; Tätigkeit; Arbeitsstelle; Job; Arbeit; Beruf II
jobless arbeitslos IV U3, 62
to **jog** joggen II
jogging Joggen II
to go **jogging** joggen gehen II
to **join** sich anschließen I; beitreten; Mitglied werden; mitmachen bei II
joke Witz; Scherz II
to **joke** Witze machen; scherzen III
to **judge** beurteilen; bewerten IV U5, 115
juice Saft I
juicy saftig; pikant; anstößig II
July Juli I
to **jump** springen I
June Juni I
junk Gerümpel; Abfall; Ramsch II
junk food Junkfood; ungesundes Essen II
just nur; einfach; gerade eben; soeben II
justice Gerechtigkeit; Justiz IV U5, 100

K

kangaroo Känguru I
kayaking Kajakfahren I
kebab Döner II
*to **keep** behalten; halten; aufbewahren II
to **keep** a record of sth über etw. Buch führen IV U2, 34
to **keep** in touch in Verbindung bleiben III
kept simple past von *to keep* II; past participle von *to keep* IV U5, 117
kettle Wasserkocher; Kessel II
keyboard Keyboard; Tastatur I
keyword Stichwort; Schlüsselbegriff I
to **kick** schießen; treten III
kid Kind II
to **kidnap** entführen IV U4, 79
to **kill** töten III
kilogramme (kg) Kilogramm III
kilometre (km) Kilometer I
kilometres per hour Kilometer pro Stunde; Stundenkilometer II
kilt Schottenrock; Kilt III
kind Art; Sorte III
Kind regards, Viele Grüße IV U4, 86
king König I
kingdom Königreich III
to **kiss** küssen IV U4, 90
kit Ausrüstung; Ausstattung; Sachen III
kitchen Küche I
knee Knie III
knee catch Fußballtrick *(bei dem der Ball mit den Knien aufgefangen und eingeklemmt wird)* III
knew simple past von *to know* II
knife Messer III
to **knock** klopfen; schlagen; stoßen III
*to **know** wissen; kennen I
to let sb **know** jmdn. informieren; jmdm. Bescheid geben; jmdm. Bescheid sagen III
known past participle von *to know* IV U4, 78

L

to **label** beschriften I
Labrador Labrador II
lacrosse Lacrosse (*Ballsportart*) IV U1, 16
lain past participle von *to lie* III
lake See I
lamp Lampe I
land Land I
to **land** landen II
landmark Wahrzeichen IV U4, 93
landscape Landschaft III
lane Fahrspur; Weg; Gasse III
language Sprache II
language detectives Sprachdetektive I
language tip Grammatikhinweis I
laptop Laptop IV U2, 42
large groß I
lasagne Lasagne II
to **last** dauern; andauern; anhalten IV U5, 112
last letzte / letzter / letztes I
late spät; zu spät I
to be **late** Verspätung haben; zu spät sein I

later später I
Latin America Lateinamerika IV U4, 77
to **laugh** lachen I
to **laugh** at auslachen II
launch Start; Abschuss IV U5, 98
launch site Raketenabschussbasis IV U5, 98
laverbread Algenpaste III
law Gesetz III
by **law** gesetzlich IV U3, 68
to pass a **law** ein Gesetz beschließen; ein Gesetz verabschieden IV U3, 68
law court Gerichtshof; Gericht *(juristisch)* IV U4, 85
lay simple past von *to lie* III
layout Layout; Anordnung I
*to **lead** leiten; führen; anführen III
leader Leiter / Leiterin; Anführer / Anführerin III
leading führend IV U3, 55
leaflet Broschüre; Informationsblatt; Prospekt II
to **learn** lernen; herausfinden; erfahren I
to **learn** about sth etwas erfahren über etw. IV U2, 31
learning Lernen II
learning platform Lernplattform III
least geringste / geringster / geringstes; am wenigsten III
at **least** mindestens; wenigstens; immerhin III
*to **leave** abfahren; verlassen; lassen I; zurücklassen IV U3, 68
to **leave** school mit der Schule fertig sein; von der Schule abgehen II
led simple past, past participle von *to lead* III
left simple past von *to leave* II; übrig IV U1, 16
left übrig; links I
on the **left** auf der linken Seite; links II
leg Bein II
legal legal; rechtlich; Rechts- IV U3, 63
legal drinking age gesetzliches Mindestalter für Alkoholkonsum IV U3, 63
legend Legende; Sage III
leisure Freizeit III
leisure centre Freizeitzentrum III
lemon Zitrone I
lemonade Limonade I
less weniger III
lesson Schulstunde; Unterricht I
*to **let** lassen I
to **let** sb know jmdn. informieren; jmdm. Bescheid geben; jmdm. Bescheid sagen III
let's lass(t) uns I
letter Buchstabe; Brief II
level Level; Niveau; Höhe; Stufe I
librarian Bibliothekar / Bibliothekarin IV U2, 45
library Bibliothek; Bücherei I
license *(AE)* Lizenz; Erlaubnis IV U5, 105
lie Lüge III
to **lie** lügen III
*to **lie** liegen III
life Leben I
life cycle Lebenszyklus; Lebensdauer; Laufzeit IV U3, 56
lifeguard Rettungsschwimmer / Rettungsschwimmerin III
lifestyle Lebensart III; Lifestyle; Lebensstil IV U4, 77
lift Aufzug; Fahrstuhl; Lift II
light Licht I
*to **light** anzünden; erhellen; beleuchten IV U2, 39
light leicht; hell IV U2, 44
lighthouse Leuchtturm I
lighting Beleuchtung II
to **like** mögen I
would **like** würde(n) gern; hätte(n) gern I
I don't **like** … Ich mag … nicht; … gefällt mir nicht. I
I'd **like** (to) … (= I would like to) Ich möchte gerne …; Ich hätte gerne …; Ich würde gerne … I
like wie II
limit Beschränkung; Begrenzung; Grenze; Limit IV U3, 63
limited begrenzt; beschränkt; limitiert IV U3, 71
line Linie; Zeile II
link Link; Verbindung IV U5, 117
lion Löwe I
list Liste IV U1, 23
to **listen** (to) zuhören; anhören; hören I
listening Hörverstehen I
lit simple past, past participle von *to light* IV U2, 39
Lithuania Litauen III
litter tray Katzenklo I
little klein I
a **little** ein bisschen II
little person Kleinwüchsiger / Kleinwüchsige IV U4, 78
*to be a **little person** kleinwüchsig sein IV U4, 78
to **live** wohnen; leben I
live live; Live- III
to **live** stream live streamen; live übertragen IV U2, 32
living Leben; Wohnen II
living history village Freilichtmuseum IV U2, 31
living room Wohnzimmer I
to **load** einräumen; laden; beladen II
to **load** the dishwasher die Spülmaschine einräumen II
lobby Eingangshalle; Empfangshalle; Foyer IV U1, 11
local örtlich; lokal II
location Ort; Standort; Lage; Drehort IV U1, 14; IV U5, 113
loch See *(in Schottland)* III
locker Schließfach; Spind II
loft Dachboden IV U1, 11
log Holzstamm III
to **log** in sich einloggen; anmelden III
lonely einsam III
long lang; lange I
no **longer** nicht mehr; nicht länger IV U2, 39
look Blick I; Look; Aussehen IV U4, 90
to **look** schauen; nachschauen; sehen; aussehen I
to **look** after aufpassen auf; hüten II; sich kümmern um III
to **look** at anschauen I
to **look** for suchen nach II
to **look** forward to (+ -ing) sich freuen auf II
to **look** up nachschauen; aufschauen I; nachschlagen IV U2, 44
loop Schleife; Schlaufe III
*to **lose** verlieren III
lost verschwunden; verloren II; simple past, past participle von *to lose* III
to get **lost** sich verlaufen; sich verirren II
lost and found Fundbüro; Fundsachen II
a **lot** viel I
a **lot** of viel(e); eine Menge I
lots of viel; jede Menge III
loud laut II
out **loud** laut III
love Liebe III
to **love** lieben; gern mögen I
I'd **love** to … (= I would love to) Ich würde sehr gern … II
low niedrig III
low tide Ebbe III
low-emission emissionsarm; schadstoffarm IV U4, 85
loyal treu; loyal III
luck Glück IV U3, 67
*to be **lucky** Glück haben II
luggage Gepäck III
lunch Mittagessen I
lunchbox Brotdose; Pausenbrotbehälter IV U2, 49
lyrics Liedtext IV U5, 111

M

macaroni Makkaroni II
macaroni cheese Makkaroni mit Käsesoße II
machine Maschine; Gerät IV U1, 18
mad wütend; verrückt IV U5, 100
to go **mad** ausrasten; überschnappen; verrückt werden III
made simple past von *to make* I; past participle von *to make* II
magazine Zeitschrift II
magic Zauberkraft; Magie; Zauberei III
main Haupt- IV U3, 62
majority Mehrheit; Mehrzahl III
*to **make** machen; tun; bilden; drehen I; herstellen II
to be **made** of hergestellt sein aus IV U3, 56
to **make** a mess Unordnung machen; Dreck machen II
to **make** friends Freundschaften schließen II
to **make** notes sich Notizen machen I
to **make** pottery töpfern III
to **make** sb feel better jmdm. helfen, sich besser zu fühlen IV U1, 22
to **make** sure dafür sorgen; sich versichern; sichergehen III

to **make** up sich ausdenken; erfinden II
make-up Make-up; Schminke IV U4, 90
mall *(AE)* Einkaufszentrum IV U1, 16
man Mann I; Mensch IV U5, 100
to **manage** verwalten IV U3, 68; leiten IV U4, 88
mango Mango I
to **manufacture** herstellen; fertigen IV U3, 57
manufacturing Produktion; Herstellung; Fertigung IV U2, 30
many viele I
map Landkarte; Stadtplan II
maple syrup Ahornsirup I
marathon Marathon IV U1, 9
March März I
march Marsch; Kundgebung IV U5, 115
to **march** marschieren IV U5, 111
margarine Margarine II
marked markiert IV U3, 65
market Markt I
*to get **married** heiraten II
Mars Mars IV U5, 106
marshmallow Mäusespeck; Marshmallow (*Schaumzuckersüßigkeit*) IV U3, 59
mashed potatoes Kartoffelbrei II
mat Matte III
match Spiel III
to **match** zuordnen; zusammenpassen; verbinden I
material Material; Stoff II
math *(AE)* Mathematik; Mathe IV U2, 32
maths Mathematik; Mathe I
to **matter** von Bedeutung sein; etw. ausmachen IV U1, 21
May Mai I
may vielleicht III; dürfen; können IV U3, 62
maybe vielleicht II
mayonnaise (mayo) Mayonnaise I
mayor Bürgermeister IV U4, 84
mayoress Bürgermeisterin IV U4, 84
me mich; mir; ich I
meal Essen; Mahlzeit II
*to **mean** bedeuten; meinen III
meaning Bedeutung III
means of transport Transportmittel; Verkehrsmittel I
meanwhile mittlerweile; in der Zwischenzeit III
meat Fleisch I
mechanic Mechaniker / Mechanikerin II
media Medien III
social **media** soziale Medien III
mediation Sprachmittlung I
medical medizinisch; ärztlich IV U3, 62
medicine Medizin; Medikamente III
meditation Meditation IV U2, 34
*to **meet** treffen; kennenlernen I
meeting Treffen; Besprechung; Meeting III
to **melt** schmelzen; zerfließen III
member Mitglied III
membership Mitglieds-; Mitgliedschaft III
memorial Denkmal; Gedenkstätte IV U1, 15
men Männer I
mental mental; geistig; psychisch IV U3, 62
menu Speisekarte; Menü I
mess Unordnung; Durcheinander II
to make a **mess** Unordnung machen; Dreck machen II
message Nachricht; SMS; Botschaft II
met simple past von *to meet* II; past participle von *to meet* III
metal Metall II
metal detector Metalldetektor; Metallsuchgerät IV U2, 32
metre (m) Meter I
Mexican mexikanisch; aus Mexiko; Mexikaner / Mexikanerin IV U5, 100
Mexico Mexiko IV U3, 61
mice Mäuse II
microphone Mikrofon I
microwave Mikrowelle II
middle Mitte II
in the **middle** of nowhere mitten im Nirgendwo II
Middle East Mittlerer Osten III
middle school Mittelschule (*weiterführende Schule in den USA, Mittelstufe*) IV U4, 78
midnight Mitternacht III
might könnte / könnten IV U5, 106
to **migrate** abwandern; wandern; umherziehen IV U4, 77
mile Meile I
milk Milch I
to **milk** melken I
million Million II
to **mind** aufpassen I
Mind the gap. Vorsicht beim Ein- und Aussteigen. I
mind map Wörternetz I
to **mine** abbauen; graben nach IV U3, 57
mine meine / meiner / meins II
mining Bergbau; Abbau; Schürfen IV U3, 67
minnow Elritze; Bitterfisch (*kleiner, schlanker Beutefisch*) IV U5, 105
minute Minute I
mirror Spiegel III
miserable elend; armselig; jämmerlich IV U1, 17
to **miss** verpassen; vermissen II; übersehen; verfehlen IV U4, 86
missing verschwunden; fehlend I
to be **missing** fehlen I
mission Mission; Auftrag; Einsatz IV U5, 98
mist Nebel I
mistake Fehler II
misty neblig I
mobile mobil; tragbar; beweglich III
mobile phone Handy; Mobiltelefon IV U5, 109
modal auxiliary modales Hilfsverb IV U5, 102
model Vorlage; Modell; Model II
modern modern II
modest bescheiden IV U4, 78
modesty Bescheidenheit IV U4, 79
mom *(AE)* Mama II
moment Moment; Augenblick II
at the **moment** im Moment; gerade; momentan; derzeit III
monarch Monarch / Monarchin II
Monday Montag I
on **Mondays** montags I
money Geld I
monster Monster; Ungeheuer III
month Monat II
mood Stimmung; Laune IV U2, 43
Moon Mond IV U5, 107
mop Mopp; Wischmopp II
more mehr; weitere I
moreover außerdem; ferner; zudem IV U5, 106
morning Morgen; Vormittag I
Good **morning**. Guten Morgen. I
this **morning** heute Morgen III
(the) **most** am meisten; die meisten; die Mehrheit II
mostly größtenteils; meistens; hauptsächlich III
mother Mutter I
to **motivate** motivieren IV U4, 82
motivated motiviert IV U4, 79
motorbike Motorrad I
mountain Berg I
mountaineering Bergsteigen III
mouse Maus II
mouth Mund; Maul III
to **move** versetzen; bewegen; umziehen I; sich bewegen III
movement Bewegung IV U5, 99
movie *(AE)* Film IV U2, 31
Mr Herr *(Anrede)* I
Mrs Frau *(Anrede)* I
Ms Frau *(Anrede)* II
much viel I
How **much** (is / are) …? Wie viel (kostet / kosten) …? I
multicultural multikulturell IV U3, 55
multimedia Multimedia-; multimedial IV U5, 117
mum Mama I
mural Wandgemälde; Wandbild III
muscle Muskel III
museum Museum I
mushroom Pilz; Champignon II
music Musik I
musician Musiker / Musikerin IV U5, 111
must müssen I
mustn't nicht dürfen II
my mein / meine I
My name is … Ich heiße … I
myself mich; mir; selbst; selber; mich selbst IV U4, 78
mysterious geheimnisvoll; rätselhaft III
mystery Rätsel; Geheimnis; Mysterium III

N

name Name I
to call sb **names** jmdn. beschimpfen IV U5, 100
to **name** benennen I
narrator Erzähler / Erzählerin II
narrow schmal; eng III
nation Nation; Land; Staat III
national National-; national II

national park Nationalpark; Naturpark III
native indigen; einheimisch; Angehöriger / Angehörige einer indigenen Bevölkerung IV U1, 9
Native American zu der amerikanischen Urbevölkerung gehörig; amerikanischer Ureinwohner / amerikanische Ureinwohnerin IV U1, 9
natural natürlich; Natur- IV U3, 68
natural resource Rohstoff; Bodenschatz; Ressource IV U5, 106
nature Natur II
Navajo Navajo / Navajo; Navajo- IV U4, 77
to **navigate** navigieren; steuern IV U5, 108
near in der Nähe von I; nah III
nearly fast; beinahe; annähernd I
necessary nötig; notwendig; erforderlich II
neck Hals; Nacken; Genick III
to **need** brauchen I
  to **need** to müssen IV U3, 57
  needn't nicht brauchen; nicht müssen III
negative Verneinungsform IV U1, 24
negative negativ; ablehnend III
  negative about ablehnend gegenüber III
neighbour Nachbar / Nachbarin I
neighbourhood Viertel; Nachbarschaft III
nephew Neffe II
nervous nervös; aufgeregt I
the **Netherlands** die Niederlande II
network Netzwerk IV U5, 107
never nie; niemals I
new neu I
New Year Neujahr I
New Year's Eve Silvesternacht III
news Nachrichten-; Nachricht(en); Neuigkeit(en) III
newspaper Zeitung III
next als Nächstes I; nächste / nächster / nächstes II
  next to neben I
nice schön; nett I; lecker II
  Nice to meet you. Schön, dich kennenzulernen. I
niece Nichte II
Nigeria Nigeria II
Nigerian nigerianisch; Nigerianer / Nigerianerin; aus Nigeria II
night Nacht; Abend I
  at **night** nachts IV U4, 76
nine neun I
nineteen neunzehn I
nineteenth neunzehnte I
ninetieth neunzigste I
ninety neunzig I
ninth neunte I
no nein; kein / keine I
  no longer nicht mehr; nicht länger IV U2, 39
  no one niemand II
to **nod** nicken II
noise Geräusch; Lärm II
noisy laut III
non-fiction Sach-; Sachliteratur III
normal normal III
Norman Normanne / Normannin; normannisch III
north Norden; nördlich; Nord- II
northeastern nordöstlich IV U1, 16
northern nördlich III
Northern Ireland Nordirland III
nose Nase II
nosy neugierig IV U1, 16
not nicht I
  not at all überhaupt nicht; gar nicht III
  not … any kein / keine II
  not … any more nicht mehr II
  not … anymore *(AE)* nicht mehr IV U5, 113
  not … anything nichts IV U1, 10
  not … either auch nicht I
  not … yet noch nicht II
note Notiz I
  to make **notes** sich Notizen machen I
to **note** notieren; aufschreiben I
nothing nichts II
noun Nomen; Hauptwort I
novel Roman III
November November I
now jetzt; nun I
  right **now** gerade; jetzt gerade; sofort III
nowhere nirgendwo; nirgendwohin; nichts II
  in the middle of **nowhere** mitten im Nirgendwo II
number Zahl; Nummer; Anzahl I
nurse Krankenpfleger / Krankenpflegerin IV U5, 107
nut Nuss II

O

o'clock Uhr *(Zeitangabe bei vollen Stunden)* I
object Gegenstand; Objekt II
obligation Verpflichtung IV U5, 116
occasion Gelegenheit; Anlass; Ereignis III
ocean Ozean; Meer IV U1, 22
October Oktober I
odd seltsam; merkwürdig; komisch IV U1, 17
of von I
  of course natürlich; selbstverständlich I
off to ab in; auf zu / nach IV U2, 30
to **offer** anbieten; bieten IV U1, 16
office Büro I; Geschäftsstelle III
officer Sprecher / Sprecherin; Beamter / Beamtin IV U2, 34
official Beamter / Beamtin; Funktionär / Funktionärin IV U1, 22
official offiziell II
official language Amtssprache III
often oft; häufig I
oh null *(bei Uhrzeiten und Telefonnummern)* I
oil Öl III
OK okay I
old alt I
old-fashioned altmodisch III
on an; auf I; über II
  on board an Bord IV U1, 22
  on foot zu Fuß I
  on Mondays montags I
  on one's own allein; für sich; ohne Hilfe IV U1, 18
  on stage auf der Bühne II
  on the left auf der linken Seite; links II
  on the other (hand) andererseits III
  on the right auf der rechten Seite; rechts I
  on time pünktlich III
once einmal II; einst IV U3, 71
one eins; ein / eine I
  a / **one** hundred einhundert; hundert I
  a / **one** thousand eintausend; tausend II
  one another einander; gegenseitig I
  one at a time immer nur eine / einer / eines IV U3, 71
  one day eines Tages II
  one of eine / einer / eins von I
one(s) *Platzhalter für ein Nomen* II
onion Zwiebel II
online online II
only nur I; einzige / einziger / einziges III
only child Einzelkind II
onto auf … hinauf I
to **open** öffnen; aufmachen I
open geöffnet; offen; unbebaut II
open day Tag der offenen Tür III
opening Öffnungs-; Öffnen II
opening times Öffnungszeiten IV U1, 14
operator Vermittlung; Telefonist / Telefonistin III
opinion Meinung IV U5, 106
  in my **opinion** meiner Meinung nach IV U5, 106
opportunity Möglichkeit; Gelegenheit; Chance IV U1, 21
opposite Gegenteil I
opposite gegenüber I
optician's Optikfachgeschäft IV U4, 85
or oder I
  either … **or** … entweder … oder … IV U3, 56
orange Orange I
orange orange I
orang-utan Orang-Utan II
orchestra Orchester IV U2, 33
order Reihenfolge; Bestell-; Bestellung II
to **order** bestellen II; befehlen IV U5, 113
organic Bio-; organisch I
to **organise** organisieren; ordnen III
to **organize** *(AE)* organisieren IV U1, 16
other andere; weitere II
  each **other** sich gegenseitig; sich; einander III
others andere II
  the **others** die anderen II
our unser / unsere I
ourselves uns (selbst); selbst II
out heraus I
  out and about unterwegs I
  out of außerhalb von IV U3, 61
  out of … aus … heraus; von … II
outdoor Outdoor-; Freiluft- I; Außen-; im Freien IV U1, 10
outdoors draußen; außen; im Freien II
outline Entwurf; Skizze IV U5, 117
to **outnumber** sb jmdm. zahlenmäßig überlegen sein III

outreach Hilfe IV U3, 62
outreach center *(AE)* Beratungsstelle IV U3, 62
outside (nach) draußen; im Freien; vor I; außerhalb III
oval Oval IV U3, 60
oven Backofen IV U2, 38
over über I; vorbei III
 over there da drüben; dort drüben II
overview Überblick; Übersicht III
overwhelmed überwältigt; überfordert IV U1, 22
to **own** besitzen III
own eigene / eigener / eigenes I
 on one's **own** allein; für sich; ohne Hilfe IV U1, 18

P

p.m. nachmittags *(Uhrzeit)* II
to **pack** packen; einpacken II
to **package** verpacken IV U3, 56
packaging Verpackung; Verpackungsmaterial IV U3, 56
packed lunch Lunchpaket; Vesper II
packet Packung; Tüte; Päckchen I
page Seite; Blatt III
paid simple past von *to pay* I
pain Schmerz III
 to be in **pain** Schmerzen haben III
to **paint** anmalen; malen; streichen II
painting Gemälde II; Mal- III
pair Paar IV U1, 23
 a **pair** of ein Paar IV U1, 23
 in **pairs** zu zweit II
pair of scissors Schere I
palace Palast II
pancake Pfannkuchen; Eierkuchen I
panel Kollektor; Paneel; Platte IV U1, 11
panic Panik IV U4, 90
paper Papier I
papers Papiere; Dokumente; Unterlagen IV U1, 23
parade Parade; Umzug IV U1, 15
paradise Paradies III
paragraph Paragraf; Absatz III
paralympic paralympisch IV U1, 25
paramedic Sanitäter / Sanitäterin II
Pardon. Entschuldigung. I
parents Eltern I
park Park I
parking lot *(AE)* Parkplatz IV U1, 11
part Teil; Stadtteil; Gegend I
 to take **part** (in) teilnehmen (an) II
particular bestimmte / bestimmter / bestimmtes III
partner Partner / Partnerin II
part-time Teilzeit IV U4, 78
party Party; Feier I
to **pass** a law ein Gesetz beschließen; ein Gesetz verabschieden IV U3, 68
to **pass** on weitergeben IV U4, 88
passage Textteil; Passage III
passenger Fluggast; Passagier / Passagierin III
passive passiv IV U3, 58
passive voice Passiv IV U3, 58
passport Pass; Reisepass III
past Vergangenheit III
past nach *(bei Uhrzeitangaben)* I; vorbei (an) II
 half **past** (six) halb (sieben) I
 quarter to / **past** Viertel vor / nach *(bei Uhrzeitangaben)* I
past progressive Verlaufsform der Vergangenheit III
pasta Nudeln; Pasta I
pastime Freizeitbeschäftigung; Zeitvertreib III
path Pfad; Weg III
patience Geduld IV U4, 79
patient Patient / Patientin III
patient geduldig IV U4, 78
pavement Bürgersteig; Gehweg II
*to **pay** bezahlen I
PE (= Physical Education) Sportunterricht I
pea Erbse II
peace Frieden III
peaceful friedlich III
peanut butter Erdnussbutter; Erdnusscreme IV U3, 59
pear Birne IV U3, 55
pecan Pekannuss IV U2, 38
peer Gleichaltriger / Gleichaltrige IV U2, 33
pen Füller; Stift I
pence (p) Pence *(brit. Währungseinheit)* I
pencil Bleistift; Buntstift II
pencil case Federmäppchen II
penguin Pinguin II
peninsula Halbinsel IV U3, 55
penknife Taschenmesser III
penny (p) Penny *(brit. Währungseinheit)* I
people Leute; Menschen I
 to put oneself in other **people's** shoes sich in jmdn. hineinversetzen IV U5, 101
pepper Paprika; Paprikaschote; Pfeffer I
per pro III
percent (%) Prozent (%) IV U1, 9
perfect perfekt; vollkommen II
to **perform** auftreten; aufführen; vortragen III
performance Aufführung; Vorstellung II
performer Künstler / Künstlerin; Darsteller / Darstellerin II
perfume Parfüm IV U1, 23
permission Erlaubnis; Genehmigung IV U1, 20
person Person I
person of color (POC) *(AE)* Person of Color *(Person mit dunkler Hautfarbe)* IV U5, 100
personal persönlich III
perspective Perspektive; Blickwinkel I
pet Haustier I
phone Handy; Telefon I
phone call Telefonanruf I
photo Foto I
 to take **photos** fotografieren; Fotos machen I
phrase Redewendung; Ausdruck; Satz I
to **pick** up aufheben; abholen II
picnic Picknick I
picture Bild I
pie Kuchen; Pastete III
pie chart Tortendiagramm; Kuchendiagramm III
piece Stück I
 a **piece** of ein Stück; eine Scheibe; ein Blatt II
pier Pier; Landungssteg II
pig Schwein III
pillow Kopfkissen I
pink pink; rosa I
pirate Seeräuber / Seeräuberin; Pirat / Piratin II
pitch Spielfeld; Platz I
pizza Pizza II
place Ort; Platz; Stelle I
 to take **place** stattfinden III
to **place** stellen; platzieren I
plain einfach; schlicht II; Ebene IV U2, 31
plan Plan III
to **plan** planen III
plan of action Aktionsplan; Einsatzplan II
plane Flugzeug II
planet Planet II
plant Pflanze II
to **plant** pflanzen II
plantain Kochbanane II
plantation Plantage IV U4, 83
plaster Pflaster III
plastic Plastik; Kunststoff II
plate Teller II
plateau Hochebene; Plateau IV U4, 77
platform Bahnsteig I; Plattform II
play Theaterstück II
to **play** spielen; abspielen I
player Spieler / Spielerin II
playground Schulhof; Pausenhof; Spielplatz I
please bitte I
pleased froh; erfreut; zufrieden I
pledge Versprechen IV U2, 32
Pledge of Allegiance Treueeid IV U2, 32
plot Handlung III
pocket Tasche; Hosentasche II
podcast Podcast II
poem Gedicht I
point Komma (bei Dezimalzahlen); Punkt III
 point of view Standpunkt; Perspektive III
to **point** (at) zeigen (auf) I; II
pointed spitz III
poison Gift III
poisonous giftig II
Poland Polen IV U1, 22
police Polizei I
police officer Polizeibeamter / Polizeibeamtin I
police station Polizeirevier; Polizeiwache IV U4, 85
Polish Polnisch; polnisch; aus Polen III
polite höflich III
political politisch III
politician Politiker / Politikerin IV U4, 84
pollution Verschmutzung IV U3, 56
pond Teich; Tümpel I
pool Teich; Tümpel; Becken III
poor arm III
popular beliebt I

population Einwohnerzahl; Einwohner *(Pl.)*; Bevölkerung III
portal Portal; Zugang IV U2, 32
portrait Portrait IV U4, 76
portrayal Darstellung; Porträt IV U4, 79
Portugal Portugal I
position Position; Stelle I
positive positiv III
possibility Möglichkeit IV U5, 108
possible möglich IV U1, 16
post Post *(online gestellte Nachricht)*; Beitrag; Eintrag IV U1, 16
to **post** online stellen; posten II
post box Briefkasten II
postcard Postkarte I
poster Poster IV U5, 101
pot Topf II
potato Kartoffel II
pottery Töpferei; Keramik III
to make **pottery** töpfern III
pound (£) Pfund (*brit. Währungseinheit*) II
power Macht; Energie; Strom; Kraft IV U4, 77
powerful stark; mächtig; bedeutend; beeindruckend IV U2, 44
powwow Versammlung (*der indigenen Völker Nordamerikas*) IV U2, 45
practical praktisch IV U3, 62
practice Probe; Übung; Training IV U1, 16
to **practice** *(AE)* üben; trainieren; praktizieren IV U2, 33
to **practise** üben; trainieren III
precious wertvoll; kostbar IV U3, 68
prediction Prophezeiung; Vorhersage; Voraussage IV U5, 108
to **prefer** vorziehen III
pregnant schwanger IV U3, 62
to **prepare** (sich) vorbereiten III
to be **prepared** bereit sein; vorbereitet sein III
preposition Präposition III
present Geschenk I; Gegenwart; Präsens IV U4, 83
to **present** präsentieren; vorstellen IV U5, 101
present perfect Perfekt II
present perfect progressive Verlaufsform des Perfekts IV U4, 92
present progressive Verlaufsform der Gegenwart II
presentation Präsentation; Vortrag II
president Präsident / Präsidentin IV U2, 31
to **press** drücken; pressen II
press officer Pressesprecher / Pressesprecherin III
to **pretend** vortäuschen; vorgeben IV U1, 12
pretty echt; ziemlich; ganz schön; hübsch III
preview Vorschau III
previously vorher; zuvor; früher III
prime minister Premierminister / Premierministerin; Ministerpräsident / Ministerpräsidentin II
prince Prinz II
print gedruckt; Druck III
print books gedruckte Bücher III
printer Drucker II
prison Gefängnis I
private Privat-; privat IV U1, 16
probably wahrscheinlich IV U2, 44
problem Problem I
process Prozess IV U3, 59
to **process** verarbeiten; aufbereiten; verstehen IV U3, 57
to **produce** herstellen; produzieren; erzeugen; anbauen IV U2, 37
producer Erzeuger / Erzeugerin; Hersteller / Herstellerin; Produzent / Produzentin IV U3, 55
product Produkt I
production Produktion; Herstellung IV U2, 32
profile Steckbrief; Profil I
program Programm; Sendung III
program *(AE)* Programm; Sendung IV U3, 61
program *(BE)* Computerprogramm IV U3, 61
to **program** programmieren IV U3, 57
programmer Programmierer / Programmiererin II
programming Programmier- IV U4, 89
project Projekt II
prom *Ball am Ende des Jahres in einer amerikanischen High School* IV U2, 32
promenade Promenade I
to **promise** versprechen III
to **promote** bewerben IV U1, 12; fördern; befördern IV U3, 66
pronoun Pronomen; Fürwort I
to **pronounce** aussprechen III
proof Beweis III
prop Requisit II
to **protect** schützen; beschützen II
protest Protest; Demonstration III
to **protest** protestieren IV U5, 99
Protestant Protestant / Protestantin; protestantisch III
protesting protestierend IV U5, 113
protestor Demonstrant / Demonstrantin IV U5, 113
proud (of) stolz (auf) IV U2, 45
to **prove** beweisen IV U5, 100
to **provide** liefern; bereitstellen; bieten; versorgen IV U4, 77
pub Kneipe; Gasthaus III
(the) **public** die Öffentlichkeit IV U5, 100
public öffentlich III
to **publish** veröffentlichen; publizieren; verlegen IV U3, 69
Pueblo Pueblo-; Angehöriger / Angehörige der Pueblovölker IV U4, 77
to **pull** ziehen III
to **pull** out herausholen; herausfahren III
to **pull** up hochhalten; hochziehen; heranziehen IV U4, 90
pumpkin Kürbis IV U2, 38
punch Punsch; Bowle IV U2, 38
purple lila; violett II
to **push** schubsen; drängeln; schieben; drücken IV U5, 100
*to **put** stellen; setzen; legen; werfen III
to **put** in hineintun; eingeben II; installieren; einsetzen III
to **put** on anziehen; anlegen; draufmachen III
*to **put** oneself in danger sich in Gefahr bringen IV U5, 101
to **put** oneself in other people's shoes sich in jmdn. hineinversetzen IV U5, 101
to **put** through verbinden; durchstellen III
to **put** together zusammensetzen; zusammenbauen IV U3, 56
to **put** up aufhängen; aufstellen; hochhalten; errichten IV U2, 39
put simple past, past participle von *to put* III
puzzle Rätsel; Puzzle III
pyjamas Schlafanzug; Pyjama III

Q

qualification Qualifikation; Abschluss; Schulabschluss IV U3, 64; IV U4, 89
quality Eigenschaft; Qualität IV U4, 84
quarter Viertel I
quarter to / past Viertel vor / nach (*bei Uhrzeitangaben*) I
question Frage I
queue Warteschlange II
quick schnell II
quiet ruhig; leise; still I
quite ziemlich II
quiz Quiz; Rätsel I
quote Zitat III

R

raccoon Waschbär I
race Wettrennen; Rennen I
racism Rassismus IV U4, 83
racist rassistisch; Rassist / Rassistin IV U5, 112
radio Radio II
radio play Hörspiel I
railroad *(AE)* Eisenbahn IV U1, 10
railway Eisenbahn III
rain Regen I
to **rain** regnen I
raincoat Regenmantel; Regenjacke III
rainy regnerisch I
to **raise** heben; anheben; hochhalten; erhöhen IV U5, 100
to **raise** awareness das Bewusstsein schärfen; jmdn. sensibilisieren IV U5, 100
to **raise** money Geld sammeln; Geld aufbringen IV U1, 9
ran simple past von *to run* I
to **rank** einstufen II
rare rar; selten IV U3, 56
raw roh; unbehandelt IV U3, 56
raw material Rohstoff; Rohmaterial IV U3, 56
RE (= Religious Education) Religionsunterricht I
to **reach** out die Hand ausstrecken IV U4, 90

read simple past, past participle von *to read* III
*to **read** lesen I
to **read** out vorlesen II
reader Leser / Leserin III
reading Lesen I
*to get **ready** sich fertig machen; sich vorbereiten IV U2, 32
real echt; richtig; wirklich II
realistic realistisch III
to **realise** bemerken; realisieren; erkennen III
to **realize** *(AE)* sich bewusst werden; erkennen; realisieren IV U4, 90
really wirklich; echt; sehr II
reason Grund III
*to **rebuild** wiederaufbauen III
to **receive** empfangen; erhalten; bekommen II
recent neueste / neuester / neuestes; letzte / letzter / letztes IV U4, 92
recently kürzlich; neulich; in letzter Zeit III
recipe Rezept IV ZI, 7
to **recognise** erkennen; anerkennen IV U2, 37
to **recommend** empfehlen IV U4, 77
record Rekord III
to **record** aufnehmen; aufzeichnen I
recording Aufnahme; Aufzeichnung I
recording studio Tonstudio I
to **recycle** recyceln; wiederverwerten II
recycled recycelt; wiederverwertet IV U3, 56
red rot I
to **reduce** reduzieren; verringern; vermindern IV U3, 56
reef Riff IV U5, 99
coral **reef** Korallenriff IV U5, 99
to **reflect** nachdenken; reflektieren IV U5, 101
refugee Geflüchteter / Geflüchtete; Flüchtling IV U1, 25
to **refuse** sich weigern; ablehnen IV U5, 112
Kind **regards**, Viele Grüße IV U4, 86
region Region; Gegend III
registration Anwesenheitskontrolle I; Anmelde-; Anmeldung III
regular regelmäßig; normal; üblich; gleichmäßig III
relative Verwandter / Verwandte III
relative clause Relativsatz IV U5, 109
to **relax** sich entspannen; sich ausruhen III
relaxing entspannend; erholsam I
relay Staffellauf; Staffel III
to **release** freilassen; loslassen; freigeben; entlassen; herausgeben IV U5, 105
reliable verlässlich; zuverlässig; vertrauenswürdig III
religion Religion III
religious religiös; gläubig III
to **remember** sich merken; sich erinnern (an) I
to **remove** entfernen II
to **renovate** renovieren; sanieren III
renovated renoviert; saniert III
renovation Sanierung; Renovierung; Umbau III
rent Miete IV U3, 62
to **rent** mieten II
to **repair** reparieren I
repair service Reparaturdienst II
to **repeat** wiederholen II
to **replace** ersetzen IV U3, 56
report Bericht III
to **report** (on) berichten (über); erzählen I
reporter Reporter / Reporterin I
to **represent** repräsentieren; stehen für; darstellen IV U1, 21
republic Republik III
the **Republic of Ireland** Irland III
request Anfrage; Bitte III
rescue Rettung III
to **rescue** retten IV U4, 79
rescuer Retter / Retterin III
research Recherche; Forschung; Untersuchung IV U3, 68
to **research** recherchieren; erforschen; untersuchen IV U1, 12
reservation Reservat IV U4, 83
reservoir Stausee IV U3, 55
resolution Vorsatz; Entschluss IV U2, 39
resource Ressource IV U5, 106
respectful respektvoll III
to **respect** respektieren III
to **respond** reagieren; erwidern; antworten IV U1, 23
response Reaktion; Antwort; Erwiderung IV U5, 112
responsible verantwortungsvoll; verantwortlich IV U2, 34; IV U3, 68
the **rest** der Rest IV U1, 22
restaurant Restaurant I
result Ergebnis I
to **return** zurückschicken; zurückgeben; zurückkehren II
to **reuse** wiederverwenden II
revenge Rache IV U4, 79
review Kritik III
revision Wiederholung; Durchsicht; Überarbeitung II
*to **rewrite** umschreiben; neu schreiben IV U4, 86
rib Rippe; Rippchen IV U5, 99
rice Reis I
rich reich I
ride Fahrt; Ritt I
*to **ride** fahren; reiten I
rifle Gewehr IV U3, 63
right Recht IV U4, 83
right richtig; korrekt; rechts I
to be **right** recht haben III
on the **right** auf der rechten Seite; rechts I
right now gerade; jetzt gerade; sofort III
ring Ring III
riot Ausschreitung; Aufruhr; Unruhe IV U5, 114
risotto Risotto II
river Fluss I
road Straße I
robin Rotkehlchen II
robot Roboter II
rock Fels; Stein III
rocky felsig; steinig IV U4, 79
rock climbing Klettern *(am Felsen)* III
rocket Rakete IV U5, 107
rode simple past von *to ride* I
rodeo Rodeo IV U4, 77
role Rolle II
role model Vorbild IV U4, 78
role play Rollenspiel I
roll Rolle II
to **roll** up zusammenrollen; aufrollen; aufkrempeln IV U4, 86
roller coaster Achterbahn I
Roman Römer / Römerin; römisch III
Romania Rumänien II
roof Dach III
room Zimmer; Raum; Platz I
rope Seil III
rose Rose II
round um … herum I; rund II
roundabout Kreisverkehr I
route Route; Strecke III
routine Routine; Ablauf I
royal königlich II
rubber Radiergummi I
rubbish Müll; Abfall I
rude unhöflich; unverschämt IV U5, 101
rug Teppich; Vorleger IV U4, 77
rugby Rugby III
rule Regel I
ruler Lineal I; Herrscher / Herrscherin III
rumour Gerücht I
run Lauf III
*to **run** rennen; laufen I
to **run** after hinterherrennen II
to **run** away weglaufen I
to **run** from … to … gehen von … bis …; dauern von … bis … IV U3, 61
runner Läufer / Läuferin III
running Laufen I
Russia Russland II
Russian Russisch; russisch; aus Russland; Russe / Russin III

S

sad traurig II
safe in Sicherheit; sicher I
Safe flight! Guten Flug! IV U2, 38
safety Sicherheit III
safety pin Sicherheitsnadel III
said simple past von *to say* I
to **sail** segeln I
sailing Segeln I
sailor Matrose / Matrosin; Seefahrer / Seefahrerin II
salad Salat I
salary Gehalt IV U4, 89
sale Verkauf; Schlussverkauf; Ausverkauf I
salt Salz IV U2, 45
salty salzig I
the **same** … derselbe / dieselbe / dasselbe …; der / die / das gleiche … II
sandwich Sandwich; Butterbrot; belegtes Brot I
sang simple past von *to sing* II

sat simple past von *to sit* II; past participle von *to sit* III
Saturday Samstag I
sauce Soße II
sausage Wurst; Bratwurst II
to **save** sparen; retten; speichern III
saw simple past von *to see* I
Saxon Sachse / Sächsin; sächsisch III
*to **say** sagen; sprechen I
Scandinavia Skandinavien III
scanning Absuchen IV U2, 39
scared verängstigt IV U1, 22
to be **scared** Angst haben; erschrocken sein III
to get **scared** Angst bekommen III
scarf Schal; Tuch II
scary beängstigend; gruselig II
scene Szene; Schauplatz; Situation II
schedule Zeitplan III
schedule *(AE)* Stundenplan; Fahrplan IV U2, 32
school Schule I
to leave **school** mit der Schule fertig sein; von der Schule abgehen II
science Wissenschaft; Naturwissenschaft I
scientific wissenschaftlich; naturwissenschaftlich IV U3, 68
scientist Wissenschaftler / Wissenschaftlerin II
scissors Schere II
scone Scone (*eine Art süßes Brötchen*) I
scooter Roller I
to **score** ein Tor schießen; punkten I
Scotland Schottland III
Scottish schottisch; Schottisch; aus Schottland III
scrapbook Scrapbook (*selbst gestaltetes Buch*); Sammelalbum III
to **scream** schreien; kreischen I
screen Leinwand; Bildschirm II
screensaver Bildschirmschoner IV U3, 61
scribble Kritzelei; Gekritzel II
script Drehbuch; Skript II
sculpture Skulptur IV U4, 85
sea Meer I
sea lion Seelöwe II
seafood Meeresfrüchte IV U1, 16
seafront Meeresufer II
seal Seehund; Robbe I
search Suche; Such- IV U5, 104
to **search** durchsuchen; suchen II
search engine Suchmaschine III
seasick seekrank IV U1, 22
seaside Küste; Meeresküste I
season Jahreszeit; Saison I
seasonal Saison-; saisonal IV U3, 55
seat Sitz; Sitzplatz IV U2, 46
seaweed Seetang IV U5, 107
second Sekunde III
second zweite / zweiter / zweites III
secondly zweitens IV U5, 106
secondary school weiterführende Schule III
second-hand gebraucht; secondhand; aus zweiter Hand III
secret geheim II; Geheimnis IV U2, 38
secretary Schriftführer / Schriftführerin III
section Abschnitt IV U4, 93
secure sicher III
*to **see** sehen I
See you … Bis … III
See you (very) soon! Bis (sehr) bald. III
See you later. Tschüss.; Bis bald. I
you **see** … weißt du …; wissen Sie … III
seed Samen; Saat II
to **seem** scheinen IV U1, 22
seen past participle von *to see* II
segment Abschnitt; Teilstück IV U3, 60
segregated getrennt IV U5, 113
segregation Rassentrennung; Trennung IV U5, 99
selfie spot Selfiestelle; Selfiespot II
self-respect Selbstachtung IV U3, 62
*to **sell** verkaufen I
*to **send** schicken; senden II
sensor Sensor; Melder II
sent simple past von *to send* II
sentence Satz I
separately getrennt; separat; verschieden I
September September I
series Serie; Reihe; Staffel III
serious schwer; ernsthaft IV U3, 62
*to take sb / sth **seriously** jmdn. / etw. ernst nehmen IV U5, 100
to **serve** bedienen; servieren; dienen III
service Dienst; Service II; Dienstleistung IV U4, 85
session Einheit; Sitzung; Stunde; Versammlung III
set Set; Kulisse II
*to **set** einstellen; setzen III
to be **set** (in) spielen (in) IV U4, 79
to **settle** (in) sich niederlassen (in); besiedeln IV U2, 31
settler Siedler / Siedlerin IV U1, 9
seven sieben I
seventeen siebzehn I
seventeenth siebzehnte I
seventh siebte I
seventieth siebzigste I
seventy siebzig I
*to **shake** schütteln; zittern II
shampoo Shampoo III
shamrock Kleeblatt III
shape Form IV U4, 84
to **share** teilen I; erzählen III
shark Hai IV U5, 105
sharp pünktlich; scharf; schneidend IV U4, 86
sharpener Spitzer I
she sie I
sheaf toss Strohgarbenwerfen (*schottische Sportart*) III
sheet Blatt II
shelf Regal; Regalbrett I
ship Schiff I
shirt Hemd; Shirt II
to **shiver** zittern; frösteln III
to **shock** schockieren IV U5, 113
shocked schockiert; geschockt IV U4, 90
shocking schockierend IV U5, 113
shoe Schuh II
shook simple past von *to shake* II
*to **shoot** drehen III; schießen IV U5, 114
to **shoot** a film einen Film drehen III
shop Laden; Geschäft I
shopping Einkaufen I
to go **shopping** einkaufen gehen I
shopping centre Einkaufszentrum I
shore Ufer; Küste IV U2, 31
short kurz II
shorts Shorts; kurze Hose II
shot Aufnahme; Einstellung; Schuss IV U2, 43; simple past, past participle von *to shoot* IV U5, 114
shot put Kugelstoßen III
should sollte II
shoulder Schulter II
to **shout** schreien; rufen II
show Show; Aufführung II
*to **show** zeigen II
to **show** sb around (a place) jmdn. (an einem Ort) herumführen II
shower Dusche III
to have a **shower** duschen; eine Dusche nehmen II
shower gel Duschgel III
shown past participle von to *show* II
shrimp Krabbe; Garnele IV U5, 99
to **shrug** mit den Achseln zucken; mit den Schultern zucken II
*to **shut** zumachen; schließen IV U2, 43
shut simple past, past participle von *to shut* IV U2, 43
shy schüchtern IV U4, 90
sibling Geschwisterkind II; Geschwister IV U2, 45
sick krank IV U3, 62
side Seite I
sidewalk *(AE)* Gehweg; Bürgersteig IV U4, 84
sight Sehenswürdigkeit II
sightseeing Besichtigungstour II; Besichtigung; Sightseeing III
to go **sightseeing** eine Besichtigungstour machen II
sign Zeichen; Schild II
to **sign** unterschreiben; unterzeichnen III
sign language Gebärdensprache I
signal Empfang; Signal; Zeichen II
signal word Signalwort IV U4, 81
signpost Schild; Wegweiser II
silent schweigsam; stumm; still III
silly blöd; dumm; doof; albern I
similar ähnlich III
simple einfach I
simple past einfache Vergangenheit I
simple present Gegenwart; Präsens II
since seit; seitdem III
Sincerely, Mit freundlichen Grüßen IV U5, 106
*to **sing** singen II
singer Sänger / Sängerin II
single alleinerziehend; alleinstehend; einzeln; einzige / einziger / einziges IV U3, 62
sink Waschbecken; Spülbecken III
sister Schwester I
*to **sit** sitzen II
to **sit** down sich hinsetzen; sich setzen I

to **sit** up sich aufrichten; aufrecht sitzen IV U4, 90
site Gelände; Ort; Schauplatz III; Platz; Anlage; Basis IV U5, 98
situation Situation III
six sechs I
sixteen sechzehn I
sixteenth sechzehnte I
sixth sechste I
sixtieth sechzigste I
sixty sechzig I
size Größe II
skate park Skatepark I
skateboard Skateboard I
skating Skateboardfahren; Inlineskaten; Schlittschuhlaufen I
skill Fertigkeit; Geschick; Kenntnis; Fähigkeit III
to **skim** überfliegen III
skimming Überfliegen IV U2, 39
skin Haut; Fell III
skirt Rock II
sky Himmel IV U5, 108
skyscraper Wolkenkratzer IV U1, 10
slave Sklave / Sklavin IV U4, 83
sleep Schlaf II
*to **sleep** schlafen I
to **sleep** late ausschlafen; lange schlafen II
sleeping bag Schlafsack III
sleeve Ärmel IV U5, 105
slept simple past von *to sleep* I
slide Folie IV U2, 42
slide show Bildschirmpräsentation IV U2, 42
slim dünn; schlank; schmal; gering IV U4, 90
slow langsam I
small klein I
smart schlau; klug; intelligent; gepflegt; schick I
*to **smell** riechen I
smelt simple past von *to smell* II
smile Lächeln III
to **smile** lächeln II
smoked geräuchert IV U5, 99
smoking Rauchen III
snack Snack; Imbiss I
snack bar Café; Imbissstube I
snail Schnecke II
snake Schlange II
snook Barsch IV U5, 105
snow Schnee I
to **snow** schneien IV U2, 38
so so; also; daher I; damit II
even **so** und doch; trotzdem; selbst dann IV U4, 90
so far bisher; bislang; bis jetzt III
so that damit; sodass II
soap Seife III
social sozial; gesellschaftlich IV U3, 62
social media soziale Medien III
social work Sozialarbeit IV U3, 62
social worker Sozialarbeiter / Sozialarbeiterin IV U4, 89
sock Socke IV U1, 23
sofa Sofa I
soft weich; sanft III
software Software IV U4, 89
solar Sonnen-; Solar-; solar IV U1, 11
solar panel Sonnenkollektor; Solarpaneel IV U1, 11
solar system Sonnensystem IV U5, 107
sold simple past von *to sell* I
solution Lösung IV U3, 61
to **solve** lösen III
some ein paar; einige; manche; etwas I
some day eines Tages III
some time irgendwann III
somebody jemand IV U1, 25
someone jemand I
something etwas II
sometimes manchmal I
son Sohn II
song Lied II
soon bald II
as **soon** as sobald III
*to be **sorry** leidtun III
Sorry. Tut mir leid.; Entschuldigung. I
I'm **sorry**. Es tut mir leid.; Entschuldigung. I
to **sort** sortieren II
sound Laut; Ton; Geräusch II
to **sound** klingen; sich anhören III
soup Suppe II
sour sauer I
source Quelle III
south Süden; südlich; Süd- II
Southerner Südstaatler / Südstaatlerin IV U5, 99
souvenir Souvenir; Andenken II
soy Soja IV U2, 30
space Weltraum I; Platz; Raum; Fläche; Ort; Stelle II
space shuttle Raumfähre IV U1, 10
space station Raumstation I
space travel Raumfahrt IV U5, 106
spacecraft Raumschiff II
spaghetti Spaghetti II
Spain Spanien I
Spanish Spanisch; spanisch; aus Spanien III
*to **speak** sprechen II
speaker Sprecher / Sprecherin; Redner / Rednerin IV U4, 84
special speziell; besonders I
specific genau; spezifisch; speziell III
spectacular spektakulär IV U1, 8
speech Rede; Sprache IV U5, 114
speech bubble Sprechblase III
*to **spell** buchstabieren I
spelling Rechtschreibung I
*to **spend** verbringen (*Zeit*); ausgeben (*Geld*) I
spent simple past von *to spend* I; past participle von *to spend* III
spice Gewürz III
spicy würzig; pikant II
spider Spinne II
spiky stachlig II
splash Platscher III
to **splash** spritzen; bespritzen I
spoke simple past von *to speak* II
spoken past participle von *to speak* III
spooky gespenstisch I
sport Sport; Sportart I
to do **sport** Sport treiben I
sports Sport- III
sports centre Sportzentrum I
to **spot** entdecken; sehen; erkennen IV U3, 68
spotlight Rampenlicht; Scheinwerfer II
spread Aufstrich IV U3, 59
spring Frühling; Frühjahr I
to **spy** entdecken; sehen I
square Platz; Quadrat II
square kilometre (km²) Quadratkilometer III
square mile Quadratmeile III
squirrel Eichhörnchen II
to **stack** befüllen; füllen III
stadium Stadion II
staff Personal; Belegschaft; Kollegium I
stage Phase; Abschnitt IV U3, 60
on **stage** auf der Bühne II
staircase Treppe; Treppenhaus IV U1, 11
stairs Treppe; Treppenhaus II
*to **stand** stehen II
to **stand** in line anstehen IV U1, 22
to **stand** up aufstehen; stehen II
to **stand** up to sb jmdm. die Stirn bieten; jmdm. gewachsen sein; sich gegen jmdn. behaupten IV U4, 78
star Stern; Star II
start Start; Anfang; Beginn IV U4, 87
to **start** anfangen; beginnen; starten I
starting point Ausgangspunkt II
start-up Start-up IV U3, 55
state Bundesstaat; Staat; Land; Zustand IV ZI, 7
statement Aussage; Behauptung; Erklärung II
station Station; Bahnhof; Haltestelle I
statue Statue; Standbild II
stay Aufenthalt III
to **stay** bleiben; übernachten I
*to **steal** stehlen III
steel Stahl IV U1, 10
STEM MINT II
step Schritt; Stufe II
to **step** treten; steigen III
step- Stief- IV U2, 44
stepbrother Stiefbruder I
stepdad Stiefvater IV U2, 44
stepfather Stiefvater I
stepmother Stiefmutter I
stepsister Stiefschwester I
stereotype Klischee; Stereotyp III
stew Eintopf II
stick Stock III
*to **stick** kleben II
sticker Aufkleber II
sticky klebrig III
sticky tape Klebeband III
still immer noch; noch; trotzdem; dennoch III
*to **sting** stechen III
stole simple past von *to steal* III
stolen past participle von *to steal* III
stomach Bauch; Magen II
stomach ache Bauchschmerzen; Bauchweh II
stone Stein III
stood simple past von *to stand* II

stop Halt; Haltestelle II
to **stop** anhalten; stoppen; stehen bleiben; aufhören; abstellen I; aufhalten; verhindern IV U4, 78
Stop it! Hör(t) auf! I
stopwatch Stoppuhr IV U3, 71
store *(AE)* Laden; Geschäft IV U1, 10
story *(AE)* Etage; Stockwerk IV U1, 10
storm Sturm; Unwetter IV U2, 43
stormy stürmisch I
story Geschichte III
storytelling Erzähl-; Geschichtenerzählen III
straight gerade; direkt II
straight away sofort; gleich III
straight on geradeaus I
to **strain** zerren; belasten; anstrengen III
strange merkwürdig; seltsam IV U1, 17
strategy Strategie; Vorgehensweise IV U5, 101
straw Stroh; Trinkhalm III
to **stream** streamen *(im Internet)* II
to live **stream** live streamen; live übertragen IV U2, 32
street Straße I
street art Straßenkunst III
strength Stärke; Kraft IV U2, 46
stress Betonung IV U5, 101
to **stretch** dehnen; strecken II
stretching exercise Dehnübung; Streckübung II
strict streng; strikt IV U3, 68
strike Streik IV U5, 114
strip Streifen II
strong stark II
structure Aufbau; Struktur IV U4, 82
to **structure** strukturieren; gliedern II
stubborn eigensinnig; störrisch IV U5, 101
stuck simple past, past participle von *to stick* II
student Schüler / Schülerin; Student / Studentin I
student council Schülerrat IV U2, 32
studio Studio I
to **study** studieren; lernen III
stung simple past, past participle von *to sting* III
stunning sensationell; fantastisch; überwältigend IV U4, 76
stupid dumm; blöd III
style Stil III
subject Schulfach I; Thema; Betreff III
submarine U-Boot IV U1, 10
subscription Abonnement III
substitute Ersatz IV U5, 116
subtitle Untertitel IV U5, 115
suburb Vorort IV U1, 16
subway *(AE)* U-Bahn IV U1, 10
to **succeed** (in) Erfolg haben (mit / bei); nachfolgen IV U1, 22
success Erfolg IV U1, 21
successful erfolgreich III
such solch III
such as wie III
all of a **sudden** plötzlich; auf einmal III
suddenly plötzlich; auf einmal II
sugar Zucker I
to **suggest** vorschlagen; nahelegen; andeuten III
suggestion Vorschlag; Anregung III
to **suit** stehen; passen II
suitable geeignet; passend IV U5, 106
suitcase Koffer IV U2, 38
to **sum** up zusammenfassen IV U5, 106
to **sum** up zusammengefasst IV U5, 106
to **summarise** zusammenfassen II
summary Zusammenfassung II
summer Sommer I
sun Sonne I
sun cream Sonnencreme II
sunbathing Sonnenbaden III
Sunday Sonntag I
sunflower Sonnenblume II
sunglasses Sonnenbrille II
sunhat Sonnenhut II
sunny sonnig I
sunrise Sonnenaufgang IV U3, 55
sunset Sonnenuntergang IV U3, 55
suntan Sonnenbräune IV U5, 108
superlative Superlativ II
supermarket Supermarkt I
support Unterstützung; Hilfe IV U3, 62
to **support** unterstützen IV U3, 62
sure sicher I
to make **sure** dafür sorgen; sich versichern; sichergehen III
surfing Surfen; Wellenreiten III
surname Nachname; Familienname III
surprised überrascht I
surprising überraschend III
survey Umfrage I
to **survive** überleben IV U5, 106
sustainable zukunftsfähig; nachhaltig IV ZI, 7
to **swap** tauschen II
to **sweat** schwitzen III
sweater Pullover II
sweet süß II
*to **swim** schwimmen I
swimmer Schwimmer / Schwimmerin IV U1, 25
swimming Schwimmen I
to go **swimming** schwimmen gehen I
swimming pool Schwimmbad I
swimwear Badebekleidung; Badesachen III
*to **swing** schwingen; schwenken III
to **switch** off ausschalten III
Switzerland die Schweiz IV U3, 68
sword Schwert III
swung simple past, past participle von *to swing* III
symbol Symbol III
synonym Synonym IV U1, 17
system System IV U5, 107

T

table Tabelle; Tisch I
tablet Tablet I; Tablette II
to **tackle** attackieren; angreifen III
*to **take** nehmen; mitnehmen; dauern I; bekommen; erhalten II; brauchen; benötigen IV U3, 56
to **take** notes sich Notizen machen *(mitschreiben)* I
to **take** off starten; abheben; durchstarten; ausziehen III
to **take** out herausnehmen; herausbringen I
to **take** part (in) teilnehmen (an) II
to **take** photos fotografieren; Fotos machen I
to **take** place stattfinden III
to **take** sb / sth seriously jmdn. / etw. ernst nehmen IV U5, 100
to **take** the dog for a walk den Hund spazieren führen I
to **take** turns sich abwechseln II
taken past participle von *to take* III
talent Talent IV U4, 79
talented talentiert; begabt IV U4, 78
talk Vortrag; Rede IV U4, 76
to **talk** (to) sprechen (mit); reden (mit) I
to **talk** about sprechen über I
tall groß; hoch I
tape Klebeband II
task Aufgabe; Auftrag I
tasty lecker; schmackhaft II
taught simple past, past participle von *to teach* III
taxi Taxi IV U1, 13
tea Tee; frühes Abendessen II
*to **teach** beibringen; unterrichten; lehren III
teacher Lehrer / Lehrerin I
team Team; Mannschaft II
*to **tear** down abreißen; zerstören; abbrechen III
teatime Teezeit I
technician Techniker / Technikerin IV U4, 89
technology Technik; Technologie II
teen Jugend-; Teenager; Jugendlicher / Jugendliche III
teenager Teenager; Jugendlicher / Jugendliche IV U1, 16
teeth Zähne II
to brush one's **teeth** sich die Zähne putzen II
telephone Telefon III
television Fernseher; Fernsehen IV U2, 43
*to **tell** sagen; erzählen I
temperature Temperatur; Fieber I
ten zehn I
tennis Tennis I
tense Zeit; Zeitform III
tent Zelt I
tenth zehnte I
term Begriff IV U5, 104
in **term** time während der Schulzeit III
terrace Terrasse IV U1, 11
terrible schrecklich; schlimm; furchtbar II
terrified verängstigt; erschrocken IV U1, 22
to be **terrified** schreckliche Angst haben IV U1, 22
terrorist Terrorist / Terroristin; Terror- IV U1, 15
to **test** testen; prüfen II
text Text I
to **text** eine SMS schreiben; texten I

text message SMS I
than als I
Thank you. Danke. I
thankful dankbar IV U2, 38
thanks danke II
Thanksgiving Erntedankfest IV U2, 38
that das I; der / die / das; dem; den; dass II; so *(Betonung)* III
after **that** danach I
so **that** damit; sodass II
That's £9.10. Das macht neun Pfund und zehn Pence. I
that's why deswegen IV U1, 16
the der; die *(auch Pl.)*; das I
the same … derselbe / dieselbe / dasselbe …; der / die / das gleiche … II
the 1800s das 19. Jahrhundert III
theater *(AE)* Theater IV U4, 78
theatre Theater II
their ihr / ihre *(Pl.)* I
theirs ihre / ihrer / ihres IV U5, 114
them sie *(Pl.)*; ihnen I
theme Thema; Motto II
themed Themen-; thematisch ausgerichtet II
themselves sich selbst; sie selbst; selbst II
then dann; danach I
theory Theorie IV U4, 82
therapy Therapie; Behandlung IV U3, 63
there da; dort I
there are es gibt; da sind I
there's (= there is) es gibt; da ist; dort ist I
these dies(e) hier II
these days heutzutage III
they sie *(Pl.)* I
thing Sache; Ding I
*to **think** finden; denken; glauben I
to **think** of sich ausdenken; sich einfallen lassen I
thirsty durstig IV U2, 44
thirteen dreizehn I
thirteenth dreizehnte I
thirtieth dreißigste I
thirty dreißig I
this das; dies I
this morning heute Morgen III
thorny dornig II
those diese dort; jene II
thought Gedanke III
thought simple past von *to think* II; past participle von *to think* III
a / one **thousand** eintausend; tausend II
three drei I
threw simple past von *to throw* II
through durch I
throw Wurf III
*to **throw** werfen II
to **throw** away wegwerfen II
to **throw** off abwerfen III
thrown past participle von *to throw* III
Thursday Donnerstag I
tick card Zeckenkarte III
ticket Fahrschein; Fahrkarte; Eintrittskarte I
ticket office Fahrkartenschalter I
tide Gezeiten III

to **tidy** (up) aufräumen; in Ordnung bringen II
tidy ordentlich; sauber III
time Zeit; Uhrzeit I; Mal II
on **time** pünktlich III
some **time** irgendwann III
time zone Zeitzone IV U2, 30
timeline Zeitstrahl III
timetable Stundenplan I
tip Tipp; Hinweis; Ratschlag II
tired müde I
title Titel; Überschrift III
to zu; in; nach; bis; vor *(bei Uhrzeitangaben)* I
quarter **to** / past Viertel vor / nach *(bei Uhrzeitangaben)* I
to sum up zusammengefasst IV U5, 106
toast Toast II
today's heutig IV U4, 79
today heute I
toe Zeh II
tofu Tofu II
together zusammen; gemeinsam; miteinander II
toilet Toilette I
told simple past von *to tell* II
tolerant tolerant IV U5, 101
tomato Tomate I
tomorrow morgen II
tonight heute Abend; heute Nacht III
too auch; zu I
took simple past von *to take* I
tool Tool; Werkzeug; Hilfsmittel; Gerät IV U3, 67
tooth Zahn II
toothbrush Zahnbürste III
top Top; Oberteil; oberes Ende; Spitze IV U1, 10
at the **top** oben II
top Top-; beste / bester / bestes II
top secret streng geheim II
topic Thema IV U5, 106
torch Taschenlampe III
tore down simple past von *to tear down* III
torn down past participle von *to tear down* III
tornado Tornado; Wirbelsturm IV U2, 31
to **toss** werfen III
total Gesamt-; gesamt IV U3, 71
totally total; völlig IV U2, 32
*to keep in **touch** in Verbindung bleiben III
to **touch** anfassen; berühren II
tour Rundgang; Tour I; Führung III
tourist Tourist / Touristin I
towards auf … zu; in Richtung III; gegenüber IV U4, 90
towel Handtuch III
tower Turm II
town Stadt I
town hall Rathaus IV U4, 84
toy Spielzeug I
track Strecke; Gleis IV U1, 10
track and field Leichtathletik IV ZI, 6
trade Handel; Gewerbe IV U5, 117
tradition Tradition III
traditional traditionell II

traffic Verkehr II
traffic light Ampel II
train Zug I
to **train** trainieren; ausbilden III
trainer Turnschuh; Trainer / Trainerin II
training Training; Ausbildung III
training session Trainingsstunde; Trainingseinheit III
tram Straßenbahn I
transfer Übertragung; Transfer IV U5, 107
transport Verkehrsmittel; Transport; Beförderung IV U4, 85
to **transport** transportieren; befördern IV U3, 56
transportation *(AE)* Verkehrsmittel; Transport; Beförderung IV U3, 56
travel Reisen IV U5, 106
to **travel** reisen; fahren III
travel agency Reisebüro IV U2, 40
travelling Reise-; Reisen II
treasure Schatz IV U3, 68
treasurer Kassenwart / Kassenwartin; Schatzmeister / Schatzmeisterin III
to **treat** behandeln III; verarbeiten; bearbeiten IV U3, 57
treatment Behandlung III
tree Baum I
tribe Stamm; Volksstamm IV U1, 9
trick Trick; Kunststück; Streich I
trip Fahrt; Trip; Ausflug; Reise I
to **trip** stolpern II
trolley Gepäckwagen; Einkaufswagen III
trouble Schwierigkeiten; Problem; Ärger III
the **Troubles** *Unruhen in Nordirland im 20. Jahrhundert* III
trousers Hose, Hosen II
true wahr I; echt; richtig II
to come **true** wahr werden; in Erfüllung gehen IV U5, 115
truth Wahrheit III
to **try** probieren; versuchen II
to **try** out ausprobieren III
T-shirt T-Shirt I
tub Becher I
the **Tube** U-Bahn *(in London)* II
tube Tube; Schlauch; Rohr I
Tuesday Dienstag I
tug of war Tauziehen III
tumble dryer Wäschetrockner II
tunnel Tunnel I
turkey Truthahn; Pute IV U2, 38
Turkey Türkei II
Turkish Türkisch; türkisch; aus der Türkei III
*to take **turns** sich abwechseln II
Your **turn**. Du bist dran. I
to **turn** abbiegen I; sich drehen; drehen; wenden; herumdrehen II
to **turn** into umwandeln in; verwandeln in I
to **turn** off ausschalten; abschalten II
to **turn** on einschalten II
to **turn** to blättern zu III
to **turn** to sb sich jmdm. zuwenden IV U2, 46
tutor Klassenlehrer / Klassenlehrerin I
tutor time Klassenstunde I

tutoring Nachhilfe IV U2, 33
TV Fernseher; Fernsehen I
to watch **TV** fernsehen I
tweezers Pinzette III
twelfth zwölfte I
twelve zwölf I
twentieth zwanzigste I
twenty zwanzig I
twenty-one einundzwanzig I
twenty-two zweiundzwanzig I
twice zweimal; doppelt III
twin Zwilling I
to **twist** verdrehen; verzerren III
two zwei I
type Sorte; Art; Typ III
typical typisch III

U

the **UK** (United Kingdom) das Vereinigte Königreich II
umbrella Regenschirm III
uncle Onkel I
under unter I
underground U-Bahn II
underground unterirdisch I
underground train U-Bahn I
to **underline** unterstreichen; hervorheben; betonen IV U5, 104
underlined unterstrichen I
*to **understand** verstehen II
understanding Verständnis IV U2, 39
understood simple past von *to understand* II; past participle von *to understand* III
underwear Unterwäsche IV U1, 23
unfair unfair III
unfortunately leider; unglücklicherweise IV U4, 84
unhappy unglücklich; traurig I
unhelpful nicht förderlich; nicht nützlich IV U4, 79
uniform Uniform I
unique einzigartig IV U5, 99
unit die Unit; die Lektion; das Kapitel III
united vereinigt III
university Universität IV U3, 65
to **unload** ausräumen; entladen; abladen; ausladen II
unpleasant unangenehm; unerfreulich IV U1, 17
untidy unordentlich; ungepflegt III
until bis I
unusual ungewöhnlich IV U1, 17
up hinauf; nach oben; oben III
up and down entlang IV U1, 9
up to bis zu I
upset aufgebracht; aufgeregt; traurig; bestürzt I
upstairs nach oben; im Obergeschoss; oben II
US US-amerikanisch IV ZI, 6
us uns; wir I
the **USA** (United States of America) die USA (Vereinigte Staaten von Amerika) II
use Gebrauch; Nutzen; Verwendung IV U3, 56
to **use** benutzen II
to be **used** for verwendet werden für III
to get **used** to (sth) sich an (etw.) gewöhnen III
useful nützlich; hilfreich II
useless nutzlos; sinnlos; unbrauchbar; zwecklos II
usually normalerweise; gewöhnlich I

V

vacation *(AE)* Urlaub; Ferien II
vacuum cleaner Staubsauger II
valley Tal III
van Lieferwagen; Transporter IV U3, 57
varied abwechslungsreich; vielseitig IV U1, 17
variety Vielfalt; Auswahl IV U3, 68
vegan Veganer / Veganerin IV U2, 49
vegetable Gemüse I
vegetarian Vegetarier / Vegetarierin IV U2, 49
vegetarian vegetarisch II
vehicle Fahrzeug I
verb Verb I
very sehr; wirklich I
vet Tierarzt / Tierärztin II
vice Vize- IV U2, 34
video Video I
view Aussicht; Sicht; Ausblick; Blick I
point of **view** Standpunkt; Perspektive III
viewing Hör- / Sehverstehen I
viewing Aussichts- IV U1, 10
Viking Wikinger / Wikingerin; Wikinger- III
village Dorf I
vinegar Essig I
violence Gewalt III
violent gewaltsam; gewalttätig; brutal III
virtual reality (VR) virtuelle Realität (VR) IV U5, 107
visit Besuch III
to **visit** besuchen I
visitor Besucher / Besucherin II
visual Bildmaterial IV U3, 71
voice Stimme III
voice message Sprachnachricht I
volcano Vulkan IV U3, 54
volleyball Volleyball IV U2, 32
volunteer Freiwilliger / Freiwillige; ehrenamtlicher Helfer / ehrenamtliche Helferin II
to **volunteer** sich ehrenamtlich engagieren; sich freiwillig melden IV U3, 65
volunteering Freiwilligenarbeit; ehrenamtliche Tätigkeit III
vote Stimme; Wahl; Stimmrecht; Abstimmung; Wahlrecht III
to **vote** wählen; abstimmen IV U5, 112

W

to **wait** warten II
wait and see wart's nur ab IV U5, 108
waiter Kellner II
*to **wake** up aufwachen II
Wales Wales II
walk Spaziergang I; Wanderung II
to go for a **walk** spazieren gehen II
to take the dog for a **walk** den Hund spazieren führen I
to **walk** laufen; gehen I
wall Wand; Mauer I
wallpaper Wandzeitung; Tapete III
to **want** (to) wollen; mögen I
war Krieg III
wardrobe Kleiderschrank IV U4, 90
warm warm I
was simple past von *to be* I
to **wash** spülen; schwemmen I; waschen II
washing machine Waschmaschine II
waste Abfall; Verschwendung II
to **waste** verschwenden II
watch Armbanduhr III
to **watch** ansehen; anschauen; beobachten I
to **watch** TV fernsehen I
watching Beobachten IV U1, 9
water Wasser I
waterfall Wasserfall IV U1, 15
wave Welle I
to **wave** winken II
way Weg; Richtung I; Art und Weise II
all the **way** to bis ganz hinunter zu III
we wir I
We're good. Uns geht es gut. II
weapon Waffe III
*to **wear** tragen; anhaben II
weather Wetter I
web-based webbasiert; internetbasiert III
website Website II
Wednesday Mittwoch I
week Woche I
weekend Wochenende I
to **weigh** wiegen III
weight Gewicht II
weird merkwürdig; seltsam; sonderbar III
to **welcome** begrüßen; willkommen heißen I
welcome (to) willkommen (bei / in) I
You're **welcome**. Gern geschehen. I
well gut I; na ja IV U2, 44
… as **well** as … sowohl … als auch … IV U2, 37
as **well** auch III
oh **well** was soll's IV U1, 10
to go **well** gut laufen III
I don't feel **well**. Mir geht es nicht gut. II
Well done! Gut gemacht! II
wellbeing Wohlbefinden IV U2, 34
well-prepared gut vorbereitet IV U3, 71
Welsh Walisisch; walisisch; aus Wales; Waliser / Waliserin III
went simple past von *to go* I
were simple past von *to be* I
west Westen; westlich; West- II
western Western *(Filmart)* IV U4, 79
wet nass I
wetland Sumpfgebiet; Feuchtgebiet IV U5, 99
whale Wal II
whale watching Walbeobachten; Whalewatching IV U1, 9
what wie; welche; was I

What about ...? Was ist mit ...? I
What about you? Und du? I
What are your names? Wie heißt ihr? I
what else was sonst; was noch II
What time is it? Wie spät ist es?; Wie viel Uhr ist es? I
what to ... was man ... III
what's on was ist los III
What's the matter? Was ist los?; Was hast du? II
What's wrong? Was ist los?; Was stimmt nicht? I
What's your name? Wie heißt du? I
wheat Weizen IV U2, 30
wheel Rad II
wheelchair Rollstuhl III
when wenn; als II
when wann I
whenever jedes Mal, wenn; wann immer; immer, wenn; jederzeit IV U5, 100
where wo; wohin; woher I
Where are you from? Woher kommst du? I
which welche; der / die / das; dem; den II
while während III
to **whisper** flüstern III
white weiß I; weiß (*soziale Kategorie*) IV U5, 112
who wer I; wen; wem III
who der / die / das; dem; den II
whole ganz I
the **whole** of ganz; der / die / das ganze ... III
whom wen; wem III
whose wessen; dessen; deren III
why warum I
wide breit II; weit IV U4, 79
wife Ehefrau IV U1, 23
wiki Wiki IV U2, 36
wild wild III
wilderness Wildnis IV U3, 68
wildfire Lauffeuer; Flächenbrand IV U3, 55
wildlife Tierwelt *(in freier Wildbahn)*; Wildtiere III
will werden II
*to **win** gewinnen; siegen I
wind Wind III
window Fenster I
windy windig I
to **wink** zwinkern II
winner Sieger / Siegerin; Gewinner / Gewinnerin I
winter Winter I
to **wish** wünschen III
with mit I
within innerhalb III
without ohne II
woke up simple past von *to wake up* II
woken up past participle von *to wake up* IV U4, 90
wolf Wolf III
woman Frau I
women Frauen I
won simple past, past participle von *to win* IV U2, 31
won't (= will not) nicht werden II
wonderful wunderbar II
to **wonder** sich fragen; sich Gedanken machen III
wood Wald; Holz II
word Wort II
wordplay Wortspiel III
wore simple past von *to wear* II
work Arbeit I
to **work** arbeiten I; funktionieren IV U3, 57
to **work** out herausfinden; ausarbeiten; herausbringen III
work experience Praktikum; Berufserfahrung III
worker Arbeiter / Arbeiterin III
working Arbeits- IV U4, 89
working hours Arbeitszeiten; Arbeitszeit IV U4, 89
workshop Workshop III
world Welt; Erde I
in the **world** der Welt; weltweit III
worried beunruhigt; besorgt II
to **worry** sich Sorgen machen III
Don't **worry**. Mach dir keine Sorgen. III
would würde(n) II
would like würde(n) gern; hätte(n) gern I
I'd love to ... (= I **would** love to) Ich würde sehr gern ... II
to **wrap** einwickeln; einpacken II
wrestling Ringen IV U2, 34
*to **write** schreiben I
writer Schriftsteller / Schriftstellerin IV U3, 68
writing Schreiben; Schreib- IV U2, 32
written past participle von *to write* III
wrong falsch I
to be **wrong** nicht stimmen; unrecht haben; sich irren III
What's **wrong**? Was ist los?; Was stimmt nicht? I
wrote simple past von *to write* III

Y

year Klasse; Jahrgangsstufe; Jahr I
a **year** pro Jahr III
yearbook Jahrbuch IV U2, 32
yellow gelb I
yes ja I
yesterday gestern I
yet schon; noch II
not ... **yet** noch nicht II
yoga Yoga IV U2, 34
yoghurt Joghurt I
you du; Sie; ihr; euch; dich; dir; Ihnen I
you see ... weißt du ...; wissen Sie ... III
You're welcome. Gern geschehen. I
young jung II
your dein / deine; euer / eure; Ihr / Ihre I
Yours, Dein / Deine (*als Briefabschluss*); Euer / Eure (*als Briefabschluss*); Ihr / Ihre (*als Briefabschluss*) III
yours deine / deiner / deins; Ihre / Ihrer / Ihres; eure / eurer / eures II
yourself dich selbst; selber IV U1, 21
yourselves ihr (selbst) / euch (selbst) / Sie (selbst); selbst III
youth Jugend III
youth club Jugendtreff I
youth hostel Jugendherberge III

Z

zero null I
zero gravity Schwerelosigkeit IV U5, 107
zip line Seilrutsche III
zone Zone IV U2, 30
time **zone** Zeitzone IV U2, 30
zoo Zoo; Tierpark I
zoom Zoom IV U1, 20
zoom in Heranzoomen I

A

ab

ab in off to IV U2, 30
Abbau mining IV U3, 67
abbauen to mine IV U3, 57
abbiegen to turn I
abbrechen to tear down III
Abend evening; night I
heute **Abend** tonight III
zu **Abend** essen to have dinner I
Abendessen dinner I
frühes **Abendessen** tea II
abends in the evening(s) I
Abenteuer adventure I
aber but I
abfahren to leave I
Abfall rubbish I; waste II; garbage *(AE)* IV U3, 68
Abgang exit II
abgeben to hand over III
von der Schule **abgehen** to leave school II
abheben to take off III
abholen to pick up II
abladen to unload II
Ablauf routine I
ablehnen to refuse IV U5, 112
ablehnend negative III
ablehnend gegenüber negative about III
Abonnement subscription III
abreißen to tear down III
absagen to cancel III
abschaffen to abolish IV U5, 112
abschalten to turn off II
Abschuss launch IV U5, 98
absolvieren to finish IV U4, 78
Abstand gap II
absteigen to get off II
abstellen to stop I
abstimmen to vote IV U5, 112
abstürzen *(Flugzeug)* to crash IV U1, 15
abwandern to migrate IV U4, 77
abwerfen to throw off III
mit den **Achseln** zucken to shrug II
außer **Acht** lassen to ignore IV U5, 100
acht eight I
achte eighth I
Achterbahn roller coaster I
achtzehn eighteen I
achtzehnte eighteenth I
achtzig eighty I
achtzigste eightieth I
Ackerbau farming III; agriculture IV U2, 30
Ackerboden farmland IV U5, 98
Ackerland farmland IV U5, 98
Acre (*Flächenmaß: 4.050 m²*) acre IV U2, 37
addieren to add III
Adjektiv adjective I
Adresse address III
Afrika Africa IV U4, 83
Afrikaner / Afrikanerin African III
afrikanisch African III
Ahnung idea I
Ahornsirup maple syrup I
akademischer Grad degree IV U4, 89
Akku battery II
Aktion campaign IV U5, 113
Aktiv active voice IV U3, 58
aktiv active IV U3, 58
Aktivist / Aktivistin activist IV U5, 112
Aktivität activity I
Akzent accent III
akzeptieren to accept III
Alarm alarm IV U4, 90
albern silly I
Algenpaste laverbread III
Alkohol alcohol III
all all I
alle all I; all of III; every IV U3, 56
alle (zusammen) everybody II
allein alone II; on one's own IV U1, 18
alleinerziehend single IV U3, 62
alleinstehend single IV U3, 62
allergisch gegen allergic to I
alles all I; everything II; anything IV U1, 10
Alligator alligator IV U3, 68
Alltags- daily I
als than I; when II; as III
also so I
alt old I; ancient IV U3, 68
Alter age II
altertümlich ancient IV U3, 68
altmodisch old-fashioned III
am wenigsten least III
American Football football *(AE)* II, American football IV U2, 31
Amerika America II
Amerikaner / Amerikanerin American II
Amerikanisch American II
amerikanisch American II
amerikanischer Ureinwohner / **amerikanische** Ureinwohnerin Native American IV U1, 9
zu der **amerikanischen** Urbevölkerung gehörig Native American IV U1, 9
amisch Amish IV U1, 18
Amischen the Amish IV U1, 18
Ampel traffic light II
Amtssprache official language III
amüsant fun III
an at; on I; by III
an Bord on board IV U1, 22
anbauen to grow II; to produce IV U2, 37
anbieten to offer IV U1, 16
andauern to last IV U5, 112
Andenken souvenir II
andere else I; other; others II
ein **anderer** / eine **andere** another I
die **anderen** the others II
(sich) **ändern** to change II
seine Meinung **ändern** to change one's mind III
anders different I
Änderung change II
Anfang beginning IV U2, 32; start IV U4, 87
anfangen to start; to begin I
anfassen to touch II
anführen to lead III
Anführer / Anführerin leader III
Angehöriger / Angehörige der Pueblovölker Pueblo IV U4, 77
Angehöriger / Angehörige einer indigenen Bevölkerung native IV U1, 9
Angelegenheit case IV U5, 112
Angeln fishing III
Angelsachse / Angelsächsin Anglo-Saxon III
angelsächsisch Anglo-Saxon III
angenehm comfortable II
von **Angesicht** zu Angesicht face-to-face IV U5, 107
Angriff attack IV U1, 15
Angst alarm IV U4, 90
Angst bekommen to get scared III
Angst haben to be afraid I; to be scared III
schreckliche **Angst** haben to be terrified IV U1, 22
ängstlich afraid II
anhaben to wear II
anhalten to stop I; to last IV U5, 112
anheben to raise IV U5, 100
anheuern to hire II
anhören to listen (to) I
sich **anhören** to sound III
ankommen to arrive I
Ankündigung announcement III
Anlage grounds IV U1, 16; site IV U5, 98
anlegen to put on III
anmalen to paint II
Anmelde- registration III
anmelden to log in III
sich **anmelden** bei to enter III
Anmeldung registration III
annähernd nearly I
annehmen to accept III
Annonce ad (= advertisement) II
anregen to inspire IV U4, 78
Anruf call II
anrufen to call I
anschauen to look at; to watch I; to check II
Anschlag attack IV U1, 15
anschließen to install IV U3, 61
sich **anschließen** to join I
Anschrift address III
ansehen to watch I
anstatt instead of IV U5, 106
anstehen to stand in line IV U1, 22
ansteigen to increase IV U2, 37
anstelle von instead of IV U5, 106
anstellen to employ IV U3, 68
anstößig juicy II
anstrengen to strain III
antreten (bei) to compete (in) III
Antwort answer I; response IV U5, 112
antworten to answer II
anweisen to direct II
Anweisungen directions III
Anwendung app III
Anzahl number I
Anzeige ad (= advertisement) II; display IV U2, 39
anziehen to put on III
sich **anziehen** to get dressed I
anzünden to light IV U2, 39
Apartment apartment IV U1, 16
Apfel apple I
gedeckter **Apfelkuchen** apple pie II
App app III
April April I
Aquarium aquarium II

Arabisch Arabic III
arabisch Arabic III
Arbeit chore; work I; job II
arbeiten to work I
Arbeiter / Arbeiterin worker III
Arbeits- working IV U4, 89
arbeitslos jobless IV U3, 62
arbeitsreich busy I
Arbeitsstelle job II
Arbeitszeit working hours IV U4, 89
Arbeitszeiten working hours IV U4, 89
Areal area II
Ärger trouble III
Arm arm II
Armbanduhr watch III
Ärmel sleeve IV U5, 105
armselig miserable IV U1, 17
arrangieren to arrange III
Art kind III
  Art und Weise way II
Artikel article III
Arzt / Ärztin doctor II
ärztlich medical IV U3, 62
Asiate / Asiatin Asian IV U3, 55
asiatisch Asian IV U3, 55
Asien Asia III
Assistent / Assistentin assistant I
Astronaut / Astronautin astronaut I
Athlet / Athletin athlete III
atmen to breathe II
Atmosphäre atmosphere IV U2, 43
Attacke attack IV U1, 15
Attraktion attraction IV U1, 10
attraktiv attractive II
auch too; also I; as well III
  auch nicht not … either I
auf in; at; on I
  auf dem Land in the country II
  auf der linken Seite on the left II
  auf der rechten Seite on the right I
  auf einmal suddenly II; all of a sudden III
  auf jeden Fall definitely III
  auf zu / nach off to IV U2, 30
  Auf Wiedersehen. Goodbye. I
  auf … hinauf onto I
  auf … zu towards III
aufbereiten to process IV U3, 57
aufbewahren to keep II
Geld **aufbringen** to raise money IV U1, 9
aufdecken to detect IV U3, 61
auffordern to invite IV U4, 90
Aufforderung call III
  letzte **Aufforderung** final call III
aufführen to perform III
Aufführung show II
Aufgabe chore I; job II
aufgeben to give up IV U4, 78
aufgebracht upset I
aufgeregt upset; nervous; excited I
aufhalten to stop IV U4, 78
aufhängen to hang up III; to put up IV U2, 39
aufheben to pick up II
aufhören to stop I; to finish II; to end IV U4, 83
  Hör(t) auf! Stop it! I
aufklären to educate IV U5, 100
Aufkleber sticker II
aufkrempeln to roll up IV U4, 86
aufladen to charge IV U3, 56
auflegen to hang up III
aufmachen to open I
Aufmerksamkeit attention IV U5, 112
Aufnahme recording I; shot IV U2, 43
aufnehmen to include II
aufpassen to mind I
aufpassen auf to look after II
aufräumen to tidy (up); to clean up II
aufrecht sitzen to sit up IV U4, 90
aufregend exciting II
Aufregung excitement III
aufreißen *(Straße)* to dig up III
sich **aufrichten** to sit up IV U4, 90
aufrollen to roll up IV U4, 86
Aufruf call III
  letzter **Aufruf** final call III
Aufruhr riot IV U5, 114
aufstehen to get up I; to stand up II
aufstellen to put up IV U2, 39
aufteilen to divide III
Auftrag mission IV U5, 98
auftragen to apply III
auftreten to perform III
Auftritt appearance IV U4, 90
aufwachen to wake up II
aufwärmen to heat II
Aufzeichnung recording I
Aufzug lift II; elevator *(AE)* IV U1, 10
Auge eye I
Augenblick moment II
August August I
aus from I
  aus dem Weg gehen to avoid IV U3, 68
  aus … heraus out of … II
ausbilden to train III
Ausbildung training III; apprenticeship IV U4, 89
Ausblick view I
Auseinandersetzung conflict; argument III
Ausfahrt exit II
Ausflug trip I
ausfüllen to fill in III
Ausgang exit II; gate III
ausgeben *(Geld)* to spend I
ausgefallen fancy IV U2, 44
ausgehen to go out I
Auskunft information desk III
auslachen to laugh at II
ausladen to unload II
ausländisch foreign IV U1, 16
ausleihen to borrow I
ausmachen to extinguish; to arrange III
  etw. **ausmachen** to matter IV U1, 21
ausprobieren to try out III
ausrasten to go mad III
ausräumen to unload II
ausrichten to host III
sich **ausruhen** to relax III
Ausrüstung kit; equipment III
ausschalten to turn off II; to switch off III
ausschlafen to sleep late II
Ausschreitung riot IV U5, 114
Aussehen look; appearance IV U4, 90
aussehen to look I
Außen- outdoor IV U1, 10
außer except IV U1, 22
  außer Acht lassen to ignore IV U5, 100
außerdem moreover IV U5, 106
außerhalb outside III
äußerst extremely IV U1, 22
Aussicht view I
Aussichts- viewing IV U1, 10
Ausstattung kit; equipment III
aussteigen to get off II
Ausstellung exhibition II; display IV U2, 39
Ausstoß emission IV U4, 85
die Hand **ausstrecken** to reach out IV U4, 90
Austausch exchange IV U2, 32
austauschen to exchange II
Australien Australia III
Ausverkauf sale I
Auswahl choice IV U5, 101; variety IV U3, 68
auswählen to choose I
ausweichen to avoid IV U3, 68
Auszeichnung award IV U4, 78
ausziehen to take off III
Auto car I
Autor / Autorin author III

B

Babysitten babysitting III
Bach creek *(AE)* IV U3, 67
backen to bake I
Bäckerei baker's I
Backofen oven IV U2, 38
Bad bathroom I
Badebekleidung swimwear III
Badesachen swimwear III
Badezimmer bathroom I
Badminton badminton I
Bahnhof station I
Bahnsteig platform I
bald soon II
  Bis (sehr) **bald**. See you (very) soon! III
Balkon balcony IV U1, 11
Ball ball II
Banane banana I
Band band II
Bank bench II; bank IV U4, 84
Bär bear IV U3, 68
Barsch snook IV U5, 105
Baseball baseball IV ZI, 6
Basis site IV U5, 98
Basketball basketball III
basteln to do handicrafts I
Batterie battery II
Bau- building III
Bauch stomach II
bauchfreies Oberteil crop top IV U2, 32
Bauchschmerzen stomach ache II
Bauchweh stomach ache II
bauen to build I
Bauer / Bäuerin farmer IV U2, 31
Bauernhof farm I
Baum tree I
Baumstamm caber III
Baumstammwerfen caber toss III
Beamter / Beamtin official IV U1, 22
beängstigend scary II

beantworten to answer II
bearbeiten to treat IV U3, 57
Bearbeitung editing III
Bearbeitungstool editing tool III
Bearbeitungswerkzeug editing tool III
Becher tub I
Becken pool III
bedeuten to mean III
bedeutend powerful IV U2, 44
von **Bedeutung** sein to matter IV U1, 21
bedienen to serve III
Bedingung condition IV U4, 78
sich **beeilen** to hurry II
beeindruckend impressive IV U1, 17; powerful IV U2, 44
beeindruckt impressed III
beeinflussen to influence III
beenden to finish II; to end IV U4, 83
beerdigen to bury III
Beerdigung funeral IV U5, 111
Beere berry II
befehlen to order IV U5, 113
befestigen to fix II
befolgen to follow II
befördern to carry I; to transport IV U3, 56
Beförderung transportation *(AE)* IV U3, 56; transport IV U4, 85
Befragung interview I
befreien to free I
befüllen to stack III
begabt talented IV U4, 78
begeistert excited I
Beginn start IV U4, 87
beginnen to start; to begin I
begraben to bury III
Begräbnis funeral IV U5, 111
begrüßen to welcome I
behalten to keep II
behandeln to treat III
Behandlung therapy IV U3, 63
sich gegen jmdn. **behaupten** to stand up to sb IV U4, 78
Behelfs- emergency IV U1, 15
Behinderung disability III
bei at I
bei Bewusstsein awake III
beibringen to teach III
beide both IV U2, 45
Bein leg II
beinahe nearly I; almost II
beinhalten to include II
Beispiel example I
zum **Beispiel** for example I
Beitrag fee III; post IV U1, 16
beitreten to join II
sich **beklagen** to complain III
bekommen to get I; to receive; to take II
Angst **bekommen** to get scared III
beladen to load II
belasten to strain III
belebt busy I
Belegschaft staff I
beleidigen to insult IV U5, 100
beleuchten to light IV U2, 39
Beleuchtung lighting II
beliebt popular I
bellen to bark III
bemerken to realise III
benachteiligen to discriminate against IV U5, 101
sich **benehmen** to behave IV U5, 101
benötigen to take IV U3, 56
benutzen to use II
Beobachten watching IV U1, 9
beobachten to watch I
bequem comfortable II
jmdn. **beraten** to advise sb IV U3, 63
Beratung counseling *(AE)* IV U3, 62
Beratungsstelle outreach center *(AE)* IV U3, 62
berechnen to charge IV U3, 56
bereit sein to be prepared III
bereits already II
bereitstellen to provide IV U4, 77
Berg mountain I; hill II
Bergbau mining IV U3, 67
Bergsteigen mountaineering III
Bericht article; report III
Beruf job II
Berufspraktikum internship III
sich **beruhigen** to calm down III
berühmt famous I
berühren to touch II
Besatzung crew II
beschädigen to damage III
beschäftigen to employ IV U3, 68
beschäftigt busy I
jmdm. **Bescheid** geben to let sb know III
jmdm. **Bescheid** sagen to let sb know III
bescheiden modest IV U4, 78
Bescheidenheit modesty IV U4, 79
jmdn. **beschimpfen** to call sb names IV U5, 100
ein Gesetz **beschließen** to pass a law IV U3, 68
beschreiben to describe III
beschützen to protect II
sich **beschweren** to complain III
beseitigen to clean up II
Besichtigung sightseeing III
Besichtigungstour sightseeing II
eine **Besichtigungstour** machen to go sightseeing II
besiedeln to settle (in) IV U2, 31
besiegen to defeat III
besitzen to have got II; to own III
Besitzer / Besitzerin owner II
besonders special I
besorgt worried II
Besprechung meeting III
bespritzen to splash I
besser better II
das **Beste** best of all IV U1, 10
am **besten** best of all IV U1, 10
beste / bester / bestes best I; top II
bester Freund / **beste** Freundin für immer BFF IV U4, 86
am **besten** best II
bestehen to exist IV U5, 112
besteigen to climb II
Bestell- order II
bestellen to order II
Bestellung order II
bestürzt upset I
Besuch visit III
besuchen to visit I; to attend IV U5, 113
Besucher / Besucherin visitor II
Betreff subject III
betreten to enter II
psychologische **Betreuung** counseling *(AE)* IV U3, 62
Bett bed I
Bettdecke blanket III
Bettzeug covers IV U4, 90
beunruhigt worried II
Bevölkerung population III
bevor before I
bewältigen to cope with IV U3, 62
bewegen to move I
sich **bewegen** to move; to get around III
Bewegung movement IV U5, 99
beweisen to prove IV U5, 100
sich **bewerben** (für / um) to apply (for) IV U4, 78
bewohnt inhabited III
sich **bewusst** werden to realize *(AE)* IV U4, 90
Bewusstsein awareness IV U5, 100
bei **Bewusstsein** awake III
das **Bewusstsein** schärfen to raise awareness IV U5, 100
bezahlen to pay I
BFF / BFF BFF IV U4, 86
Bibliothek library I
Bibliothekar / Bibliothekarin librarian IV U2, 45
Biene bee II
bieten to offer IV U1, 16; to provide IV U4, 77
jmdm. die Stirn **bieten** to stand up to sb IV U4, 78
Bild picture I; image IV U5, 113
bilden to make I; to get into IV U3, 62; to form IV U4, 77; to educate IV U5, 100
Bildschirm screen II
Bildschirmschoner screensaver IV U3, 61
billig cheap II
Bio- organic I
Biologie biology I
bionisch bionic II
Birke birch II
Birne pear IV U3, 55
bis to; until I
bis ganz hinunter zu all the way to III
bis jetzt so far III
bis zu up to I
Bis (sehr) bald. See you (very) soon! III
Bis bald. See you later. I
bisher so far III
bislang so far III
Bison bison IV U2, 31
ein **bisschen** a bit; a little II
bitte please I
Bitte schön. Here you are. I
bitten um to ask for IV U5, 100
jmdn. **bitten**, etw. zu tun to ask sb to do sth IV U4, 84
jmdn. um eine Verabredung **bitten** to ask sb on a date IV U4, 90
Bitterfisch (*kleiner, schlanker Beutefisch*) minnow IV U5, 105
Blatt page III
ein **Blatt** a piece of II

blau blue I
Blauwal blue whale II
bleiben to stay I
in Verbindung **bleiben** to keep in touch III
Bleistift pencil II
Blick view I
blöd silly I; stupid III
Blog blog II
bloggen to blog III
blond blonde III
Blume flower II
Bluse blouse IV U1, 23
Blut blood III
Boden earth I; ground II
Bodenschatz natural resource IV U5, 106
Bogengang archway III
Bohne bean IV U4, 77
Boot boat I
an **Bord** on board IV U1, 22
Böschung bank IV U4, 84
böse angry I
Botschaft message II
Bowle punch IV U2, 38
Box box I
Boykott boycott IV U5, 112
Branche business IV U4, 84
Bratwurst sausage II
brauchen to need I; to take IV U3, 56
nicht **brauchen** needn't III
braun brown I
brechen to break III
breit wide II
brennen to burn III
Brettspiel board game III
Brief letter II
Briefkasten post box II
brillant brilliant II
Brille glasses III
bringen to bring II
sich in Gefahr **bringen** to put oneself in danger IV U5, 101
die **Briten** the British III
britisch British I
die **Britischen Inseln** the British Isles III
Broschüre leaflet II
Brot bread I
belegtes **Brot** sandwich I
Brücke bridge II
Bruder brother I
Brunnen fountain II
Brust chest II
Brustkorb chest II
brutal violent III
Buch book I
gedruckte **Bücher** print books III
buchen to book II
Bücherei library I
Buchstabe letter II
buchstabieren to spell I
Bundesstaat state IV ZI, 7
bunt colourful II
Buntstift pencil II
Burg castle I
Bürgermeister mayor IV U4, 84
Bürgermeisterin mayoress IV U4, 84
Bürgerrechte civil rights IV U5, 99
Bürgersteig pavement II; sidewalk *(AE)* IV U4, 84
Büro office I
Bürste brush III
bürsten to brush II
Bus bus I
Bushaltestelle bus stop II
Butter butter I
Butterbrot sandwich I

C

Café snack bar I; café II
Cafeteria cafeteria I
Camp camp I
Camping camping III
Campingplatz campsite III
Canyon canyon IV U3, 54
Center centre I; center *(AE)* IV U1, 9
Chance opportunity; chance IV U1, 21
Charakter character III
Chat chat III
chatten to chat II
checken to check III
Cheerleader / Cheerleaderin *(jmd., der in einer Gruppe eine Sportmannschaft anfeuert)* cheerleader II
Cheerleading cheerleading IV U2, 33
Chefkoch / Chefköchin head chef IV U1, 22
Chemikalie chemical IV U3, 56
China China II
Chinese / Chinesin Chinese II
Chinesisch Chinese II
chinesisch Chinese II
Chor choir III
nach **Christus** AD (= Anno Domini) III
vor **Christus** BC (= before Christ) III
circa about I
Clog clog III
Cola cola I
College college III
Comic comic II
Comicheft comic II
Computer computer I
Computerprogramm program *(BE)* IV U3, 61
Computerunterricht IT (= Information Technology) I
cool cool I
Cousin / Cousine cousin I
Cowboy cowboy IV U4, 77
Cree Cree IV U2, 44
Cree / Cree Cree IV U2, 44
Cree- Cree IV U2, 44
Creme cream I
Crew crew II
Curry curry II

D

da there I
da drüben over there II
da ist there's (= there is) I
da sind there are I
da because I; as II
Dach roof III
Dachboden attic I; loft IV U1, 11
daher so I
damit so; so that II
Damm dam IV U4, 77
danach then; after that I; after; afterwards III
Dänemark Denmark III
danke thanks II
Danke. Thank you. I
dann then I
Darsteller / Darstellerin performer II
das the; this; that I
der / die / **das** who; which II; that III
das Beste best of all IV U1, 10
dass that II
Date date IV U4, 90
Datenbank database III
Datum date I
dauern to take I; to last IV U5, 112
davor in front of I
Debatte debate IV U2, 33
Debattier- debate IV U2, 33
Decke blanket III
definieren to define IV U2, 46
definitiv definitely III
dehnen to stretch II
Dehnübung stretching exercise II
dein / deine your I
Dein / Deine *(als Briefabschluss)* Yours, III
deine / deiner / deins yours II
Dekoration decoration IV U2, 39
dekorieren to decorate III
Delfin dolphin I
dem who; which II; that III
Demonstrant / Demonstrantin protestor IV U5, 113
Demonstration protest III
den who; which II; that III
denken to think I
Denkmal memorial IV U1, 15
dennoch still III
der the I
der / die / das who; which II; that III
deren whose III
derselbe / dieselbe / dasselbe … the same … II
derzeit at the moment III
Desaster disaster IV U5, 106
Design design IV U1, 10
Designer / Designerin designer IV U1, 10
dessen whose III
deswegen that's why IV U1, 16
Detektiv / Detektivin detective II
deutlich clear II
Deutsch German I
deutsch German I
Deutschland Germany I
Dezember December I
Diagramm chart III
dich you I
dich selbst yourself II
die *(auch Pl.)* the I
der / **die** / das who; which II; that III
Diele hall I
dienen to serve III
Dienst service II
Dienstag Tuesday I
dies this I
dies(e) hier these II
diese dort those II

digital digital III
Ding thing I
Dinosaurier dinosaur II
dir you I
direkt straight II
diskriminieren to discriminate against IV U5, 101
Diskriminierung discrimination III
Diskussion debate IV U2, 33; discussion IV U5, 106
Disziplin discipline III
und **doch** even so IV U4, 90
Dokumente papers IV U1, 23
Dollar (*Währungseinheit*) dollar ($) II; buck *(AE)* IV U4, 86
Dom cathedral III
Döner kebab II
Donnerstag Thursday I
doof silly I
Doppeldeckerbus double-decker bus II
doppelt twice III
Dorf village I
dornig thorny II
dort there I
  dort drüben over there II
  diese **dort** those II
Dose can I
Drache dragon III
Drama drama III
drängeln to push IV U5, 100
draufmachen to put on III
(nach) **draußen** outside I
Dreck machen to make a mess II
dreckig dirty I
Drehbuch script II
drehen to make I; to turn; to film II
  sich **drehen** to turn II
Drehort location IV U5, 113
drei three I
dreißig thirty I
dreißigste thirtieth I
dreizehn thirteen I
dreizehnte thirteenth I
Droge drug III
Drohne drone IV U5, 107
Druck print III
drücken to press II; to push IV U5, 100
Drucker printer II
du you I
Dudelsack bagpipes III
dumm silly I; stupid III
dunkel dark I
Dunkelheit dark III
dünn slim IV U4, 90
durch through I
  quer **durch** across III
Durcheinander mess II
Durchsage announcement III
durchschnittlich average IV U3, 56
durchstarten to take off III
durchstellen to put through III
dürfen may IV U3, 62
  nicht **dürfen** mustn't II
  Darf es sonst noch etwas sein? Anything else? I
(etw. tun) **dürfen** to be allowed to (do sth) II
durstig thirsty IV U2, 44
Dusche shower III
  eine **Dusche** nehmen to have a shower II
duschen to have a shower II
Duschgel shower gel III

E

Ebbe low tide III
Ebene plain IV U2, 31
E-Book e-book III
echt really; real; true II; pretty III
Ecke corner I
Ehefrau wife IV U1, 23
ehemalige / ehemaliger / ehemaliges former IV U1, 10
Ehemann husband III
ehrenamtlicher Helfer / **ehrenamtliche** Helferin volunteer II
ehrenamtliche Tätigkeit volunteering III
Ehrgeiz ambition IV U4, 79
ehrgeizig ambitious IV U4, 78
ehrlich honest IV U4, 90
Ei egg I
Eichel acorn III
Eichhörnchen squirrel II
Eierkuchen pancake I
eifersüchtig jealous II
eigene / eigener / eigenes own I
Eigenschaft quality IV U4, 84
Eigenschaftswort adjective I
eigensinnig stubborn IV U5, 101
eigentlich in fact III
ein paar a few II
ein / eine one; a; an I
eine / einer / eins von one of I
zum **einen** for one thing IV U5, 106
einander one another I; each other III
einbeziehen to include II
einbinden to include II
eindeutig clear II; definitely III
einerseits for one thing IV U5, 106
einfach easy I; just; plain II
einfangen to catch III
Einfluss influence IV U4, 78
einflussreich important I; influential IV U4, 79
einfrieren to freeze II
Einführung introduction IV U5, 112
Eingang entrance II
Eingangshalle lobby IV U1, 11
Eingangstür front door IV U4, 90
eingeben to put in II
einheimisch native IV U1, 9
Einheit session III
einhundert a / one hundred I
einige some I; a few II
Einigung agreement III
Einkaufen shopping I
einkaufen gehen to go shopping I
Einkaufswagen trolley III
Einkaufszentrum shopping centre I; mall *(AE)* IV U1, 16
einladen to invite II
Einlass entry III
Einleitung introduction IV U5, 112
sich **einloggen** to log in III
einmal once II
einpacken to pack; to wrap II
einräumen to load II
  die Spülmaschine **einräumen** to load the dishwasher II
Einreise immigration IV U1, 9
einrichten to install IV U3, 61; to establish IV U3, 68
Einrichtung facility IV U3, 68
eins one I
einsam lonely III
einsammeln to collect I
Einsatz mission IV U5, 98
einschalten to turn on II
einschließen to include II
einschließlich including II
einsetzen to put in III
Einsicht intelligence IV U5, 106
einsteigen to get on II
einstellen to hire II; to employ IV U3, 68
Einstellung shot IV U2, 43
einstürzen to collapse IV U1, 15
eintausend a / one thousand II
Eintopf stew II
Eintrag entry III; post IV U1, 16
eintreten to enter II
Eintritt entrance II; entry III
Eintrittskarte ticket I
Einwanderer / Einwanderin immigrant IV U1, 9
einwandern to immigrate IV U1, 21
Einwanderung immigration IV U1, 9
einwickeln to wrap II
Einwohner *(Pl.)* population III
Einwohnerzahl population III
Einzelkind only child II
einzeln single IV U3, 62
einzigartig unique IV U5, 99
einzige / einziger / einziges only III; single IV U3, 62
Eis ice cream I; ice IV U1, 16
Eisbeutel ice pack III
Eiscreme ice cream I
Eisenbahn railway III; railroad *(AE)* IV U1, 10
Eishockey ice hockey IV U1, 16
eisig icy I
Elektriker / Elektrikerin electrician IV U4, 89
elend miserable IV U1, 17
elf eleven I
elfte eleventh I
Elritze minnow IV U5, 105
Eltern parents I
E-Mail email II
  E-Mails schreiben to email III
Emission emission IV U4, 85
emissionsarm low-emission IV U4, 85
Empfang signal II
empfangen to receive II
Empfangshalle lobby IV U1, 11
empfehlen to recommend IV U4, 77
Ende end III
  etw. zu **Ende** trinken / essen to finish III
  oberes **Ende** top IV U1, 10
enden to finish II; to end IV U4, 83
endgültig final III
endlich finally II; eventually III
endlos endless IV U2, 30

Energie energy II; power IV U4, 77
eng close IV U5, 109; narrow III
England England I
die **Engländer** the English III
Englisch English I
englisch English I
enorm enormous III
entdecken to spy I; to detect IV U3, 61; to spot IV U3, 68
entfernen to remove II
entfernt away I
entführen to hijack IV U1, 15
entgegentreten to face IV U5, 113
Entkommen escape IV U1, 11
entladen to unload II
entlang along; down I; up and down IV U1, 9
entlassen to release IV U5, 105
entnehmen to extract IV U3, 57
(sich) **entscheiden** to decide IV U5, 113
entschieden determined IV U4, 78
Entschiedenheit determination IV U4, 79
(fest) **entschlossen** determined IV U4, 78
Entschlossenheit determination IV U4, 79
Entschluss resolution IV U2, 39
Entschuldigung. Pardon.; Sorry.; Excuse me!; I'm sorry. I
entsorgen to dispose (of) IV U3, 57
Entsorgung disposal IV U3, 56
sich **entspannen** to relax III
entspannend relaxing I
Entstehung formation IV U2, 31
entweder … oder … either … or … IV U3, 56
entwerfen to design IV U1, 10
entwickeln to design IV U1, 10
(sich) **entwickeln** to develop III
Entwickler / Entwicklerin designer IV U1, 10
Entwicklung development IV U3, 68
Entwurf design IV U1, 10
Enzyklopädie encyclopedia III
er he I
er / sie / es it I
Erbse pea II
Erdboden earth I; ground II
Erde earth; world I
Erdgeschoss ground floor II; ground level IV U1, 11
Erdkunde geography I
Erdteil continent III
Ereignis event III
erfahren to learn I
etwas **erfahren** über etw. to learn about sth IV U2, 31
Erfahrung experience III
erfinden to invent III
Erfinder / Erfinderin inventor III
Erfolg success IV U1, 21
Erfolg haben (mit / bei) to succeed (in) IV U1, 22
erfolgreich successful III
erforschen to explore IV U5, 107
erfreut pleased I
ergänzen to add III
erhalten to receive; to take II
erhältlich available III
erhältlich sein to come I
erheben to charge IV U3, 56
erhellen to light IV U2, 39
erhitzen to heat II
erhöhen to raise IV U5, 100
erholsam relaxing I
sich **erinnern** (an) to remember I
Erkältung cold II
erkennen to realise III; to spot IV U3, 68; to realize *(AE)* IV U4, 90
Erkrankung disease III; condition IV U4, 78
erkunden to explore IV U5, 107
erlauben to allow III
Erlaubnis license *(AE)* IV U5, 105
Erlebnis experience III
ermutigen to encourage IV U4, 78
ermitteln to detect IV U3, 61
jmdn. / etw. **ernst** nehmen to take sb / sth seriously IV U5, 100
ernsthaft serious IV U3, 62
Ernte crop IV U2, 31
Erntedankfest Thanksgiving IV U2, 38
eröffnen to establish IV U3, 68
erreichen to achieve IV U1, 21
errichten to put up IV U2, 39
erschaffen to create II
Erscheinung appearance IV U4, 90
erschließen to develop III
Erschließung development IV U3, 68
erschöpft exhausted IV U1, 22
erschrocken terrified IV U1, 22
erschrocken sein to be scared III
ersetzen to replace IV U3, 56
erstaunlich amazing II
erstaunt amazed II
erste / erster / erstes first I
als **Erstes** first III
erstens for one thing; firstly IV U5, 106
Ersthelfer / Ersthelferin first responder IV U3, 62
Erwiderung response IV U5, 112
erzählen to tell I; to share III
Erzähler / Erzählerin narrator II
erzeugen to produce IV U2, 37
Erzeuger / Erzeugerin producer IV U3, 55
erziehen to educate IV U5, 100
er / sie / **es** it I
es gibt there are; there's (= there is) I
Essen food I; meal II
ungesundes **Essen** junk food II
essen to have; to eat I
etw. fertig trinken / **essen** to finish III
etw. zu Ende trinken / **essen** to finish III
zu Abend **essen** to have dinner I
Esser / Esserin eater II
Essig vinegar I
Esszimmer dining room I
Etage floor II; story *(AE)* IV U1, 10
etwa about I
etwas some; any I; something II
euch you I
ihr (selbst) / **euch** (selbst) / Sie (selbst) yourselves III
euer / eure your I
Euer / Eure *(als Briefabschluss)* Yours, III
eure / eurer / eures yours II
Euro *(Währungseinheit)* euro (€) III
Europa Europe II
Europäer / Europäerin European IV U1, 9
europäisch European IV U1, 9
Europäische Union European Union III
ewig forever IV U3, 62
seit einer **Ewigkeit** in ages III
seit **Ewigkeiten** in ages III
Examen exam I
existieren to exist IV U5, 112
Experiment experiment I
extrem extreme IV U5, 106
exzellent excellent II

F

Fabrik factory III
Fachhochschule college III
Fähigkeit skill III
Fahne flag III
Fähre ferry III
fahren to go; to ride; to drive I; to travel III
Fahrrad **fahren** to go cycling I; to cycle II
Fahrer / Fahrerin driver II
Fahrkarte ticket I
Fahrkartenschalter ticket office I
Fahrplan schedule *(AE)* IV U2, 32
Fahrrad bike I; cycle III
Fahrrad fahren to go cycling I; to cycle II
Fahrradfahrer / Fahrradfahrerin biker II
Fahrschein ticket I
Fahrspur lane III
Fahrstuhl lift II
Fahrt trip; ride I
fair fair IV U1, 22
Fakt fact III
Fall case IV U5, 112
auf jeden **Fall** definitely III
fallen to fall I; to fall off III
falls if I
falsch wrong; false I
Familie family I
Fan fan I
Fang catch III
fangen to catch III
Fantasie fantasy III
fantastisch fantastic III; stunning IV U4, 76
Fantasy fantasy III
Farbe colour I; color *(AE)* IV U5, 100
farbenfroh colourful II
farbig colourful II
Fasching carnival IV U2, 41
fast nearly I; almost II
faszinierend fascinating IV U1, 17
Februar February I
Feder feather IV U2, 44
Federmäppchen pencil case II
Fee fairy III
fehlen to be missing I
Fehler mistake II
Feier party I; celebration III; ceremony IV U1, 15
feiern to celebrate II
Feiertag holiday I
Feld field II
Feldfrucht crop IV U2, 31

Fell skin III
Fels rock III
Fenster window I
Ferien holiday I; vacation *(AE)* II
Ferienhäuschen holiday cottage III
Ferienwohnung holiday flat III
ferner moreover IV U5, 106
Fernsehen TV I; television IV U2, 43
fernsehen to watch TV I
Fernseher TV I; television IV U2, 43
fertig finished IV U3, 57
  fertig werden mit to cope with IV U3, 62
  etw. **fertig** gemacht haben to finish doing sth IV U2, 38
  mit der Schule **fertig** sein to leave school II
  sich **fertig** machen to get ready IV U2, 32
fertigen to manufacture IV U3, 57
Fertigkeit skill III
Fertigung manufacturing IV U2, 30
Fest festival; celebration III
festhalten to hold II
Festival festival III
festnehmen to arrest IV U5, 112
Feuchtgebiet wetland IV U5, 99
Feuer fire III
Feuer (*im Freien*) bonfire I
Feuerwerk fireworks I
Fieber temperature I; fever II
Figur character III; figure II
Film film I; movie *(AE)* IV U2, 31
filmen to film II
Finanz- financial IV U1, 9
finanziell financial IV U1, 9
finden to find; to think I
Finger finger III
Firma company III
Fisch fish I
Fischen fishing III
Fischerei fishing III
fit fit IV U4, 78
Fitnessstudio gym I
fixieren to fix II
flach flat III
Fläche space II; area III
Flächenbrand wildfire IV U3, 55
Fladenbrot flatbread II
Flagge flag III
Flasche bottle I
Fleisch meat I
Fleischerei butcher's IV U4, 85
fleißig hard-working II
fliegen to fly IV U1, 15
fließen to flow IV U5, 98
Flipflop flip-flop III
Flohmarkt (*Verkauf aus dem Kofferraum*) car boot sale III
Flucht escape IV U1, 11
Flug flight III
Fluggast passenger III
Flughafen airport III
Flugsteig gate III
Flugzeug plane II; aircraft IV U1, 10
Flugzeugträger aircraft carrier IV U1, 10
Flur hall I; corridor III; hallway IV U2, 32
Fluss river I
flüstern to whisper III
Flut flood IV U5, 99
Föhn hairdryer III
folgen to follow II
Form shape IV U4, 84
  in **Form** fit IV U4, 78
Formation formation IV U2, 31
Formular form III
Forschung research IV U3, 68
fortfahren to continue III
fortführen to continue III
Forum forum III
Fossil fossil IV U2, 31
Foto photo I
  Fotos machen to take photos I
Fotoapparat camera III
fotografieren to take photos I
Foyer lobby IV U1, 11
Fracht freight III
Frage question I
fragen to ask I
  fragen nach to ask for IV U5, 100
  sich **fragen** to wonder III
Frankreich France II
  aus **Frankreich** French III
die **Franzosen** the French IV U5, 99
Französisch French III
französisch French III
Frau woman I
Frau *(Anrede)* Mrs I; Ms II
Frauen women I
frech cheeky I
frei free I
  im **Freien** outdoor IV U1, 10
freigeben to release IV U5, 105
Freiheit freedom IV U1, 15
freilassen to release IV U5, 105
Freilichtmuseum living history village IV U2, 31
Freiluft- outdoor I
Freitag Friday I
Freiwilligenarbeit volunteering III
Freiwilliger / Freiwillige volunteer II
Freizeit free time I
Freizeit- free-time I
Freizeitbeschäftigung pastime III
Freizeitzentrum leisure centre III
fremd foreign IV U1, 16
Frettchen ferret II
Freude fun I
Freudenfeuer bonfire I
sich **freuen** auf to look forward to (+ -ing) II
Freund / Freundin friend I
  bester **Freund** / beste **Freundin** für immer BFF IV U4, 86
Freundin girlfriend II
freundlich friendly I
Freundschaft friendship IV U1, 22
  Freundschaften schließen to make friends II
Frieden peace III
Friedhof cemetery IV U5, 111
friedlich calm II; peaceful III
frieren to be cold I; to freeze II
frisch fresh II
Frischkäse cream cheese I
Friseursalon hairdresser's IV U4, 85
froh pleased I; glad III
frösteln to shiver III
Frucht fruit I
fruchtbar fertile IV U5, 98
früh early I
früher previously III
frühere / früherer / früheres former IV U1, 10
Frühjahr spring I
Frühling spring I
Frühstück breakfast I
frühstücken to have breakfast I
Frühstückspension B&B (bed and breakfast) III
Fuchs fox III
(sich) **fühlen** to feel I
  jmdm. helfen, sich besser zu **fühlen** to make sb feel better IV U1, 22
führen to lead III
führend leading IV U3, 55
Führer / Führerin guide II
führerlos driverless IV U5, 107
Führung tour III
füllen to stack III
Füller pen I
Fundbüro lost and found II
Fundsachen lost and found II
fünf five I
fünfte fifth I
fünfzehn fifteen I
fünfzehnte fifteenth I
fünfzig fifty I
fünfzigste fiftieth I
Funktionär / Funktionärin official IV U1, 22
funktionieren to work IV U3, 57
für for I; in favor of *(AE)* IV U5, 106
  für immer forever IV U3, 62
  für sich on one's own IV U1, 18
furchtbar awful; terrible II
sich **fürchten** to be afraid I
Fuß foot I
  zu **Fuß** on foot I
Fuß (*Längenmaß: 30,48 cm*) foot IV U1, 8
Fußabdruck footprint IV U3, 68
Fußball football I
Fußboden floor II
Füße feet I
Fußgelenk ankle II
Fußknöchel ankle II
füttern to feed I

G

Galerie gallery II
Gang corridor III
ganz all; whole I; the whole of III
  der / die / das **ganze** … the whole of III
gar nicht not at all III
Garnele shrimp IV U5, 99
Garten garden I
Gas gas III
Gasse lane III
Gast guest II
Gastgeber / Gastgeberin host IV U2, 32
Gasthaus pub III
Gate gate III
Gebärdensprache sign language I
Gebäude building II

geben to come I; to give II
jmdm. Bescheid **geben** to let sb know III
es **gibt** there are; there's (= there is) I
Gebiet area II
geboren werden to be born III
Gebrauch use IV U3, 56
gebraucht second-hand III
gebrochen broken II
Gebühr fee III
Geburtstag birthday I
Gedanke thought III
sich **Gedanken** machen to wonder III
Gedenkstätte memorial IV U1, 15
gedruckt print III
gedruckte Bücher print books III
Geduld patience IV U4, 79
geduldig patient IV U4, 78
geeignet suitable IV U5, 106
Gefahr danger IV U5, 101
sich in **Gefahr** bringen to put oneself in danger IV U5, 101
gefährlich dangerous I
… **gefällt** mir nicht. I don't like … I
Gefängnis prison I
gefrieren to freeze II
gefroren frozen IV U4, 84
Gefühl feeling IV U2, 43
gegen against II; around III
Gegend part I; area II; region III
gegenseitig one another I
sich **gegenseitig** each other III
Gegenstand object II
gegenüber opposite I; towards IV U4, 90
sich **gegenübersehen** to face IV U5, 113
sich **gegenüberstehen** to face IV U5, 113
Gehalt salary IV U4, 89
Gehäuse case III
geheim secret II
streng **geheim** top secret II
Geheimnis mystery III; secret IV U2, 38
gehen to go; to walk I
auf die Jagd **gehen** to go hunting III
aus dem Weg **gehen** to avoid IV U3, 68
jagen **gehen** to go hunting III
joggen **gehen** to go jogging II
Gehirn brain IV U2, 46
Gehweg pavement II; sidewalk *(AE)* IV U4, 84
Geisterstadt ghost town IV U3, 67
geistig mental IV U3, 62
Gelände site III; grounds IV U1, 16
gelangweilt bored II
gelb yellow I
Geld money I
Gelegenheit opportunity; chance IV U1, 21
Gemälde painting II
Gemeinde community II
gemeinsam together II
etw. **gemeinsam** haben to have sth in common III
Gemeinschaft community II
Gemüse vegetable I
gemütlich cozy IV U1, 16
genannt werden to be called III
genau exactly III
genau genommen in fact III
Generation generation IV U3, 68
genetisch genetic IV U4, 78
Genick neck III
genießen to enjoy II
genug enough II
genügend enough II
geöffnet open II
Geografie geography I
Gepäck luggage III
Gepäckraum boot III
Gepäckwagen trolley III
gepflegt smart I
gerade straight II
gerade right now; at the moment III
gerade eben just II
geradeaus straight on I
Gerät device II; tool IV U3, 67; machine IV U1, 18
geräuchert smoked IV U5, 99
Geräusch sound; noise II
gerecht fair IV U1, 22
Gericht dish II
Gericht *(juristisch)* law court; court IV U4, 85
Gerichtshof law court IV U4, 85
gering slim IV U4, 90
geringste / geringster / geringstes least III
Gern geschehen. You're welcome. I
gern mögen to love I
hätte(n) **gern** would like I
Ich würde sehr **gern** … I'd love to … (= I would love to) II
würde(n) **gern** would like I
Geschäft shop I; store *(AE)* IV U1, 10; business IV U4, 84
Geschäftsstelle office III
geschehen to happen II
Geschenk present I
Geschichte history I; story III
geschichtlich historical IV U1, 9
Geschick skill III
geschlossen closed I
geschockt shocked IV U4, 90
Geschwister sibling IV U2, 45
Gesellschaft company III
gesellschaftlich social IV U3, 62
Gesetz law III
ein **Gesetz** beschließen to pass a law IV U3, 68
ein **Gesetz** verabschieden to pass a law IV U3, 68
gesetzlich by law IV U3, 68
Gesicht face III
gespenstisch spooky I
gesperrt closed I
Gestalt figure II
gestalten to design IV U1, 10
Gestalter / Gestalterin designer IV U1, 10
Gestaltung design IV U1, 10
gestatten to allow III
gestern yesterday I
gesund healthy II
Gesundheit health IV U3, 62
geteilt divided IV U5, 113
Getränk drink I
Getreide corn IV U2, 30
getrennt segregated; divided IV U5, 113
getrennt separately I
getrocknet dried IV U1, 23
jmdm. **gewachsen** sein to stand up to sb IV U4, 78
Gewalt violence III
gewaltig enormous III
gewaltsam violent III
gewalttätig violent III
Gewicht weight II
gewinnen to win I; to extract IV U3, 57
sich an (etw.) **gewöhnen** to get used to (sth) III
gewöhnlich usually I
Gezeiten tide III
Gift poison III
giftig poisonous II
Gitarre guitar I
Glas jar I; glass II
Glaube belief IV U1, 21
glauben to think I; to believe III
gläubig religious III
gleich equal IV U5, 100
der / die / das **gleiche** … the same … II
gleich straight away; immediately III
Gleichaltriger / Gleichaltrige peer IV U2, 33
gleichberechtigt equal IV U5, 100
Gleichgestellter / Gleichgestellte equal IV U5, 100
gleichmäßig regular III
Gleis track IV U1, 10
Gletscher glacier IV U3, 68
global global IV U3, 61
Glocke bell II
Glück luck IV U3, 67
Glück haben to be lucky II
glücklich happy I
Gold gold I
Goldrausch gold rush IV U3, 67
Goldschürfen gold-mining IV U3, 67
Grab grave III
graben to dig III
graben nach to mine IV U3, 57
Grad degree I
akademischer **Grad** degree IV U4, 89
Grad Celsius degree Celsius (°C) IV U3, 54
Grad Fahrenheit degree Fahrenheit (°F) IV U3, 54
Graffiti graffiti IV U4, 84
Gramm gram (g) III
Gras grass IV U2, 37
gratis for free II
grau grey I
Grenze border III
Grieche / Griechin Greek III
Griechenland Greece II
aus **Griechenland** Greek III
Griechisch Greek III
griechisch Greek III
Grill barbecue IV U1, 15
Grillfest barbecue IV U1, 15
Grizzlybär grizzly bear IV U3, 68
groß great; big; tall; large I; high II
große Sache big deal IV U4, 86
großartig great I; fantastic III
Großbritannien Britain I; Great Britain III
Größe size II
Großeltern grandparents I
Großstadt city I
größtenteils mostly III

grün green I
Grund reason III
gründen to found III; to establish IV U3, 68
Grundschule elementary school *(AE)* IV U5, 113
Gruppe group II
gruselig scary II
Mit freundlichen **Grüßen** Sincerely, IV U5, 106
Viele **Grüße** Kind regards, IV U4, 86
Gurke cucumber I
Gürtel belt II
gut great; good; well I
Gut gemacht! Well done! II; Good job! IV U2, 38
gut laufen to go well III
gut sein in to be good at I
Mir geht es nicht **gut**. I don't feel well. II
Guten Flug! Safe flight! IV U2, 38
Guten Morgen. Good morning. I
Güter freight III

H

Haar hair III
Haarbürste hairbrush III
Haare hair III
haben to have I; to have got II
etw. gemeinsam **haben** to have sth in common III
schreckliche Angst **haben** to be terrified IV U1, 22
Verspätung **haben** to be late I
hätte(n) gern would like I
Ich **hätte** gerne … I'd like (to) … (= I would like to) I
Hafen harbor *(AE)* IV U1, 16
Hagelkorn hailstone IV U2, 43
Hähnchen chicken II
Hai shark IV U5, 105
halb (*bei Uhrzeitangaben*) half IV U1, 10
halb (sieben) half past (six) I
Halbinsel peninsula IV U3, 55
Halle hall IV U4, 85
Hallo. Hi.; Hello. I
Hals neck III
Halt stop II
halten to keep; to hold II
halten (*Vortrag*) to give II
Haltestelle station I; stop II
Hamburger hamburger; burger II
Hammer hammer III
Hammerwerfen hammer throw III
Hand hand I
die **Hand** ausstrecken to reach out IV U4, 90
Handarbeit handicraft I
handeln to act II
handgefertigt handmade III
handgeschrieben handwritten III
Handschuh glove II
Handtuch towel III
Handwerk craft III
Handwerker / Handwerkerinnen craftspeople IV U2, 31
Handy phone I; mobile phone IV U5, 109
hart hard II
hassen to hate II
hat has I
häufig often I
Haupt- main IV U3, 62
hauptsächlich mostly III
Hauptstadt capital (city) III
Haus house I
nach **Hause** home III
zu **Hause** at home I
Hausaufgabe homework I
Hausboot houseboat III
Häuschen cottage III
Hausmeister / Hausmeisterin caretaker I
Haustier pet I
Haustür front door IV U4, 90
Haut skin III
aus **Hawaii** Hawaiian IV U3, 54
Hawaiianer / Hawaiianerin Hawaiian IV U3, 54
Hawaiianisch Hawaiian IV U3, 54
hawaiianisch Hawaiian IV U3, 54
heben to raise IV U5, 100
Hecke hedge II
Heft book I
heilen to heal III
Heim home I
Heimweh haben to be homesick II
heiraten to get married II
heiß hot I
heißen to be called III
heizen to heat II
Held hero III
helfen to help I
Helikopter helicopter II
hell light IV U2, 44
Hemd shirt II
heranziehen to pull up IV U4, 90
heraus out I
aus … **heraus** out of … II
herausbringen to take out I
herausfahren to pull out III
herausfinden to find; to learn I; to find out II
Herausforderung challenge III
herausgeben to release IV U5, 105
Herausgeber / Herausgeberin editor IV U5, 106
herausholen to get out; to pull out III
herauskommen to get out III
herausnehmen to take out I; to extract IV U3, 57
Herberge hostel III
Herbst autumn I; fall *(AE)* IV U1, 16
Herd cooker II
hereinkommen to enter II
hergestellt sein aus to be made of IV U3, 56
Herkunft background II
Herr *(Anrede)* Mr I
herstellen to make II; to produce IV U2, 37; to manufacture IV U3, 57
Hersteller / Herstellerin producer IV U3, 55
Herstellung manufacturing IV U2, 30; production IV U2, 32
herüber across III
herumdrehen to turn II
jmdn. (an einem Ort) **herumführen** to show sb around (a place) II
herumkommen to get around I
sich **herumtreiben** (mit) to hang out (with) I
herunter down I
herunterfallen to fall off III
herunterladen to download III
hervorragend excellent II
Herz heart IV U2, 45
herzzerreißend heartbreaking IV U3, 62
heute today I
heute Abend tonight III
heute Morgen this morning III
heute Nacht tonight III
hier here I
Highlight highlight III
Highschool (*weiterführende Schule, Oberstufe*) high school *(AE)* II
Hilfe help I; support; outreach IV U3, 62
ohne **Hilfe** on one's own IV U1, 18
hilflos helpless IV U5, 100
hilfreich useful II
Hilfsmittel tool IV U3, 67
hinauf up III
hinein into I
in … **hinein** inside IV U5, 113
hineingehen to enter II
hineingelangen to get into IV U3, 62
hineinkommen to get into IV U3, 62
hineintun to put in II
sich in jmdn. **hineinversetzen** to put oneself in other people's shoes IV U5, 101
hinkommen to get II
hinnehmen to accept III
sich **hinsetzen** to sit down I
hinter behind I
Hintergrund background II
hinterher afterwards III
hinterherrennen to run after II
hinüber across III
hinunter down I
bis ganz **hinunter** zu all the way to III
Hinweis tip II
hinzufügen to add III
Hip-Hop hip-hop III
Hirsch deer III
hispanisch Hispanic IV U3, 55
historisch historical IV U1, 9
hoch tall I; high II
Hochebene plateau IV U4, 77
hochhalten to raise IV U5, 100; to put up IV U2, 39; to pull up IV U4, 90
Hochland highland III
Hochschulabschluss degree IV U4, 89
Hochschule college III
Hochwasser flood IV U5, 99
hochziehen to pull up IV U4, 90
Hockey hockey III
hoffen to hope II
Hoffnung hope IV U2, 46
höflich polite III
Höhe level I
Höhepunkt highlight III
Höhle cave I
Holz wood II
Holzschuh clog III

Holzstamm log III
Hörbuch audiobook III
hören to listen (to) I; to hear II
Horn horn IV U4, 77
Hose, **Hosen** trousers II
kurze **Hose** shorts II
Hosentasche pocket II
Hospital hospital III
Hotdog (*Würstchen im Brötchen*) hot dog IV ZI, 7
Hotel hotel III
hübsch beautiful I; pretty III
Hubschrauber helicopter II
Hügel hill II
Huhn chicken II
Hund dog I
den **Hund** spazieren führen to take the dog for a walk I
Hundemarke dog tag II
hundert a / one hundred I
hundertste hundredth I
Hungersnot famine III
hungrig hungry I
Hurrikan hurricane IV U5, 99
Hut hat I
hüten to look after II
Hyperloop hyperloop IV U5, 107

I

ich I; me I
Ich heiße … My name is … I
Ich kann es kaum erwarten. I can't wait. III
Ich komme aus … I'm from … I
Ich mag … nicht I don't like … I
ich nehme … I'll take … II
Ich wünschte, du wärst hier. I wish you were here. III
Idee idea I
Igel hedgehog II
ignorieren to ignore IV U5, 100
ihm / **ihn** him I
Ihnen you I
ihnen them I
ihr you I
ihr / **ihre** her; its I
ihr / **ihre** (*Pl.*) their I
ihr (selbst) / euch (selbst) / Sie (selbst) yourselves III
Ihr / **Ihre** your I
Ihr / **Ihre** (*als Briefabschluss*) Yours, III
Ihre / **Ihrer** / **Ihres** yours II
ihre / **ihrer** / **ihrs** hers III
im Freien outside I
im Wandel changing II
Image image IV U5, 113
Imbiss snack I
Imbissstube snack bar I
immer always I
für **immer** forever IV U3, 62
immer noch still III
immer wieder again and again IV U5, 100
immer, wenn whenever IV U5, 100
immerhin at least III
Immigrant / **Immigrantin** immigrant IV U1, 9
Immigration immigration IV U1, 9
immigrieren to immigrate IV U1, 21
in to; in; at; into I; inside III
in der Woche a week II
in Form fit IV U4, 78
in Richtung towards III
in … hinein inside IV U5, 113
indem by (*+ -ing*) III
Inder / **Inderin** Indian II
Indien India II
indigen native IV U1, 9
Indisch Indian II
indisch Indian II
Industrie industry III
Industrie- industrial III
industriell industrial III
Influencer / **Influencerin** influencer II
Informatik IT (= Information Technology) I
Information information II; information desk III
Informationsblatt leaflet II
jmdn. **informieren** to let sb know III
Ingenieur / **Ingenieurin** engineer IV U3, 61
Inlineskaten skating I; inline skating III
innen in inside III
im **Innern** inside III
Insekt insect II; bug IV U5, 105
Insel isle; island III
inspirieren to inspire IV U4, 78
installieren to install IV U3, 61; to put in III
Instrument instrument I
intelligent smart I; clever III
Intelligenz intelligence IV U5, 106
künstliche **Intelligenz** (KI) artificial intelligence (AI) IV U5, 106
interessant interesting I
Interesse interest; awareness IV U5, 100
sich **interessieren** für to be interested in II; to care about III
interessiert sein an to be interested in II
international international II
Internet internet II
internetbasiert web-based III
Internettagebuch blog II
ein **Internettagebuch** führen to blog III
Interview interview I
Iran Iran II
irgendein any I
irgendetwas anything I
irgendjemand anyone III
irgendwann eventually; some time III
irgendwas any I
irgendwelche any II
Irisch Irish III
irisch Irish III
Irland the Republic of Ireland; Ireland III
aus **Irland** Irish III
sich **irren** to be wrong III
Italien Italy II
Italiener / **Italienerin** Italian II
Italienisch Italian II
italienisch Italian II

J

ja yes I
na **ja** well IV U2, 44
Jacke coat; jacket II
Jagd hunting; hunt III
auf die **Jagd** gehen to go hunting III
Jagen hunting III
jagen to hunt III; to chase IV U2, 43
jagen gehen to go hunting III
Jäger / **Jägerin** hunter III; chaser IV U2, 43
Jahr year I
pro **Jahr** a year III
Jahrbuch yearbook IV U2, 32
Jahreszeit season I
Jahrgangsstufe year I
Jahrhundert century III
das 19. **Jahrhundert** the 1800s III
Jahrmarkt fair II
Jamaika Jamaica II
jämmerlich miserable IV U1, 17
Januar January I
Jazz (*Musikrichtung*) jazz IV U5, 111
Jeans jeans I
jede / **jeder** / **jedes** every; each I
jedes Mal, wenn whenever IV U5, 100
jedenfalls anyway II
jeder everyone I; everybody II
jeder (beliebige) anyone III
jederzeit whenever IV U5, 100
jedoch however III
jegliche / **jeglicher** / **jegliches** any III
jemals ever II
jemand someone I
jene those II
jetzt now I
jetzt gerade right now III
Job job II
Joggen jogging II
joggen to jog II
joggen gehen to go jogging II
Joghurt yoghurt I
Jugend youth III
Jugendherberge youth hostel III
Jugendlicher / **Jugendliche** teenager IV U1, 16
Jugendtreff youth club I
Juli July I
jung young II
Junge boy I
Juni June I
Junkfood junk food II

K

Kabine cabin IV U1, 22
Käfer bug IV U5, 105
Kajakfahren kayaking I
Kaktus cactus IV U3, 68
Kalb calf II
kalt cold I
Kälte cold II
Kamera camera III
Kampagne campaign IV U5, 113
kämpfen to fight I
Kanada Canada III
Kanal channel II; canal III
Känguru kangaroo I
Kanufahren canoeing III
kapern to hijack IV U1, 15
Kapitän / **Kapitänin** captain II
Kapitel chapter III

Kappe cap IV U2, 32
kaputt broken II
Karneval carnival IV U2, 41
Karotte carrot II
Karte card IV U3, 56
Kartoffel potato II
Kartoffelbrei mashed potatoes II
Kartoffelchip crisp I
Karton carton I; card IV U3, 56
Käse cheese I
Kassenwart / Kassenwartin treasurer III
Katastrophe disaster IV U5, 106
Kathedrale cathedral III
Katholik / Katholikin Catholic III
katholisch Catholic III
Katze cat I
Katzenklo litter tray I
kaufen to buy I
Kaufhaus department store IV U1, 22
Kaugummi chewing gum III
Keim germ II
kein / keine no I; not … any II
Keks cookie *(AE)* I, biscuit II
Keller basement *(AE)* IV U1, 11
Kellergeschoss basement *(AE)* IV U1, 11
Kellner waiter II
Kelte / Keltin Celt III
kennen to know I
kennenlernen to meet I
Kenntnis skill III
Keramik pottery III; ceramic IV U3, 56
Kerker dungeon III
Kerl guy III; dude IV U4, 86
Kerze candle III
Kessel kettle II
Kette chain IV U5, 105
Keyboard keyboard I
Kilogramm kilogramme (kg) III
Kilometer kilometre (km) I
  Kilometer pro Stunde kilometres per hour II
Kilt kilt III
Kind child; kid II
Kinder children II
Kinderzimmer bedroom I
Kino cinema I
Kirche church I
Kirsche cherry IV U2, 37
Kiste box I
klar clear II
Klasse year; class I
Klassenkamerad / Klassenkameradin classmate II
Klassenlehrer / Klassenlehrerin tutor I
Klassenstunde tutor time I
Klassenzimmer classroom I
klatschen to clap II
Klebeband tape II; sticky tape III
kleben to stick II
Kleeblatt shamrock III
Kleid dress II
Kleider clothes I
Kleiderordnung dress code IV U2, 32
Kleiderschrank wardrobe IV U4, 90
Kleidung clothes I
klein little; small I
kleinwüchsig sein to be a little person IV U4, 78
Kleinwüchsiger / Kleinwüchsige little person IV U4, 78
Klettern climbing I
  Klettern *(am Felsen)* rock climbing III
klettern to climb II
Kletterwand climbing wall I
klicken to click II
Kliff cliff III
Klima climate IV U3, 61
Klimaanlage air conditioning unit II
klingen to sound III
Klippe cliff III
Klischee stereotype III
klopfen to knock III
Klub club I
Klubhaus clubhouse III
klug smart I; clever III
Klugheit intelligence IV U5, 106
Kneipe pub III
Knie knee III
Knopf button II
Koch / Köchin chef I
Kochbanane plantain II
kochen to cook I
Koffer suitcase IV U2, 38
Kofferraum boot III
Kohl cabbage II
kollabieren to collapse IV U1, 15
Kollegium staff I
Kollektor panel IV U1, 11
Kolonie colony III
komisch funny I; odd IV U1, 17
Komma (bei Dezimalzahlen) point III
kommen to come I
Kommentar comment IV U2, 32
Kommunikation communication II
Kompass compass III
Konfitüre jam I
Konflikt conflict III
König king I
königlich royal II
Königreich kingdom III
konkurrieren to compete (in) III
können can I; may IV U3, 62
  (etw.) **können** to be able to (do sth) II
  nicht **können** can't (= cannot) I
konnte could II
könnte could III; might IV U5, 106
kontaktieren to contact III
Kontinent continent III
Konto account III
kontrollieren to check II
Konzert concert I
Kopf head II
Kopfkissen pillow I
Kopfschmerzen headache II
Kopfweh headache II
Koralle coral IV U5, 99
Korallenriff coral reef IV U5, 99
Korn corn IV U2, 30
Körper body II
korrekt right I
Korridor hall I
kostbar precious IV U3, 68
Kosten cost IV U2, 37
kostenlos free I; for free II
Kostüm costume II
Krabbe shrimp IV U5, 99
krachen to crash IV U1, 15
Kraft energy II; strength IV U2, 46; power IV U4, 77
krank ill II; sick IV U3, 62
Krankenhaus hospital III
Krankenpfleger / Krankenpflegerin nurse IV U5, 107
Krankenwagen ambulance III
Krankheit disease III
Kraut cabbage II
kreativ creative II
Kreditkarte credit card III
Kreislauf cycle IV U3, 56
kreischen to scream I
Kreisverkehr roundabout I
Kreole / Kreolin Creole IV U5, 99
Kreolisch Creole IV U5, 99
kreolisch Creole IV U5, 99
Kreuzung crossing I
Krieg war III
Kriminalbeamter / Kriminalbeamtin detective II
Krimineller / Kriminelle criminal I
Küche kitchen I
Kuchen cake I; pie III
Kuchendiagramm pie chart III
Kugel ball II
Kugelstoßen shot put III
Kuh cow I
kühl cool I
Kühlakku ice pack III
kühlen to cool II
Kühlschrank fridge I
Kulisse set II
Kultur culture III
sich **kümmern** (um) to care (for) I
sich **kümmern** um to look after; to care about III
Kunde / Kundin customer III
Kunst art I; arts III
Kunsthandwerk arts and crafts III
Kunsthandwerker / Kunsthandwerkerin craftspeople III
Künstler / Künstlerin performer II; artist III
künstlich artificial IV U5, 106
  künstliche Intelligenz (KI) artificial intelligence (AI) IV U5, 106
Kunststoff plastic II
Kunststück trick I
Kupfer copper IV U4, 77
Kürbis pumpkin IV U2, 38
Kurs class I; course III
kurz short II
  kurze Hose shorts II
küssen to kiss IV U4, 90
Küste coast; seaside I; coastline III; shore IV U2, 31
Küsten- coastal III
Küstenpfad coastal path III
Küstenweg coastal path III

L

Lächeln smile III
lächeln to smile II
lachen to laugh I
Lacrosse *(Ballsportart)* lacrosse IV U1, 16

Laden shop I; store *(AE)* IV U1, 10
laden to load II
Ladestation charging point IV U4, 85
Lage location IV U5, 113
Lager camp I
Lampe lamp I
Land country; land I; nation; countryside III; state IV ZI, 7
auf dem **Land** in the country II
landen to land II
Landkarte map II
ländliche Gegend country I
Landschaft landscape; countryside III
Landungssteg pier II
Landwirt / Landwirtin farmer IV U2, 31
Landwirtschaft farming III; agriculture IV U2, 30
Landwirtschaftsflächen farmland IV U5, 98
lang long I
lange long I
langsam slow I
langweilig boring I
Lärm noise II
Lasagne lasagne II
lassen to let; to leave I
Lateinamerika Latin America IV U4, 77
Lateinamerikaner / Lateinamerikanerin Hispanic IV U3, 55
lateinamerikanisch Hispanic IV U3, 55
Laufen running I
laufen to run; to walk I
laufen (Veranstaltung) to be on III
gut **laufen** to go well III
Läufer / Läuferin runner III
Lauffeuer wildfire IV U3, 55
Laufzeit life cycle IV U3, 56
Laut sound II
laut loud II; noisy; out loud III
Leben life I; living II
am **Leben** alive IV U4, 77
leben to live I
Lebensdauer life cycle IV U3, 56
Lebensmittel food I
Lebensstil lifestyle IV U4, 77
Lebenszyklus life cycle IV U3, 56
lecker tasty; nice II
leer dead II; empty IV U4, 90
legen to put III
Legende legend III
Lehre apprenticeship IV U4, 89
lehren to teach III
Lehrer / Lehrerin teacher I
leicht easy I; light IV U2, 44
Leichtathlet / Leichtathletin athlete III
Leichtathletik track and field IV ZI, 6; athletics IV U4, 85
Leichtathletikbahn athletics track IV U4, 85
leider unfortunately IV U4, 84
leidtun to be sorry III
Es **tut** mir **leid**. I'm sorry. I
Tut mir **leid**. Sorry. I
Leinwand screen II
leise quiet I
leisten to achieve IV U1, 21
sich **leisten** to afford IV U3, 62
leiten to direct II; to lead III
Leiter / Leiterin leader III
Lektor / Lektorin editor IV U5, 106
lernen to learn I; to study III
lesen to read I
letzte / letzter / letztes last I; final III
letzte Aufforderung final call III
letzter Aufruf final call III
Leuchtturm lighthouse I
Leute people I; guys II
Level level I
Lexikon encyclopedia III
Licht light I
am **liebsten** best II
Liebe love III
Liebe / Lieber ..., *(Anrede in Briefen, E-Mails, ...)* Dear ..., III
lieben to love I
Lieblings- favourite I; favorite *(AE)* IV ZI, 6
Lied song II
liefern to deliver II; to distribute IV U3, 57; to provide IV U4, 77
Lieferwagen van IV U3, 57
liegen to lie III
Lifestyle lifestyle IV U4, 77
Lift lift II; elevator *(AE)* IV U1, 10
lila purple II
Limonade lemonade I
Lineal ruler I
Linie line II
links left I; on the left II
Liste list IV U1, 23
Lizenz license *(AE)* IV U5, 105
Loch hole I
lokal local II
Look look IV U4, 90
los sein to be going on III
löschen to extinguish III
lösen to solve III
loslassen to release IV U5, 105
Lösung solution IV U3, 61
Löwe lion I
loyal loyal III
Lücke gap II
Luft air II
lügen to lie III
Lunchpaket packed lunch II
lustig funny I; fun III

M

machen to make; to do I; to create II
Dreck **machen** to make a mess II
sauber **machen** to clean up II
selbst **gemacht** homemade IV U2, 38
Unordnung **machen** to make a mess II
Das **macht** neun Pfund und zehn Pence. That's £9.10. I
Gut **gemacht**! Well done! II
Mach dir keine Sorgen. Don't worry. III
Macht power IV U4, 77
mächtig powerful IV U2, 44
machtlos helpless IV U5, 100
Mädchen girl I
Magen stomach II
Magie magic III
Mahlzeit meal II
Mai May I
mailen to email III
Mais corn IV U2, 30
Maisbrot cornbread IV U2, 38
Make-up make-up IV U4, 90
Makkaroni macaroni II
Makkaroni mit Käsesoße macaroni cheese II
Mal time II
jedes **Mal**, wenn whenever IV U5, 100
malen to paint II
Mama mum I; mom *(AE)* II
manche some I
manchmal sometimes I
Mango mango I
Mann man I
Männer men I
Mannschaft crew; team II
Mantel coat II
Mappe folder I
Marathon marathon IV U1, 9
Margarine margarine II
Marke brand IV U1, 10
Markt market I
Marmelade jam I
Mars Mars IV U5, 106
marschieren to march IV U5, 111
März March I
Maschine machine IV U1, 18
Material material II
Mathe maths I; math *(AE)* IV U2, 32
Mathematik maths I; math *(AE)* IV U2, 32
Matrose / Matrosin sailor II
Matte mat III
Mauer wall I
Maul mouth III
Maus mouse II
Mäuse mice II
Mayonnaise mayonnaise (mayo) I
Mechaniker / Mechanikerin mechanic II
Medien media III
soziale **Medien** social media III
Medikamente medicine III
Medizin medicine III
medizinisch medical IV U3, 62
Meer sea I; ocean IV U1, 22
Meeresfrüchte seafood IV U1, 16
Meeresküste seaside I
Meeresufer seafront II
Meeting meeting III
Mehl flour II
mehr more I
nicht **mehr** not ... any more II; not ... anymore *(AE)* IV U5, 113
die **Mehrheit** (the) most II
meiden to avoid IV U3, 68
Meile mile I
mein / meine my I
meiner Meinung nach in my opinion IV U5, 106
meine / meiner / meins mine II
meinen to mean III
Meinung opinion IV U5, 106
meiner **Meinung** nach in my opinion IV U5, 106
seine **Meinung** ändern to change one's mind III
am **meisten** (the) most II
die **meisten** (the) most II
meistens mostly III

Melder sensor II
melken to milk I
Menge amount (of) IV U3, 56
eine **Menge** a lot of I
jede **Menge** lots of III
Mensa cafeteria I
Mensch human III; man IV U5, 100
Menschen people I
Menschen- human III
Menschenmenge crowd II
menschlich human III
mental mental IV U3, 62
sich **merken** to remember I
merkwürdig funny I; weird III; strange; odd IV U1, 17
Messe fair II
sich **messen** to compete (in) III
Messer knife III
Metall metal II
Metalldetektor metal detector IV U2, 32
Metallsuchgerät metal detector IV U2, 32
Meter metre (m) I
Metzgerei butcher's IV U4, 85
Mexikaner / Mexikanerin Mexican IV U5, 100
mexikanisch Mexican IV U5, 100
Mexiko Mexico IV U3, 61
mich me I; myself IV U4, 78
mich selbst myself IV U4, 78
Miete rent IV U3, 62
mieten to rent; to hire II
Mikrowelle microwave II
Milch milk I
Milch- dairy IV U2, 30
Milchbetrieb dairy farming IV U2, 30
Milchproduktion dairy farming IV U2, 30
Million million II
mindestens at least III
Ministerpräsident / Ministerpräsidentin prime minister II
Minute minute I
mir me I; myself IV U4, 78
Mir geht es nicht gut. I don't feel well. II
Mission mission IV U5, 98
mit with I
mit (dem Fahrrad) by (bike) I
mitbringen to bring II
miteinander together II
Mitglied member III
Mitglied werden to join II
Mitglieds- membership III
Mitgliedschaft membership III
mitmachen bei to join II
mitnehmen to take I
Mitschüler / Mitschülerin classmate II
Mittagessen lunch I
Mitte centre I; middle II; center *(AE)* IV U1, 9
Mittelschule (*weiterführende Schule in den USA, Mittelstufe*) middle school IV U4, 78
mitten im Nirgendwo in the middle of nowhere II
Mitternacht midnight III
mittlerweile meanwhile III
Mittwoch Wednesday I
Mobber / Mobberin bully IV U4, 78
Mobbing bullying III
Mobiltelefon mobile phone IV U5, 109
Mode fashion IV ZI, 7
Model model II
Modell model II
Moderator / Moderatorin host IV U2, 32
modern modern II
modisch fancy IV U2, 44
mögen to like; to want (to) I; to enjoy II
gern **mögen** to love I
nicht **mögen** to hate II
Ich **möchte** gerne … I'd like (to) … (= I would like to) I
möglich possible IV U1, 16
Möglichkeit opportunity; chance IV U1, 21
Molkerei dairy IV U2, 30
Moment moment II
im **Moment** at the moment III
momentan at the moment III
Monarch / Monarchin monarch II
Monat month II
Mond Moon IV U5, 107
Monster monster III
Montag Monday I
montags on Mondays I
montieren to assemble IV U3, 57
Mopp mop II
Morgen morning I
Guten **Morgen**. Good morning. I
heute **Morgen** this morning III
morgen tomorrow II
Motorrad motorbike I
Motorradfahrer / Motorradfahrerin biker II
müde tired I
Müll rubbish I; garbage *(AE)* IV U3, 68
Mülleimer bin I
multikulturell multicultural IV U3, 55
Mund mouth III
Münzgeld change I
Museum museum I
Musik music I
Musiker / Musikerin musician IV U5, 111
Musikgruppe band II
Muskel muscle III
Müsli cereal II
müssen must I; to have to II; to need to IV U3, 57
nicht **müssen** needn't III
mutig brave III
Mutter mother I
Mütze beanie III; cap IV U2, 32
Mysterium mystery III

N

nach to; after I
nach Hause home III
nach oben upstairs II; up III
nach unten downstairs II
nach vorne forward IV U4, 90
nach (*bei Uhrzeitangaben*) past I
Viertel vor / **nach** (*bei Uhrzeitangaben*) quarter to / past I
Nachbar / Nachbarin neighbour I
Nachbarschaft neighbourhood III
nachdem after III
nachdenken to reflect IV U5, 101
nachfolgen to succeed (in) IV U1, 22
nachhaltig sustainable IV ZI, 7
Nachhilfe tutoring IV U2, 33
Nachmittag afternoon I
nachmittags (*Uhrzeit*) p.m. II
Nachricht message II
Nachricht(en) news III
Nachrichten- news III
nachschauen to look I
Nachsitzen detention IV U2, 32
Nachspeise dessert II
nächste / nächster / nächstes next II
als **Nächstes** next I
Nacht night I
heute **Nacht** tonight III
nachts at night IV U4, 76
Nacken neck III
nah near III
in der **Nähe** von near I
nahe close IV U5, 109
Nahrung food I
Nahrungskette food chain IV U5, 105
Name name I
Nase nose II
nass wet I
Nation nation III
national national II
National- national II
Nationalpark national park III
Natur nature II
Natur- natural IV U3, 68
natürlich natural IV U3, 68
natürlich of course I
Naturpark national park III
Naturwissenschaft science I
naturwissenschaftlich scientific IV U3, 68
Navajo / Navajo Navajo IV U4, 77
Navajo- Navajo IV U4, 77
Nebel mist I; fog IV U3, 55
neben next to I; by III
neblig misty; foggy I
Neffe nephew II
negativ negative III
nehmen to take I
eine Dusche **nehmen** to have a shower II
jmdn. / etw. ernst **nehmen** to take sb / sth seriously IV U5, 100
neidisch jealous II
nein no I
nennen to call II
nervös nervous I
nett nice; friendly I
Netzwerk network IV U5, 107
neu new I
neugierig nosy IV U1, 16
Neuigkeit(en) news III
Neujahr New Year I
neun nine I
neunte ninth I
neunzehn nineteen I
neunzehnte nineteenth I
neunzig ninety I
neunzigste ninetieth I
nicht not I
auch **nicht** not … either I
nicht brauchen needn't III
nicht dürfen mustn't II

nicht können can't (= cannot) I
nicht länger no longer IV U2, 39
nicht mehr not … any more II; no longer IV U2, 39; not … anymore *(AE)* IV U5, 113
nicht mögen to hate II
nicht müssen needn't III
nicht werden won't (= will not) II
Nichte niece II
nichts nowhere; nothing II; not … anything IV U1, 10
nicken to nod II
nie never I
die **Niederlande** the Netherlands II
sich **niederlassen** (in) to settle (in) IV U2, 31
niedrig low III
niemals never I; ever IV U2, 44
niemand no one II
Nigeria Nigeria II
aus **Nigeria** Nigerian II
Nigerianer / Nigerianerin Nigerian II
nigerianisch Nigerian II
nirgendwo nowhere II
mitten im **Nirgendwo** in the middle of nowhere II
nirgendwohin nowhere II
Niveau level I
noch still; yet II; even III
noch ein another I
noch einmal again I
noch nicht not … yet II
Nord- north II
Norden north II
Nordirland Northern Ireland III
nördlich north II; northern III
nordöstlich northeastern IV U1, 16
normal regular; normal III
normalerweise usually I
Normanne / Normannin Norman III
normannisch Norman III
Not- emergency IV U1, 15
Notausgang fire escape IV U1, 11
Notdienst emergency service II
Notfall emergency III
Notfallbegleiter / Notfallbegleiterin first responder IV U3, 62
Notruf emergency call III
November November I
Nudeln pasta I
null zero I
null *(bei Uhrzeiten und Telefonnummern)* oh I
Nummer number I
nun now I
nur only I; just II
Nuss nut II
Nutzen use IV U3, 56
nützlich useful II
nutzlos useless II

O

ob if II
obdachlos homeless IV U3, 62
oben at the top; upstairs II; up III; above IV U1, 10
nach **oben** upstairs II; up III
im **Obergeschoss** upstairs II
oberhalb above IV U1, 10
Oberteil top IV U1, 10
bauchfreies **Oberteil** crop top IV U2, 32
Objekt object II
Obst fruit I
obwohl although III
oder or I
entweder … **oder** … either … or … IV U3, 56
offen open II
Tag der **offenen** Tür open day III
öffentlich public III
die **Öffentlichkeit** (the) public IV U5, 100
offiziell official II
öffnen to open I
oft often I
ohne without II
ohne Hilfe on one's own IV U1, 18
Ohr ear II
okay OK I
Ökosystem ecosystem IV U3, 68
Oktober October I
Öl oil III
Oma grandma I
Onkel uncle I
online online II
online stellen to post II
Opa grandpa I
Optikfachgeschäft optician's IV U4, 85
Orange orange I
orange orange I
Orchester orchestra IV U2, 33
ordentlich tidy III
ordnen to organise III
Ordner folder I
in **Ordnung** bringen to tidy (up) II
organisch organic I
organisieren to organise; to arrange III; to organize *(AE)* IV U1, 16
Orkan hurricane IV U5, 99
Ort place I; space II; site III; location IV U5, 113
örtlich local II
Ost- east II
Osten east II
östlich east II
Outdoor- outdoor I
Ozean ocean IV U1, 22

P

Paar pair IV U1, 23
ein **Paar** a pair of IV U1, 23
ein **paar** some I; a few II
Päckchen packet I
packen to pack II
Packung packet I
Palast palace II
Paneel panel IV U1, 11
Panik panic IV U4, 90
Papa dad I
Papier paper I
Papiere papers IV U1, 23
Pappe card IV U3, 56
Paprika pepper I
Paprikaschote pepper I
Parade parade IV U1, 15
Paradies paradise III
Parfüm perfume IV U1, 23
Park park I
Parkplatz car park I; parking lot *(AE)* IV U1, 11
Partner / Partnerin partner II
Party party I
Pass passport III
Passagier / Passagierin passenger III
passen to suit; to fit II
passend suitable IV U5, 106
passieren to happen II
Passiv passive voice IV U3, 58
passiv passive IV U3, 58
Pasta pasta I
Pastete pie III
Patient / Patientin patient III
Pause break II
Pausenhof playground I
Pekannuss pecan IV U2, 38
pelzig furry II
perfekt perfect II
Person person I
Person of Color (*Person mit dunkler Hautfarbe*) person of color (POC) *(AE)* IV U5, 100
Personal staff I
persönlich face-to-face IV U5, 107
Persönlichkeit figure II
Pfad path III
Pfannkuchen pancake I
Pfeffer pepper I
Pferd horse I
Pflanze plant II
pflanzen to plant II
Pflaster plaster III
Pfund (*brit. Währungseinheit*) pound (£) II
Picknick picnic I
Pier pier II
pikant spicy; juicy II
Pinguin penguin II
pink pink I
Pinzette tweezers III
Pizza pizza II
Plan plan III
planen to plan III
Planet planet II
Plantage plantation IV U4, 83
Plastik plastic II
Plateau plateau IV U4, 77
Platscher splash III
platt flat III
Platte panel IV U1, 11
Plattform platform II
Platz room; place; pitch I; space; square II; site IV U5, 98
plaudern to chat II
pleite broke IV U4, 86
plötzlich suddenly II; all of a sudden III
Podcast podcast II
Polen Poland IV U1, 22
aus **Polen** Polish III
Polizei police I
Polizeibeamter / Polizeibeamtin police officer I
Polizeirevier police station IV U4, 85
Polizeiwache police station IV U4, 85

Polnisch Polish III
polnisch Polish III
Pommes frites chips I
Portal portal IV U2, 32
Portugal Portugal I
positiv positive III
Post (*online gestellte Nachricht*) post IV U1, 16
posten to post II
Poster poster IV U5, 101
Praktikum internship III
praktisch practical IV U3, 62
praktizieren to practice *(AE)* IV U2, 33
Praline chocolate II
Präsentation presentation II
präsentieren to present IV U5, 101
Präsident / Präsidentin president IV U2, 31
Preis cost IV U2, 37; award IV U4, 78
Premierminister / Premierministerin prime minister II
pressen to press II
Pressesprecher / Pressesprecherin press officer III
Prinz prince II
privat private IV U1, 16
Privat- private IV U1, 16
pro per III
pro Jahr a year III
pro Woche a week II
Probe practice IV U1, 16
probieren to try II
Problem problem I; trouble III
Produkt product I
Produktion manufacturing IV U2, 30; production IV U2, 32
Produzent / Produzentin producer IV U3, 55
produzieren to produce IV U2, 37
Programm channel II; program *(AE)* IV U3, 61
Programmier- programming IV U4, 89
programmieren to program IV U3, 57
Programmierer / Programmiererin programmer II
Projekt project II
Promenade promenade I
Prospekt leaflet II
Protest protest III
Protestant / Protestantin Protestant III
protestantisch Protestant III
protestieren to protest IV U5, 99
protestierend protesting IV U5, 113
Prozent (%) percent (%) IV U1, 9
Prüfung exam I
psychisch mental IV U3, 62
publizieren to publish IV U3, 69
Pueblo- Pueblo IV U4, 77
Pullover sweater II
Punkt point III
punkten to score I
pünktlich on time III; sharp IV U4, 86
Punsch punch IV U2, 38
Pute turkey IV U2, 38
putzen to clean I; to brush II
sich die Zähne **putzen** to brush one's teeth II
Puzzle puzzle III
Pyjama pyjamas III

Q

Quadrat square II
Quadratkilometer square kilometre (km²) III
Quadratmeile square mile III
Qualität quality IV U4, 84
quer durch across III

R

Rad wheel II
Radfahren cycling I
Radiergummi rubber I
radikal extreme IV U5, 106
Radio radio II
Radweg cycle lane III
Rahm cream I
Raketenabschussbasis launch site IV U5, 98
Rampenlicht spotlight II
rar rare IV U3, 56
Rasen grass IV U2, 37
Rassentrennung segregation IV U5, 99
Rassismus racism IV U4, 83
Rassist / Rassistin racist IV U5, 112
rassistisch racist IV U5, 112
Rat advice III; council IV U2, 32
jmdm. **raten** to advise sb IV U3, 63
Rathaus town hall IV U4, 84
Ratschlag tip II; advice III
Rätsel puzzle; mystery III
Rauchen smoking III
Raum room I; space II
Raumfähre space shuttle IV U1, 10
Raumfahrt space travel IV U5, 106
Raumschiff spacecraft II
Raumstation space station I
Reaktion response IV U5, 112
realisieren to realise III; to realize *(AE)* IV U4, 90
virtuelle **Realität** (VR) virtual reality (VR) IV U5, 107
Recherche research IV U3, 68
Recht right IV U4, 83
recht haben to be right III
rechts right; on the right I
recyceln to recycle II
recycelt recycled IV U3, 56
Redakteur / Redakteurin editor IV U5, 106
Redaktion editing III
Rede speech IV U5, 114
reden (mit) to talk (to) I
Redner / Rednerin speaker IV U4, 84
reduzieren to reduce IV U3, 56
reflektieren to reflect IV U5, 101
Regal shelf I
Regalbrett shelf I
Regel rule I
regelmäßig regular III
Regen rain I
Regenjacke raincoat III
Regenmantel raincoat III
Regenschirm umbrella III
Regie führen bei to direct II
Regierung government IV U1, 9
Region region III
regnen to rain I
regnerisch rainy I
Reh deer III
reich rich I
Reihe series III
Reihenfolge order II
Reinigung cleaning I
Reis rice I
Reise trip I
Reisebüro travel agency IV U2, 40
Reisen travel IV U5, 106
reisen to travel III
Reisepass passport III
Reiseziel destination III
Reiten horse riding III
reiten to ride I
Rekord record III
Religion religion III
Religionsunterricht RE (= Religious Education) I
religiös religious III
Rennen race I
rennen to run I
renovieren to renovate III
renoviert renovated III
Reparaturdienst repair service II
reparieren to repair I
Republik republic III
Reservat reservation IV U4, 83
reservieren to book II
respektieren to respect III
respektvoll respectful III
Ressource natural resource; resource IV U5, 106
der **Rest** the rest IV U1, 22
Restaurant restaurant I
Restgeld change I
retten to save III
Retter / Retterin rescuer III
Rettungs- emergency IV U1, 15
Rettungsdienst emergency service II
Rettungskraft emergency worker IV U1, 15
Rettungssanitäter / Rettungssanitäterin emergency medical technician (EMT) IV U4, 89
Rettungsschwimmer / Rettungsschwimmerin lifeguard III
Rettungswagen ambulance III
Rezept recipe IV ZI, 7
Rhythmus beat IV U2, 44
richtig right I; real; true II
Richtung way I; direction II
in **Richtung** towards III
riechen to smell I
Riegel bar I
Riesen- giant II
riesengroß huge III
riesig great I; giant II; huge; enormous III
Riff reef IV U5, 99
Rinder cattle IV U4, 77
Rindfleisch beef II
Ring ring III
Rippchen rib IV U5, 99
Rippe rib IV U5, 99
Risotto risotto II
Ritt ride I
Robbe seal I
Roboter robot II

Rock skirt II
Rodeo rodeo IV U4, 77
roh raw IV U3, 56
Rohmaterial raw material IV U3, 56
Rohr tube I
Rohstoff raw material IV U3, 56; natural resource IV U5, 106
Rolle role; roll II
Roller scooter I
Rollstuhl wheelchair III
Roman novel III
Römer / Römerin Roman III
römisch Roman III
rosa pink I
Rose rose II
rot red I
Rotkehlchen robin II
Rotwild deer III
Route route III
Routine routine I
Rücken back II
Rückseite back II
Ruf call II
rufen to call I; to shout II; to cry III
Rugby rugby III
ruhig quiet I; calm II
Rumänien Romania II
rumhängen (mit) to hang out (with) I
Rummelplatz fairground I
rund round II
rund um around I
Rundgang tour I
Russe / Russin Russian III
Russisch Russian III
russisch Russian III
Russland Russia II
aus **Russland** Russian III

S

Saal hall IV U4, 85
Saat seed II
Sach- non-fiction III
Sache thing I
Sachen kit III
Sachliteratur non-fiction III
Sachse / Sächsin Saxon III
sächsisch Saxon III
Sack bag III
Saft juice I
saftig juicy II
Sage legend III
sagen to say; to tell I
jmdm. Bescheid **sagen** to let sb know III
Sahne cream I
Saison season I
Saison- seasonal IV U3, 55
saisonal seasonal IV U3, 55
Salat salad I
Salz salt IV U2, 45
salzig salty I
Samen seed II
Sammelalbum scrapbook III
sammeln to collect I
Geld **sammeln** to raise money IV U1, 9
Samstag Saturday I
Sandwich sandwich I
sanft soft III
Sänger / Sängerin singer II
sanieren to renovate III
saniert renovated III
Sanitäter / Sanitäterin paramedic II
Sarg coffin IV U5, 111
sauber clean I; tidy III
sauber machen to clean I; to clean up II
Saubermachen cleaning I
sauer sour I
Schachtel box I
schaden to damage III
schadstoffarm low-emission IV U4, 85
schaffen to create II; to achieve IV U1, 21
Schal scarf II
Schalter desk III
sich **schämen** für / wegen to be ashamed of IV U2, 44
scharf clear II; sharp IV U4, 86
Schatz honey *(AE)* II; treasure IV U3, 68
Schätzchen honey *(AE)* II
Schatzmeister / Schatzmeisterin treasurer III
schauen to look I
Schaukasten case III; display IV U2, 39
Schauplatz scene II; site III
Schauspiel drama III
Schauspieler / Schauspielerin actor II
eine **Scheibe** a piece of II
scheinen to seem IV U1, 22
Scheinwerfer spotlight II
Schere pair of scissors I; scissors II
Scherz joke II
scherzen to joke III
schick smart I
schicken to send II
schieben to push IV U5, 100
schießen to shoot IV U5, 114
Schiff ship I
Schiffsdeck deck IV U1, 22
Schikanieren bullying III
Schild sign; signpost II
Schinken ham I
Schlaf sleep II
Schlafanzug pyjamas III
schlafen to sleep I
lange **schlafen** to sleep late II
Schlafsack sleeping bag III
Schlafzimmer bedroom I
Schlag beat IV U2, 44
schlagen to knock; to hit III
Schlange snake II
schlank slim IV U4, 90
schlau smart I; clever III
Schlauch tube I
schlecht bad I; ill II
schlicht plain II
schließen to close I; to shut IV U2, 43
Schließfach locker II
schließlich finally II; eventually III
schlimm bad I; terrible II
Schlittschuhlaufen ice skating; skating I
Schloss castle I
Schlucht canyon IV U3, 54
Schluss end III
zum **Schluss** finally II
Schlussverkauf sale I
schmackhaft tasty II
schmal narrow III; slim IV U4, 90
schmelzen to melt III
Schmerz ache II; pain III
Schmerzen haben to be in pain III
Schmerzen ache II
Schmetterling butterfly II
Schminke make-up IV U4, 90
Schmuck jewellery I; decoration IV U2, 39
schmücken to decorate III
schmutzig dirty I
Schnecke snail II
Schnee snow I
(sich) **schneiden** to cut II
schneidend sharp IV U4, 86
schneien to snow IV U2, 38
schnell quick II; fast I
Schnupfen cold II
schockieren to shock IV U5, 113
schockierend shocking IV U5, 113
schockiert shocked IV U4, 90
Schokolade chocolate I
schön nice; beautiful I
ganz **schön** pretty III
Schön, dich kennenzulernen. Nice to meet you. I
schon already; yet II
Schottenrock kilt III
Schottisch Scottish III
schottisch Scottish III
Schottland Scotland III
aus **Schottland** Scottish III
Schrank cupboard I
schrecklich awful; terrible II
Schreib- writing IV U2, 32
Schreiben writing IV U2, 32
schreiben to write I
eine SMS **schreiben** to text I
E-Mails **schreiben** to email III
Schreibtisch desk III
schreien to scream I; to shout II; to cry III
Schriftführer / Schriftführerin secretary III
Schriftsteller / Schriftstellerin writer IV U3, 68
Schritt step II
Schublade drawer I
schubsen to push IV U5, 100
schüchtern shy IV U4, 90
Schuh shoe II
Schul-AG club I
Schulden debt IV U3, 62
Schule school I
mit der **Schule** fertig sein to leave school II
Schüler / Schülerin student I
Schülerrat student council IV U2, 32
Schulfach subject I
Schulhof playground I
Schulstunde lesson I
Schulter shoulder II
mit den **Schultern** zucken to shrug II
Schürfen mining IV U3, 67
schürfen to dig III
Schuss shot IV U2, 43
schütteln to shake II
Schutzbrille goggles III
schützen to protect II
schwanger pregnant IV U3, 62

schwarz black I
schwarz (*soziale Kategorie*) Black IV U4, 83
schweigsam silent III
Schwein pig III
die **Schweiz** Switzerland IV U3, 68
schwemmen to wash I
schwenken to swing III
schwer heavy I; hard II; serious IV U3, 62
Schwere gravity IV U5, 107
Schwerelosigkeit zero gravity IV U5, 107
Schwerkraft gravity IV U5, 107
Schwert sword III
Schwester sister I
schwierig difficult I; hard II
Schwierigkeiten trouble III
Schwimmbad swimming pool I
Schwimmbrille goggles III
Schwimmen swimming I
schwimmen to swim I
  schwimmen gehen to go swimming I
schwingen to swing III
schwitzen to sweat III
Scrapbook (*selbst gestaltetes Buch*) scrapbook III
sechs six I
sechste sixth I
sechzehn sixteen I
sechzehnte sixteenth I
sechzig sixty I
sechzigste sixtieth I
secondhand second-hand III
See lake I
See (*in Schottland*) loch III
Seefahrer / Seefahrerin sailor II
Seehund seal I
seekrank seasick IV U1, 22
Seetang seaweed IV U5, 107
Segeln sailing I
segeln to sail I
sehen to see; to look; to spy I; to spot IV U3, 68
Sehenswürdigkeit sight II; attraction IV U1, 10
sehr very I; really II; highly III; extremely IV U1, 22
Seife soap III
Seil rope III
Seilbahn cable car I
Seilrutsche zip line III
sein to be I
  los **sein** to be going on III
  mit der Schule fertig **sein** to leave school II
sein / seine his; its I
seit since III; for IV U4, 78
  seit einer Ewigkeit in ages III
  seit Ewigkeiten in ages III
seitdem since III
Seite side I; page III
Sekunde second III
selber myself IV U4, 78; yourself II
selbst myself IV U4, 78; themselves; ourselves II; himself; yourselves III
  dich **selbst** yourself II
  er **selbst** himself III
  mich **selbst** myself IV U4, 78
  sie **selbst** themselves II
  selbst dann even so IV U4, 90
  selbst gemacht homemade IV U2, 38
Selbstachtung self-respect IV U3, 62
selbstbewusst confident II
selbstsicher confident II
selbstverständlich of course I
Selfiespot selfie spot II
Selfiestelle selfie spot II
selten rare IV U3, 56
seltsam funny I; weird III; strange; odd IV U1, 17
senden to send II
Sendung program *(AE)* IV U3, 61
sensationell stunning IV U4, 76
jmdn. **sensibilisieren** to raise awareness IV U5, 100
Sensor sensor II
separat separately I
September September I
Serie series III
Service service II
servieren to serve III
Set set II
setzen to put III
  sich **setzen** to sit down I
Shampoo shampoo III
Shirt shirt II
Shorts shorts II
Show show II
sich each other III
  sich gegenseitig each other III
  sich kümmern (um) to care (for) I
sicher sure; safe I; secure III
sichergehen to make sure III
Sicherheit safety III
  in **Sicherheit** safe I
Sicherheitsnadel safety pin III
Sicht view I
Sie you I
sie *(Pl.)* they; them I
sie she; her I
  er / **sie** / es it I
sieben seven I
siebte seventh I
siebzehn seventeen I
siebzehnte seventeenth I
siebzig seventy I
siebzigste seventieth I
Siedler / Siedlerin settler IV U1, 9
siegen to win I
Sightseeing sightseeing III
Signal signal II
Silvesternacht (*in Schottland*) Hogmanay III
Silvesternacht New Year's Eve III
singen to sing II
sinnlos useless II
Situation scene II; situation III
Sitz seat IV U2, 46
Sitzbank bench II
sitzen to sit II
  aufrecht **sitzen** to sit up IV U4, 90
Sitzplatz seat IV U2, 46
Sitzung session III
Skandinavien Scandinavia III
Skateboard skateboard I
Skateboardfahren skating I
Skatepark skate park I
Skibrille goggles III
Sklave / Sklavin slave IV U4, 83
Sklaverei slavery IV U4, 83
Skript script II
Skulptur sculpture IV U4, 85
smaragdgrün emerald III
SMS message II
  eine **SMS** schreiben to text I
Snack snack I
so so I
  so … wie as … as III
so (*Betonung*) that III
sobald as soon as III
Socke sock IV U1, 23
sodass so that II
soeben just II
Sofa sofa I
sofort right now; straight away; immediately III
Software software IV U4, 89
sogar even III
Sohn son II
Soja soy IV U2, 30
solar solar IV U1, 11
Solar- solar IV U1, 11
Solarpaneel solar panel IV U1, 11
solch such III
was **soll's** oh well IV U1, 10
sollte should II
Sommer summer I
sonderbar weird III
Sonne sun I
Sonnen- solar IV U1, 11
Sonnenaufgang sunrise IV U3, 55
Sonnenbaden sunbathing III
Sonnenblume sunflower II
Sonnenbrille sunglasses II
Sonnencreme sun cream II
Sonnenhut sunhat II
Sonnenkollektor solar panel IV U1, 11
Sonnensystem solar system IV U5, 107
Sonnenuntergang sunset IV U3, 55
sonnig sunny I
Sonntag Sunday I
sonst else I
Mach dir keine **Sorgen**. Don't worry. III
sich **Sorgen** machen to worry III
dafür **sorgen** to make sure III
sorgfältig careful II
Sorte kind III
Soße sauce II
Souvenir souvenir II
sowieso anyway III
sowohl … als auch … both … and … III
sozial social IV U3, 62
  soziale Medien social media III
Sozialarbeit social work IV U3, 62
Sozialarbeiter / Sozialarbeiterin social worker IV U4, 89
Spaghetti spaghetti II
Spalt gap II
Spanien Spain I
  aus **Spanien** Spanish III
Spanisch Spanish III
spanisch Spanish III
spannend exciting II
sparen to save III
Spaß fun I

Spaß machen to be fun I
spaßig fun III
spät late I
zu **spät** late I
zu **spät** sein to be late I
später later I; after III
spazieren gehen to go for a walk II
Spaziergang walk I
Spediteur carrier IV U1, 10
speichern to save III
Speise dish II
spektakulär spectacular IV U1, 8
spenden to donate IV U2, 39
speziell special I
Spiegel mirror III
Spiel game I; match III
spielen to play I; to act II
Spieler / Spielerin player II
Spielfeld pitch I; court III
Spielplatz playground I
Spielzeug toy I
Spind locker II
Spinne spider II
spitz pointed III
Spitze top IV U1, 10
spitze awesome II
Spitzer sharpener I
Sport sport I
Sport treiben to do sport I
Sport- sports III
Sportart sport I
Sportunterricht PE (= Physical Education) I
Sprache language II; speech IV U5, 114
sprechen to say I; to speak II
sprechen (mit) to talk (to) I
Sprecher / Sprecherin speaker IV U4, 84
Springbrunnen fountain II
springen to jump I
spritzen to splash I
sprudelnd fizzy I
Spülbecken sink III
spülen to wash I
Spülmaschine dishwasher II
die **Spülmaschine** einräumen to load the dishwasher II
Staat nation III; state IV ZI, 7
Staatsangehöriger / Staatsangehörige citizen IV U1, 15
Staatsbürger / Staatsbürgerin citizen IV U1, 15
stachlig spiky II
Stadion arena I; stadium II
Stadt city; town I
Städtereise city break III
Stadtplan map II
Stadtteil part I
Staffel relay; series III
Staffellauf relay III
Stahl steel IV U1, 10
Stamm tribe IV U1, 9
Standbild statue II
Standort location IV U5, 113
Stange bar I
Star star II
stark heavy I; strong II; powerful IV U2, 44
Stärke strength IV U2, 46
Start start IV U4, 87; launch IV U5, 98
starten to start I; to take off III
Start-up start-up IV U3, 55
Station station I
statt instead of IV U5, 106
stattdessen instead II
stattfinden to take place; to be on III
Statue statue II
Staubsauger vacuum cleaner II
Staumauer dam IV U4, 77
Stausee reservoir IV U3, 55
stechen to sting III
stehen to stand up; to stand; to suit II
stehen bleiben to stop I
stehlen to steal III
steigen to climb II; to step III
Stein stone; rock III
Stelle place I; space II
stellen to put III
online **stellen** to post II
sterben to die III
Stereotyp stereotype III
Stern star II
Stief- step- IV U2, 44
Stiefbruder stepbrother I
Stiefel boot II
Stiefmutter stepmother I
Stiefschwester stepsister I
Stiefvater stepfather I; stepdad IV U2, 44
Stift pen I
stiften to donate IV U2, 39
Stiftung charity I
still quiet I; silent III
Stimme voice III
nicht **stimmen** to be wrong III
Stimmung atmosphere IV U2, 43
jmdm. die **Stirn** bieten to stand up to sb IV U4, 78
Stock stick III
Stockwerk floor II; story *(AE)* IV U1, 10
Stoff material II
stolpern to trip II
stolz (auf) proud (of) IV U2, 45
stoppen to stop I
stornieren to cancel III
störrisch stubborn IV U5, 101
stoßen to knock III
Strand beach I
Straße street; road I
Straßenbahn tram I
Straßenkunst street art III
Strategie strategy IV U5, 101
streamen *(im Internet)* to stream II
live **streamen** to live stream IV U2, 32
Strecke route III; track IV U1, 10
strecken to stretch II
Streckübung stretching exercise II
Streich trick I
streichen to paint II
Streifen strip II
Streik strike IV U5, 114
Streit argument III
(sich) **streiten** to fight I
streng strict IV U3, 68
streng geheim top secret II
strikt strict IV U3, 68
Stroh straw III
Strohgarbenwerfen *(schottische Sportart)* sheaf toss III
Strom power IV U4, 77
strömen to flow IV U5, 98
ein **Stück** a piece of II
Student / Studentin student I
studieren to study III
Studio studio I
Stufe level I; step II
Stuhl chair I
stumm silent III
Stunde hour I; session III
Kilometer pro **Stunde** kilometres per hour II
Stundenkilometer kilometres per hour II
Stundenplan schedule *(AE)* IV U2, 32
Sturm storm IV U2, 43
stürmisch stormy I
suchen nach to look for II
süchtig (nach) addicted (to) IV U3, 62
Süd- south II
Süden south II
südlich south II
Südstaatler / Südstaatlerin Southerner IV U5, 99
Summe amount (of) IV U3, 56
Sumpfgebiet wetland IV U5, 99
super cool I; awesome II
Supermarkt supermarket I
Suppe soup II
Surfen surfing III
süß sweet II
Symbol symbol III
System system IV U5, 107
Szene scene II

T

Tabelle chart III
Tablet tablet I
Tablette tablet II
Tafel board; bar I
Tag day I
Tag der offenen Tür open day III
eines **Tages** one day II; some day III
Tagebuch diary IV U1, 23
Tageslicht daylight IV U3, 55
täglich daily I
Takt beat IV U2, 44
Tal valley III
Talent talent IV U4, 79
talentiert talented IV U4, 78
Talsperre dam IV U4, 77
Tante aunt I
Tanz dance I
Tanz- dancing I
Tanzen dancing I
tanzen to dance II
Tänzer / Tänzerin dancer II
tapezieren to decorate III
tapfer brave III
Tasche bag I; pocket II
Taschenlampe torch III
Taschenmesser penknife III
Tastatur keyboard I
Taste button II
Tätigkeit job II
ehrenamtliche **Tätigkeit** volunteering III
Tatsache fact III

tatsächlich in fact III
tauschen to exchange; to swap II
tausend a / one thousand II
Tauziehen tug of war III
Taxi taxi IV U1, 13
Team team II
Technik technology II
Techniker / Technikerin engineer IV U3, 61; technician IV U4, 89
Technologie technology II
Tee tea II
Teenager teenager IV U1, 16
Teich pond I; pool III
Teil part I
teilen to share I; to divide III
teilnehmen (an) to take part (in) II; to compete (in) III; to attend IV U5, 113
teilnehmen an to enter III
Teilzeit part-time IV U4, 78
Telefon phone I; telephone III
Telefonist / Telefonistin operator III
Teller plate II
Temperatur temperature I
Tennis tennis I
Teppich carpet I; rug IV U4, 77
Terrasse terrace IV U1, 11
Terror- terrorist IV U1, 15
Terrorist / Terroristin terrorist IV U1, 15
teuer expensive II
Text text I
texten to text I
Theater drama III; theatre II; theater *(AE)* IV U4, 78
Theaterstück play II
Thema subject III; topic IV U5, 106
Therapie therapy IV U3, 63
tief deep III
tiefgefroren frozen IV U4, 84
Tiefkühlschrank freezer II
Tiefkühltruhe freezer II
Tier animal I
Tierarzt / Tierärztin vet II
Tierheim animal home II
Tierpark zoo I
Tierwelt *(in freier Wildbahn)* wildlife III
Tipp tip II
Tisch table I
Tischler / Tischlerin carpenter IV U4, 89
Titel title III
Toast toast II
Tochter daughter II
Tofu tofu II
Toilette toilet I
tolerant tolerant IV U5, 101
toll great I; amazing; brilliant II
Tomate tomato I
Ton sound II
Tonstudio recording studio I
Tool tool IV U3, 67
Top top IV U1, 10
Top- top II
Topf pot II
Töpferei pottery III
töpfern to make pottery III
Tor goal I; gate III
ein **Tor** schießen to score I
Torbogen archway III
Tornado tornado IV U2, 31
Tortendiagramm pie chart III
tot dead II
total totally IV U2, 32
töten to kill III
Tour tour I
Tourist / Touristin tourist I
Tradition tradition III
traditionell traditional II
tragen to carry I; to wear II
Träger carrier IV U1, 10
Trainer / Trainerin trainer II; coach III
trainieren to practise; to train III; to practice *(AE)* IV U2, 33
Training training III; practice IV U1, 16
Trainingseinheit training session III
Trainingsstunde training session III
Transfer transfer IV U5, 107
Transport transportation *(AE)* IV U3, 56; transport IV U4, 85
Transporter van IV U3, 57
transportieren to transport IV U3, 56
Traube grape IV U3, 55
Traum dream II
träumen to dream IV U1, 16
traurig upset; unhappy I; sad II
Treffen meeting III
treffen to meet I; to hit III
sich **treffen** (mit) to hang out (with) I
treiben to drive I
Trennung segregation IV U5, 99
Treppe stairs II; staircase IV U1, 11
Treppenhaus stairs II; staircase IV U1, 11
treten to step III
treu loyal III
Treue allegiance IV U2, 32
Treueeid Pledge of Allegiance IV U2, 32
Trick trick I
trinken to drink I
etw. fertig **trinken** / essen to finish III
etw. zu Ende **trinken** / essen to finish III
Trinkhalm straw III
Trip trip I
trocken dry I
Trocken- dried IV U1, 23
Trockenfrüchte dried fruit IV U1, 23
Trockenobst dried fruit IV U1, 23
trocknen to dry II
Trommel drum IV U2, 44
tropfen to drip III
trotzdem anyway II; still III; even so IV U4, 90
Truthahn turkey IV U2, 38
Tschüss. See you later.; Bye. I
T-Shirt T-shirt I
Tube tube I
Tümpel pond I; pool III
tun to make; to do I
etw. gern **tun** to be happy to do sth IV U4, 84
etw. **tun** können to be happy to do sth IV U4, 84
Tunnel tunnel I
Tür door I
Türkei Turkey II
aus der **Türkei** Turkish III
Türkisch Turkish III
türkisch Turkish III
Turm tower II
Turnhalle gym I
Turnier competition III
Turnschuh trainer II
Tüte bag; packet I
Typ guy III; dude IV U4, 86
typisch typical III
Tyrann / Tyrannin bully IV U4, 78
Tyrannisieren bullying III

U

U-Bahn underground train I; underground II; subway *(AE)* IV U1, 10
U-Bahn (*in London*) the Tube II
üben to practise III; to practice *(AE)* IV U2, 33
über about; across III; over I; on II; above IV U1, 10
überall everywhere; all over III
Überfall attack IV U1, 15
überfordert overwhelmed IV U1, 22
überfüllt crowded III
übergeben to hand over III
überhaupt nicht not at all III
überleben to survive IV U5, 106
übernachten to stay I
überprüfen to check II
überqueren to cross I
überrascht surprised I
überschnappen to go mad III
Überschrift title III
Überschwemmung flood IV U5, 99
übersehen to miss IV U4, 86
live **übertragen** to live stream IV U2, 32
Übertragung transfer IV U5, 107
überwältigend stunning IV U4, 76
überwältigt overwhelmed IV U1, 22
überzeugt convinced IV U3, 68
Überzeugung belief IV U1, 21
üblich regular III
U-Boot submarine IV U1, 10
übrig left IV U1, 16
Übung exercise (Ex.) II; practice IV U1, 16
Übungsheft exercise book I
Ufer bank IV U4, 84; shore IV U2, 31
Uhr clock II
Uhr (*Zeitangabe bei vollen Stunden*) o'clock I
Uhrenturm clock tower II
Uhrzeit time I
um at I; by III
um … herum round I; around I
Umarmung hug III
Umfrage survey I
Umgebung environment II
umgraben to dig up III
umherziehen to migrate IV U4, 77
umsonst for free II
umsteigen to change II
umtauschen to exchange II
Umwelt environment II
umziehen to move I
Umzug parade IV U1, 15
unabhängig independent III
Unabhängigkeit independence; freedom IV U1, 15
unangenehm unpleasant IV U1, 17
unbebaut open II

unbehandelt raw IV U3, 56
unbeholfen clumsy II
unbrauchbar useless II
und and I
und doch even so IV U4, 90
unerfreulich unpleasant IV U1, 17
Unfähigkeit disability III
unfair unfair III
Unfall accident IV U4, 80
ungefähr about I; around III
Ungeheuer monster III
ungepflegt untidy III
ungeschickt clumsy II
ungesundes Essen junk food II
ungewöhnlich unusual IV U1, 17
unglaublich amazing; incredible II
Unglück disaster IV U5, 106
unglücklich unhappy I
unglücklicherweise unfortunately IV U4, 84
unhöflich rude IV U5, 101
Uniform uniform I
unordentlich untidy III
Unordnung mess II
Unordnung machen to make a mess II
unrecht haben to be wrong III
Unruhe riot IV U5, 114
uns us I
uns (selbst) ourselves II
unser / unsere our I
unten below; downstairs II
unter under I; below II
Untergeschoss basement *(AE)* IV U1, 11
im **Untergeschoss** downstairs II
unterhalb below II
unterhalten to entertain II
Unterhaltung chat; entertainment III
unterirdisch underground I
Unterlagen papers IV U1, 23
Unternehmen company III; business IV U4, 84
Unterricht class; lesson I
unterrichten to teach III
Unterrichtsstunde class I
Unterschied difference III
unterschiedlich different I
unterschreiben to sign III
unterstützen to support IV U3, 62; to encourage IV U4, 78
Unterstützung support IV U3, 62
Untersuchung research IV U3, 68
Unterwäsche underwear IV U1, 23
unterwegs out and about I
unterzeichnen to sign III
untröstlich heartbroken IV U1, 17
unverschämt rude IV U5, 101
Unwetter storm IV U2, 43
zu der amerikanischen **Urbevölkerung** gehörig Native American IV U1, 9
Urgroßeltern great-grandparents I
Urlaub holiday I; vacation *(AE)* II
die **USA** (Vereinigte Staaten von Amerika) the USA (United States of America) II
US-amerikanisch US IV ZI, 6

V

Vater father I
vegetarisch vegetarian II
Verabredung date IV U4, 90
jmdn. um eine **Verabredung** bitten to ask sb on a date IV U4, 90
ein Gesetz **verabschieden** to pass a law IV U3, 68
(sich) **verändern** to change II
sich **verändernd** changing II
Veränderung change II
verängstigt scared; terrified IV U1, 22
Veranstaltung event III
verantwortlich responsible IV U3, 68
verantwortungsvoll responsible IV U3, 68
verarbeiten to process; to treat IV U3, 57
verärgert angry I; annoyed III
verärgert sein to feel annoyed III
Verb verb I
Verband bandage III
verbessern to improve IV U4, 84
Verbesserung improvement III
verbieten to forbid IV U2, 44
verbinden to connect; to put through III
sich **verbinden** to connect III
Verbindung connection IV U3, 61
in **Verbindung** bleiben to keep in touch III
sich in **Verbindung** setzen mit to contact III
verblüfft amazed II
Verbrecher / Verbrecherin criminal I
verbrennen to burn III
verbringen *(Zeit)* to spend I
verdrehen to twist III
Verein club III
Vereinbarung agreement III
vereinigt united III
das **Vereinigte Königreich** the UK (United Kingdom) II
Vereinsheim clubhouse III
verfehlen to miss IV U4, 86
verfolgen to chase IV U2, 43
Verfolger / Verfolgerin chaser IV U2, 43
verfügbar available III
Vergangenheit past III
vergessen to forget I
vergleichen to compare III
vergrößern to increase IV U2, 37
verhaften to arrest IV U5, 112
sich **verhalten** to act II; to behave IV U5, 101
verhindern to stop IV U4, 78
sich **verirren** to get lost II
Verkauf sale I
verkaufen to sell I
Verkäufer / Verkäuferin assistant I
Verkehr traffic II
Verkehrsmittel transportation *(AE)* IV U3, 56; transport IV U4, 85
verlangen to charge IV U3, 56
verlassen to leave I
sich **verlaufen** to get lost II
verlegen embarrassed II
verlegen to publish IV U3, 69
verletzen to hurt II
sich **verletzen** to get hurt IV U2, 43
verletzt werden to get hurt IV U2, 43
Verletzung injury III
verlieren to lose III
Verlies dungeon III
vermeiden to avoid IV U3, 68
vermindern to reduce IV U3, 56
vermissen to miss II
Vermittlung operator III
veröffentlichen to publish IV U3, 69
verpacken to package IV U3, 56
Verpackung packaging IV U3, 56
Verpackungsmaterial packaging IV U3, 56
verpassen to miss II
verringern to reduce IV U3, 56
verrückt crazy I; mad IV U5, 100
verrückt werden to go mad III
Versammlung session III
Versammlung *(der indigenen Völker Nordamerikas)* powwow IV U2, 45
verschieden different; separately I
Verschmutzung pollution IV U3, 56
sich **verschulden** to get into debt IV U3, 62
verschwenden to waste II
Verschwendung waste II
verschwinden to disappear III
versetzen to move I
sich **versichern** to make sure III
versorgen to provide IV U4, 77
verspätet delayed III
Verspätung haben to be late I
Versprechen pledge IV U2, 32
versprechen to promise III
verstehen to understand II; to process IV U3, 57
Versteinerung fossil IV U2, 31
Versuch experiment I
versuchen to try II
verteidigen to defend IV U5, 113
verteilen to distribute IV U3, 57
Vertrag agreement III
verursachen to cause IV U5, 99
verwalten to manage IV U3, 68
Verwandter / Verwandte relative III
verwendet werden für to be used for III
Verwendung use IV U3, 56
verwirrt confused IV U4, 90
verzerren to twist III
verzieren to decorate III
Vesper packed lunch II
Video video I
Vieh cattle IV U4, 77
viel a lot; much I; lots of III
Viel Glück! Good luck! II
Viele Grüße Kind regards, IV U4, 86
viel(e) a lot of I
viele many I
Vielfalt variety IV U3, 68
vielleicht maybe II
vier four I
vierte fourth I
Viertel quarter I; neighbourhood III
Viertel nach *(bei Uhrzeitangaben)* past I
Viertel vor / nach *(bei Uhrzeitangaben)* quarter to / past I
vierzehn fourteen I
vierzehnte fourteenth I
vierzig forty I
vierzigste fortieth I
violett purple II

virtuelle Realität (VR) virtual reality (VR) IV U5, 107
Vogel bird I
Volksstamm tribe IV U1, 9
voll full III
voller full of III
  voller Menschen busy III
Volleyball volleyball IV U2, 32
völlig totally IV U2, 32
vollkommen perfect II
von from; of I; by II
  von der Schule abgehen to leave school II
  von … out of … II
vor in front of; outside; before I
vor (*zeitlich*) ago I
  vor Christus BC (= before Christ) III
vor (*bei Uhrzeitangaben*) to I
  Viertel **vor** / nach (*bei Uhrzeitangaben*) quarter to / past I
vorbei over III
  vorbei (an) past II
sich **vorbereiten** to get ready IV U2, 32
(sich) **vorbereiten** to prepare III
vorbereitet sein to be prepared III
Vorbild role model IV U4, 78
Vorder- front II
Vordergrund foreground II
Vorderseite front II
Vorfahre / Vorfahrin ancestor III
Vorführung display IV U2, 39
Vorgehensweise strategy IV U5, 101
Vorhang curtain I
vorher previously III
vorher before I
Vorlage model II
Vorleger rug IV U4, 77
Vormittag morning I
vormittags (*Uhrzeit*) a.m. II
nach **vorne** forward IV U4, 90
Vorort suburb IV U1, 16
Vorrichtung device II
Vorsatz resolution IV U2, 39
Vorsicht beim Ein- und Aussteigen. Mind the gap. I
vorsichtig careful II
Vorsitzender / Vorsitzende chairperson III
vorstellen to present IV U5, 101
  sich (etw.) **vorstellen** to imagine (sth) IV U5, 101
Vortrag presentation II
vortragen to perform III
vorwärts forward IV U4, 90
vorziehen to prefer III
Vulkan volcano IV U3, 54

W

wach awake III
wachsen to grow II; to increase IV U2, 37
Waffe weapon III
Wahl choice IV U5, 101
wählen to choose I; to vote IV U5, 112
wählen (*Nummer*) to dial II
Wahlfach elective IV U2, 32
wahr true I
während during II; while III
Wahrheit truth III
wahrscheinlich probably IV U2, 44
Währung currency IV ZI, 6
Wal whale II
Walbeobachten whale watching IV U1, 9
Wald forest I; wood II
Wales Wales II
  aus **Wales** Welsh III
Waliser / Waliserin Welsh III
Walisisch Welsh III
walisisch Welsh III
Wand wall I
Wandbild mural III
im **Wandel** changing II
Wandern hiking II
wandern to hike II; to migrate IV U4, 77
  wandern gehen to go hiking II
Wanderung walk II
Wandgemälde mural III
wann when I
  wann immer whenever IV U5, 100
warm warm I
warten to wait II
Warteschlange queue II
warum why I
was what I
  Was hast du? What's the matter? II
  was ist los what's on III
  Was ist los? What's wrong? I; What's the matter? II
  Was ist mit …? What about …? I
  was man … what to … III
  was noch what else II
  was soll's oh well IV U1, 10
  was sonst what else II
  Was stimmt nicht? What's wrong? I
Waschbär raccoon I
Waschbecken sink III
waschen to wash II
Wäschetrockner tumble dryer II
Waschmaschine washing machine II
Wasser water I
Wasserfall waterfall IV U1, 15
Wasserkocher kettle II
webbasiert web-based III
Website website II
Wechsel change II
Wechselgeld change I
wechseln to change II
wechselnd changing II
Wecker alarm IV U4, 90
Weg way I; lane; path III
  aus dem **Weg** gehen to avoid IV U3, 68
weg away I
Wegbeschreibung directions III
wegen because of III
weglaufen to run away I
Wegweiser signpost II
wegwerfen to throw away II
weh tun to hurt II
weich soft III
Weide field II
sich **weigern** to refuse IV U5, 112
Weihnachten Christmas I
weil because I; as II
weinen to cry III
Art und **Weise** way II
weiß white I
weiß (*soziale Kategorie*) white IV U5, 112
weit far I
weitere more I; other II; another III
weitergehen to continue III
weitermachen to continue III
Weizen wheat IV U2, 30
welche what I; which II
Welle wave I
Wellenreiten surfing III
Welt world I
  der **Welt** in the world III
Weltraum space I
weltweit global IV U3, 61
weltweit in the world III
wem who III
wen who III
wenden to turn II
ein **wenig** a bit II
am **wenigsten** least III
wenige a few II; few III
weniger less III
wenigstens at least III
wenn if I; when II
wer who I
Werbespot ad (= advertisement) II
werden to get; to become I; will II
  etw. tun **werden** to be going to do sth II
  genannt **werden** to be called III
  nicht **werden** won't (= will not) II
  würde(n) would II
  würde(n) gern would like I
  Ich **würde** gerne … I'd like (to) … (= I would like to) I
werfen to throw II; to put; to toss III
Werk factory III
Werkzeug tool IV U3, 67
wertvoll precious IV U3, 68
wessen whose III
West- west II
Westen west II
westlich west II
Wettbewerb competition III
Wetter weather I
Wettkampf competition III
Wettrennen race I
Whalewatching whale watching IV U1, 9
wichtig important I
  wichtig nehmen to care about III
wie what; how I; like II; as IV U4, 83
  so … **wie** as … as III
  wie auch immer anyway II
  Wie alt bist du? How old are you? I
  Wie geht es dir? How are you? I
  Wie heißt du? What's your name? I
  Wie spät ist es? What time is it? I
  Wie viel (kostet / kosten) …? How much (is / are) …? I
  Wie viel Uhr ist es? What time is it? I
wieder again I
wiederaufbauen to rebuild III
Auf **Wiedersehen**. Goodbye. I
wiederverwenden to reuse II
wiederverwerten to recycle II
wiederverwertet recycled IV U3, 56
Wiege cradle III
wiegen to weigh III
Wiese field II
Wikinger / Wikingerin Viking III

Wikinger- Viking III
wild wild III
Wildnis wilderness IV U3, 68
Wildtiere wildlife III
willkommen (bei / in) welcome (to) I
  willkommen heißen to welcome I
Wind wind III
windig windy I
winken to wave II
Winter winter I
wir we; us I
Wirbelsturm tornado IV U2, 31; hurricane IV U5, 99
wirklich very I; really; real II
wirr confused IV U4, 90
Wirtschaft economy IV U1, 9
Wischmopp mop II
wissen to know I
  weißt du … you see … III
  wissen Sie … you see … III
Wissenschaft science I
Wissenschaftler / Wissenschaftlerin scientist II
wissenschaftlich scientific IV U3, 68
Witz joke II
  Witze machen to joke III
witzig funny I
  witzig sein to be fun I
wo where I
Woche week I
  in der **Woche** a week II
  pro **Woche** a week II
Wochenende weekend I
woher where I
  Woher kommst du? Where are you from? I
wohin where I
sich **wohlfühlen** to feel comfortable II
Wohltätigkeitsorganisation charity I
Wohnen living II
wohnen to live I
Wohnmobil campervan III
Wohnung flat I; apartment IV U1, 16
wohnungslos homeless IV U3, 62
Wohnungstür front door IV U4, 90
Wohnwagen caravan III
Wohnzimmer living room I
Wolf wolf III
Wolke cloud I
Wolkenkratzer skyscraper IV U1, 10
wolkig cloudy I
Wolldecke blanket III
wollen to want (to) I
Workshop workshop III
Wort word II
Wörterbuch dictionary III
wunderbar wonderful II
wünschen to wish III
Wurf throw III
Wurst sausage II
würzig spicy II
Wüste desert IV U3, 54
wütend angry I; mad IV U5, 100

Z

Zahl number I
zählen to count II
Zahn tooth II
Zahnbürste toothbrush III
Zähne teeth II
  sich die **Zähne** putzen to brush one's teeth II
Zauberei magic III
Zauberkraft magic III
Zaun fence I
Zeckenkarte tick card III
Zeh toe II
zehn ten I
zehnte tenth I
Zeichen sign; signal II
zeichnen to draw I
zeigen to show II
zeigen (auf) to point (at) II
Zeile line II
Zeit time I; hours IV U4, 89
Zeitalter age II
Zeiten hours IV U4, 89
Zeitplan schedule III
Zeitschrift magazine II
Zeitung newspaper III
Zeitvertreib pastime III
Zeitzone time zone IV U2, 30
Zelt tent I
Zelten camping III
Zeltplatz campsite III
Zentimeter centimetre (cm) II
zentral central III
Zentrum centre I; center *(AE)* IV U1, 9
zerbrechen to break III
Zeremonie ceremony IV U1, 15
zerfließen to melt III
zerren to strain III
zerstören to tear down III; to destroy IV U5, 106
Ziege goat II
ziehen to grow II; to pull III
Ziel goal I; destination III; ambition IV U4, 79
zielstrebig determined IV U4, 78
ziemlich quite II; pretty III
Zimmer room I
Zimmermann / Zimmerin carpenter IV U4, 89
Zimt cinnamon IV U2, 38
Zitrone lemon I
zittern to shake II; to shiver III
Zone zone IV U2, 30
Zoo zoo I
zornig angry I
zu too; to I
  auf … **zu** towards III
  zu Fuß on foot I
  zu Hause at home I
  zu spät late I
  zum einen for one thing IV U5, 106
züchten to grow II
mit den Achseln **zucken** to shrug II
mit den Schultern **zucken** to shrug II
Zucker sugar I
zudem moreover IV U5, 106
zuerst at first II; first III; firstly IV U5, 106
zufrieden pleased I
Zug train I
Zugang portal IV U2, 32; access IV U5, 100
zugunsten von in favor of *(AE)* IV U5, 106
Zuhause home I
zuhören to listen (to) I
Zukunft future II
zukünftig future IV U3, 68
Zukunfts- future IV U3, 68
zukunftsfähig sustainable IV ZI, 7
zum Schluss finally II
zumachen to shut IV U2, 43
zumachen to close I
zunächst at first II
zunehmen to increase IV U2, 37
zurück back I
zurückgeben to return II
zurückkehren to return II
zurücklassen to leave IV U3, 68
zurückschicken to return II
zusammen together II
zusammenbauen to put together IV U3, 56; to assemble IV U3, 57
zusammenbrechen to collapse IV U1, 15
zusammenfassen to sum up IV U5, 106
zusammengefasst to sum up IV U5, 106
zusammenrollen to roll up IV U4, 86
zusammensetzen to put together IV U3, 56
zusammenstoßen to crash IV U1, 15
Zusatz- extra I
zusätzlich extra I
Zustand state IV ZI, 7; condition IV U4, 78
zustimmen to agree II
Zustimmung agreement III
Zutat ingredient IV U5, 99
Zutritt access IV U5, 100
zuvor before I; previously III
Zuwanderung immigration IV U1, 9
sich jmdm. **zuwenden** to turn to sb IV U2, 46
zwanzig twenty I
zwanzigste twentieth I
zwecklos useless II
zwei two I
zweimal twice III
zweite / zweiter / zweites second III
  aus **zweiter** Hand second-hand III
zweitens secondly IV U5, 106
Zwiebel onion II
Zwilling twin I
zwinkern to wink II
zwischen between I
in der **Zwischenzeit** meanwhile III
zwölf twelve I
zwölfte twelfth I
Zyklus cycle IV U3, 56

Quellennachweis

Alamy stock photo, Abingdon (PhotoStock-Israel / Ohad Shahar), **112.1**; Benecke, Lars, Hannover, **206.3**; Bláha, Marek, Offenbach am Main, **7.5; 14.1; 17.4; 21.4; 28.2; 29.2; 39.7; 47.1; 52.3; 53.7; 58.1; 66.1; 71.1; 71.2; 74.2; 81.7; 83.2; 88.1; 91.1; 96.2; 97.3; 103.1; 104.1; 107.1; 117.1; 120.3; 121.2; 124.1; 125.3; 130.1; 130.3; 131.7; 133.1; 133.2; 134.1; 137.7; 144.1; 146.1; 146.2; 148.1; 150.1; 150.2; 152.1; 155.1; 156.1; 156.2; 157.1; 158.1; 159.1; 160.1; 160.2; 162.1; 164.1; 166.1; 176.1; 177.1; 178.1; 180.1; 181.1; 182.1; 183.1; 184.1; 190.1; 191.1; 192.1; 193.1; 193.2; 194.1; 196.1; 197.1; 198.1; 199.1; 228.3; Vorsatz_vorn.1**; Burghart-Vollhardt, Martina, Kamenz, **212.1; 219.1**; CartoonStock Ltd, Bath (Baloo), **40.1; 129.7**; Charles Clyde Ebbets "Lunch atop a Skyscraper" 1932, **12.5**; Chudinskiy, Kirill, Köln, **35.1; 35.2; 35.3; 35.4; 35.5; 35.6; 128.1; 128.2; 128.3; 128.4; 128.5; 128.6**; Dekelver, Christian, Weinstadt, **224.1**; Florian, Andreas, Lübeck, **204.2**; Fröhlich, Anke, Leipzig, **207.1; 221.1; 227.1**; Getty Images Plus, München (AGENZIA SINTESI / Alamy), **78.2**; Getty Images Plus, München (Anna_Om/iStock), **197.7**; Getty Images Plus, München (AscentXmedia/E+), **73.4**; Getty Images Plus, München (Collection Mix: Subjects / Michael Nolan/robertharding), **73.2**; Getty Images Plus, München (Corbis Documentary / Layne Kennedy), **51.1; 51.3**; Getty Images Plus, München (COROIMAGE/Moment), **101.1; 136.1**; Getty Images Plus, München (DigitalVision / Ariel Skelley), **17.1**; Getty Images Plus, München (DigitalVision / EMS-FORSTER-PRODUCTIONS), **95.3**; Getty Images Plus, München (DigitalVision / Hill Street Studios), **234.4; 234.10**; Getty Images Plus, München (DigitalVision / Paul Souders), **68.1**; Getty Images Plus, München (DigitalVision / Riou), **102.3; 137.3**; Getty Images Plus, München (DigitalVision/Hill Street Studios), **33.1**; Getty Images Plus, München (DigitalVision/Mike Powell), **33.4; 48.1**; Getty Images Plus, München (DigitalVision/MoMo Productions), **34.4**; Getty Images Plus, München (dszc / iStock), **53.4**; Getty Images Plus, München (Elena Pejchinova/Moment), **87.5**; Getty Images Plus, München (E+ / Alex Potemkin), **65.1**; Getty Images Plus, München (E+ / DenisTangneyJr), **27.2**; Getty Images Plus, München (E+ / doug4537), **50.2**; Getty Images Plus, München (E+ / dszc), **67.1; 94.2**; Getty Images Plus, München (E+ / FrankRamspott), **50.1; 99.4**; Getty Images Plus, München (E+ / Hirurg), **62.1**; Getty Images Plus, München (E+ / LeoPatrizi), **15.1**; Getty Images Plus, München (E+ / LordHenriVoton), **99.3**; Getty Images Plus, München (E+ / SDI Productions), **163.1**; Getty Images Plus, München (E+/Ankit Sah), **39.5; 129.5**; Getty Images Plus, München (E+/AzmanL), **77.4**; Getty Images Plus, München (E+/Drazen_), **6.1**; Getty Images Plus, München (E+/eyecrave productions), **34.1**; Getty Images Plus, München (E+/FG Trade Latin), **78.3**; Getty Images Plus, München (E+/FG Trade), **41.1; 78.4; 96.1; 130.2**; Getty Images Plus, München (E+/Giselleflissak), **39.3; 129.3**; Getty Images Plus, München (E+/izusek), **84.1**; Getty Images Plus, München (E+/kali9), **83.1; 89.1; 89.2; 89.5**; Getty Images Plus, München (E+/ kupicoo), **85.1**; Getty Images Plus, München (E+/PeopleImages), **6.3; 78.1; 81.3; 134.4**; Getty Images Plus, München (E+/RichLegg), **77.1**; Getty Images Plus, München (E+/SDI Productions), **32.1; 89.7; 126.1**; Getty Images Plus, München (E+/skynesher), **89.3**; Getty Images Plus, München (E+/Terryfic3D), **87.2**; Getty Images Plus, München (E+/yorkfoto), **31.2**; Getty Images Plus, München (gerenme / iStock), **238.3**; Getty Images Plus, München (Goodboy Picture Company/E+), **104.2**; Getty Images Plus, München (Image Source), **52.1**; Getty Images Plus, München (iStock Unreleased / DoraDalton), **72.3**; Getty Images Plus, München (iStock Unreleased/ChristiLaLiberte), **47.2**; Getty Images Plus, München (iStock / Fitzer), **163.3**; Getty Images Plus, München (iStock / Juanmonino), **12.4; 122.5**; Getty Images Plus, München (iStock / mshch), **12.2; 122.3**; Getty Images Plus, München (iStock/SeventyFour), **89.8**; Getty Images Plus, München (Leland Bobbe), **Cover.1**; Getty Images Plus, München (Masterfile / Jeremy Woodhous), **77.2**; Getty Images Plus, München (Moment Open / Enzo Figueres), **19.3; 125.2**; Getty Images Plus, München (Moment / Carmen Martínez Torrón), **68.2**; Getty Images Plus, München (Moment / Daniel A. Leifheit), **95.1**; Getty Images Plus, München (Moment / Jia Liu), **72.2**; Getty Images Plus, München (Moment / Jultud), **55.2**; Getty Images Plus, München (Moment / Scott Suriano), **50.3**; Getty Images Plus, München (Moment/Anjelika Gretskaia), **76.1**; Getty Images Plus, München (Moment/Boris SV), **87.4**; Getty Images Plus, München (Moment/Halfpoint Images), **34.2**; Getty Images Plus, München (Moment/Jasmin Merdan), **6.4; 7.1; 38.1**; Getty Images Plus, München (Moment/Jose A. Bernat Bacete), **39.1; 129.1**; Getty Images Plus, München (Moment/Laura Olivas), **7.2; 56.1**; Getty Images Plus, München (Moment/the_burtons), **39.6; 129.6**; Getty Images Plus, München (Monkey Business Images), **234.1**; Getty Images Plus, München (Photodisc / GeoStock), **67.4**; Getty Images Plus, München (Photodisc / Image Source), **21.2**; Getty Images Plus, München (SDI Productions), **234.9**; Getty Images Plus, München (Stocktrek Images), **98.2**; Getty Images Plus, München (Tatyana Aksenova / Tatyana Aksenova), **20.1**; Getty Images Plus, München (The Image Bank / Danny Lehman), **9.2**; Getty Images Plus, München (The Image Bank / Siegfried Layda), **76.2; 92.1**; Getty Images Plus, München (The Image Bank / Steve Prezant), **21.3**; Getty Images Plus, München (The Image Bank/David Zaitz), **39.4; 129.4**; Getty Images Plus, München (tobiasjo/iStock), **197.5; 197.6**; Getty Images Plus, München (urbazon/E+), **112.3**; Getty Images Plus, München (valentinrussanov / E+), **42.1**; Getty Images Plus, München (1971yes / iStock), **240.1**; Getty Images, München (Ada Summer/Corbis/VCG), **7.3; 10.1**; Getty Images, München (Archive Photos / Kean Collection), **26.2**; Getty Images, München (Cavan / Regula Heeb-Zweifel), **18.2**; Getty Images, München (Corbis Historical / Stefano Bianchetti), **27.3**; Getty Images, München (Corbis Historical / Sunset Boulevard), **118.3**; Getty Images, München (Corbis / Robert Llewellyn), **111.5**; Getty Images, München (Corbis/Hal Beral), **95.2**; Getty Images, München (David Redfern), **118.1**; Getty Images, München (Gamma-Rapho / Patrick PIEL), **119.1**; Getty Images, München (Getty Images Entertainment / Frazer Harrison), **119.3**; Getty Images, München (Getty Images North America / Roy Rochlin), **10.2**; Getty Images, München (Icon Sportswire), **31.3**; Getty Images, München (Mint Images), **94.3**; Getty Images, München (MJ Zheng / 500px), **72.1**; Getty Images, München (Photographer's Choice RF / Richard Handwerk), **10.5**; Getty Images, München (Stone / Justin Lewis), **55.1**; Getty Images, München (Stone/Peter Unger), **77.3**; Getty Images, München (Tetra images / PT Images), **17.2**; Getty Images, München (Tetra Images), **27.4**; Getty Images, München (WireImage / Theo Wargo), **119.2**; graphitecture book & edition, Bernau am Chiemsee ; Source: Pew Research Center analysis of 2014-2017 American Time Use Survey (IPUMS), **140.1**; Graphi-Ogre/GEOATLAS, Hendaye, **Vorsatz_hinten.1**; Hammen, Josef, Trierweiler, **215.3**; Hesselbarth, Susann, Leipzig, **220.2**; Hochmann, Carmen, Gütersloh, **209.2**; Hoppe-Engbring, Yvonne, Steinfurt, **215.4**; Jähde, Steffen, Sundhagen, **215.1; 225.1**; jani lunablau, Barcelona, **178.2; 178.3; 178.4; 178.5; 183.2; 183.3**; Joswig, Dominik, Wandlitz, **213.1**; Katja Kassler Grafik Design, Leipzig, **228.2**; Kramer, Peer, Schneverdingen, **44.1; 45.1; 45.2; 46.1; 90.1**; Kranenberg, Hendrik, Drolshagen, **205.1; 206.1; 209.1; 212.3; 213.2; 214.1; 227.2**; Mahnkopf, Dorothee, Diez a.d. Lahn, **226.1**; Marzell, Alfred, Schwäbisch Gmünd, **206.2**; Mauritius Images, Mittenwald (age fotostock), **37.1**; Mauritius Images, Mittenwald (Alamy Stock Photos / Jim West), **112.5**; Mauritius Images, Mittenwald (Alamy / Alpha Historica), **112.4; 114.2**; Mauritius Images, Mittenwald (Alamy / Beth Hall), **111.1**; Mauritius Images, Mittenwald (Alamy / CrackerClips Stock Media), **99.2**; Mauritius Images, Mittenwald (Alamy / Dennis Hallinan), **109.2; 139.5**; Mauritius Images, Mittenwald (Alamy / Jeffrey Isaac Greenberg 7+), **105.1**; Mauritius Images, Mittenwald (Alamy / Jeffrey Isaac Greenberg 9+), **113.4**; Mauritius Images, Mittenwald (Alamy / Mark Stevens), **102.1; 116.1; 137.1**; Mauritius Images, Mittenwald (Alamy / Matthew Williams), **102.2; 137.2**; Mauritius Images, Mittenwald (Alamy / Wavebreak Media

Premium), **109.1**; Mauritius Images, Mittenwald (Bob Daemmrich / Alamy), **234.8**; Mauritius Images, Mittenwald (Cavan Images), **30.1**; Mauritius Images, Mittenwald (CNMages / Alamy), **111.2**; Mauritius Images, Mittenwald (dcphoto / Alamy), **115.1**; Mauritius Images, Mittenwald (Erik Pendzich / Alamy), **53.2**; Mauritius Images, Mittenwald (FLHC JN8 / Alamy / Alamy Stock Photos), **25.1**; Mauritius Images, Mittenwald (Hanna Tor / Alamy), **31.1**; Mauritius Images, Mittenwald (Hansrad Collection / Alamy), **112.2**; Mauritius Images, Mittenwald (Jeffrey Isaac Greenberg 9+ / Alamy / Alamy Stock Photos), **18.5**; **124.2**; Mauritius Images, Mittenwald (Jeffrey Wickett / Alamy), **51.2**; Mauritius Images, Mittenwald (Jim West), **30.2**; Mauritius Images, Mittenwald (Jit Lim / Alamy), **67.8**; Mauritius Images, Mittenwald (JT Vintage), **113.1**; Mauritius Images, Mittenwald (Keith Jefferies / Stockimo / Alamy), **63.1**; **132.9**; Mauritius Images, Mittenwald (KGPA Ltd), **67.5**; Mauritius Images, Mittenwald (Lightspruch / Alamy), **111.6**; Mauritius Images, Mittenwald (Maryna Kolechyna / Alamy / Alamy Stock Photos), **18.1**; Mauritius Images, Mittenwald (Maskot), **102.6**; **137.6**; Mauritius Images, Mittenwald (mauritius images / William Morgan / Alamy), **111.4**; Mauritius Images, Mittenwald (Mytopshelf / Alamy), **67.3**; Mauritius Images, Mittenwald (NASA Photo / Alamy), **167.1**; Mauritius Images, Mittenwald (nature picture library), **55.4**; **98.1**; Mauritius Images, Mittenwald (Norbert Eisele-Hein / imageBROKER), **13.1**; Mauritius Images, Mittenwald (Pictorial Press Ltd / Alamy), **118.2**; Mauritius Images, Mittenwald (Pixel-shot / Alamy), **53.6**; Mauritius Images, Mittenwald (Raga), **14.2**; **24.1**; Mauritius Images, Mittenwald (Ron Buskirk / Alamy), **111.7**; Mauritius Images, Mittenwald (Science Photo Library), **106.1**; **138.1**; Mauritius Images, Mittenwald (Tetra Images, LLC / Alamy Stock Photo), **34.3**; Mauritius Images, Mittenwald (Thislife pictures / Alamy / Alamy Stock Photos), **22.3**; Mauritius Images, Mittenwald (Thomas Haensgen), **10.4**; Mauritius Images, Mittenwald (TopFoto), **113.3**; Mauritius Images, Mittenwald (Wavebreakmedia), **81.5**; **134.6**; Mauritius Images, Mittenwald (Westend61), **31.4**; Mauritius Images, Mittenwald (Witold Skrypczak / Alamy), **67.7**; Mauritius Images, Mittenwald (World Book Inc.), **113.2**; Mauritius Images, Mittenwald (World History Archive / Alamy), **26.1**; Oser, Liliane, Hamburg, **6.2**; **6.5**; **7.4**; **8.3**; **10.6**; **11.1**; **16.1**; **16.2**; **16.3**; **19.1**; **30.3**; **54.3**; **57.1**; **57.2**; **57.3**; **57.4**; **57.5**; **57.6**; **59.2**; **59.3**; **59.4**; **59.5**; **59.6**; **59.7**; **59.8**; **59.9**; **76.3**; **98.3**; **100.1**; **100.2**; **100.3**; **100.4**; **107.2**; **107.3**; **107.4**; **107.5**; **122.1**; **131.1**; **131.2**; **131.3**; **131.4**; **131.5**; **131.6**; **132.1**; **132.2**; **132.3**; **132.4**; **132.5**; **132.6**; **132.7**; **132.8**; **139.1**; **139.2**; **139.3**; **139.4**; **219.2**; **233.1**; **233.2**; **233.3**; **233.4**; **233.5**; **233.6**; **233.7**; **233.8**; **236.1**; **236.2**; **236.3**; **236.4**; **236.5**; **236.6**; **236.7**; **236.8**; **236.9**; **236.10**; **236.11**; **236.12**; **236.13**; **236.14**; **236.15**; **236.16**; **237.4**; Palmowski, Sven, Barcelona, El Prat de Llobregat, **218.1**; plainpicture GmbH & Co. KG, Hamburg (Bias), **67.6**; plainpicture GmbH & Co. KG, Hamburg (Carmen Spitznagel), **55.3**; plainpicture GmbH & Co. KG, Hamburg (Dave Wall), **18.4**; plainpicture GmbH & Co. KG, Hamburg (DEEPOL by plainpicture/Cate Brown), **26.3**; plainpicture GmbH & Co. KG, Hamburg (DEEPOL by plainpicture/Christian Vorhofer), **54.2**; plainpicture GmbH & Co. KG, Hamburg (DEEPOL by plainpicture/Josefsson), **59.1**; plainpicture GmbH & Co. KG, Hamburg (DEEPOL by plainpicture/Konstantin Trubavin), **54.1**; plainpicture GmbH & Co. KG, Hamburg (DEEPOL by plainpicture), **58.2**; **70.1**; plainpicture GmbH & Co. KG, Hamburg (DEEPOL / Johan Alp), **102.5**; **137.5**; plainpicture GmbH & Co. KG, Hamburg (DEEPOL /Eva Blanco), **81.1**; **134.2**; plainpicture GmbH & Co. KG, Hamburg (DEEPOL /Fotofeeling), **80.3**; plainpicture GmbH & Co. KG, Hamburg (DEEPOL/Lena Granefelt), **33.2**; plainpicture GmbH & Co. KG, Hamburg (DEEPOL/Marie Linnär), **33.3**; plainpicture GmbH & Co. KG, Hamburg (DEEPOL/Rainer Berg), **87.6**; plainpicture GmbH & Co. KG, Hamburg (DEEPOL/Simona Pilolla), **89.6**; plainpicture GmbH & Co. KG, Hamburg (DEEPOL/Winslow Productions), **80.1**; plainpicture GmbH & Co. KG, Hamburg (DEEPOL/Zero Creatives), **87.1**; plainpicture GmbH & Co. KG, Hamburg (DEEPOL/zerocreatives), **89.4**; plainpicture GmbH & Co. KG, Hamburg (DEEPOL), **93.1**; **102.4**; **137.4**; plainpicture GmbH & Co. KG, Hamburg (Design Pics/Carl Johnson), **73.3**; plainpicture GmbH & Co. KG, Hamburg (Design Pics/John Hyde), **9.3**; plainpicture GmbH & Co. KG, Hamburg (Design Pics/John Stubbs), **21.1**; plainpicture GmbH & Co. KG, Hamburg (Design Pics/Ken Gillespie), **8.1**; plainpicture GmbH & Co. KG, Hamburg (Design Pics/Yvonne Duivenvoorden), **39.2**; **129.2**; plainpicture GmbH & Co. KG, Hamburg (Frank Baquet), **19.2**; **125.1**; plainpicture GmbH & Co. KG, Hamburg (Jerry Monkman), **8.2**; plainpicture GmbH & Co. KG, Hamburg (Leander Hopf), **17.3**; plainpicture GmbH & Co. KG, Hamburg (Lena Granefelt), **9.4**; plainpicture GmbH & Co. KG, Hamburg (Marcus Windus), **18.3**; plainpicture GmbH & Co. KG, Hamburg (Michael Jonsson), **13.2**; **123.1**; plainpicture GmbH & Co. KG, Hamburg (Nordic Life/Terje Rakke), **67.2**; plainpicture GmbH & Co. KG, Hamburg (Patrick Strattner), **94.1**; plainpicture GmbH & Co. KG, Hamburg (Paul Tait), **87.3**; plainpicture GmbH & Co. KG, Hamburg (p426m2309845), **99.1**; plainpicture GmbH & Co. KG, Hamburg (R. Schönebaum), **36.1**; plainpicture GmbH & Co. KG, Hamburg (Sibylle Pietrek), **10.3**; plainpicture GmbH & Co. KG, Hamburg (Tandem Stills + Motion/DeYoung, Michael), **80.2**; plainpicture GmbH & Co. KG, Hamburg (Tony Arruza), **111.3**; plainpicture GmbH & Co. KG, Hamburg (Valerie Schmidt), **64.1**; Rau, Katja, Berglen, **212.2**; Rockstroh, Myrtia, Berlin, **210.1**; **210.3**; Schumann, Friederike, Berlin, **215.2**; Schwarzstein, Jaroslaw, Hannover, **142.1**; **142.2**; **143.1**; **224.2**; ShutterStock.com RF, New York (Africa Studio), **235.2**; ShutterStock.com RF, New York (AjayJangra_123), **29.1**; ShutterStock.com RF, New York (AlessandroBiascioli), **235.5**; ShutterStock.com RF, New York (Amy Richmond), **53.3**; ShutterStock.com RF, New York (Anil Varma), **197.4**; ShutterStock.com RF, New York (APIWAN BORRIKONRATCHATA), **75.1**; ShutterStock.com RF, New York (Billion Photos), **81.2**; **134.3**; ShutterStock.com RF, New York (Chekyravaa), **163.6**; ShutterStock.com RF, New York (ChiccoDodiFC), **238.4**; ShutterStock.com RF, New York (David Papazian), **232.6**; ShutterStock.com RF, New York (Ekaterina Pokrovsky), **74.1**; ShutterStock.com RF, New York (engel.ac), **240.9**; ShutterStock.com RF, New York (Er_On), **232.13**; ShutterStock.com RF, New York (Evgeny Karandaev), **147.1**; ShutterStock.com RF, New York (Framepersecond), **240.7**; ShutterStock.com RF, New York (Grindstone Media Group), **97.2**; ShutterStock.com RF, New York (Grustock), **163.4**; ShutterStock.com RF, New York (HannaTor), **53.8**; ShutterStock.com RF, New York (Have a nice day Photo), **240.8**; ShutterStock.com RF, New York (Irina Wilhauk), **121.1**; ShutterStock.com RF, New York (Ivanova Ksenia), **73.1**; ShutterStock.com RF, New York (JabaWeba), **232.11**; ShutterStock.com RF, New York (Jane Rix), **197.2**; ShutterStock.com RF, New York (Jne Valokuvaus), **52.2**; ShutterStock.com RF, New York (Jordan Roper), **240.4**; ShutterStock.com RF, New York (Kinga), **235.7**; ShutterStock.com RF, New York (Lazhko Svetlana), **49.1**; ShutterStock.com RF, New York (Le Do), **234.12**; ShutterStock.com RF, New York (Leigha Perales), **235.6**; ShutterStock.com RF, New York (LeManna), **75.7**; ShutterStock.com RF, New York (lev radin), **28.1**; ShutterStock.com RF, New York (Lightspring), **239.1**; ShutterStock.com RF, New York (LN team), **75.3**; ShutterStock.com RF, New York (Lotta Axing), **197.3**; ShutterStock.com RF, New York (Marcus Friedrich), **163.2**; ShutterStock.com RF, New York (mariakray), **12.3**; **122.4**; ShutterStock.com RF, New York (MilanMarkovic78), **238.6**; ShutterStock.com RF, New York (Monkey Business Images), **75.6**; **120.2**; ShutterStock.com RF, New York (msheldrake), **53.1**; ShutterStock.com RF, New York (Nagel Photography), **234.6**; ShutterStock.com RF, New York (nampix), **238.7**; ShutterStock.com RF, New York (Nanci Santos Iglesias), **238.2**; ShutterStock.com RF, New York (New Africa), **235.4**; ShutterStock.com RF, New York (Owlie Productions), **238.5**; ShutterStock.com RF, New York (PeopleImages.com - Yuri A), **238.8**; **238.9**; **240.6**; ShutterStock.com RF, New York (Peshkova), **232.4**; ShutterStock.com RF, New York (Peter Titmuss), **238.1**; ShutterStock.com RF, New York (Philip Lange), **12.1**; **122.2**; ShutterStock.com RF, New York (Pixel-Shot), **75.5**; **182.2**; **234.11**; ShutterStock.com RF, New York (Proxima Studio), **75.2**; ShutterStock.com RF, New York (Q3kiaPictures), **22.1**; **22.2**; **22.4**; **23.1**; **23.2**; **25.2**; ShutterStock.com RF, New York (RaiDztor), **232.12**;

ShutterStock.com RF, New York (Ratchat), **232.9**; ShutterStock.com RF, New York (Robert Kneschke), **232.2**; ShutterStock.com RF, New York (Roman Zaiets), **120.1**; ShutterStock.com RF, New York (Sergio Foto), **232.3**; ShutterStock.com RF, New York (Simon Dannhauer), **75.8**; ShutterStock.com RF, New York (Smit), **81.4; 134.5**; ShutterStock.com RF, New York (ss.photography), **97.1**; ShutterStock.com RF, New York (Stefano Garau), **189.1**; ShutterStock.com RF, New York (Suzanne Tucker), **235.8**; ShutterStock.com RF, New York (u3d), **232.14**; ShutterStock.com RF, New York (Veja), **159.2**; ShutterStock.com RF, New York (vipflash), **81.6**; ShutterStock.com RF, New York (Vlad Linev), **53.5**; ShutterStock.com RF, New York (wayfarerlife), **232.16**; ShutterStock.com RF, New York (WoodysPhotos), **74.3**; ShutterStock.com RF, New York (YanLev Alexey), **75.4**; ShutterStock.com RF, New York (YIUCHEUNG), **238.12**; ShutterStock.com RF, New York (Your Hand Please), **238.11**; ShutterStock.com RF, New York (8 income), **232.15**; Slawski, Wolfgang, Kiel, **228.1**; stock.adobe.com, Dublin (AboutLife), **27.1**; stock.adobe.com, Dublin (bongkarn), **159.3**; stock.adobe.com, Dublin (Casa imágenes), **232.1**; stock.adobe.com, Dublin (Dolores Harvey), **237.2**; stock.adobe.com, Dublin (Gerald Zaffuts), **114.1**; stock.adobe.com, Dublin (ImageFlow), **234.7**; stock.adobe.com, Dublin (Interstellar), **240.2**; stock.adobe.com, Dublin (J Bettencourt/peopleimages.com), **234.2**; stock.adobe.com, Dublin (JackF), **235.1**; stock.adobe.com, Dublin (lovelyday12), **240.3**; stock.adobe.com, Dublin (Mark), **238.10**; stock.adobe.com, Dublin (Mary Perry), **235.9**; stock.adobe.com, Dublin (phonlamaiphoto), **240.5**; stock.adobe.com, Dublin (Pormezz), **237.1**; stock.adobe.com, Dublin (pressmaster), **234.3**; stock.adobe.com, Dublin (Prostock-studio), **235.3**; stock.adobe.com, Dublin (sborisov), **9.1**; stock.adobe.com, Dublin (shine), **234.5**; stock.adobe.com, Dublin (Stephen), **61.1**; stock.adobe.com, Dublin (stockphoto mania), **163.5**; stock.adobe.com, Dublin (Surachetsh), **232.7**; stock.adobe.com, Dublin (S.Kobold), **237.3**; stock.adobe.com, Dublin (tiero), **232.5**; stock.adobe.com, Dublin (Who is Danny), **232.8**; stock.adobe.com, Dublin (2mmedia), **232.10**; Unsplash, Montréal, QC (Caleb Perez), **Cover.2**; Voets, Inge, Berlin, **207.2**; Wolff, Steffen, Herzogenrath, **204.1; 210.2; 210.4; 220.1**; Wolf, Sylvia, Wiesbaden, **206.4; 216.1**; Wolters, Dorothee, Köln, **223.1**; www.CartoonStock.com, Bath (Bill Whitehead), **86.1**; www.CartoonStock.com, Bath (Jim Sizemore), **86.2**; 2021, TMW Media, powered by Boclips, **105.2**; © Digital Learning Associates Ltd 2019, **43.1; 43.2**;

Text:
Bundesministerium für Familie, Senioren, Frauen und Jugend, Berlin: Jugend stärken – Brücken in die Eigenständigkeit, 2022; Zur besseren altersgemäßen Verständlichkeit wurde der Originaltext verändert, ohne den Inhalt und/oder Sinn zu verändern., **64**; Fancy Dancer in: Ancestor Approved: Intertribal Stories for Kids ©2021 Monique Gray Smith; Zur besseren altersgemäßen Verständlichkeit wurde der Originaltext verändert, ohne den Inhalt und/oder Sinn zu verändern., **44-46**; From: Fancy Dancer in: Ancestor Approved: Intertribal Stories for Kids ©2021 Monique Gray Smith; Zur besseren altersgemäßen Verständlichkeit wurde der Originaltext verändert, ohne den Inhalt und/oder Sinn zu verändern., **47.1; 47.2**; Martin Luther King, Jr.: I Have a Dream, delivered 28 August 1963, at the Lincoln Memorial, Washington D.C., **115**; Source: Pew Research Center analysis of 2014-2017 American Time Use Survey (IPUMS); Zur besseren altersgemäßen Verständlichkeit wurde der Originaltext verändert, ohne den Inhalt und/oder Sinn zu verändern., **140**; William Henry Davies †1940, **140**; Wörterbucheintrag „awesome", aufgerufen unter https://de.pons.com/%C3%BCbersetzung/englisch-deutsch/awesome am 14.12.2022; © PONS Langenscheidt GmbH, **195.1**; Wörterbucheintrag „show" - aus PONS Schülerwörterbuch Englisch (978-3-12-517539-6), © PONS GmbH, Stuttgart 2016, **194.2**; Written by Mark Twain. Adapted by Gina D.B. Clemen © 2016 Black Cat – A brand of De Agostini Scuola Spa.; Zur besseren altersgemäßen Verständlichkeit wurde der Originaltext verändert, ohne den Inhalt und/oder Sinn zu verändern., **142-143**;

Stand: März 2025

CANADA
Calgary
Vancouver
Vancouver I.
Columbia
ROCKY MOUNTAINS
WASHINGTON
Seattle
Tacoma
Olympia
Spokane
Portland
Salem
Eugene
OREGON
MONTANA
Helena
Billings
Missouri
NORTH DAKOTA
Bismarck
Fargo
SOUTH DAKOTA
MOUNT RUSHMORE
Pierre
BADLANDS
Custer County
OGLALA LAKOTA COUNTY
IDAHO
Boise
Snake
Yellowstone
WYOMING
Cheyenne
NEBRASKA
Omaha
Lincoln
GREAT PLAINS
Great Salt Lake
Salt Lake City
NEVADA
GREAT BASIN
Reno
Carson City
UTAH
COLORADO
Denver
Colorado Springs
Saint Elmo
KANSAS
Wichita
Rio Grande
CALIFORNIA
Santa Rosa
Sacramento
Stockton
San Francisco
Oakland
Mountain View
San Jose
Salinas
Fresno
YOSEMITE
SEQUOIA
DEATH VALLEY
Las Vegas
Bakersfield
HOLLYWOOD
Los Angeles
Long Beach
Riverside
San Diego
Tijuana
Mexicali
GRAND CANYON
NAVAJO NATION
Flagstaff
ARIZONA
Colorado
Show Low
Phoenix
Tucson
SAGUARO
NEW MEXICO
Taos Pueblo
Santa Fe
Albuquerque
CIBOLA N.F.
Socorro
GILA N.F.
El Paso
Ciudad Juárez
OKLAHOMA
Oklahoma City
TEXAS
Abilene
Fort Worth
Austin
San Ant
Corpus
Brow
PACIFIC OCEAN
Guadalupe Mexico
Monterrey
Culiacán
MEXICO
Tamp
Guadalajara
CIUDAD DE MEXICO
Acapulco
120°
105°
45°
30°
Alaska at 25%
165°
150°
135°
Chukchi Sea
Beaufort Sea
ALASKA
GATES OF THE ARCTIC
ARCTIC CIRCLE
Bering Strait
Fairbanks
DENALI NP
Anchorage
WRANGELL ST ELIAS
Seward
Juneau
60°
Bering Sea
Queen Charlotte Islands
Aleutian Islands
PACIFIC OCEAN
0 km
800
1600 km
Hawaii (at the same scale)
165°
Hawaiian Islands
Kauai
Oahu
Honolulu
Maui
20°
PACIFIC OCEAN
HAWAII
Hawaii
Kilauea